Rachilde and French Women's Authorship

RACHILDE
AND FRENCH WOMEN'S AUTHORSHIP

From Decadence to Modernism

Melanie C. Hawthorne

UNIVERSITY OF NEBRASKA PRESS

LINCOLN AND LONDON

Portions of the chapter
"1900, December 10"
were previously published as
"To the Lighthouse: Fictions of
Masculine Identity in Rachilde's
La Tour d'amour,"
L'Esprit créateur
32.4 (winter 1992).

The author
gratefully acknowledges
Mme Edith Silve
for permission to quote
from those titles by Rachilde
that remain protected under copyright law.

Library of Congress Cataloging-in-Publication Data
Hawthorne, Melanie.
Rachilde and French women's authorship : from decadence to
modernism / Melanie C. Hawthorne.
p.   cm.
Includes bibliographical references and index.
ISBN 0-8032-2402-8 (cloth : alk. paper)
1. Rachilde, 1860–1953.   2. Authors, French—19th century—
Biography.   3. Authors, French—20th century—Biography.
4. Women and literature—France.   I. Title.
PQ2643.A323 Z74 2001
843'.912—dc21
[B]   2001027148

N

For Mum and Dad.
Thanks.

CONTENTS

ILLUSTRATIONS

ACKNOWLEDGMENTS

Since this book ended up taking over ten years to complete, I have accumulated more debts to more people than I can ever hope to repay, but let me begin to acknowledge some of them here. First, I must thank the person without whom I would never have heard of Rachilde, Patsy Baudoin. It was Patsy who, while working at Schoenhofs in Cambridge, sent me a book that had just come across her desk and that she thought might interest me. The book was *Monsieur Vénus*. I had never heard of the author but wanted to know more about her. I quickly discovered how little had been written and decided that it would be a simple project to gather what was known in an article or a short book. Easy enough to do, I thought.

Many institutional grants have made this book possible. I have benefited greatly from various programs at Texas A&M University, such as the Women's Studies Program, the Honors Program, and the International Research Travel Assistance Grant Program as well as other grant programs administered through the College of Liberal Arts (I thank Dean Woodrow Jones Jr.) and through the Department of Modern and Classical Languages (I am grateful to its former head, Luis Costa, as well as to the current head, Steven Oberhelman, both of whom have so consistently supported this research). The Association of Former Students deserves special recognition for funding the development leave (sabbatical) program, which makes it possible for faculty to devote an extended period of time to research without the competing demands of teaching and administration. The South Central Modern Language Association and the Harry Ransom Humanities Research Center (HRC) at the University of Texas at Austin also made important contributions, sponsoring an extended period of research at the HRC. I am also grateful to the staff of the many libraries and archives I consulted; these are listed in the bibliography. In particular, I would like to thank the Inter-Library Loan Services of the Sterling Evans Library at Texas A&M and Pat at the HRC.

In addition, there are those who read the manuscript—Willa Silverman and Richard Shryock—whom I cannot thank enough for their thoughtful responses and suggestions. A writer can be paid no greater compliment than to have readers who engage with the text, who take it seriously, and who are anything but indifferent to its arguments, and I consider myself fortunate to have had two such readers. I count them among a host of friends who have contributed to this book in tangible and intangible ways that range from sending me clippings and references, to putting me up and putting up with me in Paris, to acting as a "research buddy," someone with whom to share the trials and tribulations of a hard day at the library. In addition to those already named, let me mention Michael Finn, Lynne Huffer, Elspeth Kennedy, Line Koïs, Leonard Koos, Anne Laroche, Cheryl Morgan, Catherine Perry, Catherine Ploye, Gretchen van Slyke, Margaret Waller, and all the regulars of the Nineteenth-Century French Studies Association, who have provided a community of scholars with whom to share my progress on Rachilde over the years. My thanks to the students who participated in the 1999 Texas A&M summer study abroad in France program and who indulged my detour to Rachilde's home and continue to inquire so kindly about the progress of the book. I am also grateful to Edith Silve and Romana Severini-Brunori, who gave their permission to consult certain archival collections, especially Edith Silve for agreeing to meet with me on many occasions and share her insights. I owe a special debt to Christian Laucou, whose extraordinary generosity puts him in a category of his own.

I cannot end this list without thanking my writing group; as tradition now has it, its members remain nameless, but they know who they are. What I wrote above about being fortunate to have good readers goes double for them, and they know how much I shall forever be indebted to them in ways that defy words. Finally, in the world of Too-Much-Coffee-Man (created by Shannon Wheeler), having to go to France again "for my high-paying job" is one of the things a person is not allowed to complain about. But nothing says that everyone else has to keep quiet about it, so, last but not least, thanks to Patty for ten years of putting up with "I just have to go to France again one more time this summer to look for this one last thing."

ABBREVIATIONS FOR WORKS BY RACHILDE

AJ	*Alfred Jarry; ou, Le Surmâle de lettres*
AM	*A mort*
AR	*L'Amazone rouge*
MN	*Monsieur de la Nouveauté*
MS	*La Marquise de Sade*
PM	*Le Parc du mystère*
Pourquoi	*Pourquoi je ne suis pas féministe*
QJJ	*Quand j'étais jeune*
RHS	*Le Roman d'un homme sérieux*
TB	*Le Théâtre des bêtes*

Rachilde and French Women's Authorship

On Writing Biography

In which the author pays a visit to Périgueux and
makes a detour to Galveston

It is early July, and I am sitting in a café in Périgueux, Rachilde's home-town, after a sudden summer thunderstorm. I am drenched. The clouds blow away as suddenly as they came, the swallows resume their spiral-ing antics, and I contemplate my predicament. I have just come from a fruitless search at the Bibliothèque Municipale de Périgueux, where I have been looking for *L'Exposition sans chemise: Lanterne périgourdine hebdomadaire*, a rare journal of the 1880s produced by a local group of avant-garde writers and one of the first periodicals with literary preten-sions to which Rachilde contributed. Rachilde used many pseudonyms (other than that of "Rachilde") and probably wrote under yet another one in *L'Exposition sans chemise* so I am not even sure what I might learn from this publication, but I feel a need to look at everything just in case. Perhaps it would reveal something about the transition from writer of regional color "à la Ponson du Terrail" to self-consciously ar-tistic writer of the decadent movement. Perhaps it would reveal more about the somewhat mysterious and enigmatic figure of Léo d'Orfer (Marius Pouget), who seems to have been an early love interest. But I will probably never know because the municipal library has the only copy of this rare journal, and no one seems able to locate it for me.

This story of dead ends has been a recurring motif during this trip. The helpful *conservateur* with whom I had been corresponding before my trip has recently taken another job in another area. His replacement is not unsympathetic and wants to help, but he does not seem really to know what is in the collection, at least this part of it. In addition, the municipal library is open only during limited hours, so in the meantime I have been to the regional archives—the "archives départementales"—where I hope to trace some members of Rachilde's family through rec-ords of births, marriages, and deaths. I have also been told to contact Pierre Pommarède, a priest and local historian who has been working on the same subject, or so I am told by helpful archivists. They give me

The Cathedral of Saint-Front in Périgueux. Reprinted from Pommarède, *Périgueux oublié.*

his address, but I am not surprised to learn that he is out of town. Moreover, the archives themselves, I discover, will close in two days for the annual holiday. I panic. I should have thought of this, I think; everyone knows that things close in France in August. Of course, had it been August, I might have anticipated this, but it is only the beginning of July. Nevertheless, I am embarrassed that it did not occur to me to check this detail (you can never be too sure, and, besides, I *know* that libraries sometimes close at odd times in France, even large bureaucratic offices like regional archives).

My own shortcomings as a researcher seem all too obvious and all but drive me to despair. Getting soaked in the sudden downpour seems merely to offer divine confirmation. Each individual check on my progress drives home the point that is becoming increasingly clear: this trip is not working out as I had planned. Before these failures, I had not been aware that I had even had expectations, but, like so many other things, they began to make their existence felt only when they failed to be realized. As I dry off in the café, I begin to think about what it was that I had expected to accomplish during this week in Périgueux. Somehow I had gradually evolved a fantasy of what this trip would bring, and realizing what a simplistic wish fulfillment it was now made me wonder how I could have been so naive. Without quite being aware of it, I had imagined that I would arrive in this backwater of the Midi and casually strike up a conversation with the *patron* of the local café. The conversation would eventually turn to the purpose of my visit, and I would smile and confess that actually I was not a tourist but that I was researching the life of one of Périgueux's forgotten daughters, Rachilde; perhaps the *patron* had heard of her? This B-movie fantasy would continue with the patron exclaiming, "But of course," and he would send me to talk to someone or other, an old-timer who had actually known Rachilde (since she did not die until 1953, this seemed, alas, all too possible in my fantasy). The old-timer would share all sorts of colorful stories, delighted to find someone interested at last in hearing about the past. My work would be done for me.

I look up from my thoughts. The café has the kind of glass doors that can be folded back, opening up the entire front of the café. The tables and chairs spill out onto the sidewalk. As I look out across the street to the old quarter of Périgueux with its narrow medieval streets, I realize that there had been a brief moment when the fantasy had almost come true. It was the morning on which I had first set eyes on the Cathedral of Saint-Front in Périgueux, the cathedral where Rachilde's great-grandfather had supposedly been a canon and that therefore seemed inextricably linked to her family. Having seen so many northern French cathedrals, from the smiling angels of Rheims and spidery unfinished Beauvais to the husk of bomb-torn Rouen and the curious zodiacs of Amiens, I felt perfectly well acquainted with the Gothic style and was fully prepared to interpret something in this vein. Nothing (not even other Romanesque buildings) prepared me for what I saw. The cathedral of Périgueux defies easy description. When attempting to categorize it, the guidebooks usually make some reference to St. Mark's Cathedral in Venice because St. Mark's is the other unique cathedral and because *Byzantine* is about the only adjective that can be applied to the cathedral of Périgueux (sometimes it is the best adjective that comes to mind to describe Rachilde's work, too). It has nothing of the lacy, graceful verticals of Gothic aspiration. Instead, the chunky stones of the square basilica rest heavily on the earth, while the huge rounded domes of its roof hug the building tightly like the lids of primitive earthenware jars. Whatever spirit resides in the cathedral is not that of an ethereal Gothic soul but that of a superstitious mystic rooted in ritual.

Quasimodo lived here, surely, not in Paris. Around the cathedral is a dense, medieval quarter with narrow cobbled streets. Many stone buildings dating to the Renaissance remain, and it requires little imagination to see the medieval character of other houses, even if they are really much later in origin. The narrow, twisting streets, odd angles, and misshapen windows and doorways all speak of an age before urban planning, before standardized building codes, before the age of reason and rationalization.

The cathedral at the center of this maze seemed to provide a key to Rachilde's work. It symbolized the Byzantine elements of her work, the cruelty shrouded in mysticism, the thrill of blasphemy, the assertion of difference. It was easy to imagine that the atmosphere of the cloisters was partly responsible for certain scenes of *Le Meneur de louves*, for example, and I pictured the young Rachilde absorbing the sight of this almost monstrous cathedral, this proud statement of willful difference, as she accompanied her nurse on trips to market (held on the square in front of the cathedral). It all seemed to fit. My research trip to Périgueux would be worth it.

Then I discovered that, since the seventeenth century, the cupolas of the cathedral had been covered up with a wood-frame roof. Though they are visible today, by the mid-nineteenth century no one had seen them in years. They could not have exercised the kind of influence over the local imagination that I had been attributing to them. The key to Rachilde's work was not going to offer itself quite as easily as I had thought.

This exercise in projection should have served as a warning to me not to get carried away, but I did not heed it. Instead, I just dug a little deeper into local history and discovered (thanks to a book by the elusive Pierre Pommarède) that between 1850 and 1890 the cathedral was "restored" by the architect Abadie. As part of the restoration he had uncovered the Byzantine cupolas. So perhaps the Byzantine nature of the cathedral was being rediscovered when Rachilde was a girl? Perhaps it was being reevaluated by eyes that brought a fresh perspective because they were seeing the cupolas again for the first time? Now I had a new question: What did Rachilde see, and when did she see it?

No, the trip was not turning out as I had expected. So what was I learning from it? I looked out from the café at the view across the rain-soaked streets now glistening in the sun. We were on the avenue Montaigne, one of the main streets. Strictly speaking, Montaigne was not from Périgueux but from the little town of, well, Montaigne not far away, but the capital city of the province was proud to acknowledge him all the same. The same was true for Cyrano de Bergerac. In addition to the avenue Montaigne, there were streets named for other notable statesmen and writers, including Victor Hugo (not "from" the region, but he did visit Périgueux in 1843), but I found no "rue Rachilde." (Ironically, there is a street named after her grandfather, Urbain Feytaud, in Thiviers, not far from Périgueux, but the honor was no doubt intended to recognize his status as a local journalist and magistrate rather than his role as progenitor of a writer.) With so many famous sons to remember, Périgueux could not keep track of everyone, but it tried. Just down the street from the café, in front of the Monoprix, for example, was the place Bugeaud, the site of the outdoor market some days and a parking lot the others, making it something of a social center. Bugeaud is honored by a statue. Since I had never heard of him, I was pleased to be instructed by the inscription on the statue that his contribution to the nation was to have been a "colonialist." He led the African army (in which Rachilde's father served as a career officer) in the colonization of Algeria (though of course there is no mention of Captain Eymery on Bugeaud's statue). Bugeaud is a son the city gratefully remembers, but, like her father, Rachilde remains a foundling no one wants to claim.

No, Périgueux was not at all what I had imagined. Of course it wasn't. Before seeing it with my own eyes, I had had only Rachilde's descriptions of it to go on, and these descriptions always presented it as a backward, provincial, nineteenth-century town. I knew we were no longer in the nineteenth century. I had, after all, reached Bordeaux (from Paris, of course) by TGV—France's modern, rapid train—even though I had had to switch to a slower, local train for the final part of my journey. As the wishfully named "express" train trundled steadily along, it did sometimes seem as though, for every inch we moved forward in distance, we moved a day back in time, but I realized that this increasing oppressiveness was in part due to the close heat that presaged a storm. It was not until after another storm, the one that brought me to the café, that I realized how much I had absorbed Rachilde's version of things. I would come to understand just how much I had underestimated this effect as I struggled to compose the biography of Rachilde I had initially set out to write. I realized now that Périgueux was a lot more modern, cosmopolitan than my patronizing fantasy had allowed. Everyone hastened to tell me how "les Anglais" were returning to the parts of France relinquished mere centuries ago, buying up the land now that the Common Market was making international living easier. Although every other postcard proudly depicted the grotesque but "traditional" art of force-feeding geese for the regional specialty pâté de foie gras and tradition was everywhere, Périgueux had little use for old-timers telling anecdotes.

So where on earth had I gotten this fantasy about writing biography? Where indeed. As I began to interrogate my presuppositions, I realized that I had acquired a very specific model of what biography entailed. I realized that I had been imagining I would write the kind of biography that I had read as an undergraduate. I had devoured large, authoritative biographies, particularly those by Enid Starkie (a fearless and redoubtable figure, I imagined, rather like the actress Margaret Rutherford's version of Miss Marple in some of the old films), who had written monumental and scholarly books on such major French writers as Baudelaire and Rimbaud. (I recently looked at the biography of Baudelaire, which I still have. It runs over six hundred pages in paperback.) My imagination had been particularly gripped by the biography of Rimbaud. Someone had had to go and check what he been up to in "Abyssinia," verify or disprove the rumors that he had been a gunrunner and slave trader. (Was it really Enid Starkie who had done this? In my imagination it was.) I realized that this was my image of what a biographer did, especially a female one. She was adventurous, she was tough, she trekked across dark, unknown continents to unearth a few bare facts about a writer and probably contracted malaria into the bargain. In short, the biographer was a colonialist, a cross between David Livingstone and one of those intrepid Victorian lady travelers.

Another example of biographical research that lingered in the back of my mind concerned the poet Apollinaire (an acquaintance of Rachilde's), whom I had also studied as an undergraduate. I had recollections of Francis Steegmuller's book—which I read in sturdy Penguin paperback (like Starkie's *Baudelaire*)—in which he revealed to the world (or so I thought) that he had succeeded in tracking down Annie Playden. Part of the charm of this sleuthing was that the innocent Annie had no idea that the young man with whom she had briefly been in love in Europe had gone on to become a world-famous poet. Because of Apollinaire's poem "Annie," which describes a woman (unnamed except in the title) who walks in a garden "Sur la côte du Texas / Entre Mobile et Galveston" (Apollinaire, *Oeuvres poétiques* 65), I always pictured Annie Playden in Galveston.[1] I pictured the earnest young scholar Steegmuller walking along a sandy Texas Gulf Coast explaining to a charmingly unspoiled Annie Playden how she had been immortalized in some of the world's most beautiful love poetry. It was a pleasing image that inverted the usual relationship between source and scholar. In most biographical research, the scholar is the supplicant, while the source is privileged, the one who knows, but the Annie story reversed these roles: Steegmuller brought the news to Annie that all this time she had been famous without knowing it. Annie was grateful.

When I began more actively to revisit these texts, I was living in Texas; Galveston was not far away. I was now close enough to know that the way I had always imagined Galveston was just that: imaginary. Moreover, if the site was the product of imagination, so was a good deal more of my conceptualization of the interaction between the biographer and the source. For me, "Galveston" represented simultaneously the exotic and the provincial. It was the place where one could remain unaware of the rest of the world (as Annie apparently had), where news did not travel fast, where poetry was an unnecessary luxury, a place of nostalgia immortalized by Glen Campbell, the antipodes of equally mythical cosmopolitan centers such as the "City of Lights" and the "Big Apple." "Galveston" explained everything about how Annie had remained so innocent.

I rationalized this image by telling myself that, in the 1960s, when Steegmuller made his discovery (as I thought), Galveston would have been somewhat remote, perhaps somewhat provincial. But, living just a few hours away from Galveston, I realized that "Galveston" had little to do with Galveston, the 1960s oil-boom city just minutes from the command control center of a space-age project that would arguably come to represent the pinnacle of twentieth-century technological achievement, putting a man on the moon. "Galveston" was a trope for the underlying patronizing attitude of the scholar who knows more, an attitude I had not consciously recognized but that had nevertheless structured my mental re-creation of the Annie story.

The projection was all the clearer when I reread Steegmuller's account of his visit to Annie Playden.[2] The interview with Annie had taken place, not in Galveston at all, but in a suburb of—of all places—New York City, the Big Apple (345). Moreover, it was not clear that Annie had ever lived in Galveston, although she had worked for a number of years in Santa Barbara, California.[3] And I had misremembered much else, too. Steegmuller was not the one who had discovered Annie Playden's identity and whereabouts, nor was this the first time that she had received a visit from an Apollinaire scholar. Steegmuller credits the discovery to an anonymous "Belgian Apollinairien" ten years previously. The Belgian had only corresponded with her, however, and it fell to LeRoy Breunig, then a professor of French at Barnard, to be the first to visit her.

Despite the misremembered details, my displacement of events to

Galveston proved to be a way of encoding what today seems the patronizing tone of Steegmuller's account. Annie is "the most delightful-looking person imaginable, plump, white-haired, rosy-cheeked" (346), like a grandmother in a children's story. She needs to be reminded of Apollinaire's fame, and when she is told that "Annie is immortal," her natural modesty manifests itself charmingly: "she broke off her reminiscing and bowed her head, and we could see her pink cheeks flush brighter" (347).[4] She contritely admits, "I was such an ignorant little English goose at the time. . . . I was so *mean* to Kostro! [Apollinaire's real name was Kostrowitzky]" (348). Annie behaves like the perfect "Beatrice, . . . Laura, . . . Dark Lady of the Sonnets" (345): unassuming, modest, indifferent to literary fame, with no desire to bask in the glory of her role or to seek profit—financial or emotional—from the acquaintance. She and her sister display jewelry given them by "Kostro," and Steegmuller uses the occasion once again to demonstrate his superiority. He describes Annie's pendant: "Probably the last word in Paris when Kostro offered it to Annie, the pendant passed through whole decades in which it would have been classified by a jeweler or a person of fashion as démodé and impossible; now there is a revival of Art Nouveau among the more or less sophisticated" (351). Although Steegmuller considers it "more showy than valuable," I cannot help but wonder how much a genuine Art Nouveau pendant would be worth today (not to mention one given by Apollinaire to one of his muses). Not as much as Jackie O.'s faux pearls, no doubt, and perhaps not as much as artifacts associated with other writers, but certainly more than Steegmuller's valuation. Steegmuller (perhaps to his credit) views the piece not as an asset but merely as an index of Annie's naive and uncultivated artistic sense, of her lack of sophistication.

Annie, the informant who knows her place, and Steegmuller, the scholar who knows, together represent a certain version of the scholarly enterprise of biography. Annie gives her knowledge freely, modestly, and unconditionally. There is no hint that it would ever occur to her to demand editorial control over the interview (indeed, the reader suspects that she never even read it), and her feminine sensibilities are flattered merely by the chance to share her memories of the poet who made her famous. She remains unimpressed, unchanged, unaffected by her own encounter with greatness. Had a bundle of Apollinaire's letters been in her possession, she would surely have handed them over to Steegmuller to publish, insisting demurely that, if the world wanted to know more about Kostro, she owed it to the world to make the letters available, never dreaming of seeking publicity by publishing them herself.

How I wanted to be Steegmuller! I dreamed of generous informants, unexploited archives, sources there for the taking. And in all this I would play the heroic scholar who knows. Alas, like so many other examples of the quest genre, the hero is always male, and I came to realize how much I had underestimated the gendered script of Steegmuller's encounter, imagining that I could fill his shoes by an act of sheer will.

It was while I was in Périgueux that I recognized and renounced the fantasy of writing what I have come to think of as "colonialist" biography. There would be no Annie Playden equivalent in my work, and rather than appropriating someone else's narrative, I needed to generate my own. Périgueux marked a watershed because there I confronted some of the issues faced, overcome, and described by other contemporary biographers: dealing with estates; how to handle sensitive information about the subject's private life; integrating unconventional sources of information.[5] Thanks to the work of Blanche Wiesen Cook, Carolyn Heilbrun, Diane Middlebrook, and others (see n. 5 above), biography as a genre has been challenged and reinvigorated, and other narrative paths have been opened up for biographers. The recognition that the biographer is a kind of colonialist who plunders the raw materials of others renders possible a kind of consciously "postcolonialist" biography in which the subject is not merely a resource to be exploited by a more "knowing" writer. Postcolonialism has altered biography, the narrative of an individual, just as postmodernism has altered ethnography, the narrative of a group.

In the case of Rachilde, I began to notice that, although several biographies of her had already been written, they all told the same version of her life, the "official" story. The authors of the first two biographies (Gaubert; David, *Rachilde*), published during Rachilde's lifetime, were in fact acquainted with her, but such access to the "source" made the resulting texts, not more reliable, but partisan. Although the subject of a biography is an important source of information about her own life, she is rarely the most objective. The third biography, a more recent and scholarly work by Claude Dauphiné (*Rachilde*, 1985/1991), was a vast improvement, but it still treated earlier works as reliable and so, unwittingly perhaps, reproduced some of the same errors even as it corrected others. In a sense, then, my biography is also an account of the life of those earlier biographies, the story of their rhetoric.

Having examined those narratives to see how they work, I needed to come up with my own, and this is where I had got stuck in Périgueux. Having decided that previous biographies did not tell the truth, or enough of the truth, I still thought that the truth—a singular, authoritative narrative—was out there, waiting to be discovered. But the trip to Périgueux—and the "detour" to "Galveston"—had made me see that no such simple, single discovery would be possible. I had found a handful of bureaucratic facts (births, marriages, deaths) that did make it possible to verify certain dates but that mostly served to destabilize what was thought to be known—without providing a "thick" enough narrative to replace the displaced truths. In Périgueux, I realized that trying to offer a single, stable narrative would not do justice to the complexity of the subject. I would continue to seek out information, but such research would produce multiple and complex truths. I would continue to scour archives (such as the military archives at Vincennes) for whatever meager and shriveled bits of information I could turn up. I would continue my detective work, which would lead me to all manner of sources, including the records of the mental asylum of Charenton made famous by the marquis de Sade. I would continue to visit relevant sites (leading a group of American undergraduates on a detour from their planned itinerary to visit the house where Rachilde was born). But none of this research would exhaust the truth.

The result of my research would not be the linear narrative of discovery, I decided. Instead, the book that I would write would be a layered and sometimes nonlinear series of overlapping excursions, readings of Rachilde and readings of other biographies of Rachilde structured around those points in the bureaucratic record at which facts do emerge and make themselves known. Those facts, expressed as dates that introduce the chapter headings, are arranged chronologically and serve as the pretext to investigate some aspect of Rachilde's life as it is presented through a number of sources. Each chapter also then opens onto a discussion of elements of thematic importance, a discussion that is not limited to the chronological moment but ranges both backward and forward in time. Thus, the narrative that follows begins, more or less, with Rachilde's birth and ends with her death, but in between are stories of werewolves and ghosts, stories of bohemians and surrealists, and stories of an equally mythical creature, a nineteenth-century French woman writer.

Taken together, what these chapters show is that Rachilde was not the exception that she has so often been described as. Rather, she used the claim of exceptionality as a way to exist within the status quo. In using this strategy (and many others), she was very much the product of her time. The late nineteenth century saw the beginnings of modern advertising, *la publicité* as it is called in French. Advertising was part of Rachilde's milieu: in places like the Chat Noir cabaret (known today for its striking posters that continue to sell in reproduction), she mixed with artists such as Henri de Toulouse-Lautrec, who would produce some of the earliest examples of the advertisement poster, a genre now treated as art. A child of her times, Rachilde exploited the connection between publicity and publishing, as many of these chapters will show. To publish her work, she publicized herself and in so doing became aware of the need for managing her self-presentation. Seeing the person behind the various poses is not always easy (or even possible), but the following chapters attempt to understand the poses of the "publicizing woman" and, through this example, the modes of being imposed on the typical late nineteenth-century woman writer in France.

Women as Outsiders

In which Marguerite Eymery (Rachilde) is born,
a werewolf appears, and traps are both set and sprung

> Marguerite Eymery naquit le 11 février 1860 (1), à minuit, dans
> un milieu familial et un décor dessinés pour le roman.
>
> Gaubert, *Rachilde*

An examination of the way in which Rachilde's birth is presented in the
three biographies already available illustrates something of the unacknowledged stakes and assumptions in biography.[1] Analyzing the way
others have framed a central event—Rachilde's birth—shows that,
in addition to addressing questions of truth and error, a broader issue
is also at stake in the biographical endeavor: the problem of reading
in general. A representative work of fiction by Rachilde (*Minette*) will
illustrate the argument that focusing only on the image that Rachilde
presented of herself—as exceptional—distracts from an important dimension of her story, namely, her self-conscious manipulation and exploitation of social codes.

The quotation presented as the epigraph to this chapter is the description of Rachilde's birth given by Ernest Gaubert on page 5 of his
1907 biography, the first book devoted to her, and the first of two biographies to be published during her lifetime (the other would be by
André David in 1924). Gaubert relegates the fact that this date places
Rachilde's birth under the sign of Aquarius to a footnote (n. 1). David
gives more importance to the zodiac in his account of Rachilde's birth
but otherwise repeats, in hiccupy syntax fragmented by commas, a similar story: "Sous le signe zodiacal du Verseau, qui représente, disent Vir-
gile et Ovide, Ganymède que Jupiter fit enlever par un aigle pour lui
servir le nectar, à la place d'Hébé, naquit, le 11 février 1860, dans le Périgord, au fond de la vallée très resserrée de Beauronne, Marguerite
Eymery" (*Rachilde* 11). Where Gaubert makes "Marguerite Eymery" the
first words of his birth announcement, David, while keeping her as the
grammatical subject, shunts her appearance to the end of a series of pre-
saging clauses. But differences of style and order aside, both versions offer the "received wisdom" about Rachilde's birth. The elements are zodiacal sign, time of birth, place, and literary connections.

Le Cros today. Courtesy of the author.

Gaubert and David should be equally reliable sources. Both counted Rachilde among their personal friends and probably received this information directly from her. David, for example, makes it explicit in the course of his biography that the work is based on personal acquaintance, and, in the paragraph preceding the description of her birth, he records a moment in the present tense during which he is her guest at her country residence, les Bas-Vignons. She talks; he (passively) listens: "Aujourd'hui, je suis son hôte dans sa petite maison de campagne. . . . Elle parle; j'écoute ses souvenirs" (*Rachilde* 10).

One detail stands out in both accounts: both Gaubert and David accurately give Rachilde's date of birth as 1860. Rachilde liked to mislead people about this, claiming to be—or allowing people to believe that she was—born in 1862, a misconception so widespread that *Le Monde* gave 1862 as her date of birth in her obituary in 1953. To judge from this single point alone, it would seem that the biographies of Rachilde give us the facts we need to know, but that impression is misleading.

On the "point de départ" of 1860 the biographers are agreed, but they also agree that Rachilde was born at the liminal time of midnight. Imagine the surprise, then, when, in the course of revising her 1985 biography of Rachilde, Claude Dauphiné actually checked the facts. Here is Dauphiné's account; the italicized part appears in both versions of her *Rachilde* (1985 and 1991), the roman section only in the revised edition:

> *C'est en 1860 que Marguerite Eymery voit le jour, en Périgord vert, dans la vieille demeure familiale du Cros, non loin de Château-l'Evêque et tout près de Périgueux. La petite fille, promise à une étonnante destinée littéraire sous le pseudonyme de Rachilde, arrive au monde un 11 février à minuit, dans cette province excentrée qui avait déjà donné au pays un Brantôme, et, plus récemment, un Eugène Le Roy.* Minuit . . . détail fourni par Ernest Gaubert qui s'en remettait à Rachilde, détail mensonger puisque l'acte de naissance de Marie Marguerite Eymery, rédigé le 12 février 1860, à la mairie de Château-l'Evêque, indique qu'elle est née à "six heures du matin."
>
> *Saturnienne, du signe du Verseau, elle* choisit *pour sa naissance l'heure romanesque par excellence et le décor le plus sombre autant que le plus romantique.* (23)

In both versions, the narrative continues with exactly the same phrase "elle choisit pour sa naissance." In a sense, then, the new information changes nothing in Dauphiné's text (it is inserted into a text that remains unchanged before it and only slightly modified in emphasis after it), but in a sense it changes everything. Before, Rachilde chose to be *born* at midnight; after, she chose to *say* she was born at midnight.

Change of emphasis aside, the same elements (astrological sign, time of birth, place, and literary connections) go into Dauphiné's account—though in a slightly different order—as go into those of Gaubert and David and as indeed go into mine. While the topos of Aquarius will come up later in this book, the focus of this chapter is the when, where, and who of Rachilde's birth, the time, the place, and the family of origin. In pursuing these aspects of Rachilde's biography, there is also a larger point to be made. Dauphiné notes that the (now) demonstrably false detail about being born at midnight can be traced directly back to Rachilde. In other words, Dauphiné reminds us of what an unreliable narrator Rachilde can be. I shall argue that, far from making any claim to reliability, Rachilde goes so far as to warn her readers not to fall into her narrative traps. If the warnings are not heeded, Rachilde's autobiographical novels can be misleading. If read more cautiously, however, her fiction may indeed be a useful source of information.

In giving her natal hour as midnight, Rachilde proves to be unreliable about the very first thing she does in life—being born—and having been "wrong" in some absolute, factual sense from the very beginning, she will prove to be unreliable about many things that come afterward.[2] All three biographers stress the literary connections with Rachilde's birth, Gaubert and David perhaps prompted by Rachilde herself, as though to offer a veiled warning that Rachilde is a born storyteller. *Telling stories* refers to the act of narrating, but it is also a euphemism for lying, and in Rachilde's case the two are inseparable. The accuracy of individual details will always be sacrificed to the needs of the overall narrative, and if the narrative can be improved by substituting the more resonant *midnight* for a more accurate but prosaic time, then Rachilde will always serve art before accuracy, treating life as a work of art in true decadent fashion. In reading Rachilde, one should not fail to consider the paramount importance of narrative, of what makes a good story. With this in mind, it is difficult to read Rachilde's work—even the most blatantly autobiographical—naively in the belief that every detail corresponds to a "truth" about Rachilde's life. Rather than individual details, what emerge are patterns, recurrent configurations that had meaning for Rachilde. Indirectly, these patterns tell a great deal about Rachilde, but I have come to be skeptical of what appears to be direct self-revelation, and this chapter recommends such skepticism to others.

What patterns are at work in Rachilde's (auto)biography, in the account of her birth and origins? Consistently, what is emphasized are those elements that tie Rachilde to other writers. Whether it concerns where she was born or the family she was born to, all narratives stress that she was born to be a writer. The clues to this "destiny" (Dauphiné's word) lie, not only in the time of birth, but also in the nature of her surroundings—from the cultural associations of the Périgord and Gascony to the individual details of the family home—and in the nature of her family of origin, which overlaps with the collective family of other Périgourdin writers, as well as her animal relatives. In each case, just as Rachilde "chose" to be born at midnight, she selects the elements she wishes to stress.

The ur-narrative of Rachilde's birth—drawn on in all three biographies—is an autobiographical text, the preface to the novel *A mort*, published in 1886 after Rachilde had become famous as the author of *Monsieur Vénus* in 1884. I shall have occasion to return to this preface in more detail later, but for now the mere fact that Rachilde writes about herself in the third person throughout it might be enough to suggest that she presents herself here as a fictional character. Yet biographers have used this text uncritically as a source of information, rather than treating it as a literary text. This chapter examines both the high degree of reliance on this ur-narrative (by focusing on the similarities among the three biographies) and the modulations added by each biographer (by noting the rhetoric of individual authors). Ultimately, if all the biographical accounts derive from the preface to *A mort*, and if this preface is unreliable, then "what we know" about Rachilde also becomes much more unstable.

In the accounts of Rachilde's birth, sooner or later everyone mentions that she was born at the family home of le Cros, adds that in local dialect this means "hole," and then offers some description of it. Here is Rachilde's ur-version from the preface to *A mort*:

> *Mademoiselle Rachilde naquît en 1860 au Cros (ça veut dire trou en patois) entre Château-l'Evêque et Périgueux. Ce Cros était une propriété humide autour de laquelle poussait trop de pervenche, trop de lierre, trop de vigne vierge, trop de saules et trop de truffes. Devant la maison, des grenouilles dans un étang; derrière, des fermes remplies de petits enfants peu légitimes, malpropres. Au jardin l'humidité empêchait les fraises de rougir, les radis étaient mangés par une bête qu'on ne voyait jamais, et les vaches de l'étable, quand elles s'égaraient dans ce jardin, tarissaient. Les confitures de cerises prenaient des moustaches quinze jours après leur fabrication; en revanche il y avait des folles-avoines s'agitant partout avec l'insolence morgue d'une aigrette de reine.*
>
> *Rachilde vint donc au monde dans une chambre du Cros en face de la mare aux grenouilles, côté des folles-avoines. (v)*

All three biographers (Gaubert, David, Dauphiné) re-create slightly different, though ultimately similar, visions of this home setting. That they are drawing on this autobiographical version is suggested by the recurring similarities, but there are differences that will be significant also. The first account, chronologically, is by Gaubert, who mentions the "milieu familial" (5) when presenting Rachilde's birth and shortly afterward returns to elaborate on this scene:

> *Ce fut une fille pâle et chétive qui vint au monde, par une nuit d'hiver, dans le lugubre décor du Cros, vaste domaine de pâturages et de bois entre Château-l'Evêque et Chancelade, à quelques kilomètres de Périgueux. Là, s'étaient retirés les grands-parents de Rachilde, dans une spacieuse maison de maître, sise au fond d'une dépression de terrain, humide, fréquentée du vent, familière des eaux*

et des roseaux palustres, parmi des bouquets de noisetiers sauvages,
de tamaris, de peupliers, tout enlacés de vigne vierge. . . . La bise
d'octobre réveillait, sous les chênes, les hurlements de l'ancêtre
maléficié. Il y avait un sort sur les récoltes. On croyait voir errer, au-
tour des trois fermes qui dépendait du Cros, les yeux ardents du
loup-garou. Toute une atmosphère d'humidité, de cauchemar, pro-
pre aux sabbats, y enveloppa l'enfant craintive et charmée. (6–7)

The birth of a "pale and sickly child" is implicitly explained for Gaubert
by the place of birth, as though Rachilde were a character in a Balzac
novel. Le Cros is portrayed in the wintry season of Rachilde's birth (in
February, although Gaubert also refers to the October winds) as damp
and humid, the house oppressed by shadowy trees and clinging vines.
For Gaubert, le Cros is the setting for a nightmare of supernatural
origins: haunted by werewolves with burning eyes, it offers everything
needed for a witches' sabbat. According to folk wisdom, the baby with
a spell on it would not live long since an owl had hooted to the north at
its birth. Most of the decor of le Cros is drawn from Rachilde's version,
though Gaubert omits the references to other children to underscore
Rachilde's loneliness and uniqueness and adds a supernatural overlay as
well as literary references. "Cette demeure tenait de la Maison Usher,"
continues Gaubert, "du couvent maudit de Robert-le-Diable et du
cloître des alchimistes. Là, on ne pouvait naître que romantique. On
devine les premières impressions de la fillette" (7). The impressions of
the child do not need to be guessed at when they seem so clearly to have
made themselves known ventriloquially through the narrative of Gaubert, yet the sensations attributed to the "fillette" were not offered in
Rachilde's narrative.

Rachilde's voice is both openly acknowledged and silently appropri-
ated in David's account, which touches on the same topoi as the preface
to *A mort*, via Gaubert, though with different modulations:

Situé entre Château-l'Evêque et Périgueux, le Cros était très sombre,
couvert de lierre, de vignes-vierges, entouré de peupliers, de saules,
de noisetiers sauvages; il y poussait aussi des pervenches, des angé-
liques et des roses du Bengale. Un étang peuplé de grenouilles s'éta-
lait devant la maison, éloignée de tout village; derrière s'étalaient les
fermes et les dépendances. Au jardin, assure Rachilde, l'humidité
empêchait les fraises de rougir, les radis étaient mangés par une
bête qu'on ne voyait jamais, et les vaches de l'étable, quand elles
s'égaraient dans ce jardin, tarissaient. Les yeux de Rachilde s'ou-
vrirent sur la folle-avoine et sur l'eau trouble de la mare aux

grenouilles. D'une paleur mortelle, elle se mit à grandir dans l'ombre humide de ces murs romantiques et subit l'influence d'un décor digne de plaire à Edgar Poë. (Rachilde 12)

Still a pale child, Rachilde here seems to owe this failure to thrive to the dark and humid garden that keeps out the sunlight—a human analogue of the strawberries that will not ripen—rather than to a supernatural curse at birth. Nevertheless, David hints at the existence of inexplicable forces, though in less satanic terms than Gaubert: the invisible "beast" is never actually seen, and in any case it eats only radishes, while the worst that happens to the cows is that their milk dries up. The most haunting part of the garden seems to be the troubled waters of the frog-filled pond, also mentioned by Gaubert, although not in the passage cited, but what exactly is so disturbing about this pond is not made clear (and readers of both David and this book will have to wait for an explanation). In these details, David is more "faithful" to Rachilde's version; indeed, a large section of it is plagiarized directly from the preface to *A mort* with only a casual "assure Rachilde" to acknowledge the borrowing. Like Gaubert, however, David likens the setting to something from Edgar Allan Poe, something "romantique" (an adjective used by both Gaubert and David), something that situated Rachilde from birth as the heroine of a Poe-esque tale of fantasy, terror, and death. Although Poe's melancholy House of Usher does not share the prolific vegetation of le Cros (it has only "a few white trunks of decayed trees" [231] when seen at the beginning of Poe's story), both houses share the uncanny ability to induce in the viewer a feeling of gloom and depression emanating from their "pestilent and mystic vapour" (233).

Dauphiné, the third and most recent biographer, omits the reference to Poe altogether, and varies the descriptive language, but goes through the same motions: "La maison des Eymery, voisine de la très ancienne abbaye de Chancelade, tapie au fond de la vallée de la Beauronne, a tout pour modeler une âme originale, voire une vocation d'écrivain. Sombre à souhait, elle est envahie par une végétation exubérante. Le lierre la couvre, ainsi que la vigne vierge. Les peupliers, les saules, les noisetiers sauvages l'entourent. Elle possède sa pièce d'eau, un étang trouble, où coassent les grenouilles" (*Rachilde* [1991] 23). Stripped of the suggestive language of the supernatural, this account still succeeds in implying that the landscape created and nurtured the writer, that Rachilde, in other words, is still the product of another narrative already unfolding at her birth. Dauphiné proceeds to cite passages from the preface to *A mort* to supply the rest of the description. Thus, she is more explicit about and conscious of her inclusion of Rachilde's words but not of the underlying architecture of the narrative that she follows, a narrative topology in which Rachilde the writer is always already leading us up the garden path.

Although the reference to Poe is lacking in both Rachilde (earliest) and Dauphiné (latest), the similarities in all four narratives illustrate the way in which knowledge about Rachilde has circulated. She is the original source of information about herself, and in her self-presentation she is always already the heroine of a story (at first merely a narrative in which she is described in the third person, but later one belonging to an established genre, such as "a tale by Edgar Allan Poe"). Each successive biography borrows from previous versions, adding or subtracting a note or an emphasis here and there, yet substantially retelling the same story. I am aware that in some ways I too am doing the same: as a result of having read my predecessors, I tread the same ground and increase the chances that others will follow me in their turn. But whereas Gaubert, David, and Dauphiné tell Rachilde's life as if it were a novel, this biography is an attempt to *read* her life knowing that she has made a novel of it.

One of the compulsory stations of Rachildian biographical narrative consists of a recitation of her ancestors, distant and not so far removed, famous and less well-known, writers and men (for they are all men) of action, but all colorful and eccentric. The list includes as its stock characters the sixteenth-century writer Brantôme; the Dominican inquisitor; and the great-grandfather, a canon of the Périgueux cathedral, who renounced his calling during the Revolution (everyone repeats the phrase "jeta son froc aux orties" at this point).[3]

The list of relatives unfolds reverently, almost biblically, and indeed the point of the recitation seems to be that just as Old Testament figures typologically announce those of the New and signal their preordained role in human history, so Rachilde comes to appear the inevitable product of such a genealogy. The ancestors reassuringly guarantee that her appearance on the face of the earth was meant to be, that her eminence as a writer was preordained, and even that her suffering and misunderstanding were inevitable, part of a grander plan, to be redeemed by some higher meaning. That the writer Brantôme (1540–1614), for example, is not only a fellow Périgourdin but in fact claimed as a distant relative appears significant. What could be more natural than to repeat his formula, combining court gossip about the rich and (in)famous with salacious hearsay about everyone's sex life? Translated into late nineteenth-century vernacular, drawing on the streets of bourgeois Paris (and occasionally the provinces) for its sources rather than the restricted circles of the court, Brantôme's memoirs might well have supplied the anecdotal raw material for Rachilde's novels.

Similarly, the Spanish grand inquisitor Dom Faytos—"ou mieux *Fétos*" adds Gaubert in a footnote (5)—seems to explain the mix of religious fervor, superstition, and cruelty that marked Rachilde's childhood background and that passed into her novels. As might be predicted, this inquisitor reputedly had an illegitimate child (by one Maria-Libeira Sandoval). The child, François-Marie Feytaud (a fanciful spelling of the French pronunciation of Faytos), was raised in Languedoc before becoming a legal functionary (*tabellion*) in the Périgord and marrying a propertied member of the Brantôme family, thereby fusing the literary and the religious elements of Rachilde's heritage (Gaubert 5; David, *Rachilde* 11).[4] The Feytaud name remained in the family—the Feytaud Woods just outside Périgueux are so named to this day—and it was the family name of Rachilde's mother, Gabrielle Feytaud.

Rachilde thus traced the connection to these literary ancestors through her mother's side of the family (a point I shall have occasion to return to later). Rachilde probably heard stories about this lineage from childhood on. (She also claimed the "plumitive" poisoner Madame Lafarge as a relative.) Whether or not she believed in this family mythology, assuming it as an adult retroactively reconstructed her writing as foreordained rather than chosen.

In the less distant past, the Spanish inquisitor was echoed by the life of one of Rachilde's great-grandfathers (the father of her maternal grandfather, Urbain Feytaud), here described by Dauphiné: "Quant à l'arrière-grand-père de Rachilde, chanoine de la cathédrale Saint-Front à Périgueux, promis à l'épiscopat, il jeta le froc aux orties sous la terreur, fit un mariage d'amour et obtint une notoriété enviable comme avocat de la ville" (*Rachilde* [1991] 26). This great-grandfather illustrates once again the rebellious career path of Rachilde's relatives: from religious vocation to the people's defender via defiance of authority. The anecdote about this figure always includes mention of the fact that as a lawyer he was so well loved by the people that, on his death, they erected a tombstone inscribed with the words: "A l'avocat des pauvres, le peuple reconnaissant." A touching story, but the whereabouts of this tombstone are unknown, and the Cathedral of Saint-Front in Périgueux has no cemetery attached to it.[5] Moreover, in the retelling of the story, an important qualification gets dropped: according to Gaubert, this great-grandfather was only an "honorary" canon (5). Like so many other details about Rachilde's family background, the mythology cannot stand up to scrutiny, but as mythology it works admirably well. Her ancestors proved more appropriate than any that could have been supplied by fiction. They proclaim that she is born to be a writer, and they even suggest what kind of writer she will be. It is as though Rachilde herself were born in a novel, just as her biographers imply.

The "honorary" canon is a link in another important family chain for Rachilde, tying her to a family of animals like a totem. Because he turned his back on the church, the great-grandfather is cursed, or at least so the local superstition ran: like all such priests, he and his descendants for five generations would be werewolves. Such a curse is no doubt much more effective and dramatic when visited on "full" canons instead of honorary ones, but it was enough to make the more suggestible of Rachilde's neighbors keep a wary eye on her; after all, she was only the fourth generation (her daughter would be the fifth—and indeed the last—generation: she died on November 18, 1984).[6] If the superstition were true, then every year on the feast of Candlemas (February 2, the day commemorating the Purification of the Virgin Mary) Rachilde, too, would become a werewolf.

Had Rachilde known about this curse as a child, as she seems to have, it is likely that she would have relished rather than feared the idea of turning into a wolf. Regardless of the curse, the wolf came to represent the persecuted outsider for Rachilde. To the extent that she also felt like an outsider, the werewolf was her alter ego, the wild, untamed, and even sometimes frightening side of herself that rebelled. Through a combination of firsthand experience, family associations, and general cultural beliefs, the wolf was the totem animal with which she formed a lasting identification.

Among the firsthand experiences, one of the most dramatic is the account—different versions of which were told at different times—of how an adolescent Rachilde defied (or, in some versions, obeyed) her father and freed a wolf that had been left to die, pinned to the ground by a stake through the thigh (the then-customary method of killing wolves that was supposed to serve as a warning to other wolves). In an early version of the story, Rachilde describes what she claims is the first such instance, in which her father presents the act as a test of courage and rewards her with a watch (*PM* 236–43). In later versions—for example, in *Face à la peur* (1942)—Rachilde accompanies her father on the hunt and defies him, releasing the animal to an uncertain future. The Périgord could be a cruel and brutal world, and Rachilde learned very quickly the low value placed on animal life, as anyone familiar with her fiction knows. Yet the persecution of the wolf affected her even more than the repeated and thoughtless destruction of family pets and domestic animals, and the wolf rivals the rat in her affection for the misunderstood and the maligned.

On another occasion, recorded in her memoirs *Quand j'étais jeune* (1947), a trap set for a wolf instead caught a poacher. On this occasion, too, Rachilde defied her father's order to guard the prisoner while he fetched the police, and she used the butt of her rifle to prize open the trap and free the "bête humaine" (111), as Rachilde calls him. The anecdote would be almost without importance were it not that the youth, named le Césarien, later came to the house to demand money from her in order to leave the region and start a new life elsewhere. When Rachilde—a teenager several years younger than the youth—wonders why he is appealing to her, she learns that he claims to be her half brother, evidently the illegitimate fruit of an adulterous relationship of her father's. Rachilde repeatedly stresses her disbelief of this rumor, but her protestations are hollow and unconvincing (her father was illegitimate himself and would never, imagines Rachilde, visit the same misfortune on his own offspring [*QJJ* 121–22]).

Perhaps what causes Rachilde to doubt her own conviction that le Césarien cannot be her brother, however, is that at some level he, like she, is a wolf. Something of a wild child to begin with, with "des yeux de bête sauvage" (*QJJ* 111), le Césarien must be a wolf because what else would a wolf trap catch? Thus, at least in some part of Rachilde's imagination, not only was the wolf her figurative brother, but he was her literal brother as well. Furthermore, when Rachilde is summoned to meet with le Césarien, she is sitting at the same table at which she sits "pour écrire les nuits de pleine lune" (119). She wrote by the light of the full moon, Rachilde explains, because her parents would not allow her any candles (see, for example, *QJJ* 8), but she chooses not to remind us of that fact at this particular point. Is it thus just a coincidence that the full moon is also when werewolves traditionally appear? The inclusion of this detail (why else mention it?) serves to remind the reader that it is when she writes that the adolescent Rachilde turns into a teenage werewolf. If the nineteenth-century woman writer must "examine, assimilate, and transcend the extreme images of 'angel' and 'monster' which male authors have generated for her," as Sandra Gilbert and Susan Gubar have suggested in the case of the British woman writer (*Madwoman in the Attic* 17), the werewolf served to express what Rachilde perceived as the monstrosity of her desire to write. Yet the reminder of that monstrous alter ego at this juncture of the narrative also explains why, despite her professions of disbelief, Rachilde was inclined to accept le Césarien as her brother and to give him a family heirloom in lieu of cash.

That Rachilde's father, Captain Eymery, did not share this sense of clan loyalty and was, on the contrary, the sworn enemy of the wolf did not in any way invalidate Rachilde's sense of totemic allegiance; rather, in some ways, his opposition confirmed its relevance. The symbolic and sometimes literal hostility between mother and father, as well as between the maternal and the paternal sides of the family, is a theme that recurs throughout Rachilde's work and serves to organize and structure a number of conflicts she experienced. As mentioned above, the connection both to the (were)wolf (via the honorary canon) and to the family of writers (via Brantôme) came from Rachilde's mother's side of the family, while her father's side of the family represented very different values. If Rachilde belonged to a family of writers through her mother, her father scorned and hated what he called "des plumitifs" (see, for example, *QJJ* 166). If Rachilde experienced some conflict about the fact that she idolized her father while he rejected her for not being the son he wanted (the son he had but did *not* want having turned out a bit sheepish in wolf's trappings), she expressed that conflict by becoming the very thing her father most despised: a writer/werewolf writing/howling under a full moon. Given the displaced and indirect way in which these hostilities get expressed, it seems perfectly appropriate that, after retiring from the military, Captain Eymery should join the *louveterie*, the paramilitary community organization devoted to the hunting down and extermination of the wolf, "his natural enemy." If a "natural" son (like le Césarien) is a child who is really "family," though one you cannot or will not admit, then perhaps a "natural" enemy (such as a wolf) may also be denied (cast as an enemy), even when a *legitimate* member of the family (such as Rachilde).

Given the resonance of the wolf image (as I have tried to show), it is not surprising to note the insistent recurrence of wolves in Rachilde's fiction. From early novels such as *Minette* (1889), through mid-career works such as "La Fille du louvetier" in *L'Imitation de la mort* (1903) and *Le Meneur de louves* (1905), to later works such as *Le Parc du mystère* (1923), *L'Amazone rouge* (1932), and even her final publication, *Quand j'étais jeune* (1947), which contains the chapter on le Césarien, the wolf is one of the most enduring figures (see also Santon 7–8). But the wolf trap, the significance of which has been explored briefly with reference to le Césarien, is also a metaphor that guides the reading of all Rachilde's fiction, whether explicitly about wolves or not, as an analysis of one of her works will illustrate.

One of her early novels, *Minette*, an otherwise fairly unremarkable effort, focuses on the threat of wolves. Although this novel was not published until 1889, Rachilde was working on obtaining a contract for it as early as 1886 (RHS 24–25). *Minette* was not her choice of title but the publisher's, and the manuscript of the novel, dated 1889 and preserved in the Fonds Doucet, bears the title "Le Loup-Garou" (The werewolf).[7]

Set in the Corrèze, the novel focuses on the story of Hermine de Messiange (part angel, part messiah, part sparrow). Hermine is also known by the nickname Minette, the two names signaling a split personality and the resulting conflict between the two sides of her character, one good, one bad. Minette falls in love with her (married) guardian and cousin, Laurent Bruon, but resists the temptation to give in to her love ("Hermine n'a pas cédé à Minette" ["Bibliographie générale" 126]).

Minette opens with the death of the baroness de Messiange, making Minette (then only sixteen) the last of the Messiange family. Minette is thus a typical Rachildian (and decadent) heroine, but, whereas Rachilde inherited the curse of the werewolf through her mother's side of the family, Minette is "garou par son père" (38). Her father is not the baron, however; she is the lo(u)ve child of the curé of Sorges, with whom her mother evidently had an adulterous affair. Like Rachilde's maternal great-grandfather, however, the curé is cursed because he abandons the church, although in his case he abandons it by going against church teaching on adultery. Not only is the curé rumored to be a werewolf, but he is also reputed to be the king of the wolves (34–35) and is compared to a wolf in the way "il va rôder autour de la maison [des Messiange] comme un loup en quête de son louveteau" (18).

The action of the novel covers approximately a year in Minette's life, beginning and ending in the depths of winter. After her mother's death, Minette lives with Laurent Bruon and his wife, Marie. Attracted initially by her money, Laurent gradually falls in love with Minette. She resists his advances at first but eventually admits that she loves him. Her sense of virtue, however, prevents her from acting on those feelings, and, as a result, she goes insane. Finding her husband about to shoot himself in misery, Maria gives her blessing to the consummation of the adulterous affair, and she sends Minette to the bedroom where Laurent is now sleeping. As she is about to enter the bedroom, however, Minette thinks that she sees the ghost of her recently deceased father, the curé, and she flees into the snowy night and dies.

Because so much of the action concerns illicit and covert activities, much of it takes place at night. For example, Minette exchanges letters with the curé, but, since their correspondence is clandestine, they leave the letters for each other hidden in a tree, Minette leaving hers and collecting his only at night. Because Laurent's attentions make her uncomfortable, she tries to avoid sleeping under the same roof as he. When he responds by locking her in at night, Minette escapes through the bedroom window and sleeps in the garden, yet another setting for nocturnal encounters. Finally, when farmwork peaks in the summertime, Laurent takes advantage of the full moon to work at night. For these various reasons, then, characters are always running into each other in half-deserted settings where shadows lurk and the only light is provided by the moon.

Although wolves are normally less of a problem in the summer than in the winter (197), the sheer amount of nocturnal activity increases the chances both of encounters with actual wolves and of tricks of the light that make people *think* they have seen a wolf (or a werewolf). Thus, it is when Minette collects one of the curé's letters that she runs into a real wolf. At first, she thinks it is just the dog, Canteau, but then "le chien ouvrit, dans un bâillement féroce, sa gueule qui sembla se distendre comme un étau d'acier brillant" (93), and she realizes that she is about to be attacked by a wolf. She is saved on this occasion by Laurent, who had been following her and who kills the wolf and collects the bounty.

The roles are reversed when Laurent finds Minette sleeping in the garden. As Laurent declares his love and urges her to abandon herself to him, Minette suddenly sees a ghost, an apparition with distinctly lupine qualities: "On aperçut des mèches de cheveux argentés, deux yeux caves, éclairés d'une farouche lueur" (147). Laurent is convinced that it is a werewolf, although it turns out to be the curé keeping a protective eye on Minette. Laurent thus saves Minette from the wolf, while a werewolf saves Minette from Laurent.

This reversal illustrates how wolves proliferate in this novel. Laurent, for example, is not merely a wolf hunter (he kills the wolf that threatens Minette); he is himself a wolf in the predatory way he stalks Minette. After he kills the real wolf, Minette is hardly reassured: "Elle ne s'était pas trompée, un loup ne va pas seul . . . et elle se trouvait, maintenant, face à face avec le plus cruel des deux" (99). This moment is evoked later, when Minette again feels threatened by Laurent's advances (141). Fur-

ther, if Laurent is a wolf, it makes sense that the rest of his family belong
to the same genus. Thus, Maria acts "comme une louve" (169), and Laurent and Maria's son Charlot is described as a "louveteau" (282), or wolf
cub, even as he accuses Minette of being a werewolf.

Similarly, if the curé is a werewolf, as the rumors claim, and if he is
Minette's real father, as the rumors also claim, it is hardly surprising that
Minette, too, is part (were)wolf. When gossiping neighbors hear a disembodied voice (later identified as Minette's), they naturally assume it
is that of a werewolf (40), and Laurent's children openly refer to Minette
as the "garou" (185, 218). As an extension of this lupine identity, Minette
imagines her future husband to be a werewolf (88), and Laurent imagines that she is after a werewolf (138).

The profusion of references succeeds in blurring the separation between human and wolf. Sometimes, people are indistinguishable from
wolves (because they are werewolves or because of their predatory behavior). Some people are part wolf (like Minette), yet they are not
immune to attack from their own species (both real and figurative).
Wolves prey on people, but people also hunt wolves. People set traps for
wolves, but sometimes they have as much to fear from the traps as from
the wolves that the traps are intended to catch.

The ending of *Minette* offers a *mise en abyme* of these interpretive
problems and also offers a warning to readers. In the last two pages of
the novel, a peasant returning home at dawn sings a song about a shepherdess. Ignoring the advice of her parents, this shepherdess went to the
ball, returning only late at night, along a dark path, where she encounters, not the wolf that the reader is by now expecting, but a wolf trap, in
which she is caught. It is at this point that the singing peasant catches
sight of Minette's body. The last time the reader saw her, she was lying
naked in the snow, lulled to sleep by the cold. Now, we learn, she is
dead. What killed her? Did she meet a wolf once again, one who took
advantage of her weakened state? Did her own inner wolf manifest itself—we know it is a moonlit night (312); perhaps that brought about
the metamorphosis? After all, when the peasant catches sight of Minette's body, he interrupts his song: "'Quand on parle du loup . . . !
Sacré bon sort!' jura-t-il, 'c'est *le garou* de la Messiange! c'est la petite
demoiselle'" (314). Not only is it sufficient to mention a wolf for one to
appear, but in death it seems that Minette has assumed—or reverted
to—her true form, that of a werewolf.

But the conclusion of the peasant's song suggests another reading:
the "moral" of the shepherdess's story, it turns out, is not "beware of
wolves," or even "obey your parents," but "ne tendez plus le piège au

loup." Don't set traps for wolves because it is not wolves they catch but people (people like the shepherdess, people like le Césarien). The real enemy, in other words, is not the wolf but the notion that it can be eliminated.

The fact is, wolves have nothing to do with the death of either the shepherdess or Minette. The shepherdess, we are told, dies, not from a wolf attack, or even from the wolf trap, but "de peur" (314), while Minette dies simply of cold. In the end, then, what proves fatal is nothing to do with wolves at all, despite the ever-present threat that they pose. Besides, wolves and traps are interchangeable: the trap that "bites" the shepherdess is described in terms of a wolf's grip—"douze dents d'acier" (313)—while, as indicated above, the wolf's jaws resemble the trap, "un étau d'acier brillant." The insistence on wolves and wolf traps, then, is a narrative trap. It is human failings like madness and fear, as well as their antecedents love and foolishness, that kill people.

The puzzling thing about the ending of *Minette*, then, is that after all the hints spread along the way, the cautions about not falling into a wolf trap, this is not Minette's fate. In a sense, the warnings succeed: wolf traps are successfully avoided by all in the novel. Yet the (wolf) traps succeed in trapping the reader by creating the expectation that the warnings will go unheeded. As readers, we think that we are smarter than the characters in the novel. We will avoid the wolf, like the characters themselves do, but we will go one step further and also avoid the equally dangerous wolf trap. But a careful reading of *Minette* suggests that wolves are really red herrings. To be caught by a wolf—or even a wolf trap—is the exception, not the rule. Rachilde is very much like her heroine Minette in turning out, finally, to be quite ordinary. All the talk of wolves is really only a smoke screen. And, in Rachilde's case, all the talk about exceptional things (ghosts, spirits, hysteria, persecution) serves to disguise the fact that, when the smoke clears, Rachilde's life is much more ordinary by far than she would have us believe. Narratives create expectations, set (wolf) traps for the reader. But the real story is the one that the narrative tells only reluctantly, the banal one of a girl who dies of fright or cold.

The lesson Rachilde's readers must learn is not to be misled by wolves. There are other narrative traps out there, most notably that of paying attention only to the exceptions. The critic who reads Rachilde's life as that of an exceptional woman will miss the ways in which, when it comes right down to it, that life is, in fact, quite ordinary.

This observation leads to the more sweeping judgment that the criticism that women writers in general—and Rachilde in particular—

wrote only about their own lives is a dangerous oversimplification. This criticism was leveled specifically at Rachilde, I suspect, because it made her work either more piquant, and therefore more marketable, or more tame and less threatening—depending on whether you were trying to drum up sales or reassure her fellow writers, or yourself, that she was not a threat to anyone else's literary career. A good example would later be furnished by Maurice Barrès's preface to the 1889 edition of *Monsieur Vénus*, in which he describes the novel as the dream of the young virgin author.

The chapters that follow, then, will be trying to show what is at stake in some of the distortions and misprisions that Rachilde allows and fosters. I maintain that Rachilde is typical of a generation of (French) women writers whose audience was unused to women authors—unused, not because women necessarily do write differently from men (although that belief was widespread), but because the sight of a woman's name on the cover of a book was rare. While acknowledging what is unique about Rachilde's fictional preoccupations, then, I shall also be concerned to point out what I believe was typical for women writers of turn-of-the-century France.

The Ambivalence of the Paternal

In which Captain Eymery is taken prisoner

> Le 29 octobre 1870, remis aux Prussiens 89 hommes et 85 che-
> vaux dont 75 de troupe et 10 d'officiers.
>
> Rachilde, *Les Rageac*

One of the most significant events of Rachilde's childhood was also an event of national and international importance: the Franco-Prussian War of 1870. It was the first of three Franco-German conflicts that Rachilde would witness, and, although she would experience World Wars I and II more directly, arguably it was the Franco-Prussian conflict that caused the most long-term disruptions in her life, for the national crisis of 1870–71 mirrored a personal, familial one. Just as this war led to a series of transformations from the relative order of the Second Empire via the bloody upheavals of the Commune to the national reconstruction begun during the Third Republic, so the war and its aftermath marked the end of childhood innocence and the beginnings of awareness of family conflict.

Before the war, Rachilde's childhood was not particularly happy, but there was a certain stability to it. The family traveled around the country from garrison to garrison as her father changed posts, and, although this constant movement was not conducive to putting down roots, the fact that army routine was the same everywhere provided a certain continuity.

Some of Rachilde's recollections of this early period were recorded by Auriant (see *Souvenirs*). In this presentation, Rachilde's father and his lifestyle affected her directly and profoundly, while her mother remained a shadowy, background figure, removed from the day-to-day routines of the infant's life. At six weeks old, Rachilde claimed, she was traveling on the knees of her nurse, Louise-la-Rousse (Rachilde also called her "Lala"), from garrison to garrison (see also *AM* vi; Gaubert 7; David, *Rachilde* 12). Although there were emotional stresses, Rachilde's early life was relatively free of material cares and pressures. From early infancy, Louise-la-Rousse gave her both love and freedom. Rather than restrict the child's movements with cumbersome swaddling, Louise placed the naked baby in a box of bran. Cold, the baby could burrow into the box; warm, she could lie closer to the surface (Auriant, *Souvenirs* 26). When the child grew a little older, Louise provided a menagerie of animal friends, including large hunting dogs that would act as substitute child minders, hauling Rachilde back to her chair by the scruff of the neck if she wandered off while Louise was busy chopping vegetables. Since her nurse could not read, Rachilde herself showed little inclination to learn, preferring to ride in Lala's shopping basket on their trips to market. As a young girl, Rachilde had more dresses than she could wear and horses and carriages at her disposal (*QJJ* 122). These conditions had much to do with the situation of Rachilde's immediate family, a product, on one side, of several generations of increasingly prosperous provincial bourgeois and, on the other, of a struggle to overcome illegitimacy.

Rachilde's mother's side of the family can be traced back fairly easily to the honorary canon (the one who became the werewolf), and from there Feytaud family tradition held that Urbain-François Feytaud could trace his ancestry back to François-Marie Feytaud, the illegitimate son of the Spanish inquisitor (see "1860: Women as Outsiders"). The third child of Urbain-François Feytaud and his wife, Charlotte Deglane Feytaud, was born Urbain Raymond Feytaud in Périgueux on July 3, 1807.[1] In later life, Urbain Raymond would return to his native Périgord, become a justice of the peace in Thiviers, and acquire a reputation for an interest in the occult and especially séances, which he organized, but before he could settle into such distinguished retirement, he had to go out into the world and make a reputation for himself, as had his two older brothers.[2]

After attending the lycée de Périgueux, Urbain Raymond made his way to Paris, where he took part in the July Days of 1830 and became a typesetter (*typographe*). Back in Nontron in 1834, he set up a print shop, published a newspaper, and founded a credit union. In 1847, having made his way to Valenciennes, in the "France instruite du Nord-Est" (Chartier and Martin 18), the political journalist became editor in chief of the *Courrier du Nord* (Pommarède, "Le Sol et le sang" 812). The grandfather figure in *Les Rageac*—perhaps based on Urbain—is a "révolutionnaire de 48" and "possédait le caractère brouillon des gens qui ont essayé de tous les régimes en s'y opposant" (55). Urbain Feytaud was also an author, having published a number of books and pamphlets on topics ranging from agricultural and labor reform to spiritualism (a number of which are listed in the catalog of the Bibliothèque Nationale). With his wife, Marie-Etiennette Izaline Desmond,[3] a widow (Pommarède, "Le Sol et le sang" 812), he had one child, a daughter named Marie-Gabrielle, born on May 28, 1837, in Nontron.[4]

Rachilde later described Izaline and Gabrielle, mother and daughter, as "deux oppositions très classiques du type de la femme: la 1830, *la romantique*, et la 1870, *l'excentrique*, celle qui devait précéder la *révoltée moderne*" (*Pourquoi* 13). She went on to give a more detailed portrait of her grandmother: "Ma grand'mère (elle s'appelait *Isaline* et ce petit nom en dit long sur les franfreluches sentimentales de son époque) était une corpulente dame, encore fort jolie, une blonde cendrée portant des *anglaises* [ringlets] et dont il restait des jambes parfaites, des pieds minuscules, plus une perpétuelle faculté de s'attendrir sur n'importe qui, à propos de n'importe quoi avec un frémissement de sa bouche en coeur tout à fait puéril" (14).

Izaline and Urbain Feytaud raised their daughter with every advantage. A talented musician (she won a first prize at the Conservatory of Valenciennes), Gabrielle was presented at the court of Napoleon III by her Belgian violin teacher, Henri Vieuxtemps (1820–81), another event described in *Les Rageac* (80). At twenty-one, she seemed destined to become a virtuoso and make a good match in life when she met and fell in love with a handsome young career soldier without fame or name on that fateful evening when she performed at court (*Les Rageac* 80). "Ce fut le coup de foudre, pas pour lui, pour elle!" claimed Rachilde (*QJJ* 127).

The ancestry of Rachilde's father, Joseph Eymery, proves difficult to trace more than one generation back. According to Rachilde, this "soldier of fortune without a fortune" (*QJJ* 128) was the illegitimate son of a country squire (*hobereau*) named the marquis d'Ormoy—"un de ces nobles absolument inutile à la société, parce qu'il est l'objet de luxe sans emploi et presque toujours nuisible" (*QJJ* 67)—and Jeanne Eymery, "une pauvre fille sans fortune, une de ces jeunes filles orphelines que les riches protégeaient pour leur jolie figure ou leur science de la bonne compagnie" (*QJJ* 68). This girl, described here as a tutor (*lectrice*) for a certain Madame de Lidonne, was seduced by the feckless marquis, an inveterate "skirt chaser" who declined to marry her because she had no fortune.[5] Rachilde claims that the marquis offered to recognize his son Joseph legally when he reached the age of majority but that Joseph refused the title he would have inherited.[6]

Once again, the story Rachilde tells diverges somewhat from the one that can be reconstructed today from the available records. Joseph Eymery's birth is not recorded under the name Eymery or even under "Aimeri," which Rachilde claims as "le vrai nom de mon père" (*QJJ* 68).[7] Instead, it can be found in an entry under the name "Padres Jean trouvé" that states that a male child was found on the doorstep of a hospice in Périgueux at two o'clock in the morning on January 22, 1822, and was given the name Jean Padres.[8] An annotation in the margin has been added later: "L'enfant ci contre a été reconnu le vingt deux juin 1839 [seventeen and a half years to the day after his abandonment], devant Gaillard, notaire à Périgueux. Il est dit dans cet acte que désormais cet enfant portera le nom et prénom de Joseph Eymery comme étant fils naturel de Jeanne Eymery, comparante." The child was thus a foundling for the first seventeen and a half years of his life.[9]

Whether or not his father ever offered to recognize him, as Rachilde claimed, is not recorded, but even his mother did not recognize him (legally) until he was nearly eighteen (of course it is possible that she had some contact with him before doing so). It was also at this time that he legally acquired the new identity of Joseph Eymery. His mother's name is clearly given as Eymery (there is no mention of "Aimeri"), and there is no reference at all to his father. When births were registered, it was usual to give information such as the age, occupation, and place of residence of the parents, but the belated act of recognition by Jeanne Eymery includes none of these facts, except to correct her occupation to that of *gouvernante* (housekeeper).[10] There is no allusion to any aristocratic connection, and no trace of the marquis has been found subsequently. Perhaps Rachilde's knowledge of family history came directly from her paternal grandmother, or perhaps it was pure wishful thinking. As she states in *L'Autre Crime* (1937), "un bâtard qui n'a pas de parents connus ça peut être fils de prince, naturellement" (66).

Madame de Lidonne (Jeanne's employer), on the other hand, has been identified as Louise-Thérèse Dessalles de Marzat (ca. 1754–1845), daughter of a bourgeois family well established in Périgueux by the seventeenth century. She had one son, Jean-Baptiste, by her first marriage to Pierre Tamarelle de Boisset. Her second marriage (to Jacques-François de Lidonne, grandson of Nicolas Lidonne, who came to Périgueux in 1727) took place in 1785. It is tempting to speculate that Joseph Eymery's father may have been a member of the Lidonne household, but there is no direct evidence for this hypothesis (not even a hint of an Ormoy in the family tree) other than the interest that the Lidonne family seems to have taken in the illegitimate offspring of one of its servants. Jean-Baptiste de Lidonne, for example, married a Mademoiselle de Benoit de Laubresset, and it was a member of the Benoit de Laubresset family—Jean Joseph Benoit de Laubresset "adjoint au maire, officier de l'état civil de la commune de Périgueux département de la Dordogne par délégation du maire"—who officially recorded the birth of the infant Jean Padres. Madame de Lidonne also left Joseph Eymery one thousand francs in her will, a generous act for one who is not a blood relative (Pommarède, "Le Sol et le sang" 804–5).

Whoever his father was, somehow Joseph escaped the fate of many foundlings—poverty and obscurity. When Rachilde knew her paternal grandmother, Jeanne Eymery seems to have lived on the place du Coderc, now part of the historic center of Périgueux,[11] and one of the pieces of property described as belonging to Joseph in his marriage contract was located not far away from this square, on the corner of the rue des Chaînes and the rue de l'Arc, also in the heart of Périgueux. On the basis of these facts, one might speculate that Jeanne had or acquired the means to care for her son. Perhaps their financial needs were taken care of by the elusive marquis d'Ormoy or some member of the Lidonne family who had employed the girl. If, as Rachilde claims, Jeanne Eymery was an orphan from a respectable family (*QJJ* 68), perhaps she had a little education and some modest means of her own. Either way, she is described as a "propriétaire" in Joseph's marriage contract in 1858.[12] And, whether it had been settled on him by his mother or father or purchased with his own savings, Joseph also himself had a claim to property by the time he decided to marry.

Joseph Eymery also attained bourgeois status through his career in the army. He joined up as a volunteer in the fifth cavalry regiment (*chasseurs*) on June 14, 1842. The regiment was then stationed in Tarbes, but in October it moved to Tarascon. By December, Joseph had been promoted to *brigadier élève fourrier* (brigadier apprentice quartermaster), and, by the following summer (July 19, 1844), he had become *maréchal des logis fourrier*. He thus was part of the unit responsible for the regiment's accommodations.

The fifth regiment was composed of five squadrons (*escadrons*), four of them designated as combat units (*de guerre*) and one as a supply squadron (*dépôt*) responsible for recruiting, training, maintenance, and procurement or foraging. In October 1845, the four combat squadrons were sent to Algeria, Joseph Eymery among them. He would spend the next four years in North Africa.

The specifics of his actions in North Africa have not been recorded, but we can get some idea of what his life was like from official records. While in Algeria, the squadrons went on expeditions and occasionally took part in combat, but, as the regimental historian notes, "à l'époque dont il s'agit, la guerre d'Afrique était, à la fois, une épreuve et une école pour les troupes appelées à y prendre part, et que, même dans les expeditions où on ne trouvait pas devant soi un ennemi groupé et prêt à la résistance, il ne fallait pas moins faire preuve de sérieuses qualités militaires pour les mener à bien" ("Historique" 242). Having conceded this point, however, it should be said that Joseph Eymery's continued responsibilities as *maréchal des logis* (he was promoted to *maréchal des lo-*

gis chef, or marshal of the supply chief, on December 10, 1845, that is, shortly after his arrival in Algeria) probably kept him away from much of the action. He received no decorations or special mentions for his service in Algeria, although he did receive another promotion, this time to sublieutenant, on May 9, 1848.

The regiment returned to Tarbes on September 21, 1849, where it was reorganized, and Eymery began a decade of service in garrisons around France. In October 1849, the regiment left in two columns for Vendôme to become part of the armée de Paris. After a few years, Joseph Eymery was again promoted, this time to lieutenant, on March 10, 1854, while the four combat squadrons were sent in July 1854 to Boulogne to take part in maneuvers. Shortly after this, Joseph Eymery left his regiment temporarily, and while his regiment moved on to yet another garrison (Napoléonville, Morbihan), he spent nearly two years (December 31, 1854–October 1, 1856) at the Ecole impériale de cavalerie in Saumur training to become an officer. When he finished his training, he rejoined the regiment and shortly after (in October 1857) moved with it to a new garrison in Valenciennes, where a new chapter in his life began.

For one thing, he was now a captain, having been promoted on October 30, 1857, and he would soon be promoted again, to adjutant major captain, on January 12, 1858. Joseph Eymery had evidently climbed high enough in the hierarchy to be acceptable as a son-in-law to the bourgeois Feytauds, with whose only daughter, Gabrielle, he would contract an alliance in October 1858. No record remains of how he met the Feytauds, but it is not hard to imagine how their common origin in the Périgord may have brought them together when they found themselves far from home in Valenciennes, on the Belgian border. Within a few years, Joseph Eymery would make a financially advantageous match, start a family, and become a knight of the Legion of Honor (this last on December 31, 1862).

It may have been love at first sight, at least for Gabrielle Feytaud, as Rachilde would later claim, but it was apparently not so for Joseph Eymery, a Don Juan who "changeait de maîtresse aussi souvent qu'il changeait de garnison" (*Pourquoi* 16). Joseph's initial attraction, or so Rachilde claimed, was to Izaline Feytaud,[13] but he subsequently transferred his attentions to her daughter, Gabrielle. Rachilde wrote that she never understood what drew her parents together, other than the fact that "les extrêmes s'attirent naturellement" (*Pourquoi* 16), but, whatever the foundation of their relationship, it led to marriage in 1858.[14] Marie-Marguerite, the only offspring of their union, was born some fifteen months later back in the Périgord. Gabrielle's parents, too, moved back there in time to receive visits from their granddaughter. Urbain Feytaud founded a newspaper in Périgueux, the *Progrès de la Dordogne*, ran for office in 1869, and was named a justice of the peace in Thiviers on October 14, 1870 (Pommarède, "Le Sol et le sang" 812).

The family rifts that would become further apparent after the Franco-Prussian War had already begun by the time of Rachilde's birth. Joseph and Gabrielle had separate bedrooms (*QJJ* 129), as did many married couples of their time and class, but Gabrielle apparently carried things further and after her daughter's birth refused further conjugal relations with her husband, perhaps to avoid a second pregnancy. The couple's devotion to each other was short-lived, if indeed it had ever existed at all. While Rachilde was cared for by Lala, she could remain ignorant of such stresses and strains between her parents, but the older she grew, the harder they were to miss.

While Gabrielle did not yet speak openly of the problems in her marriage, she dropped dark hints. Despite her nickname "the angel Gabriel," Rachilde's mother was not compassionate and merciful but strict and judgmental. This "dragon of virtue" (*Pourquoi* 15) actively encouraged Rachilde to disobey men because "l'homme: 'animal immonde et égoïste' n'a pas le droit d'exercer sa détestable influence sur les gens vertueux. La vraie, la seule famille, c'est la mère, elle porte seule son enfant . . . et les responsabilités de sa naissance, etc., etc." (*Pourquoi* 17). Reading between the lines of this bitterness, one can see that Gabrielle's Second Empire rhetoric of female propriety masked deep grievances. Despite—or perhaps because of—her whirlwind romance with Joseph Eymery, Gabrielle perhaps soon realized that she had made a mistake in marrying a military Don Juan, a mistake that was irreversible in an era and a provincial society that did not allow divorce either legally or socially. Her complaints about men in general were perhaps the specific regrets of a woman who saw that her life was henceforth constrained and her ambitions curtailed, that her talents as a musician and her acquaintances at court were to be sacrificed to a stultifying life as a provincial matron.

Unfortunately, this bitterness carried over into a rejection of her child. This deformed little being (Rachilde's right leg was slightly shorter than her left, which caused her to walk with a limp) would cling to her crinoline skirts, a constant reminder of imperfection that Gabrielle would push away with the only partially affectionate nickname "little slug" (Auriant, *Souvenirs* 27). This "slug" proved a much slower and clumsier companion for Gabrielle than the pet monkey, Favorite, so appropriately named, who quickly usurped Rachilde's place in the family.

Favorite would eat at the same table as Rachilde (children ate separately from adults), steal her food, pull her hair, and trip her up. The behavior was irritating to say the least, but more hurtful than any physical trial were the demeaning comparisons that her mother made: "Ma mère prétendait que Favorite était plus *humaine* que moi et quand elle se mettait au piano la fort grande musicienne qu'était la dame Napoléon III prenait sa singesse sur ses genoux et lui faisait plaquer quelques accords. Je l'entends dire à une de ses amies: 'Vous me croirez si vous voulez, ma chère, Favorite a plus de sens artistique et plus d'oreille que ma fille: elle ne fera pas de fausses notes'" (Auriant, *Souvenirs* 27). Whatever the underlying reasons for Gabrielle's "favoritism," Rachilde soon learned that her mother found her wanting and artistically inferior to a pet monkey.

As Rachilde learned to expect such behavior from her mother, it is not surprising that she turned to her father instead. In this family dynamic we see the beginnings of the two opposite poles that would structure Rachilde's universe: the maternal, with its promise of a legitimate connection to writing but with psychological rejection, and the paternal, the illegitimate, anti-intellectual inheritance that offered a more direct and less complicated form of mistreatment. As the heroine Mary Barbe learns in *La Marquise de Sade*: "Aimer, c'est souffrir" (84).[15]

Joseph Eymery's treatment of his daughter was scarcely more affectionate than Gabrielle's, at least overtly—"mon père . . . m'écartait du bout de sa cravache sans d'ailleurs me faire grand mal, mais avec un mépris qui me terrorisait, me donnait de moi-même la plus humiliante opinion" (Auriant, *Souvenirs* 26)—but at least there was something about him that Rachilde could idealize, whereas Gabrielle's bitterness about men was alienating. Despite her mother's admonishments, and despite the beatings from his whip that she took on her hand, Rachilde secretly admired her father "parce qu'il pouvait regarder le soleil en face, comme les aigles; parce qu'il montait très bien à cheval et qu'il avait fait la guerre" (*Pourquoi* 17).

Rachilde knew that her father wished to remain distant, however, and she did not dare give him any sign of sympathy. Such perverse admiration and childish idealization were also somewhat pathetic responses to intense rejection. Joseph Eymery had desperately wanted a son (a *legitimate* son—I have already discussed the rumors of the illegitimate son, le Césarien), and from the beginning Rachilde was made perfectly aware of her shortcomings. Paradoxically, however, she did not resent her father's rejection in the same way she did her mother's. She desperately sought to compensate her father for his disappointment, as though pleasing him would also bring the gratifying approval that she craved. She turned to physical training, hanging around the stables and learning to ride at an early age, the first of many episodes in a lifelong attempt to win his attention.[16]

Her attempts to infiltrate his affections were hampered by the fact that, even at the best of times, Joseph Eymery was not a demonstrative man. Rachilde offered this portrait of him in her memoirs: "Mon père ne parlait pas, ne s'expliquait pas; il savait beaucoup de choses, et les subissait sans se plaindre: était-il très fort par endurance de son métier militaire, ou par indifférence naturelle? Je lui ai souvent entendu dire que la plus grande noblesse est de *savoir garder le silence*, se taire, sous les armes . . . en guerre, comme pendant la paix. Je ne lui ai jamais connu d'opinion politique autre que sa haine instinctive du désordre. Il ne connaissait qu'un devoir: servir son pays, avant de défendre un régime" (*QJJ* 70). Joseph Eymery was thus the quintessential strong, silent type. The supreme virtue was silence, a standard that must have caused conflict for the part of Rachilde that sought self-expression.

During the early years of Rachilde's childhood, the fifth cavalry regiment moved regularly. Shortly after her birth, for example, on April 3, 1860, the combat squadrons were sent to Paris while the depot squadron went to Joigny. Then, in May 1861, the regiment was sent to Chartres (except for one squadron that went to Châteaudun). This was followed by moves to Clermont-Ferrand in April 1863 (still minus one squadron, this one stationed at Riom), to Lyon (for the combat squadrons) and Dôle (for the depot) in 1866, and to Vienne in 1867. (The movements of Colonel Barbe's regiment in *La Marquise de Sade* follow exactly the same itinerary: Clermont-Ferrand, Dôle, Vienne.) On September 2, 1867, Joseph Eymery's entire regiment was stationed in Haguenau (a move also mirrored in *La Marquise de Sade*), except for one platoon (*peloton*) sent to Strasbourg. It was in Strasbourg that Joseph Eymery's career problems and physical decline began.

Despite his air of aloofness and indifference, Joseph Eymery committed himself quickly and easily when personal honor was at stake. Thus, it was impossible for him to let pass a reference to his illegitimacy by the baron "Bontaud-Guiron" (as Rachilde calls him in a thinly disguised reference to Gontaud-Biron) without settling the matter in a duel. Though technically illegal, dueling was a socially accepted way of settling disputes, but it was also a way of "performing" masculinity, as some historians have argued.[17] The encounter is retold in Rachilde's *Les Rageac* (a duel also figures in chap. 6 of *La Marquise de Sade*).[18] As punishment for engaging in the duel, Eymery was sentenced to six months in the military prison of Strasbourg. Using her court connec-

tions, Gabrielle solicited the empress to intervene on her husband's behalf, and Joseph was in fact released after only four months, but, as a result of conditions in the prison, Joseph had become deaf.

Rachilde's description of "capitaine Rageac" after four months in
prison captures the changes that the young Marguerite must have noted
when she saw her father again: "En quatre mois, il avait maigri, blanchi,
s'était atrophié, diminué qu'il était par d'abominables douleurs névral-
giques dont il n'avait soufflé mot à personne, car l'idée d'être transporté
à l'infirmerie pour un mal d'oreille lui semblait humiliante" (*Les Rageac*
101). If before he was aloof and reserved by choice, now he found himself surrounded by enforced silence, which no doubt intensified his air
of indifference. "Ce n'est plus un homme qui nous revient, c'est un
spectre," says the character Gabrielle in *Les Rageac* (106). The incident
says much about what life must have been like for Rachilde: her father
was absent a great deal (four months in prison was just one example),
while her mother was put in the ambivalent position of having to seek
favors at court. The trials of military life did not improve Joseph's communication skills, and, since an imperial decision placed him on reserve
status as of May 15, 1869, "par retrait d'emploi," apparently as punishment for the duel, throwing himself into his career was no longer an
option.

As a child, then, Rachilde may have spent little time with her parents
and more with the household staff. When not with Lala, Rachilde enjoyed the company of her maternal grandmother, a simpleminded soul
who epitomized for Rachilde the frivolous and sentimental woman of
the 1830s. Izaline was *gourmande* and pious in equal proportions (there
being bakeries on the way to church, as Rachilde noted) and had no intellectual pretensions whatsoever: "Elle ne discutait pas, ne tançait pas,
ne lisait aucun roman, n'étudiait pas les philosophes et ne se lançait pas
en théories subversives. Elle semblait très peu cultivée, se servait d'une
orthographe des plus fantaisistes, avait des superstitions amusantes et
croyait, par exemple, que lorsqu'on égarait son dé, ses ciseaux ou une
aiguille, il arrivait un malheur dans la journée" (*Pourquoi* 18). Rachilde's
mother taught her to ridicule and even despise Izaline, and, unlike the
lesson on men, this one took root. Rachilde thus learned to dismiss one
of the few apparent sources of genuine acceptance and tenderness in her
life, albeit a tenderness mingled with sentimentality.

Ironically, unlike the dragon mother and the stoic father, both removed in their respective ways, it was the frivolous Izaline who perceived the loneliness of the only child and recognized her need for fun
and entertainment. When she came to visit the family in the country,

she cried over her granddaughter and offered what distractions she could: "Vois-tu, Magui, je ne peux pas te dire l'effet que ça me fait de te voir toute seule, ici, dans cette grande maison triste. Il faudrait t'amuser. Viens à la messe avec moi. Tu verras d'autres enfants que nous ramènerons pour goûter. Ton grand-père fera marcher la lanterne magique et nous jouerons aux grâces et aux volant!" (*Pourquoi* 18–19). Izaline thus encouraged "Magui" to get out and enjoy her childhood, to play with other children, to let herself be seduced by the scenes of the magic lantern (an experience captured instead by Proust). In contrast to the lugubrious le Cros, Izaline and Urbain had a pleasant old family house in Thiviers called "the house with green balconies" (*QJJ* 83) because all the ironwork was painted an "aggressive" (Rachilde's term) shade of green. It had three stories jammed with old furniture as well as a stable that could accommodate a coach and six horses. The only blot on this scene, at least as far as Rachilde was concerned, was that Joseph refused to set foot in the house after he quarreled with Urbain (*QJJ* 84).

Unlike the "angel" Gabrielle, Izaline never lectured "Magui" on the tiresome duties of the virtuous woman or on the turpitude of men. Instead, she showered her with jewelry and knickknacks. It must have been her good nature and lack of judgmental cynicism that made Urbain Feytaud cherish and protect his wife, but these were qualities Rachilde could not appreciate. It was not the approval of a grandmother—there for the asking—that she sought but that of her father—an approval that she believed could and should be earned. Although the Feytaud household was "le modèle de la paix par la douceur et le désarmement" (*Pourquoi* 19), it was not a model that Rachilde found it in herself to want to emulate.

The example of her paternal grandmother, Jeanne, was hardly more comforting. Rachilde saw her rarely. Jeanne Eymery lived in the old center of Périgueux, where Rachilde was occasionally taken to visit (perhaps the inspiration for certain scenes of *L'Amazone rouge*). Her memories of these occasions are limited to details: her grandmother knitted stockings for her that were as fine as lace; Gabrielle respectfully addressed her mother-in-law as "Madame"; and Jeanne would dab her eyes as she contemplated her young granddaughter (Dauphiné, *Rachilde* [1991] 25).

Although she seldom saw her paternal grandmother, these visits serve as a reminder that Rachilde was acquainted with old Périgueux from a young age. The town was still a provincial capital, cut off from the politics and fashions of Paris, and change came slowly. Rachilde's arrival in the world coincided with that of the railway in Périgueux. The first line had been inaugurated in 1857, and the ground-breaking ceremony for the new railway station took place on September 12, 1860. In addition, the town was undergoing renovation and modernization, partly as a result of floods in 1860 that destroyed the Pont-Vieux (a new bridge, the pont des Barris, was opened in 1862). The new quays along the river were opened to traffic on May 1, 1860, and, between 1857 and 1861, the rue Saint-Front was built, entailing the destruction of some of the old town center. This new construction also coincided with renewed appreciation of Périgueux's past as it often led to the discovery of old sites: it was during construction work on the canal, for example, that workers discovered the ancient springs of Vésona, while an amateur archaeologist discovered prehistoric remains in 1874. This was also the moment when the Cathedral of Saint-Front underwent the transformations referred to in the introduction.

When she was not in town, the greater part of Rachilde's young life was spent either in the kitchen or in the stable. With these influences, Rachilde at the age of eight was still *un enfant sauvage*, a wild child: quiet and pale, solitary and taciturn. Unable to count, she preferred a shiny ten-sous coin to the more valuable but less glittering gold ten-franc piece, much to the amusement of her father (*QJJ* 122). (The value of money was something she would never quite learn.)

This, then, was the picture of Rachilde's life—its routines and rhythms—in her first decade, but that routine would be destroyed forever by the July 19, 1870, declaration of war. Of course, the immediate threat that the war posed to the family was the death of Joseph, who found himself at the battlefront shortly after war was declared. Coping with the possibility of his imminent death proved a challenge for both Rachilde and her mother, a challenge that neither confronted particularly well. Joseph managed to avoid a premature death—by being taken prisoner—but the few months during which his fate remained uncertain were enough to bring to the fore the underlying problems in the marriage. Indeed, the personal toll exacted by war caused each member of the family to confront personal demons, with repercussions that lasted long after the cessation of hostilities. Rachilde suffered acutely from isolation and loneliness, Gabrielle was torn between the fear of losing her husband and the fear of getting him back, and Joseph returned from prison camp a broken hero, no longer of any use to his country (the one thing that really mattered to him). Rachilde imagined her mother's difficult situation in *Les Rageac*: "Gabrielle sentait, entre elle et son mari, se dresser cette affreuse barrière de la surdité. Fatalement on ne se comprenait plus" (105).

The causes, events, and consequences of the Franco-Prussian War have been minutely analyzed elsewhere and need not be repeated here (see Audoin-Rouzeau; Howard). What is important for our purposes are rather the reactions of those involved—combatants and noncombatants alike—to the experiences of war and its aftermath. As far as those who stayed behind in the Périgord were concerned, life remained relatively safe and stable. Unlike families living closer to the front, Rachilde and her mother had no need to worry about their own immediate survival (at least, no more than usual). There was even some general enthusiasm for the war—even though rural communities are notoriously more inclined to worry about who will bring in the harvest than about who will defend the nation's honor (see, for example, Tindall)—since the French fully expected to trounce Prussia rapidly and thoroughly. It turned out, however, that the French troops were totally unprepared for Bismarck's careful planning, especially with defense forces drawn primarily from the African army. Anticipated triumph gave way very quickly to humiliation and defeat, an experience that not only brought down a regime (the Second Empire) but also shaped a generation of resentful patriots and xenophobes (Rachilde included) who came of age and assumed leadership roles in the Third Republic.

Captain Joseph Eymery did not question his allegiance. Although he avoided politics personally,[19] he knew where his duty lay: he belonged to the world of Napoleon III socially (Gabrielle had been presented at court, after all), and he even wore his beard and mustache in the style known as "imperial," after the emperor who had popularized it. He performed the duties that his country expected and demanded, and, when summoned, he joined the twelfth cavalry (to which he had been appointed, with the rank of captain, on August 8, 1869), which formed part of the Third Corps of the Rhine army under Marshal Bazaine.[20]

Captain Eymery's contribution to the war effort consisted of covering the retreat of Marshal Bazaine to Metz. This episode, a major strategic blunder, was not one of the more glorious chapters of the war. Indeed, in hindsight, Bazaine's decision to retreat can be seen as leading to the loss of the war, the capture of the emperor, and the fall of the empire—more significant consequences would be hard to imagine. Bazaine's forces were quickly surrounded by the Prussians and besieged. Marshal Mac-Mahon's army attempted to break through the Prussian lines and rejoin Bazaine's beleaguered forces, engaging the enemy at Sedan, but the effort was a disaster. The battle was lost, the emperor was captured by the Prussians, and republican forces back in Paris declared a republic. Meanwhile, after a two-month siege, Bazaine was left with no choice but to surrender, which he did on October 27, handing everything over to the Prussians, including weapons and ammunition and items of paramount symbolic importance, such as flags. These poor choices led to his court-martial, and, on December 10, 1873, he was found guilty of having capitulated to the enemy without having exhausted all other possibilities and was exiled from France (a relatively lenient sentence seeing as the offense of which he was convicted was punishable by death).

This is the unheroic chapter of French history with which Captain Eymery is linked, but in Rachilde's retelling of events, none of these unfortunate contextual details are ever mentioned. The shame and betrayal of Bazaine's retreat and surrender are erased, and the focus is on the endurance and devotion to duty of her father. Captain Eymery was indeed commended by General Lapasset for his efforts in covering Bazaine's retreat, and Rachilde incorporated the full text of the general's commendation in her memoirs. On the eve of World War I, she also published her father's diary of the siege of Metz ("Carnet de guerre d'un officier de 1870"), and, a few years later, she incorporated the material into *Les Rageac* (113–32).[21] Captain Eymery shrugged off any praise whenever the matter was discussed; he was only doing his job. His report to the Ministry of War on his "situation militaire . . . depuis l'origine de la dernière guerre jusqu'à la fin de la lutte contre l'insurrection," completed at Château-l'Evêque on October 10, 1871, gives a succinct report of his activities from the moment he left Joigny (also one of the garrisons in *La Marquise de Sade*) with his regiment on July 25, 1870, until the time he left the Hamburg prison (at his own expense) to return to France and arrived in Clermont-Ferrand on April 20, 1871. The final paragraph of the form leaves room to report any "récompenses" (compensation or reward) received during this time. The officer has written—in somewhat larger letters—only one word: "néant" (nothing) (Archives de l'Armée, *dossier de veuve*, 77.504/3).

Given the scandalous overtones that the whole incident of Bazaine's retreat had acquired at the national level, the fact that Captain Eymery would not press his claim further should not be surprising. A closely watched military court had decided that Bazaine had failed to do *his* job, so Captain Eymery's modesty could be seen as disingenuous: even a claim to have done one's job could be subject to dispute. But Rachilde mentions nothing of this. Nothing about Bazaine's failure rubs off on her father, and his heroic picture remains untarnished.

Capatin Eymery had surrendered himself (along with eighty-eight other men and eighty-five horses) to the Prussians on October 29, 1870

(*Les Rageac*, 131), in an antithesis of military glory. He was taken prisoner and held until the following year in Hamburg prison, where he contracted the smallpox that scarred his face for the rest of his life. In *Les Rageac*, "capitaine Rageac" writes a letter to "Gabrielle" dated March 1871 in which he describes himself as almost blind and goes on: "Je vais mieux mais je ne suis pas beau. J'ai la tête comme un ballon. Mon visage est criblé comme par du plomb de chasse. J'ai eu la petite vérole noire, une espèce de typhus" (136). Whether Captain Eymery ever wrote such a letter to his wife, or whether Rachilde fabricated this letter for her novel, remains unknown.

Rachilde's feelings of being unwanted were no doubt intensified by the tensions introduced into her parents' relationship by the stress of separation during the war. Gabrielle fretted that her husband would not return from the war, but whether she feared that he would die or that he would desert her is not clear. According to an anecdote in the preface to *A mort*, Captain Eymery had gone off to fight wearing a white cloak so that the enemy would be able to see him clearly (vi), an act of bravado that also increased his chances of injury. His wife had therefore every reason to fear the worst. But in a twist worthy of Rachilde's fiction (and, since it is recounted in the preface to *A mort*, it may indeed be fiction), it was Gabrielle herself who had made the cloak for her husband.

Given the troubled marriage and his infidelities, Gabrielle may have wished Joseph dead, but the war could have brought her an even worse fate. Had he abandoned her, she would have been left to face not only social stigma, but material deprivation, exacerbated by the fact that, in France at the time, a married woman had no legal control over her own property or income. Even legally sanctioned separation could cause problems since the husband's consent was still required for all legal matters (see H. D. Lewis).

Whatever her reasons, the result of her worry was a paralyzing depression, as Rachilde described:

> *Ma mère ne vivait plus que pour le tourment de l'absence et elle n'attendait plus que la nouvelle de la séparation définitive. Elle ne sortait, ni ne bougeait, assise au coin de son feu, ou devant sa fenêtre, et elle qui avait été si vaillante, lors de l'affaire de l'internement de mon père à la forteresse de Strasbourg, elle qui avait tenu tête si crânement au plus terrible général de l'armée française, le général Ducros, elle se minait, se rongeait dans son désespoir, sans essayer de réagir le moins du monde, ne s'occupant pas plus de sa fille que de son piano. Elle semblait frappée de vertige pour toute sa vie. Il ne re-*

viendrait pas, elle en était certaine et le disait à qui voulait l'enten-
dre, ceux qui essayaient de la consoler. (QJJ 128–29)

Before the war, her only interests had been her piano (sometimes) and her embroidery, pastimes that had displaced any interest that she might have taken in her daughter, but now even those diversions failed her. Fatalistically, she would tell Rachilde: "Fais ce que tu voudras, Marguerite, tu n'échapperas jamais à la malédiction qui pèse sur nous. Tu es la dernière des *loups-garous* et tu feras le malheur de tous ceux qui t'approcheront!" (QJJ 52–53). Such words were hardly likely to inspire confidence and optimism. Rachilde's tutors, the abbés Raoul and Granger, watched and listened to Gabrielle and shook their heads. Rachilde claims that at this stage Gabrielle knew nothing of le Césarien, Rachilde's reputed half brother, but there must have been other rumors that fueled her suspicions, for she was convinced that Joseph was unfaithful (or so Rachilde suggests in *Les Rageac* 194–96). The white cloak served as the symbol of her ambivalence: she herself had created the very object that made her husband an easier target for the enemy, and she seems to have been racked by the contradictory emotions that its fabrication entailed. If the cloak worked, that is, if it made Joseph more visible to the enemy, he might be killed and not return. Widowhood was perhaps preferable to separation, but, if Joseph were killed, she would have to endure the guilt. On the other hand, if Joseph survived, there would be nothing to feel guilty about, but all the unresolved problems of the marriage would still remain to be faced. In short, Gabrielle feared both that Joseph would not come back from the war and that he would, hence the paralyzing impasse that Rachilde describes as her "lifelong vertigo."

Eventually, Joseph did return (at least in body, though arguably not in spirit), but in the meantime Rachilde had formed one of the strongest images of her mother, one that would remain with her for the rest of her life—the image of a neglectful mother, paralyzed by incomprehensible fears, unable to function, and consumed with worry.

For those who remained at le Cros, the events of the war on the eastern borders, as well as the later upheavals of the Commune in Paris, seemed remote. Of more immediate concern were the hardships caused by the harsh winter of 1870. Rachilde loyally strove to imitate her father by playing war games with local peasant children: "[Elle] dirigea une armée de petits paysans mal nourris, sans souliers, mais ayant des pistolets de plomb" (AM vii).

Despite such patriotic efforts, the war was lost, governments and times changed. The Second Empire had been a period of elegance and glamour for the likes of Rachilde's family. The nation had been expanding its colonies and overseas interests and developing banking and industry at home. There were fortunes to be made, social ladders to be climbed (with plenty of shortcuts to the top), and peers to be impressed by conspicuous consumption. But these facades crumbled when the emperor himself was unexpectedly and humiliatingly captured and forced to surrender at Sedan. France was declared a republic and a defense cobbled together, but the Prussians advanced as far as Paris, which was besieged until 1871, when the government capitulated. Even then, France's trials were not over, for there remained the bloody upheavals of the Commune and its repression to be endured before peace would return. Although buffered from the suffering in the capital, Rachilde and her family shared the smart of humiliation with the rest of the nation, and, for Rachilde, at the impressionable age of eleven, it was the first in a series of German invasions that she would witness (the last being the occupation during World War II), an experience that laid the foundation for her lifelong hatred of everything German.

After his release from prison, Joseph Eymery once again allowed himself to be placed on inactive status on December 28, 1872.[22] It was not his definitive retirement, which would come in 1877 when he would write a formal letter of resignation; his official *état des services* shows that he served as "chef d'escadrons" in 1875 and 1876, but that same document also shows that this was the highest rank he attained. After his return home in 1871, however, he inexplicably became a colonel (*Les Rageac* 145), and Rachilde frequently promoted him in her fictional representations. In *Nono* (1885), for example, the father figure is *General Fayor*, while in *La Marquise de Sade* (1887) Mary Barbe's father is *Colonel Daniel Barbe*. In *Les Hors-Nature* (1897), the baron de Fertzen is a Prussian "officier d'état major." In André David's biography, too, Rachilde's father is "Colonel Eymery."

In *Les Rageac*, Rachilde acknowledges some of this confusion: "Le commandant Rageac . . . depuis qu'il était colonel, c'est-à-dire démissionnaire, ne commandait plus rien du tout ni chez lui ni ailleurs" (181). Strictly speaking, he is neither a commander nor a colonel but a "lieutenant de louveterie" (181).

After retirement, Joseph Eymery devoted himself to the estates of le Cros. "Plus de départ tous les six mois, plus de chevaux à dresser et des conscrits à punir" (AM vii). He occupied himself instead with the pleasures of hunting, maintaining a pack of seven fine hounds, and with his duties as a lieutenant in the wolf patrol and gave more attention to his child.

Questions about the marriage remained unsettled. If *Les Rageac* is to be believed, Gabrielle wanted a separation, and it was partly to provide for their daughter after the breakup of the family that Joseph and Gabrielle planned to settle Rachilde in a marriage and sell le Cros (195–96).[23] But of course things did not turn out this way since Rachilde refused to be married. According to some retellings, this is the time when Joseph drank and beat and verbally abused both his wife and his child—until one day Rachilde stood up to him.[24]

Joseph could at the same time be a pathetic figure, as he is portrayed in *Quand j'étais jeune*. Also noteworthy here is the theme of forgiveness that runs through this text and that is taken up later. Joseph claims to have had Rachilde's best interests at heart when he tried to marry her off, and, when she set out on her own, he sold his prized hunting pack to raise a substantial sum of cash in order to give her a start in her chosen profession, even though he opposed her decision.[25]

Eventually, after Rachilde left home, Joseph and Gabrielle Eymery did sell le Cros and go their separate ways, Gabrielle alternating between Paris and her parents' house in Thiviers, Joseph moving to another property near Périgueux (see "1885: Marriage and the Woman Writer"). To what extent the Franco-Prussian War was a precipitating factor in this informal separation must remain speculation. What is clear, however, is that the war crystallized the two poles in Rachilde's family.

On the one hand, her mother's side of the family offered a legitimate connection to literary tradition. While the connection was conferred through the distaff line, however, the writers themselves were men, and, given the very legitimacy of this side of the family, it was not clear how women could themselves be writers. One possibility was the way in which this family tradition also incorporated the outcast, the (were)-wolf, but in this way lay madness, and Gabrielle was already showing signs of mental instability, signs that would become increasingly apparent.

On the other hand, Rachilde's father and his family traditions represented illegitimacy but with all the possibilities that such illegitimacy confers. Joseph's lack of established family history favored creative rewriting: where a factual genealogical record was lacking, a more interesting one supplying mysteriously suppressed links to the aristocracy (the marquis d'Ormoy) or to medieval knights (such as Aimeri [see "1877: Authority, Authorship, and Authorization"]) could be imagined to supply legitimacy.

Rachilde's family history, as embodied in the stories about ancestors that circulated in the family and as crystallized during the Franco-Prussian War, presented her with two paths: she could try to claim a legiti-

mate place in a bourgeois literary tradition, or she could embrace illegitimacy as a way of claiming distinction despite social convention.
Both paths supposed a male subject, however, and Rachilde's writing
career will tell the story of her repeated efforts to negotiate these two
poles as a person assigned the status *female* at birth.

The Cultural Injunction to Silence

*In which Rachilde is engaged, appears to attempt suicide,
and meets a ghost who delivers an important message*

On la fiança à quatorze ans, par devant le curé. Elle ne voulut
rien entendre et essaya de se noyer dans la pièce d'eau entre les
saules.

Gaubert, *Rachilde*

Despite being educated by priests (Rachilde's education is described in
more detail in "1900: Women and Education"), Rachilde remained a religious skeptic, thinking of herself as owing more to Voltaire and Sade
than to religious or mystical patterns of thought.[1] This skepticism co-
existed, however, alongside a healthy imagination, one prone to superstition and mysticism, as the family myths about werewolves have
already illustrated (see "1860: Women as Outsiders"). A religious ceremony was an invitation to superstitious indulgence, even when undertaken in the name of piety, as Rachilde's account of her confirmation illustrates. In spite of a general lack of religious faith in the household,
socially expected rituals such as confirmation could not be avoided.
While Rachilde's account of her experiences on this solemn occasion is
every bit as much a manifestation of her talent for self-dramatization as
are her other autobiographical writings, the narrative also provides an
important perspective on a recurrent motif in Rachilde mythology: the
figure of the *noyé*, or drowned man.

This figure first manifested itself around the time of Rachilde's confirmation, in early adolescence.[2] Despite her skepticism, the sheer sol-
emnity and ceremony of the occasion put Rachilde in a suggestive frame
of mind, as she freely acknowledges in the autobiographical preface to
A mort. Following her confirmation, she was prone to flights of imagination: "Aux soirs des mois de mai, quand la nuit semble n'être qu'une
longue aurore criblée de lune, d'étoiles, de mouches phosphorescentes
et de ces rayons incertains qui paraissent monter des eaux dormantes, la
fillette, en jupe presque longue déjà, descendait les collines le chapelet à
la main, les yeux vagues, cherchant Dieu: elle trouva la poésie" (*AM* vii).
Rachilde would end her wanderings by going home and writing in a diary a highly literary version of her adventures. Stealing a peach, for ex-

ample, would become "madame la Poésie née d'Eglantier-moussu permet de voler les pêches du voisin et même de laisser inachever [*sic*] un chapelet commencé" (viii). In this manner, the religious ceremony nurtured the superstitious and suggestive parts of her nature that expressed themselves in writing.

As the reference in the preceding paragraph to the mysterious rays rising from still waters hints, the natural outcome of this state of mind is "la névrose": "Par une de ces nuits de mai pendant laquelle la petite, assise devant sa fenêtre ouvrant sur le lac aux grenouilles, songea que tout ce qui finit est bien court, selon saint Augustin" (*AM* ix). Rachilde begins a long series of meditations, but she is interrupted by a vision: "A ce moment de son monologue Rachilde vit une chose monstrueuse s'élever au-dessus de l'eau sombre du mystérieux étang, une sorte de grand, d'immense cadavre blême les bras tendus en avant, la tête ballottant sur les épaules, et l'eau tout autour semblait se soulever d'horreur en grosses vagues muettes." She opens her mouth to cry out, but she is frozen and can only watch as the *noyé* walks out of the pond and between the willow trees, crying out in an unearthly voice, "Tu ne parleras jamais, jamais" (x).

The next morning, Rachilde convinces herself that she has been dreaming, but the nightmare recurs: "De semaine en semaine elle eut ce cauchemar: elle se mettait à la fenêtre, le noyé faisait de grands gestes désespérés ou bien levait la tête, une tête verte et gonflée; de son côté, la pauvre demeurait là, cramponnée à cette fenêtre, le lendemain elle se réveillait dans son lit." This recurrent nightmare preyed on her mind to the extent that one day she decided to investigate. She approached the pond "et tomba dedans, en criant: Maman! On fit courir le sot bruit qu'elle s'était suicidée. . . . Mais non . . ." (*AM* xi).

This narrative of Rachilde's "coming to writing" (to borrow Cixous's phrase) takes her confirmation as its starting point and leads, through the account of her juvenile writing in her diary, to the recurrent nightmare of the ghost of a drowned man that assures her she will never "speak," never find a voice. This vision leads to what Rachilde acknowledges was framed by others as a suicide attempt, although she explicitly denies that self-destructive intention in the version of events written as part of the preface to *A mort*. This novel, published in 1886, was a follow-up to the success of *Monsieur Vénus* in 1884. Rachilde establishes the context of the preface by recounting that, when the publisher comes to print her latest novel, it is several pages short of the specified length, so she hurriedly pens a preface to make up the difference, drawing on her own life as an easy subject.

There will be occasion to return to many of the things claimed in this preface, and, as already discussed above, it is a more complicated text than appears at first sight. Far from being an autobiographical tale dashed off as filler, the seemingly casual surface of the text is in fact carefully constructed, and the effect of the preface is to present to a public familiar with *Monsieur Vénus* an author worthy of their expectations. In other words, Rachilde used the occasion to create an image of herself that would perpetuate the mythological author created by her earlier success. Before there was *Roland Barthes* by Roland Barthes, there was "Rachilde" by Rachilde.

This is not to say that everything in the preface is untrue or unreliable, but it is to offer a warning about reading too literally. In a moment of despair during World War II, when, just for an instant, Rachilde considered drowning herself, she concludes: "Le suicide est un peu ridicule à mon âge. C'était drôle à mes quinze ans . . . *en guise de préface!*" (*Face à la peur* 35). Rachilde warned readers about falling into what was characterized above as a literary "wolf trap," and the preface to *A mort* is an example of just such a pitfall, particularly the confirmation story. It is a highly artful and writerly account of Rachilde's own coming to writing. Although parading as naive, as self-mockingly ironic, it is full of rhetorical flourishes: the merry month of May is when all writing begins, and personifications such as "madame la Poésie" blend rhetoric with a child's clever self-exculpation. Moreover, it is dramatically presented (the use of the present tense, the imaginary interruptions of the publisher, M. Monnier, that retard the action and build suspense). It is not just a very consciously written narrative; it is a narrative about becoming, consciously, a writer. In this story, the moment of confirmation is less about Rachilde becoming an accepted member of the church and more about a sign that she will become an accepted member of the literary fraternity. Of course, like most signs of predestination, it is recognized and narrated only in retrospect.

While this preface may not be a reliable source of information about Rachilde's childhood, however, it contains important patterns of information that should not be dismissed. In particular, in this narrative, Rachilde presents the figure of the *noyé*, which will haunt many of her other writings; she explicitly rejects the notion of a suicide attempt, an event in her life that has received too little critical analysis; and, finally, she links the pseudosuicide to the figure of the *noyé*, and therefore to writing, in a highly suggestive way. The *noyé* and the threat that it poses have everything to do with writing. Previous biographies have presented Rachilde's suicide attempt as linked to her rejection of marriage;

through a reexamination of the rumors surrounding Rachilde's attempted suicide, this chapter returns the emphasis to the figure of the ghostly *noyé* and shows how this creates a more meaningful network of associations to illuminate the problems that Rachilde faced as a woman writer at the turn of the century. In this story, the *noyé* is a *noyau*, or "kernel," at the center of a network of complex associations.

In recounting Rachilde's suicide attempt, few critical or biographical accounts mention either the (religious) confirmation or the ghostly and ghastly figure of the *noyé*. All three previous biographies of Rachilde place the suicide attempt in the context of a rejected suitor. Both Gaubert and David based their work on personal acquaintance with Rachilde, but a comparison of the three relevant passages suggests that David and Dauphiné also drew on their predecessors, as the descriptions accumulate more and more detail while retaining a core narrative first set forth by Gaubert in 1907. The core of this anecdote is that Rachilde's parents (her father in particular) tried to force her to marry against her will and that, rather than submit, she threw herself in the pond in front of the family home, Le Cros (the same pond that figured so prominently in the Poe-esque descriptions of Rachilde's birthplace discussed above and therefore a site already linked to her writerly destiny). For Gaubert and subsequent biographers, the anecdote crystallizes everything about Rachilde's adolescence: her parents' tyranny, a forced marriage (with the concomitant overtones of sexual violation), and a defiance of authority that finds death preferable to dishonor.

Here, for example, is how Rachilde's first biographer, Ernest Gaubert, frames the event: "On voulut la précipiter dans un mariage de raison, on la fiança à quatorze ans, par devant le curé. Elle ne voulut rien entendre et essaya de se noyer dans la pièce d'eau entre les saules. Elle en ressortit, envoûtée par tout le mystère de son désespoir, du site et des ombres entrevues" (8). Gaubert's businesslike account, with the impersonal "on" imposing the marriage, the succession of action verbs in the *passé simple*, and the allusion to precipitous action, clearly frames Rachilde's suicide attempt as a response to the arranged marriage. This account pays little attention to mystical phenomena other than the mention of vague and unspecified "ombres entrevues."

André David adds one or two colorful details but otherwise maintains the same narrative framework: "A quatorze ans, son père la fiança brutalement à un de ses officiers.[3] Elle essaya de s'habituer à l'idée d'aller s'expatrier deux ans en Afrique, puis au bout d'un an, refusa catégoriquement, et tenta de se noyer dans la pièce d'eau, au bord de laquelle fleurissaient les pervenches et les roses. Pour chasser cette crise de tristesse incohérente et chimérique, elle se remit à lire beaucoup" (*Rachilde* 15). David expands on Gaubert—the engagement is brutal rather than precipitous; Rachilde must contemplate two years in exile in Africa—but eliminates any reference to mystical phenomena; the only thing that remains unclear and chimerical is Rachilde's sadness. David presents the events in a less telescoped manner, however, indicating that a year had elapsed between the engagement and the suicide attempt (Gaubert's version almost seems to suggest that Rachilde rushed right home from the curé's and threw herself into the pond). David's account also makes the connection between the refusal to marry and the turn to literature, although in his version it is in the passive form of reading rather than the active form of writing.

Claude Dauphiné takes a more synthetic approach, blending multiple sources both fictional and autobiographical (for example, the information about Joseph Eymery's motives gleaned from *Quand j'étais jeune*), but still relies on Gaubert and David, as the opening of her account suggests: "Brutalement, alors qu'elle n'a pas quinze ans, son père, désireux de la soustraire au climat familial de plus en plus tendu, et spécialement à l'influence d'une mère malade nerveusement, la fiance à l'un de ses officiers, Jacques de La Hullière." She conscientiously cites her sources (*Les Rageac*) before continuing: "Le promis n'enthousiasme guère Rachilde qui songe déjà plus à la carrière littéraire qu'aux joies relatives du ménage." Dauphiné then proceeds to explain that Rachilde was subsequently confined to a convent and that it is only on her return from this sojourn that an "incident mystérieux" takes place: "La jeune fille se jette dans l'étang du Cros, peut-être après une altercation avec sa mère, peut-être pour marquer encore son refus d'entrer dans l'existence qu'on lui prépare aux côtés de Monsieur de La Hullière" (*Rachilde* [1991] 30).[4] In this account, then, the engagement and the suicide attempt are separated by a significant amount of time, so much so that some ambivalence enters in as to whether the incident is in fact linked to the proposed marriage or the result of her mother's interference (in unrelated matters?), though this indeterminacy is the only "mysterious" thing that remains about the event, all references to ghosts and drowned men having been omitted.

Although an evolution can be traced in these three narratives— more and more time elapses between the engagement and the suicide attempt, and the supernatural elements are gradually eliminated— all three versions continue to relate the suicide to the engagement, and all three present Rachilde's reaction as implicit evidence of her exceptionalism.

By challenging this presentation of events, I do not intend to suggest that the claim of an unwanted engagement is unfounded. It seems clear that Joseph Eymery did indeed attempt to broker a marriage between his daughter and an officer of his regiment and acquaintance, called variously Jacques de La Hullière (*QJJ* 166; Dauphiné, *Rachilde* [1991] 30), Jacques de la Huillière ("Chronologie" 8), Jacques du Tilliers (*Les Rageac*), and even simply Jacquiat (*La Marquise de Sade*). If *Les Rageac* is to be trusted, Captain Eymery was contemplating the match as early as his imprisonment in Hamburg in 1870–71 (140–41).[5]

Rachilde herself offers different accounts of her suicide attempt. In the preface to *A mort* (1886), she situates it around the time of her confirmation and relates the anecdote to her desire to write—the engagement is not even mentioned—while in *Les Rageac* (1921), it is presented as a rejection of marriage. This is not to say that one of these autobiographical accounts is true and the others false but simply that Rachilde stressed different aspects of the story at different moments. An analysis of these different elements suggests a way of understanding this event that relates writing to marriage and shows that, far from being exceptional, Rachilde was operating within narrative conventions typical of her time when presenting female desire.

In her memoirs, *Quand j'étais jeune*, for example, she presents her father as explaining that his intentions had been to protect her from what he felt were dangerous influences: "J'avais mes raisons de chercher à t'éloigner d'une famille un peu *originale*, une famille de *plumitifs*, pour tout dire, et qui, sans doute, t'a donné les idées bizarres que tu as." He cannot understand why she would want to go to Paris and be a writer, a choice that entailed "une certaine misère" (166), when he had arranged for such a comfortable and secure future through marriage. This account also makes it clear that one of the perceived dangers was the "scribbling" ("plumitif") influence of the family, which underscores the fact that, in rejecting the match, Rachilde was not so much rejecting marriage per se, or even simply defying her parents' authority, as asserting her determination not to be separated or distanced ("éloigné") from her connection to writing (traced, as shown above, through the maternal line).

Thus, while Rachilde ultimately rejected the match, that rejection may have had little to do with her feelings for her fiancé; indeed, a photograph (in a private collection) of a smiling adolescent Rachilde with a young man who, in all probability, is the lucky fiancé suggests that she was not necessarily unhappy, at least not all the time.[6] In *L'Amazone rouge*, Rachilde even explores an alternative-universe fantasy in which the heroine murders her brother—the male double usually associated in Rachilde's fiction with the writing self—because he forces her to renounce marriage with an officer. The puzzle in this chapter is to understand how throwing herself in the pond gets recast as a suicide attempt and why the event becomes attached to the rejected marriage proposal (as in later works such as *Les Rageac* and *Quand j'étais jeune*) rather than the confirmation (as in the preface to *A mort*).

The key to this recasting of events is suggested by Rachilde's father in the conversation already referred to above, where he goes on to state: "Une femme ne doit pas s'émanciper autrement que par le mariage" (*QJJ* 166). For a society used to thinking of marriage as women's only avenue to "emancipation," it was more acceptable and understandable for Rachilde to present her break with her family as an act of resistance to an arranged marriage than it would have been for her to suggest that she wanted to free herself ("s'émanciper") in order to become a writer. For a woman to aspire to be a writer was still an incomprehensible goal, whereas an arranged marriage might be more readily understood as an intolerable imposition. Yet the script of marriage and domestication is precisely what Rachilde is rejecting in her early aspirations, so the anecdote in some ways is a very accurate representation of what she finds unacceptable. Two aspects of the story signal its ambivalence, however. The first is the highly gendered aspect of Rachilde's suicide attempt, the second the troubling presence of the *noyé*, which recurs in several narratives, albeit in different ways, suggesting the complex set of associations that it (dis)embodies.

Rachilde's suicide attempt is often presented as a unique act, evidence of her strong will and defiant nature, but it can also be argued that Rachilde was not deviating from but conforming to a very feminine nineteenth-century script, even as she was adapting that script to suit her own ends. Both the choice to attempt suicide and the method chosen are embedded in perceptions of suicide and other general cultural expectations shared in Europe at the end of the nineteenth century.

In the late nineteenth century, it was widely feared that people were committing suicide simply because it had become fashionable (see O. Anderson; Stokes; and Gates). The cliché of suicide as fashionable had been inherited in part from the early nineteenth century and "Wertherism," the wave of suicides inspired by Goethe's *The Sorrows of Young Werther*. While actual suicide rates for the period do not seem to bear out such fears, a number of high-profile cases kept the phenomenon in the public eye.[7] In June 1886, the eccentric King Ludwig II of Bavaria drowned himself in Lake Starnberg, an event commemorated in a poem

by Paul Verlaine that appeared in *Le Décadent* (July 31, 1886),[8] but by far
the most notorious "celebrity" suicide was the Mayerling Affair of 1889,
in which the crown prince of the Hapsburg Empire, Rudolf, and his
mistress died in a royal hunting lodge just outside Vienna, fulfilling a
suicide pact.[9] By the end of the century, suicide had become the object
of sociological study. For example, the French sociologist Emile Durkheim's *Le Suicide* would be published in 1897. This scientific interest was
preceded and shaped, however, by a fascination that found expression
in popular writing.

Rachilde's suicide attempt would have taken place in the mid-1870s,
but since she did not come to write about it until the mid-1880s, when
attitudes toward suicide were changing, particularly among "aesthetes
and would-be bohemians" (O. Anderson 242), her shaping of events
reflects the reading expectations of a somewhat later period. By the
1890s, a clear set of expectations had evolved around *reading* suicide (as
opposed to actually committing suicide). An expression of the "unnat-
ural" desire to kill oneself had become proof either of the degenerative
tendencies deplored by the middle class or of the superior sensitivity
that characterized decadent attempts to distance oneself from bourgeois society. Examples of the latter include Villiers de l'Isle-Adam's famous dismissal of the business of living in his influential play *Axël*—
"Vivre? les serviteurs feront cela pour nous" (*Oeuvres complètes* 2:
672)—as well as Ibsen's formulation in *Hedda Gabler* of suicide as a
beautiful act. Those who viewed it as a form of degeneration could point
to the "coming universal wish not to live" of *Jude the Obscure*'s children in Thomas Hardy's novel.

Rachilde was writing, at least to begin with, before such clear and
concise formulations of this cultural stereotype had become widely disseminated but at a time when such attitudes were in the process of
forming. The depiction of suicide found, for example, in the preface to
A mort (1886) is one of the ways in which Rachilde contributed to a nas-
cent decadent sensibility as well as larger cultural paradigms. Suicide
continued to be an important theme in Rachilde's work, in which a series of heroes and heroines choose to end their lives in spectacular ways
(like the knife thrower Eliante Donalger in *La Jongleuse*).

In the 1880s and 1890s, suicide was a topic of enormous interest to
the general public (see Stokes). The media fed that interest, contributing to the perception of suicide as a social problem. For example, in order to increase sales and lure readers away from its rival, the *Daily Mail*,
the *Daily Express* joined forces with William Booth, the founder of the
Salvation Army, to establish an "Anti-Suicide Bureau." Booth received

free publicity for his work through the newspaper, while, in a major publishing coup, the *Express* both gained a reputation for philanthropy and scooped the *Mail* by running banner headlines and sensationalist copy that boosted readership (O. Anderson 335–36). This example of the symbiotic relationship between capitalism and philanthropy illustrates the way in which the development of advertising practices in Europe in general could serve simultaneously to promote an individual and to sell mass-produced merchandise.

While suicide carried literary connotations, it also reflected widely held cultural assumptions about gendered behavior. Again, these assumptions have more to do with perception than reality, as Olive Anderson has shown. For example, it was believed in England that men who committed suicide had suffered financial ruin, women moral ruin, even though a survey of case histories does not seem to bear this out. Gender was thought to influence not only the motive but also the means. In both England and France, women were frequently perceived to favor drowning, though again this was often more a case of perception than reality.[10] As Barbara Gates has stated in her study of Victorian attitudes toward suicide, "It was as though women drowned in their own tears, or returned to the water of the womb, or, as Freud believed, were delivered of a child when they made their final retreat into water" (135).[11]

Rachilde's suicide narrative displays elements of the popular assumptions about suicide prevalent at the time. For example, because suicide was sinful, it was widely thought to be the work of the devil. O. Anderson, for example, cites the case of a woman who in 1864 attempted to drown herself in a farm pond and subsequently apologized for her actions, saying that "the Devil pulled her in" (162–63, 235). Rachilde could not have known of this example, yet she offers a similar script. Although she did not attribute her action directly to the devil, one of the connotations of the figure of the *noyé* is indeed that of a demon who both tempts and punishes. Rachilde thus seems to be drawing on widely shared perceptions.

Comparisons to two of Rachilde's contemporaries will illustrate the way in which Rachilde was both deploying and contributing to a well-known script. The first comparison is to Pauline Tarn, better known to literature as the fin-de-siècle francophone poet Renée Vivien. It has been suggested that Vivien ultimately succeeded in committing suicide through anorexia, but earlier in her life she also seems to have contemplated drowning herself. Drawing on letters in the Bibliothèque Nationale, Karla Jay describes Vivien's infatuation with the fifty-year-old poet Amédée Moullé in 1894: "Suspicious that Vivien was planning to flee to

Paris and/or elope with Moullé, Mary Tarn locked Vivien up. . . . Finally, Vivien escaped through an open window. After pawning a brooch, she had enough money to pay for lodging for five days and eat one meal a day. Just as she had run out of money and *was about to throw herself into the Thames*, she was discovered by one of her mother's maids. This is the story as Vivien recounts it, and it seems a bit theatrical" (7; emphasis added). The theatricality of the story indicates, not that Vivien was a bad storyteller, but that she was invoking cultural stereotypes in order to emphasize the extremity of her circumstances.[12]

The second comparison is to Sarah Bernhardt. Bernhardt provides an even better counterpoint both because she published a first-hand account (see Bernhardt) of the event, which can be compared to Rachilde's narrative, and because of the role that she played in Rachilde's life.

Rachilde was introduced to Bernhardt by her cousin Marie de Saverny (alias Mademoiselle de Feytaud),[13] and it is clear that, as an immensely successful female public figure, Bernhardt became something of a role model. Rachilde left several accounts of her acquaintance with Bernhardt, from the early "portrait" that she published as a young (and hungry) journalist (reprinted in *L'Estafette* on January 12, 1880 [see Soulignac, "Bibliographie"]), to the chapter "Une Visite chez Sarah Bernhardt" published nearly seventy years later in *Quand j'étais jeune* (1947).[14] In addition to serving as a commercially viable subject for Rachilde's works, Bernhardt boosted Rachilde's career in more direct ways; Marie de Saverny assured her young cousin that "c'est elle qui vous fera obtenir une préface pour votre premier livre; sans ça, vous n'aurez jamais d'éditeur" (*QJJ* 43). De Saverny had also introduced Rachilde to Arsène Houssaye, but, according to David, Bernhardt took matters further (perhaps her association with the Comédie-Française gave her an edge—among his other accomplishments, Houssaye had been the theater's director from 1849 to 1856): "La merveilleuse tragédienne promit à la débutante qu'elle lui ferait avoir sa préface, l'invita à dîner avec Houssaye et obtint ce qu'elle avait promis" (*Rachilde* 19). *Monsieur de la Nouveauté* duly arrived before the public in 1880 with a recommendation from the great man of letters (he is also thought to have provided a preface for *Monsieur Vénus* four years later).

Given the role that Bernhardt played, then, it is instructive to examine her memoirs (first published in 1907), noting the similarities to Rachilde's. Bernhardt's memoirs were entitled, appropriately, *Ma double vie*, and, as Bernhardt's biographers Arthur Gold and Robert Fizdale note, the autobiography "promises more than it fulfills for while it seems to present a woman of disarming frankness, a closer reading reveals the prototypical actress impersonating—and consummately—a character called Myself" (9). The description fits Rachilde's autobiographical writings equally well. Even the minor qualification that, while Bernhardt was "the prototypical actress," Rachilde was the prototypical woman writer remains superfluous, for actress and woman writer were professions so closely linked at the turn of the century—beyond mere talent, both required the creation and promotion of "Myself"—that the difference in job title is insignificant. The similarities are not confined simply to the degree of obfuscation in which the two texts engage, although Gold and Fizdale record that the same unreliability that may confound the reader of Rachilde's autobiographical texts also hampered their efforts to write Bernhardt's biography: "Tales about her origins are unreliable at best. Some she invented; others were the fantasies of journalists bent on revealing 'the truth about Sarah Bernhardt' whether they knew it or not" (10). In addition to the general similarity in self-presentation, a certain resonance between specific episodes in Bernhardt's and Rachilde's memoirs can also be identified.[15]

For example, after Bernhardt had received some preliminary schooling at the Institution Fressard, her mother decided that Sarah needed to be sent to a convent school in order to be made marriageable. When the news was broken to the young Bernhardt, she reacted violently:

> *L'idée qu'on violentait à nouveau mes goûts, mes habitudes, sans me consulter, me mit dans une rage indicible. Je me roulai par terre; je poussai des cris déchirants; je hurlai des reproches contre maman, mes tantes, Mme Fressard qui ne savait pas me garder.*
>
> *Après deux heures de luttes pendant lesquelles je m'échappai deux fois des mains qui essayaient de me vêtir, pour me sauver dans le jardin, grimper aux arbres, me jeter dans le petit bassin dans lequel il y avait plus de vase que d'eau; enfin, épuisée, domptée, sanglotante, on m'emporta dans la voiture de ma tante.*
>
> *Je restai trois jours chez elle avec une telle fièvre, qu'on craignit pour ma vie. (Bernhardt 15)*

Here, Bernhardt freely acknowledges, then, that her gesture was symbolic, noting that the ornamental pond ("bassin") contained more mud than water.

Bernhardt's experience thus follows the same outlines as Rachilde's. Both Bernhardt and Rachilde use a halfhearted suicide attempt to resist the marriage plot: in Bernhardt's case, the plot is only implied by the convent education, but, in Rachilde's, it is explicit in the formal engagement (and resistance would be followed by the imposition of a more indirect route to the same end, namely, convent education). In both cases, however, part of the point of the reaction is to assert agency, to protest the lack of consultation. It is clear in both memoirs, however, that neither subject knew exactly what it was that she wanted to do, only what she did *not* want to do. Bernhardt had yet even to set foot on a stage, while, even though she had begun to write, Rachilde was far from conceiving of writing as a *career*, with all the connotations, including professional legitimacy, that the term carries today. Marriage was being rejected, not for its own sake (both would eventually marry), but for what it represented at that stage of life—the inevitable outcome of a conventional, convent-oriented narrative closing off other possible but as yet inchoate alternatives. More than the casual echo found in Vivien's life, the strong similarity between Rachilde's and Bernhardt's autobiographical representations of suicide underscores the extent to which both accounts appealed to a reading public prepared to see such suicide attempts as evidence of impotent resistance in a feminine mode rather than as a morbid death wish or evidence of a seriously unbalanced mind.

This is not to suggest that Rachilde's suicide attempt never took place but rather to question the seriousness of her intent and the role that the attempt has come to occupy in Rachildian mythology.[16] If Rachilde did not really want to die, what other explanations of her actions can be offered? Those actions express defiance and willfulness, and these are significant factors, but the event deserves to be read in a broader context, one that places Rachilde's actions alongside the visions of the *noyé*. Rachilde explicitly makes this connection in some of her accounts of the suicide attempt, for example, in *Les Rageac* (1921) where she describes her fiancé as a "fantôme nouveau qui la menaçait plus directement" (190), as one more ghost threatening silence. These accounts vary widely in some of their details, but the point to underscore is that, in attempting suicide by drowning, Rachilde is expressing a desire to *become* herself a *noyée*. To explore this further, it is necessary to examine the various aspects of this ghost figure in order to see the related yet distinct meanings that it came to hold for her.

Insofar as it is the devil who tempts the weak to commit the sin of self-murder, Rachilde's example signals her diabolical intent. Like the woman (cited above) who saw the devil in the pond and jumped in af-

ter him, Rachilde also saw a (sort of) devil—the *noyé*—who made her
jump; it was the devil made her do it. The "simple" version of events
holds that Rachilde threw herself in the pond to avoid marriage (as her
biographers have emphasized), but some accounts, notably that of *A
mort*, clearly signal that her action was meant, not only to avoid one fate
(marriage), but actively to pursue another (one with diabolical connotations, moreover, at least in the eyes of late nineteenth-century French
society).

In the confirmation story, for example, the drowned man speaks.
He tells Rachilde that she will not speak. Since this tale is related in
her memoirs (those of a writer's life), the reader is invited to contemplate the drowned man's failure to carry out his threat—Rachilde *does*
speak—even as the drowned man is being presented at his most frightening. Within the context of the story itself, however, Rachilde does not
know as she experiences the vision that she will succeed in her endeavors. The drowned man is a patriarchal figure, and his interdiction represents both the culturally imposed silence of women as well as the disapproval of Rachilde's father, who considered writers "des plumitifs."
(Rachilde dedicated *Les Rageac* to her father with the words "au héros
qui m'aurait défendu de l'écrire.") Moreover, Rachilde's father, the parent she idolized, was the one who thought that "la plus grande noblesse
est de savoir garder le silence" (*QJJ* 70), as discussed earlier (see "1870:
The Ambivalence of the Paternal"). The two figures of Patriarchy and
the Paternal are thus fused and internalized (Joseph's original name
was, after all, "Padres," the fathers). In a word, the *noyé* is the Lacanian
"nom/non du père."

The drowned man goes on to figure prominently in Rachilde's writing, often representing the anxieties just outlined. Repeatedly, Rachilde's characters find themselves (to use the title of one of her books
of memoirs) "face à la peur," confronting a terrifying image of the
corpse of a drowned man. However, the *noyé* also took on an additional
role when real life (possibly) conspired to take what had been merely a
symbolic figure and make it real.

La Vierge-Réclame (1887), by Gisèle d'Estoc (about whom see "1895:
"Marriage and the Woman Writer"), a roman à clef about Rachilde,
contains a chapter entitled "L'Histoire d'un caissier trop curieux," according to which a clerk "barbu et blanc" (40) who had read "L'Homme-
Vénus" (d'Estoc's transparent code for *Monsieur Vénus*) follows the
character based on Rachilde home and falls in love with her. Rachilde
agrees to go out with him, but his attentions soon became tiresome (he
insists on biting her neck in public), and she refuses to receive him any

more. A respectable "père de famille," he drowns himself one winter night in the Seine. D'Estoc concludes the story: "Dans ses bons moments, [Rachilde] avoue que ce souvenir l'a un peu gênée pendant quinze jours, car elle s'imaginait, la nuit, que le suicidé allait venir la tirer par les pieds" (44–45).

D'Estoc undercuts the anecdote by implying that it lacks credibility: Rachilde thought that all men were after her, and besides, as a Gascon, she was prone to exaggeration (45–46). If the story were true, however, it would explain an otherwise obscure allusion in Vallette's correspondence to not doing "comme *l'autre*" (RHS 100), perhaps a response to Rachilde's fear that he too would drown himself if rejected. The incident is also referred to by Rachilde in *Face à la peur* when she describes a man "qui se tue parce qu'il ne comprend pas qu'ayant écrit un certain livre tu ne veuilles pas le vivre" (142). Here, Rachilde gives the man's name as Le Henaff.

The story of the "curious clerk" only further complicates the figure of the drowned man, who comes to represent all that is rejected (parents' values, imposed in childhood; the unwanted attentions of would-be lovers) as well as the potentially terrifying consequences of rejecting others' demands. He personifies guilt and conscience while also threatening self-realization. Becoming a writer thus means being willing to sacrifice, not just oneself, but also others. No wonder Rachilde finds the figure haunting.

The importance of the drowned man is evident from the way the figure of the *noyé* haunts Rachilde's fiction, recurring with obsessive regularity. In *La Sanglante Ironie* (1891), for example, the reader learns through flashbacks how the (male) narrator, Sylvain de Hautcrac, comes to be in prison awaiting execution, having been found guilty of murder. It turns out that, while his impulses were at first self-destructive, a series of crises convinced him instead to target life itself through others (115).[17]

One of the early crises takes place around the time of his first communion, when he discovers that the woman he has been led to believe is his mother is not in fact his real mother. This revelation is followed by a prolonged period of melancholy during which he constructs a fantasy about his *real* mother, who exists as a ghost, and also turns to writing. He decides that suicide is the solution but then catches sight of his own reflection in the river: "J'avais la mine d'un exténué, les pommettes de mes joues saillaient, à peine carminées, mon nez se pinçait aux narines, mes lèvres se tiraient en un rictus désagréable, mes cheveux, d'un noir d'encre, éparpillaient leurs mèches tristes comme des cheveux de noyé, mes yeux se creusaient pleins d'une flamme de fièvre" (116–17). In a sense, then, Sylvain is already dead: his face looks like that of a corpse, and he has the hair of a drowned man. Later, Sylvain discovers that his real mother went mad and committed suicide (143–44), a discovery that precipitates his first murder, that of his mistress.

Although this synopsis is necessarily brief (the novel itself is nearly three hundred pages long), it serves to illustrate the elements that Sylvain's story shares with Rachilde's suicide attempt. The parallels, however, are not exact. Sylvain contemplates suicide, not because he is being pressured to marry against his will (on the contrary, he *wants* to get married), but because of the (delayed) discovery of his dead mother's madness and his turn to writing. Also, rather than being haunted by the *noyé*, Sylvain himself is the drowned man.

La Sanglante Ironie, then, illustrates a somewhat different way of combining the elements of the suicide story, one that emphasizes not so much the interdictions of the father (though these are present, too) but as the link (through the mother) to a legacy of madness and literature. This example shows how protean the constellation of associations grouped around the suicide attempt can be in Rachilde's prose. (Later chapters will address the recurrence of the figure of the *noyé* in other texts.)

To summarize the importance of Rachilde's attempted suicide is a challenge. In narratives in which Rachilde or her protagonist seek to evade the ghost (narratives in which the connection to the rejection of a suitor is deemphasized), the figure of the drowned man represents a prohibitive presence, the voice of both the patriarch and her own father. Here, she is haunted by forces that threaten to prevent her from expressing herself. In other retellings of the drowning story, the suicide attempt signals a desire to *join* the *noyé*. In these stories, however, the emphasis is less on the wish to die per se and more on the symbolic rejection of marriage (and what it represents) and the desire to embrace a maternal connection to writing. Here, the ghost is both Rachilde herself and her mother, a vision of what she could become if she gives in to a potentially self-destructive identification with her mother. Finally, the ghost is also a reminder that her success as a writer threatens others. This *noyé* is a personification of haunting guilt.

Ultimately, the figure of the *noyé* is so overdetermined as to make simple generalizations impossible, but, wherever it recurs, one can expect to see a blend of all these elements, elements that both reflect and give shape to the predicament of a girl "coming to writing" in the early years of the Third Republic.

Woman as Medium

In which séances are held, Madame Eymery
meets "Rachilde," and doubles mysteriously appear

Part of what must have frightened Rachilde about the figure of the *noyé* was that it told her that she would never find a voice. "Tu ne parleras jamais," he prophesied. It must have been difficult to separate those elements of this forbidding voice that sounded like her father from those that seemed to represent a broader societal voice that enjoined all women to remain silent. Whether Rachilde really believed in the ghost, or whether it was a story she made up, the threat of silence that the *noyé* represented was a real one. This cultural injunction may have modulated over time, but certainly in Rachilde's time and place there remained a strong expectation that women would keep quiet, especially in public matters.[1]

Rachilde eventually overcame this interdiction enough to publish her work, although at first she stopped short of publicly claiming authorship. Her first story, "La Création de l'oiseau-mouche," was published on June 23, 1877, under the initials "M. E." (Soulignac, "Bibliographie" 198). The use of initials, rather than a full name, provided a certain kind of anonymity, but, within a short period of time, a new authorial persona emerged. The second published work by Marguerite Eymery, "Un Chapitre à la Ponson du Terrail," appeared just a few weeks after the first (on July 8, 1877). It was signed "Rachilde." If Marie-Marguerite Eymery was born in 1860, "Rachilde" was "born" in 1876, as this chapter will show. Marguerite Eymery, as we shall see, never published anything (with the exception of one story that can be attributed to her only through the use of the initials "M. E."), but "Rachilde" went on to become a prolific writer. In some ways, then, the *noyé* was proved right: Marguerite would not speak, but "Rachilde" would, and it is the story of the split between these two personae—the mostly silent Marguerite and the garrulous Rachilde—that will be traced here. Marguerite obeyed, at least in one sense, the ghost's injunction not to speak, but the disembodied narrative voice of Rachilde (even more disembodied that the ghost's own voice) could talk back.

The encouragement of other writers whom Marguerite/Rachilde admired must be taken into consideration as a factor in her decision to

publish and persevere, and the next chapter ("1877: Authority, Authorship, and Authorization") discusses Victor Hugo's encouragement and
his role in "authorizing" her to write. That chapter will show how *authorization* meant both that Hugo gave her "permission" to write, as it
were, and that he made an author of her by inscribing her in a French
literary tradition. But Rachilde had already begun writing when she
sought Hugo's encouragement to continue publishing; this chapter
continues the discussion of Rachilde's "coming to writing" by focusing
on how she began to see herself as a writer and find a voice. Specifically,
this chapter is about the role of *dédoublement*, or doubling, in the evolution of "Marguerite" into "Rachilde." Like numerous other women
writers, Marguerite used the device of *dédoublement* to create a public
authorial persona and voice. Forbidden by cultural expectations to address others, Marguerite began by addressing herself, but, in the course
of making this split, Marguerite also discovered the position of being a
"medium" for a male voice. The story of Rachilde's role as a medium
also leads to a consideration of the underexplored question of Gabrielle
Eymery's role in her daughter's evolution as a writer.

In using *dédoublement*, Rachilde was once again representative of a
number of writers rather than being the exception. While not all the
writers who employed *dédoublement* were women, and while it is certainly possible to argue that all writers use the device to some extent,
this strategy is particularly important to writers who feel, at least at the
start of their careers, that they lack an audience. To the extent that
women were excluded from thinking of themselves as routinely addressing a public audience by cultural expectations of silence, then, the
strategy of *dédoublement* may have been especially important to them.
Kathryn Crecelius has shown how George Sand used this device to
get started as a writer (see esp. her chap. 1), and I shall have occasion
to point out in a number of other contexts how Rachilde consciously
or unconsciously used Sand as a point of reference in her own self-
presentation as a writer.

For the general public, Sand was the paradigm of a certain kind
of French woman writer in the nineteenth century. Kathryn Crecelius
shows how, in Sand's early works, the writer split herself into two so that
she was both author and *destinataire* of her work. She was, in other
words, her own audience to begin with, until she found a "real" public
for her work. Crecelius documents the gradual separation of author and
reader in Sand's early work and has pointed out how Sand constituted
for herself an authorial persona—"Sand"—as well as thinking of herself as her own reader in the person of Aurore Dudevant. Sand thereby

represents both parties in the communicative contract, and, in an era when women writers were not sure of their audience or reading public, this strategy enabled women to overcome some of the anxiety of female authorship. The (woman) writer creates an alter ego (often male), the alter ego becomes a writer, and the "self" is the reader for whom the author writes.

This strategy continues to be used by women right up to the present. Under the name "bell hooks," for example, Gloria Watkins writes: "Sometimes . . . it seems like I am living two separate lives. . . . One way I cope with these two identities is to have different names. As a writer I use the name bell hooks. This is the name of my mother's mother's mother. . . . Talking like her meant that I spoke my mind—clearly and decisively. Two names will help me to practice detachment—remind me always that I am not my writing always something more" (hooks 158). In a sense, then, Watkins, too, is a medium for the voice of a dead spirit, that of her great-grandmother. The split (or "detachment") gives her a voice to speak *with* (a voice that speaks what is on her mind) as well as someone to speak *to* (the part of herself that exceeds her writing).

Rachilde discovered a similar distribution of responsibilities, thanks perhaps in part to having been forced to play different roles within the family in order to manage the various strong but conflicting family influences. She later described herself as "avant tout, une actrice *de la vie privée*, un être double qui a l'habitude de quitter un rôle pour un autre" (*QJJ* 86), so it is clear that multiple roles were familiar to her from early on.

Jean-Paul Sartre once explained the concept of *dédoublement* by reference to Superman's dual identity as both a superhero and the journalist Clark Kent. If the ordinary Clark Kent corresponds to the mortal Marguerite Eymery, the alter ego that Marguerite eventually invented for herself was no less superhuman than Superman and no less endowed with superpowers. For "Rachilde" was, so Marguerite would claim, a Swedish courtier who contacted her during a séance (*QJJ* 149). Before she could invent this persona, however, she needed the experience of *dédoublement* in order to apprehend and exploit the split consciousness that would enable her to be her own audience, to have someone to write for.

The patriarchal voice that threatened her with silence was sometimes embodied in her forbidding father. In addition to representing cultural beliefs about "des plumitifs" and about women's proper place, this former "writer in stone" (his profession was given as "écrivain lithographe" on the official act when his mother legally recognized him) who had turned his back on publishing sometimes silenced his daughter in a curiously specific way.[2] His unwitting attempt to censor her, however, turns out to have created the very split consciousness that may have taught her the value of *dédoublement*.

As noted above, Rachilde's first story was signed only with the initials "M. E.," and subsequent stories appeared above the name "Rachilde," a name known to her mother but evidently not to her father, who disdained the spiritualist activities. The lack of (known) signature disguised the source of the stories, making for a curious case of mistaken identity. André David recounts that Joseph Eymery would read aloud stories from the local newspaper, unaware that the author was seated next to him (David, *Rachilde* 15).[3] The irony of this situation would not have gone unnoticed by Rachilde, but there is yet a further twist that adds piquancy, namely, that Eymery would censor parts of the stories as he read them. This would not be Rachilde's last encounter with censorship, by any means, but the modifications made by her father effected a distinction between the persona of the author and that of the reader/hearer of the text. Rachilde was placed in the interesting position of being both sender and receiver of her work, but with the realization that the text that returned to her was slightly different than that which she had originally placed in circulation. The discrepancy underscored her different positions as author and audience.

For Marguerite/Rachilde, as for Aurore Dudevant/George Sand, this splitting of roles was clarified and consolidated through the use of a pseudonym. While the newspaper stories were published pseudonymously or with initials, it is the writing of her first *novel* that impels Marguerite toward the creation of an identifiable alter ego (QJJ 145). Marguerite Eymery may have had many reasons for wanting to write pseudonymously, but one of the uses of such a disguise is to mark the distinction between author and reader and to mark the boundaries between the two personae. Marguerite invented Rachilde in 1876 in order to "essayer d'acquérir la *liberté littéraire* qu'on ne voulait pas me donner et habituer mes parents à un tour de langage qu'ils n'eussent pas supporté de moi sans un habile préambule" (PM 165–66). Although Marguerite later became known to the world as Rachilde and adopted this identity for the rest of her life, it began as an alibi, as a form of impersonation.

Rachilde claimed in memoirs that the idea had been suggested by her family's interest in spiritualism, a popular bourgeois pastime in many countries in the nineteenth century. Her family resembled many others in Second Empire France that were in the grip of this craze. Spiritualism was taken up with particular enthusiasm by her grandparents, who indulged in table turning and murmured invitations to speak to the spirits who responded to their invocations (*QJJ* 52). Her maternal grandfather, Urbain Feytaud, later went on to write a book on the subject.[4] It was left to Joseph Eymery to remain the skeptical rationalist. Rachilde's fictionalized representation of him, Captain Rageac, comments, apparently in response to his wife's description of how the family passed the time during the long winter of 1870–71 in the company of refugees from Paris: "Que l'on soulage ses amis dans l'infortune est une chose bien naturelle mais un Monsieur qu'on n'a jamais vu, qui vous tombe de la lune et qui s'occupe de faire tourner les tables, ceci me surpasse et chagrine beaucoup"(*Les Rageac* 139). Perhaps the craze for spiritualism was transported in similar fashion to the Eymery family in the Périgord by refugees from Paris, the cultural capital, during the war.

One day, Marguerite claimed to be possessed by the spirit of a Swedish courtier (named Rachilde) who spoke through her. She thus used the gullibility of certain members of her family to indulge her talent for storytelling in a mutually enabling symbiosis, or at least this is how it appears in her memoirs. In *Quand j'étais jeune*, she confesses to the astronomer Camille Flammarion (whose wife was an old school friend of Gabrielle's) "que j'avais inventé cette histoire d'un gentilhomme *suédois* (pourquoi suédois?) de toute pièce pour éclairer mes parents . . . aux dépens de leurs croyances si vraiment particulières à propos des esprits frappeurs" (149).

If the possession was indeed all Marguerite's own invention, it was a happy one, for, not only did it "turn the tables" on her family and force them to legitimate the products of her imagination, but it also mobilized and countered the cultural assumptions of women's passivity through an act of ventriloquism. Being possessed by a spirit speaking through her, Marguerite made no claim to speak in her own right and indeed according to the logic of spiritualism was powerless to refuse the injunction to lend her voice to a higher force. By presenting the female body merely as a medium for the transmission of the words of a man, however, Marguerite Eymery could find her own voice. The idea was not entirely original, but Marguerite was the one to realize how to exploit the possibilities and in the process once again used the maternal side of the family as a conduit to writing.

Why Marguerite chose a Swedish connection ("pourquoi suédois?" as she herself wonders) must remain speculation,[5] but two factors seem relevant. First, the "historic" Rachilde lived during the reign of John III, who ruled from 1568 to 1592, making him a contemporary of Brantôme's (1540–1614). Second, Rachilde lived at the court of a certain "Christine" in Upper Bothnia (*PM* 163), which serves to evoke the legendary Queen Christina of Sweden, about whom several works appeared in France in the nineteenth century.[6]

There were many reasons why Marguerite might have wished to recall Christina, whose life offered so many parallels with her own. Christina (1626–89) was the only surviving child of King Gustavus II Adolphus and his wife, Marie Eleonore. She is most famous for her abdication in 1654 and for the repeated invocation of her as a figure of female rebellion against gender rules. Raised as a boy, she disparaged women's intellectual weakness, but though she preferred the company of men, she refused to marry one. Rumors circulated about her cross-dressing and about her sexual preferences, especially her reputation as a tribade.[7] The French did more than their share to fan these rumors: a forged volume of letters, for example, appeared in France—and in French—in 1761, some addressed to a French marquise (see Lacombe).

There are also specific details that Marguerite might have known. Christina had a slight physical defect (her left shoulder was higher than her right as the result of a childhood accident), a characteristic shared by both the spirit Rachilde (*PM* 152) and Marguerite Eymery. And Christina's parents were like the Eymerys: Christina's father was a war hero, a veteran of the Thirty Years' War, while her mother was neurotic and hysterical. Even if Marguerite was not acquainted with the specifics of Christina's reputation, she may have picked up enough to think of her as a dashing, aristocratic figure who defied gender conventions and therefore chose a pseudonym that signaled an embryonic sense of identification or kinship with such a person.

Whatever the Swedish connection may have been, the myth of the medium meant that Marguerite could not be held responsible for her words, and this too was a liberating aspect of her feigned possession. She recounts in *Quand j'étais jeune* that she invented her story with the collusion of her Jesuit tutor and the local curé. Her accomplices' goal was to punish the family for its heretical beliefs, and Marguerite appeared to go along with the scheme, but once again the strategy of appropriating another's voice also strengthened Marguerite's own voice: "Lorsque j'inventais, d'accord avec mes directeurs de conscience, toute une histoire *spirite*, sinon *spirituelle*, pour leur prouver que rien ne nous vient de *l'au-delà*, au moins en fait de littérature profane, je voulais d'abord m'émanciper sous le rapport de l'imagination, les habituer à un langage plus hardi que celui d'une jeune fille du meilleur monde . . ." (*QJJ* 146). Both the motive for this invention—altruistic cure—and the form—

mere dictation—were serviceable pretexts for a girl who wanted to write. Yet, had Marguerite truly wanted to dupe her parents, why choose such an unstereotypically Swedish name unless at some level she wanted to be found out, wanted her role as the real author to be recognized?

One of the neglected stories of Rachilde's life is how much this girl who wanted to write might have been aided and abetted by her mother. Gabrielle Eymery made many contributions to her daughter's career— when Marguerite/Rachilde's first application to become a member of the Société des gens de lettres was rejected in 1879, it was Gabrielle who wrote a follow-up letter challenging the decision (see Caradec)—but the invention of the persona of Rachilde the writer must rank as the most important.

Rachilde took full credit for her own self-invention in *Quand j'étais jeune*, as though the only help she received was from her tutor and her confessor, but the notion that Gabrielle might have had a role in the creation of Rachilde should not be dismissed without further consideration. In *Le Parc du mystère* (1923), Rachilde transcribes a manuscript written, she claims, in her mother's hand that recounts the spirit Rachilde's first manifestations (149–65). Is Gabrielle merely recording events (why write it down for her daughter?), or did she play a more active role in this invention? By marking the appearance of the spirit Rachilde, Gabrielle helps fix this persona, which her daughter can then exploit. It would seem, then, that it was Gabrielle who started out writing down what the voices told her and that her daughter merely copied her, thereby transforming madness into literature.[8] Gabrielle's ability to believe in the voices would turn from a charming gullibility into a liability (see "1900: Women and Education"); thus, Rachilde may have chosen to repress or distance herself from the knowledge that it was such an ability to hear voices, to give voice to disembodied persons, that had enabled her to write in the first place. The traces of Gabrielle's collaboration in the creation of Rachilde are removed in *Quand j'étais jeune*, but they remain perfectly legible elsewhere.

Whether by serendipity or by calculation, Marguerite had discovered a very enabling myth in the Swedish nobleman Rachilde, one that facilitated her writing at an age when she was still dependent on her parents and moving in a society that disapproved of women writing. To be chosen as the vehicle for such a noble and distinguished voice was an honor that a girl could hardly be expected to refuse. The choice of pseudonym was similarly fortuitous. Whether the young Marguerite simply borrowed the name Rachilde,[9] or whether it was her own invention, she chose a name that was rich in connotations, at least some of which she seems knowingly to have exploited. The name is morphologically quite French and presents a certain gender ambiguity: the mute final -*e* adds a feminine connotation, especially if it is viewed as a first, rather than as a last, name. Although many people did assume it to be a family (last) name, it also evokes the first name Rachel, recalling the famous actress known throughout France.[10] (Rachel had performed at the theater in Périgueux in 1849, for example, just after the switch from oil to gas lighting lit up the stage.) It was certainly an association that occurred to at least one Parisian, the editor of *Le Figaro* (see below). Later, during World War II, the occupying Germans ironically placed the antisemitic Rachilde on the infamous "Otto" list, the blacklist of (predominantly) Jewish authors, perhaps because they, too, assumed the name to be a variation on Rachel (Auriant, *Souvenirs* 16).

Rachilde came to be known by this name for the rest of her life. The public, authorial persona gradually replaced the private one of Marguerite Eymery, and, as Rachilde gained a public, Marguerite the reader became redundant and disappeared completely. The fact that the name Rachilde blended both feminine and masculine elements made it the perfect mask for its wearer, for it defied any definitive categorization. Its fictional masculine referent, the Swedish nobleman, provided the kind of protective gender shield sought by many women writers of the nineteenth century who wanted to place their work in the public sphere without incurring immediate condemnation. Nineteenth-century French literature offers the precedents of George Sand, Daniel Stern, and the vicomte de Launay (in addition to many others less well known today).

At the same time as it purported to identify a man, however, the name also evoked a woman writer, specifically, the British Gothic novelist Ann Radcliffe, author of *The Mysteries of Udolpho*. Not only would the name Raclife be used as a transparent reference by one of Rachilde's critics, but, according to Paul Léautaud, one of Rachilde's colleagues at the *Mercure*, a literary dictionary published in the 1920s went so far as to attribute the works of Ann Radcliffe to Rachilde. Léautaud also recalled the words of Marcel Schwob: "Rachilde? C'est Anne [*sic*] Radcliffe" (1: 1534–35).

Like numerous other writers, Rachilde did not keep her true identity a secret for long, however, and thus the pseudonym rapidly became unnecessary as protection. The fact that Rachilde continued to use it therefore suggests that it served other purposes as well. Not the least of these was that it consolidated the masculine identity that she had assumed since childhood to please her father. She even went so far as to refer to herself using masculine linguistic forms (pronouns, adjectival endings, etc.). At the same time, however, the possible feminization of the name underscored the fact that the masculine role was an assumed one. The result was a pleasant confusion, as both strangers and acquaintances tried to cope with the mixed signals. Some referred to her as "Margot Rachilde," as "Monsieur Rachilde" (this one even in person), as "Madame Rachilde," and some simply as "Rachilde," either acknowledging defeat or assimilating the name with the Arabic title *rashid*, made known by colonialism and popular by Orientalism.

The name thus contains a number of different layers of meaning, but it clearly functioned both as an important and complex form of self-representation for Rachilde and eventually as a model for other writers such as Colette (who adopted this single label at the turn of the century, long after Rachilde's identity was established).[11] Rachilde might well congratulate her imagination for guaranteeing her existence with the words, "Je pense . . . donc je suis" (*QJJ* 149), but it would have been more accurate to conclude, "I write, therefore I am," for her pseudonymous writing endowed her with the voice, and by extension the existence, that had been threatened by the *noyé*. The Swedish nobleman was thus a fantastic discovery, one ghost that seemed to offer protection from another (the *noyé*), although he would also come back to haunt Rachilde in ways she could not possibly have imagined at the time.

In addition to learning about *dédoublement* through the spirit world, Marguerite was learning to live a double life through a very material experience, one that taught her something of the different reception of male and female voices. At around the time that Marguerite was beginning to think about publishing her work, she also established a relationship with a publisher that made her aware of some of the possibilities of *dédoublement* and that cemented its association with publication and authorship. This curious relationship developed with the editor of the *Echo de la Dordogne*, a regional newspaper based in Périgueux. It was here that Marguerite would publish that first short story ("La Création de l'oiseau-mouche") in 1877. She would continue to publish work there regularly, and she credited this contact as an important development in her career: "Je dois à cet homme bien élevé et de grande érudition les meilleurs conseils littéraires que j'ai reçus" (*QJJ* 56).

The information about this relationship comes from Rachilde's reminiscences *Quand j'étais jeune*, and as already noted, these memoirs are unreliable when it comes to ages and dates. Thus, Rachilde writes here that she was allowed to ride alone to Périgueux at "quinze ou seize ans" (54) and that one day, accessorized with riding boots and a whip, she used this freedom to call on the editor of the *Echo*, who had accepted a number of articles and stories from her in the past, in order to ask his permission to write an article about army maneuvers in Thiviers (55–57). As already noted, however, her publications began only in 1877, when she would have been seventeen, and the article about the maneuvers appeared in 1879 (Rachilde kept a copy of this publication in a scrapbook of press cuttings, so she could easily have checked the date.) While unreliable as to dates, *Quand j'étais jeune* nevertheless provides a valuable document concerning the way in which Marguerite liked to present herself and enables us to situate her contacts with the (unnamed) editor of the Périgueux paper generally in her teenage years, her formative years as a writer, the years of her "coming to writing."

The account in *Quand j'étais jeune* focuses on Rachilde's request to cover the maneuvers, but, in the course of the narration, Rachilde tells the reader something of her previous contacts with this editor. She would ride alone on her favorite horse, Lison, from Château-l'Evêque to Périgueux to meet with him and sell him her work. The offices of the *Echo* were located in the old city center, "dans une petite rue sombre, où l'on pouvait venir à cheval, mais pas en voiture" (56). No doubt the need to travel on horseback determined to some extent the costume in which Marguerite would present herself: she was accustomed to wearing male clothing for riding purposes and thus would occasionally appear "en homme," though sometimes also "en femme." The editor would accept her work without comment:

> *Quand j'étais* en homme, *il ne discutait jamais avec moi mais souvent insinuait qu'il serait bon de dire à Mlle Rachilde de faire attention à* la presse avancée.
> *Quand j'étais* en femme, *il me chargeait de ses amitiés pour* mon frère. *(56–57)*

If *Quand j'étais jeune* can be trusted, it appears, then, that the relationship with this editor may have suggested to Marguerite/Rachilde a connection between writing and sibling relationships. The editor's assumption that the two figures that he saw were brother and sister gave a concrete—and gendered—relationship to the two "doubles" in Rachilde's personal fiction of *dédoublement*, a relationship subsequently explored in her novels.

The adoption of the male pseudonym Rachilde originated within the family circle of the séance and predated the contacts with the editor of the *Echo*. It originated, then, as a way of making Marguerite's writing acceptable to her parents, but she ended up adopting this pseudonymous identity on a permanent basis, no doubt in conformity with social expectations that writing was a masculine activity.

Marguerite did not become Rachilde in name only, however. Part of the apprenticeship in *dédoublement* involved cross-dressing. I shall discuss later how cross-dressing was something that Rachilde would continue to do, in various ways, throughout her life (see "1884: Writing as Cross-Dressing" and "1885: Marriage and the Woman Writer"), but the realization that she could present herself as either male or female is connected to the splitting of self represented in *dédoublement*. In childhood, this may go back in part to the fact that her parents had wanted a boy and her father in particular treated her as a boy in her infancy, teaching her to ride and fence. The association with riding and cross-dressing was, then, an important nexus of symbolic meaning for Rachilde. Dressing as a boy in order to ride horses more freely was one of the earliest manifestations of Rachilde's cross-dressing. Perhaps, owing to her parents' desire for a son, she had also developed the idea of a twin male sibling, but what started out as perhaps mere convenience or the indulgence of a collective family fantasy seems, thanks to the editor of the *Echo*, to have become associated with the role of author. Marguerite became an author (Rachilde) when she put on male clothing and discovered that she had to put on male clothing in order to become an author.

The story of Marguerite's encounter with the editor of the *Echo* thus fuses several strands in the development of her authorial persona. On the one hand, she adopted the literary voice of Rachilde, the male authorial voice still expected by the average French reader at the turn of the century. At the same time, she explored a relationship with a male sibling persona through her cross-dressing (Anne Freadman reports that George Sand, too, was mistaken for a brother/sister pair). Rachilde's contacts with her first publisher linked two factors already present in her early life: cross-dressing as an equestrian and cross-dressing as an author. Both were simultaneously symbolic and practical.

Whether the editor of the *Echo* was really confused about these siblings, or whether he was just humoring his eccentric young author, a self-described "riche héritière" (*QJJ* 57), we cannot know. It suits Rachilde's authorial purposes in *Quand j'étais jeune* to present him as naive and phlegmatic. She describes him as "un grand garçon un peu triste, d'allure extrêmement pondérée, ne s'animant jamais, ne blâmant jamais, et sachant son métier d'écrivain averti, tout en évitant les polémiques d'ordre (ou de désordre) local" (56). He did not leave us his version of events.

What has been left behind, however, is the trace of Rachilde's association of a sibling relationship with writing. The device of *dédoublement*
occurs in a number of Rachilde's novels, but the motif of confused sibling identity is prominently foregrounded in one published some ten
years after Rachilde's first dealings with the editor of the *Echo*, *Madame
Adonis* (1888). The book also deals indirectly with the problems of writing as a woman, a point to which I shall return below.

Madame Adonis is something of a companion piece to *Monsieur
Vénus*. Both titles evoke androgyny through the conjunction of a gendered form of address (Monsieur/Madame) and the name of a classical
figure of the opposite sex (Venus/Adonis). Both figures are associated
with eroticism—Venus because she is the goddess of love, Adonis because he is loved by Venus—hence the novels proclaim that they will
treat the sexual adventures of ambiguously gendered figures.[12] Perhaps
Rachilde (or her publisher) was hoping to capitalize on the success of
Monsieur Vénus by explicitly inviting a comparison in *Madame Adonis*.
The titles also announce a kind of *dédoublement* marked by the gender
duality.

Unlike *Monsieur Vénus*, however, *Madame Adonis* is not about cosmopolitan morals; rather, it is one of Rachilde's provincial novels. The
principal setting in Tours invites a comparison between Rachilde and
Balzac, and other similarities between the two writers' work can be ad-
duced, Rachilde's work, taken as a whole, offering, for example, a kind
of *comédie humaine*. But, while Balzac focuses on the permutations of
ambition and fortune, Rachilde's unifying themes involve the permutations of human sex and gender systems, offering an overview of the
ways sex is never simple. The contribution of *Madame Adonis* to this
larger panorama is to show, as one critic puts it, how a man can be
cuckolded by his mistress ("Bibliographie générale" 125). The Balzacian
depiction of the provinces, the Flaubertian sense of irony, and the Mo-
lieresque sense of character and timing are among the novel's strengths.

Madame Adonis concerns the complicated relationships between
two couples, one married, the other apparently brother and sister. Louis
and Louise Bartau, young provincial newlyweds, are echoed by Marcel
Carini and his sister, Marcelle Desambres. Onomastically, the novel
presents a problem: while the first or given names of both couples suggest two parallel pairs (Louis/Louise; Marcel/Marcelle), the last or family names are curiously asymmetrical. Louis and Louise form a cohesive
social unit (symbolized by the fact that they carry the same last name):
"Monsieur et Madame Bartau, de la maison Bartau (douves en chêne),
de Tours" (8). But Marcel and Marcelle do not share the same last name,

even though they are supposedly brother and sister. As the novel will reveal, Marcel and Marcelle turn out to be one and the same. The difference in last name helps prolong the reader's ignorance of this fact yet also, in anticipation of the dénouement, draws attention to the fact that there is something "wrong" with this couple. The exaggeration of difference spelled out by the unexpectedly mismatched last names also draws attention to the play of difference and pseudodifference characteristic of *dédoublement*.

Louis and Louise first meet the Adonis-like Marcel in the Château d'Amboise through his brother, Hector Carini, a sculptor working on a restoration. Curiously, however, Marcel is introduced as Marcel *Desambres*, that is, as a brother, but one who does not share the same last name as Hector. Hector's explanation is that "c'est un frère que j'ai qu'on appelle ainsi pour le distinguer" (18), as though a different first name were not enough, but the inconsistency of the naming system is later further commented on by Louise when she meets Marcel's sister, Marcelle Carini Desambres: "Ainsi, dans cette famille, le frère et la soeur portaient le même nom. L'étrange famille!" (173). Marcel is known, not by his family name (Carini), but by his sister's married name (Desambres). As the novel will show, the confusion around the sameness and difference of names acts as a symptom of sexual confusion.

For Louise, the meeting with Marcel represents a *coup de foudre*, for he is like the prince of her dreams (26) and fills her with strange, inexplicable feelings. Her unforgettable encounter with this "other" spells the beginning of marital problems. Throughout the main part of the novel, it is Louise's adulterous relationship with Marcel that seems to form the principle threat to the married couple. Several months after the meeting with Marcel, however, Marcelle, now coincidentally a resident of Louis and Louise's hometown, Tours, becomes a customer of the Bartaus' and gradually becomes, first, Louis's confidant and adviser and, finally, his mistress. Her house also serves as a rendezvous for Louise and Marcel. For the reader, the coincidences quickly become all too apparent—Marcel and Marcelle are never seen together, for example—but it is not until nearly the end of the novel that Louise realizes that Marcelle bears an uncanny resemblance to Marcel (279). The novel ends in a climactic erotic scene: Louis, tipped off by Marcelle, catches Louise and Marcel in flagrante delicto and stabs Marcel. Only then does Louise realize that Marcel and Marcelle are the same person (a woman, as it turns out—Adonis is a [ma]dame), Louis that he has murdered his mistress.

While hardly surprising (except to Louis and Louise), this denouement fulfills the titillating conventions of decadent fiction. After all, *Madame Adonis* clearly situates itself in relation to *Monsieur Vénus*, echoing in its title both the structure and the gender confusion of the 1884 novel that earned Rachilde her reputation as the queen of decadence.

The privileging of the somewhat Shakespearean plot of a brother and sister who turn out to be the same person foregrounds as a theme the device that Rachilde had used in the early days of her writing career. In some senses, *Madame Adonis* (re)tells Rachilde's experiences with the editor of the *Echo de la Dordogne*. (Although Rachilde did not *write* about these experiences directly until the memoir *Quand j'étais jeune* in 1947, she would have *lived* them some ten years before the publication of *Madame Adonis* in 1888.) That the novel *Madame Adonis* is about the situation of the woman writer is not readily apparent, however, until the main narrative is read in the context of the preface, "L'Art de se faire injurier."

As she had done in her earlier novel *A mort* (1886), Rachilde introduces *Madame Adonis* with an apparently autobiographical preface. Like the preface to *A mort*, this preface deals explicitly with the writing process, and in particular with an anecdote from 1880 about a woman writer. Like the novel, the anecdote relates an incident of *dédoublement* in that, in it, Rachilde, an aspiring woman writer, is waiting to talk to a publisher when a beautiful and successful woman writer breezes in to consult with him. To this woman's face, the publisher is charming and polite, but, as soon as she leaves, he comments, "Vieille bique" (4), a remark that "haunts" (v) Rachilde. Rachilde both is witness to this event and at the same time identifies with one of the participants, the woman writer, hence the *dédoublement*. The lesson Rachilde derives from the anecdote is that even the most successful woman writer is not above insult. The anecdote is presented in order to explain to the public why Rachilde has adopted a masculine authorial persona: "Je porte des chapeaux d'homme, des cheveux courts" (x). Although people consider her to be hysterical (to be locked up in Charenton [x], though this would turn out to be her mother's fate, not hers), she explains her deviance as the logical consequence of an illogical world.

The combination of *dédoublement* through siblings who turn out to be a single person and of the need to explain herself as a writer suggests a reading of *Madame Adonis* as a fictional metacommentary on the situation of the woman writer in fin-de-siècle France. Marcel(le) is the woman writer who must present herself as a man to seduce the reading public. Read in this light, the ending of the novel suggests something about the violence done to the woman writer who risks such a deception. A telling detail not mentioned in the earlier summary, moreover, is that Louis stabs Marcel with a knife used to cut the pages of new books, a very literary weapon.

One could read the ending of *Madame Adonis* as a straightforward Girardian intolerance of doubles (see, for example, Girard, *To Double Business Bound*), but, given the ways in which, as I have indicated, *dédoublement* is linked to authorship in the Rachildian world, the simple suppression of doubles seems insufficient as an explanation. The character of Marcel(le) seems to evoke Rachilde herself, and the violence that is done to her at the end of the novel is perhaps an expression of the violence to which she is subjected as an author by the provincial and provincially minded reading public.[13]

The preface to *Madame Adonis*, dated November 1887, was written in part in response to one such public attack on Rachilde as a writer, Gisèle d'Estoc's scathing critique *La Vierge-Réclame*, published earlier that year. Referring to Rachilde as "Mlle Raclife," d'Estoc accuses her, among other things, of writing badly and of immorality in her personal life. Typical of the criticisms are such comments as, "Les ouvrages de Mlle Raclife nous font l'effet de contes de fées, à l'usage des grands enfants corrompus et des assassins latents" (105), and a recurrent theme aired at length is whether or not "Mlle Raclife" could really claim to be a virgin. The strongest criticism leveled against Rachilde (and further discussed below), the criticism behind the title of d'Estoc's work, was the accusation that Rachilde was a shameless self-promoter: "Mlle Raclife . . . est, au même degré qu'une comédienne célèbre [Bernhardt?] possédée d'une manie furieuse de réclame" (107). Rachilde, then, was being treated like the "vieille bique" of her preface, the only difference being that she was insulted to her face as well as behind her back.

Rachilde had discovered that literal and metaphoric cross-dressing was one way to get around such prejudice against the "vieilles biques" of fin-de-siècle France, just as it had served to get her stories published in Périgueux. But once readers began to love her, as some did after *Monsieur Vénus*, she became increasingly subject to scrutiny. The revelation of the female identity behind the male face presented to the public occasioned violent reactions, character assassination that Rachilde represented as literal assassination in *Madame Adonis*. Thanks to the later account of Rachilde's early relationship with the editor of the *Echo de la Dordogne* made available in *Quand j'étais jeune*, the contemporary reader can glean some appreciation of the underlying symbolic meaning of the *dédoublement* in novels such as *Madame Adonis*.

Authority, Authorship, and Authorization

*In which Rachilde publishes her first story
and Victor Hugo authorizes her*

Rachilde was extremely proud of her first publication, "La Création de l'oiseau-mouche," a "legend" describing the creation of the humming bird. Some of the circumstances connected with its appearance were discussed in the previous chapter. The story was quickly followed by others (see Soulignac, "Bibliographie" 198–205), and Rachilde sent a copy of one of her next works ("Premier amour," first published in 1878) to her idol, Victor Hugo (1802–85), for his assessment. Anxiously, she waited for a reply from the great man:

> *Elle est venue attendre le facteur, loin de la maison de ses parents.*
> *Voici bientôt une semaine qu'elle espère cette lettre. (QJJ 5)*

This anecdote begins Rachilde's memoirs, *Quand j'étais jeune* (published in 1947), the first two chapters of which—"La Lettre" and "Présentation au Dieu"—deal with Rachilde's idolization of Hugo. She did eventually receive the reply she was waiting for, and Hugo's words of encouragement were important in motivating her to continue writing. But beyond offering a pat on the back from a famous writer, why were the words of Victor Hugo in particular of such paramount importance?

In retelling the story of the letter, Rachilde distorts her age, underestimating it by two years. Just after the passage quoted above, she continues: "Elles sont rares, les filles de quinze ans qui savent ce qu'elles disent en écrivant! Oui, elle n'a que quinze ans, et elle a osé une chose défendue entre toutes: écrire à un homme qu'elle ne connaît pas, qui ne la connaît pas . . ." (5). She states that she was only fifteen years old, not once, but twice, stressing her young years. On the one hand, this distortion has the effect of heightening her daring. Although her first publication did not appear until she was seventeen (and the story that she claims to have sent Hugo was not published until she was eighteen), to write to an unknown man is a more powerful act of defiance when one is only fifteen.

But could there be another reason for distorting her age and ignoring so cavalierly her own publication record (easily available in the book of press clippings that she kept, now in the Fonds Doucet)? Later in this first brief chapter of her memoirs, she describes her writing as an act of defiance directed against her parents, one that she is compelled to carry out under a full moon since her parents will not allow her a lamp or candles at night.[1] From her parents' point of view, she is just "une jeune fille [qui] doit se coucher à 9 heures et dormir toute sa nuit" (8). They have anticipated a safe future for her: "Elle est fiancée à un monsieur très bien, un officier, comme l'a été son père, un homme sérieux ayant tout ce qu'il faut de noblesse, de fortune, pour diriger dans le monde une petite personne dont l'imagination, les caprices, toutes les fantaisies sont vraiment des choses inquiétantes pour des gens soucieux du savoir-vivre" (8–9). As already suggested, Rachilde's rejection of the marriage script was a vehicle through which to convey her desire to become a writer. If she described her first contact with Hugo at age seventeen, when she was no longer engaged to be married, she would not be able to link her writing to the rejection of the bourgeois future that her parents planned for her quite as effectively. By being still engaged when she receives Hugo's letter, she can intimate to the reader that it was partly due to his encouragement that she was able to break the engagement.

This is a useful fiction, but it still does not exhaust the question of why Hugo, a question that becomes only more complicated once it is posed. It is true that Hugo was the idol of an entire generation of writers, but few carried their enthusiasm so long and so far as Rachilde.

In part, Rachilde's awe can be attributed to the fact that Hugo did eventually respond. He sent only a few words, it is true, but they were enough to raise the spirits of the aspiring writer. He wrote two sentences (four words, all nouns): "Remerciements, applaudissements. Courage, mademoiselle" (9). Rachilde was ecstatic.

The reaction of the fifteen-year-old (or even seventeen-year-old) can be easily understood, but Rachilde writes her memoirs as an eighty-year-old, yet age has clearly given her no sense of distance from this moment. What distance would the reader expect her to have? For one thing, as an adult member of the bohemian crowd in Paris in the 1880s, she would have discovered that *every* aspiring writer in Paris could produce such a letter from Hugo.

If Rachilde never discovered this fact, it is surprising indeed because it quickly became apparent to one of her friends and contemporaries, Emile Goudeau. Goudeau, a fellow Périgourdin, was a well-known member of the bohemian crowd that Rachilde frequented in her early days in Paris. Most notably, Goudeau founded (on Friday, October 11, 1878, at the Café de la Rive Gauche on the corner of the rue Cujas and the boulevard St.-Michel) the bohemian group "les Hydropathes," of

which Rachilde was a celebrated member. The unusual name has been
explained in several different ways. It is said to have been derived from
a waltz by Joseph Gung'l, but members of the group also liked to play
with the pun "hydro*patte*" as well as the etymology: one with a pathological aversion to water (and hence, it is implied, who prefers alcohol).
Rachilde seems to have liked this latter association since on numerous
occasions she asserted that she drank only water, a paradox that she
would have relished: that one who drank only water should be wel-
comed among those who feared it, the rabid bohemians.

    Bohemian literary circles were flourishing in the 1880s, and Rachilde
associated with many of them.[2] The most well-known today, perhaps,
was the circle that met at the Chat Noir, but there was also the zutistes,
the fumistes, and the hirsutes, among others. The general format was
similar from one group to the next: members would meet regularly on
a designated evening in the back room of a café and listen to each other
recite poetry and songs while drinking, smoking, and talking.[3] Some
had journals in which they published members' contributions; thus, for
example, Rachilde published "Les Lépilliers" in *Le Chat noir* on January 16, 1886. Although, in order to avoid scandal, women were not allowed officially to join some of these groups (see, for example, Goudeau
172–73), nevertheless Rachilde, as well as other women, participated
actively.

    In addition to *Le Chat noir*, Rachilde was affiliated with a number
of literary reviews and periodicals in the 1880s when she was establish-
ing her literary reputation. Thus, for example, she contributed to the
weekly *Lutèce* (founded in November 1882 as *La Nouvelle Rive gauche*,
the publication took its new name—the Roman name for Paris—in
April 1883), edited by Léo Trézenik (who would later serve as one of the
witnesses at Rachilde's wedding). Here, Rachilde would have encountered other writers such as Jean Moréas, Jules Laforgue, Laurent Tailhade, Paul Adam, Georges d'Esparbès, Henri de Régnier, Francis Vielé-
Griffin, and Ernest Raynaud. This last would begin his three-volume
memoir of "la mêlée symboliste" by referring to the letters of encouragement the new poets had solicited from Victor Hugo, letters with a by
now familiar ring: "Courage, vous réussirez. Vous n'êtes pas seulement
des talents. Vous êtes des consciences" (Raynaud 1:1–2).

    It is surprising, then, that in all this activity, Rachilde never came
across the situation described by Goudeau in his memoirs *Dix ans de
Bohème* (published in 1888) of a literary circle in the process of formation. Goudeau responded to an announcement in a literary review
inviting those interested in founding a new review or journal "pour les

jeunes" to a meeting. In retelling the story of this meeting, Goudeau recalls the naive assumptions that he held as he arrived at the specified address. He is concerned to find only two other people there ("un blond et un brun") but holds his impatience in check until their convener arrives. Goudeau's doubts only grow, however, when the convener, Monsieur T., addresses the company, presenting the excuses of some poets who were unable to attend (Banville, Leconte de Lisle) and then brandishing a letter from Victor Hugo: "L'heure est aux poètes. Votre entreprise est noble. Je suis avec vous. V. H." (19).

The telegraphic cadences of Hugo's reply are unmistakably the same as those of the long-awaited letter received by Rachilde, and this much alone of Goudeau's story might have alerted her to the formulaic, perfunctory nature of Hugo's correspondence, but Goudeau's narrative continues. The two other men laugh and introduce themselves (they are M. Adelphe Froger and M. Edmond Nodaret). Names alone are not enough, suggests Monsieur T., and he invites the poets to read aloud a sample of their work:

> *A cette invitation, le blond Adelphe tira de sa poche un manuscrit, et lut des vers très parnassiens: des images, des allitérations, des rimes riches, pour la forme; pour le fond, un rassemblement de jolis nuages dans un tunnel. Nous applaudîmes. Le blond svelte, triomphant, exhiba aussitôt une lettre de Victor Hugo, qu'il avait gardée pour la bonne bouche. Le maître lui écrivait: "Toujours en avant, et vers la lumière!—V. H."*
>
> *Ce fut au tour d'Edmond Nodaret, le petit brun. Il lut des vers quasi-classiques: de l'esprit, une forme lâchée, un prosaïsme drôle de chroniqueur débutant, qui sera très amusant plus tard. Quand il eut achevé, il prit dans son portefeuille une lettre que Victor Hugo lui avait adressée et nous en donna connaissance: "Ossa et Pélion ne sont rien, il faut gravir le Parnasse; vous êtes en chemin. Continuez.—V. H." (20–21)*

When it is his turn to submit his work to the judgment of his peers, the naive Goudeau feels ashamed and humiliated to have no recommendation from the Master to embellish his recitation. He might have been completely discouraged by his lack of credentials, and his literary career might have stalled there and then, had not the convener decided to end the evening with a recitation of his own work. The dramatic poem chosen for the occasion was so bad that the three listeners could barely conceal their hilarity. It was an important lesson for Goudeau: "Je compris, en entendant ces choses innomables, que les brevets du maître étaient une simple formule de bienveillance, et ne tiraient pas à con-séquence" (22; see also Lefrère 22).

Although Rachilde may herself never have been faced with the same situation as Goudeau (and, indeed, would not have been in the embar-rassing situation of having no letter to show), she might well have learned from others, including Goudeau himself, that Hugo's endorse-ment was meaningless. And perhaps she did hear such tales but chose to cling to the cherished idea that somehow she had been singled out for the favor of the Master.

Rachilde was aware of her naiveté in another interaction with Hugo, the story of which forms the second chapter of *Quand j'étais jeune*, "Présentation au Dieu," in which she recounts her first meeting with her idol. Rachilde claimed that she was only seventeen at the time of this en-counter (19), yet at the same time she states that it was when she had al-ready written "un livre et des contes qu'on avait bien voulu publier dans des journaux parisiens" (16). Since none of her work appeared in Pa-risian newspapers until 1878 (Soulignac, "Bibliographie" 200), and since her first book, the novel *Monsieur de la Nouveauté*, was not published until late 1879,[4] she seems once again to have exaggerated her youth. Yet the meeting with Hugo involved staying at a hotel in the rue de Valois, suggesting that Rachilde was not yet living in Paris permanently, and Rachilde was still being escorted by her mother (10), so her estimate is probably not too far from the mark. She had obtained her mother's per-mission to wear her best dress, "une de celles que je mettais pour aller au bal de la préfecture de Périgueux les jours de gala officiel," and, al-though her mother was convinced that it would look ridiculous, she had granted permission for Rachilde to don this "robe rose en tarlatane gar-nie de dentelles blanches" (17). The evening dress was covered by a "macfarlane" coat.

Before the presentation, Rachilde lunched with three "messieurs de littérature" (15)—Catulle Mendès, Villiers de l'Isle-Adam, and Briffault, "[qui] n'était pas de littérature" (18)—who were to present her to Hugo but who conducted themselves like conspirators. They informed her that it was customary for those presented to the Master, then in his sev-enties, to go down on their knees and ask for his blessing. Rachilde found this perfectly credible and duly did so when presented to the great man. At first, he looked angry at this act of hommage: "Puis il se mit à rire, d'un petit rire toussotant, se baissa en me prenant par la taille et, d'un seul effort, comme on se saisirait d'une poupée pour s'assurer qu'elle n'est pas trop lourde, il m'assit sur ses genoux." Rachilde's reac-tion to this unexpected turn of events was mixed: "J'étais à la fois confuse, déçue, enchantée, peut-être très effrayée" (19). But she does not analyze this mixture of conflicting emotions.

Rachilde was, no doubt, embarrassed to have been made to look foolish by the three gentlemen who had preyed on her innocence, but another violation of innocence seems to have been perpetrated by Hugo himself. Even if she were only seventeen, and certainly if she were eighteen or nineteen, to be seated on a man's lap was something her mother surely would not have condoned. If it was unthinkable for a proper young lady to write to an unknown man, as Rachilde had asserted in the first chapter of her memoirs, how much less appropriate to sit on his lap? Yet doing so had not been her idea, the compliments and attentions of the great writer were surely flattering, and surely such a great man could only ever conduct himself in the most proper way.

Rachilde was soon to learn that great men did not always have pure intentions when they sat young ladies on their knee. Indeed, it was a lesson she had perhaps already learned by the time she published *Monsieur de la Nouveauté* (and therefore by the time she was presented to Hugo). This book had originally been published in serial form in the newspaper *L'Estafette*, where her first Parisian publications (also alluded to in "Présentation au dieu") had appeared. Serialization of *Monsieur de la Nouveauté* began in June 1878; when it appeared in book form, it was dedicated to Léonce Détroyat, the "directeur politique" of *L'Estafette*. Détroyat's name comes up again in the preface to *A mort*, where it is once again a question of sitting on a gentleman's lap:

> M. Détroyat, ex-directeur de L'Estafette, après avoir offert une collaboration payée dans un des ses nombreux journaux, prétendit que cette pauvre Rachilde entendait de travers ce qu'on lui disait et se plaignait de persécutions imaginaires . . ., il abandonna naturellement sa protégée quand elle aurait eu le plus besoin de ses appointements . . . aussi Rachilde ne se plaignit plus! Tant pis pour toi . . . petite . . . tes écrits sont légers, légère tu dois être, eh! saute, enfant, sur les genoux de nous, les hommes miséricordieux! (AM xvi)

Here, in 1886, one year after Hugo's death, Rachilde looks back on an example of the way in which her innocence was abused in her collaboration with Détroyat. She was grateful for the offer of work, but not for the unwanted sexual attentions, and, when she protested, it was maintained that she had misunderstood. She recounts this episode with a bitterness and irony that seem completely lacking from her memoirs, which assume a more nostalgic tone and in which the bitterness has been softened by the distance of time. Can the vehemence and biting irony of her attack on Détroyat be read, in part, as a displaced reaction to her disillusioning meeting with Hugo? Her disappointment on that occasion must have been sharp, indeed: someone she idolized was treating her, in her words, like a doll.

Still the need to believe that Hugo was perfect colors her memoirs over half a century later. Even though in 1947 she could rail against the hypocrisy of "les hommes miséricordieux," she could not place Hugo in that category. She continued to maintain that his behavior was benevolent, paternalistic—in a word, innocent.

Thus, Rachilde maintained a lifelong denial about two aspects of Hugo. In the first place, she continued to act as though she believed that his encouragement of her writing really meant something. Second, although she was able to articulate her anger at the way she was sexually harassed, dismissed, and belittled by other men, she ignored this same behavior in Hugo, even though he had humiliated her (in a way that might today be described as sexual harassment) and dismissed her like a doll rather than treating her as the serious writer that (at least she thought) he should have known her to be.

What could account for such persistent denial? Why did Rachilde remain so resolutely blind to Hugo's shortcomings? One reason might be that Hugo stood for everything that her father rejected. Although Rachilde idolized her father (just like she idolized Hugo), the idolization was laced with ambivalence: her father beat her, rejected her, wished she were a boy, wished she were different. Was it to punish this father that she became a writer, the thing he despised most? And was it to drive home her rejection of him that she modeled herself on the writer he hated the most?

This would certainly be justification enough, but, in Rachilde's universe, there was another reason to be grateful for Hugo, and that was *La Légende des siècles*, Hugo's epic poem about the history of France. Rachilde's gratitude was not so much for the poem itself—as an aesthetic object and a contribution to literature—although such a response would not have been inappropriate and doubtless others have felt the same way. Rachilde was, I believe, grateful to Hugo for another reason.

In the preface by "F. P." (François Porché?) to Rachilde's *Le Théâtre des bêtes* (1926), the author first gives a brief biography of Rachilde, devoting some considerable attention to her real name, Marguerite Eymery. It is an evocative name, one that seems to have "une allure romantique d'un charme un peu lointain peut-être aujourd'hui" (viii). The author then introduces an extensive quote from Hugo's *Légende des siècles*, an episode from the reign of Charlemagne ("lointain," indeed).

The quotation is repeated in full here in order to reproduce the effect of conjoining the name of Rachilde / Marguerite Eymery to the following image:

> ... *Ainsi Charles de France appelé Charlemagne,*
> *Exarque de Ravenne, empereur d'Allemagne,*
> *Parlait dans la montagne avec sa grande voix.*
> ... *Les barons consternés fixaient les yeux à terre.*
> *Soudain comme chacun demeurait interdit,*
> *Un jeune homme bien fait sortit des rangs et dit:*
> *Que Monsieur Saint-Denis garde le Roi de France.*
> *L'empereur fut surpris de ce ton d'assurance*
> *Il regarda celui qui s'avançait et vit,*
> *Comme le roi Saül lorsqu'apparut David,*
> *Une espèce d'enfant au teint rose, aux mains blanches,*
> *Que d'abord les soudards dont l'estoc bat les hanches*
> *Prirent pour une fille habillée en garçon,*
> *Doux, frêle, confiant, serein, sans écusson*
> *Et sans panache, ayant sous ses habits de serge,*
> *L'air grave d'un gendarme et l'air froid d'une vierge.*
> ... *L'enfant parlait ainsi d'un air de loyauté*
> *Regardant tout le monde avec simplicité.*

This is the verbal portrait painted by Hugo of the young legendary hero Aymery (or Aimeri).

The medieval "geste" of Aimeri de Narbonne was one of the many examples of early French literature "rediscovered" by medievalists of the nineteenth century and given new life by Hugo's legend. The plot forms part of the Roland cycle: after the defeat and vengeance of Roncevaux, Charlemagne sees a fortified city (Narbonne) that he wants to win back from the Saracens. He offers a reward to the knight who will capture the city, but each of the noblest peers declines the honor. Charlemagne laments the cowardice of his knights and the loss of Roland and Olivier, who would not have failed him thus, and dismisses the knights. It is at this point that the young and inexperienced Aimeri steps forward to accept the challenge. Since the rest, as they say, is history, the dramatic center of Hugo's narrative is the confrontation between the older knights, tired of battle, and the young Aimeri, ambitious and hungry for a chance to earn a reputation. After Aimeri accepts the challenge and Charlemagne praises him and dubs him "Aymery de Narbonne," Hugo ends with the laconic "Le lendemain Aymery prit la ville."

The reader of the preface to *Théâtre des bêtes* would thus probably

have some general idea of Aimeri de Narbonne as the hero who succeeded where his betters had failed or, to use the comparison suggested
by Hugo himself, as a David who defeated a Goliath. This was certainly
a flattering way to describe Rachilde—and in keeping with her image of
herself as the underdog—but the quotation chosen by "F. P." contains
a further set of resonant images. If Aymery was an ancestor of the Eymery family, Marguerite Eymery was living up to her name. Her ancestor
had androgynous qualities: he looked like "une fille habillée en garçon,"
not a real knight but a girl dressed up as one. Where Aymery *looked* like
a girl dressed up as a boy, Rachilde sometimes really was one. Rachilde
also shared Aymery's "air froid d'une vierge." Many critics used the
contrast between the knowledge of human sexuality displayed in her
works and her reputedly virginal status to heighten the piquancy of her
work. The introduction by Barrès to the 1889 edition of *Monsieur Vénus*,
where he describes the novel as offering "ce vice savant éclatant dans le
rêve d'une vierge" (6), is a perfect example, but there is also the case of
Gisèle d'Estoc's *La Vierge-Réclame*, in which challenging and debunking
the myth of Rachilde's virginity constitutes an obsessively recurrent
theme. In short, as depicted by Hugo, Rachilde's ancestor had all the
qualities that Rachilde could have wished for: an ambiguously gendered
but pure, plucky boy who steps forward to save France when his betters
have all given up.

Part of Rachilde's debt to Hugo, then, is this flattering depiction of
her ancestor, one that conformed to the image that she had developed
of herself. I do not know when Rachilde became aware of the *Légende*—
the epic was published in installments from 1859 to 1883—but, given
her idolization of Hugo, it does not seem far-fetched to suppose that she
learned of it early on, well before *Théâtre des bêtes* (1926). It is certain
that as early as 1879 she gave the name Vicomte Aimeri de Cros to one
of her heroes (see her "Gemma," serialized in the *Echo de la Dordogne*)
and later returned to the name for the crusader Aimeri in *Notre Dame
des rats* (1931).

Hugo's poem also accomplishes two other things for Rachilde. First,
it places Rachilde, as Aimeri, squarely within mainstream French tradition. Aimeri is there at the dawn of French history and plays a foundational role. Despite the outsider, "David" status of Aimeri, then,
Rachilde is in some ways positioned as an insider. By identifying with
this famous ancestor (whether or not he was really related, Rachilde
imagined that he was), Rachilde was not the provincial outsider in Paris
but the descendant of a member of the emperor's inner circle. Moreover, the *Chanson de Roland* is a foundational text of French literature,

and Hugo's poem also acknowledges that Aimeri/Eymery has always been associated—even if peripherally—with that literary tradition. Thus, not only is Rachilde an insider, but she has always been literary. She was there, as it were, when Roland *et compagnie* crossed the Pyrenees and "founded" French literature by providing the material for what has now become the first work in the accepted canon, the *Chanson de Roland*.

Hugo's words of encouragement—thanks, applause, and courage—might have been addressed to Aimeri as well as to (Marguerite) Eymery. With these words, Rachilde was author(iz)ed as a writer.

The Politics of Publishing

In which Monsieur Vénus *is published and
the French police take an interest in Rachilde*

It has been said that while *Monsieur Vénus* was not Rachilde's first novel, it was the first one that counts (Coulon 547). To understand why, let us begin by stating a banal yet significant fact: *Monsieur Vénus* was published not in France but in Belgium. The edition most readily available today is the first *French* edition, published in 1889 (with the notorious preface by Maurice Barrès that fueled so many rumors and misconceptions over the years by presenting Rachilde as a twenty-year-old prodigy), but the original—that is to say, the 1884—edition, the one published jointly under the names of both Rachilde and the enigmatic Francis Talman, was published in Brussels by an obscure publisher.

The identity of Talman remains something of a mystery. Some people have speculated that Talman never really existed, but Rachilde claimed that he was someone she met while taking fencing lessons and who agreed to be her coauthor in order to fight any duels that might be provoked by the publication of the book:

> *J'ai rencontré le François* [sic] *Talman qui signe avec moi sur cette première couverture dans une salle d'armes que je hantais assez souvent autrefois. . . . Donc, j'ai rencontré dans une salle d'armes de Paris un jeune journaliste qui prétendait dans une autre salle, celle-là de rédaction, où je faisais des chroniques* PEU PAYÉES, *que l'on ne peut pas bien lancer un livre sans un duel . . . c'était la mode. Alors, il devait collaborer (le moins possible) au livre en question, mais se battre à la première polémique contenant une injure à mon adresse. J'attendis sa collaboration de plume trois mois. . . . Or, le roman était fini; mais comme je ne voulais pas qu'il se mît à me défendre pour rien, j'ai laissé sa signature. (Auriant,* Souvenirs *29)*

Talman's contributions to the actual writing were minimal and were suppressed in subsequent editions because, according to Rachilde, the writing was so bad.[1] Whether Talman ever existed remains open to debate, but, regardless, the fact remains that Rachilde thought, or, more precisely, wanted the public to believe that she thought, that the publication of the novel might provoke duels.[2]

On its original publication sometime before July 1884 (Soulignac, "Bibliographie" 215), the novel carried the subtitle "Un Roman matérialiste." Why characterize *Monsieur Vénus* as a materialist novel? For one thing, the term *decadent* had not yet gained wide acceptance.[3] Another clue is offered by an article in *La Revue indépendente* that announced the defeat of "romanciers idéalistes" who want to ignore science: "Longtemps le gouvernement du monde a été dévolu aux idées mythiques et mystiques, à l'hypothèse subjective, en un mot; il est temps qu'il passe aux mains de la science experimentale, de la certitude objective, c'est-à-dire du matérialisme" (*La Revue indépendente* 1). Thus, "materialism" shared many of the properties of literary naturalism, although the author of this article takes pains to point out that the materialist rejects the implicitly moralizing tone of naturalism by characterizing the materialist as "négateur de tout ordre social et de toute grandeur morale" (3). The subtitle thus reveals both that the authors, Rachilde and Talman, did not yet perceive themselves as part of a "decadent" movement and also that they may have seen themselves as rejecting literary idealism. Given the way in which idealism came to have certain feminized connotations in the context of the novel (see Schor), the subtitle was also a statement of literary virility.

By far the most interesting thing about *Monsieur Vénus* from a contemporary point of view, however, is that in 1884 it appeared in two almost identical editions, both published by Auguste Brancart in Brussels. Brancart initially issued three *éditions* (or "printings") of the novel.[4] This "*first* first edition" (in the English sense) had the address of the publisher on the title page (4, rue de Loxum) and a short preface signed with the authors' initials ("R. et F. T.") that simply invited readers to consider "qu'au moment où ils coupent ces premiers feuillets, l'héroïne de notre histoire passe peut-être devant leur porte."[5] The "*second* first edition" (the fourth printing) is distinguished by an addition to the publisher's address (4, rue de Loxum *et Rue d'Aremberg, 30*) and by the replacement of the authors' cryptic preface by an anonymous one thought to be by Arsène Houssaye.[6]

The most interesting difference, however, was the suppression of part of a sentence in the penultimate paragraph of the novel. At the end of the novel, an epilogue (chap. 17 in the 1884 and 1885 editions, chap. 16 in later editions) narrates the nocturnal visits of mysterious figures (both of whom we guess to be Raoule de Vénérande in various disguises) to a wax mannequin (the one incorporating the relics of Jacques Silvert).[7] According to the edition of *Monsieur Vénus* most widely used today (the 1977 Flammarion reprint of the 1889 edition), when the nocturnal visitor kisses the wax figure, "un ressort disposé à l'intérieur des flancs correspond à la bouche et l'anime" (228). In the *first* first edition, however, the sentence does not end there but continues: ". . . en même temps qu'il fait s'écarter les cuisses" (228). No chaste kiss this but instead a very clear suggestion of necrophilia.

Can we attribute the reaction to the initial publication of *Monsieur Vénus* to this suggestive phrase, suppressed in later editions? True, the Belgian authorities reacted swiftly and judged the book to be pornographic. The physical copies and the manuscript of the book were seized (probably all the remaining copies of the three *éditions*), and the author was fined and sentenced to prison. But were the authorities reacting only to content, or did other factors (for example, the fact that Brancart was a somewhat shady character, one already known to the police)[8]— shape public reaction?

Rachilde avoided most of the inconveniences caused by the Belgian reaction by not setting foot in Belgium, a small price to pay for the notoriety that she achieved in France, especially when Brancart brought out the *second* first edition (with the suggestion of necrophilia suppressed). Rachilde described the reception of the book in France in the preface to *A mort* (1886): "Le *Gil Blas* déclara que c'était là un livre obscène. Sully Prudhomme dit devant quelques-uns 'c'est un curieux ouvrage!' Les femmes en défendirent la lecture à leurs maris. M. Henri Fouquier, sous le pseudonyme de Colombine, hurla que l'auteur, qui avait les cheveux jaunes et les yeux verts, était un monstre dangereux" (AM xx). The book also attracted the attention of figures whose witty assessments have become part of the mythology of *Monsieur Vénus*. From Barbey d'Aurevilly's "pornographe, soit, mais tellement distingué" to Verlaine's ultimately negative but intriguingly provocative declaration that, if Rachilde had succeeded in inventing a new vice, she would have been the benefactor of humanity, critical opinion made the book essential reading for those with literary pretensions. The mythology surrounding *Monsieur Vénus* created a very simple narrative: the book was pornographic, it was banned; it got read, Rachilde got noticed.

Was Rachilde using the Belgian authorities who took the first step in creating this mythology by banning the book as part of a larger publicity move? The answer to this question seems to reside less in yet another analysis of the sexual politics of the novel[9] and more in an examination of the politics of publishing pornography in France under the Third Republic.

The history of censorship during the Third Republic involves a lot more than just moral outrage, although that certainly was a factor (see

Angenot and Stora-Lamarre). There were economic interests at work of
which Rachilde was aware and on which she capitalized in order to
launch her career. These interests had to do with the censorship laws
and the publishing industry (which was experiencing explosive growth
at the end of the nineteenth century).

In the 1870s, France had had repressive publishing laws, and a number of those who wished to publish sensitive material had turned to Belgian publishers, who were not subject to French law but yet published
for a francophone reading public. *Sensitive material* was not synony-
mous with *pornography* (though it included that): political writings
such as those of the Communards were published in exile, as were works
by such literary figures as Victor Hugo (*encore lui!*) and naturalist dis-
ciples of Zola. Around 1880, however, the market dynamics shifted. In
1879, the Communards were officially amnestied, meaning that their
works were no longer forbidden in France, and in 1881 the Ferry laws re-
laxed the censorship of the press. As a result, books that had previously
generated revenue for Belgian publishers could now be published in
France. To offset the loss, Belgian publishers needed to develop new
sources of income. Pornography was one such possibility. Of course,
these changes did not happen overnight, and the early 1880s saw intense
competition between French and Belgian publishers as both struggled
to renegotiate their place in the market and test the limits of the law.

The case of the Belgian publisher Henry Kistemaeckers (1851–1934)
offers a paradigmatic example that illustrates the shifting dynamics of
the market. Kistemaeckers was never Rachilde's publisher, although he
corresponded with her and contributed to the *Mercure de France* (ironically, an article about his legal trials and tribulations as a publisher entitled "Mes procès littéraires"), but he was typical of Belgian publishers
who acquired a reputation for pornography.

In the 1870s, Kistemaeckers considered himself a socialist and a supporter of the Communards, and his work in publishing was explicitly
political: not only was he making political works available (by publishing them), but he also made sure there was a place people could buy
them by operating a bookstore (Baudet). When the market changed in
the 1880s, he could no longer make a living publishing only such material and consequently set out to explore other options. One possibility was to publish young, relatively unknown Belgian writers, among
whom he already had some contacts, but public opinion considered
some of this new, experimental literature indistinguishable from pornography (the reason that a number of naturalists had been publishing
in Belgium in the first place). Kistemaeckers thus became the publisher

of, for example, Paul Bonnetain's controversial depiction of mastur-
bation *Charlot s'amuse* in 1883. This novel was intended as a naturalist
work of literature, but the sensitive subject matter meant that it quickly
became embroiled in controversy. (It was also one of the works that
inspired *Monsieur Vénus*, as discussed below.) Kistemaeckers proved
good at recruiting literary talent but poor at retaining it. Thus, he published the works of Camille Lemonnier but broke with him after 1885
and never quite succeeded in becoming *the* publisher of the younger
generation of Belgian writers. His efforts to publish literature, even
questionable literature such as *Charlot s'amuse*, were not enough to
sustain his business; he could not afford to neglect other sources of
income, such as pornography (the kind without literary pretensions).
Kistemaeckers began a series of *réimpressions galantes* in 1880. The reputation for publishing pornography was thus based on these "hard-
core" publications, but it also derived from the risky literary ventures
that seemed pornographic to the general public.

Of course, Kistemaeckers did not confine his efforts to the Belgian
market but was assiduous in promoting his authors in France. The development of the railway system over the course of the nineteenth century meant that foreign markets were increasingly easily accessible, and
chances were that most shipments of questionable material would escape the detection of the overworked customs officials. Kistemaeckers,
too, would travel to Paris and make deals with publishers of reviews and
journals for them to publish extracts of his novels in return for his dis-
tributing their journals in Belgium. His regular Friday dinners were frequented by some of the most prominent, if controversial, writers of the
day, including Jean Richepin, Catulle Mendès, Joris-Karl Huysmans,
Lucien Descaves, and Oscar Méténier (Baudet 54).

This brief and relative but undeniable commercial success did not
make Kistemaeckers any friends among French publishers. Between
1884 and 1889, jealous Parisian publishers used the remaining censorship laws to attack Kistemaeckers and his business, perceived as based
on an unfair advantage (the greater freedom of the press in Belgium).
The *parquet* (public prosecutor) went after bookstores that so much as
displayed Kistemaeckers's books. Not surprisingly, those books disappeared from shelves, and his business suffered. In one spectacular incident, in the spring of 1884 (the year *Monsieur Vénus* was published), the
parquet sent a strong signal by carrying out searches of the Paris bookstores, confiscating a large number of books on display (Baudet 62). The
police also interrogated customers as far away as the Persian Gulf and
Cairo in an attempt at intimidation (Kistemaeckers 676–77).

The campaign by French publishers appears to have been successful: Kistemaeckers served a brief prison sentence in 1885–86, then tried to pick up the threads of his business again, but was unable to reestablish himself completely. In once instance, all copies of a book were seized, along with a list of its subscribers, each of whom was subsequently interrogated—and all this happened even before the book had been officially declared obscene (Baudet 68ff.). Finally, Kistemaeckers left Belgium to live in exile in 1903 and died in Paris in 1934, all but completely forgotten.

In his article in the *Mercure de France*, Kistemaeckers attributed his problems to the settling of old political scores, specifically, politically motivated reprisals against the former publisher of the Communards and other French exiles, but he acknowledged that this was not the explanation usually given: "En haut lieu le prétexte qu'on invoquait pour justifier cette persécution contre la littérature était que, depuis quelque temps, une certaine partie de la presse française menait une campagne contre les 'livres belges,' et que le gouvernement belge, pour protester contre l'accusation d'encourager la pornographie, se voyait forcé d'entreprendre une répression à outrance, sans se soucier de faire une distinction entre le vrai et l'ivraie" (672). To judge from Kistemaeckers's perspective, then, it was widely acknowledged that the campaign against "Belgian books" was being orchestrated by French interests and that the Belgian authorities were overreacting in order not to appear "soft on crime."

The case of Kistemaeckers illustrates that, in the mid-1880s, a lot more was at stake in labeling a book *pornographic* than just a moral issue. A book with dubious content could be published in Belgium, ostensibly because it was too pornographic to be published in France, but it could still be bought and sold and read in France. It would be bought and sold and read, however, only if the public knew about the book, if there was, in other words, some publicity. One way to generate such public awareness was to create scandal, as in the case of *Charlot s'amuse*—just not enough scandal to result in total suppression. Thus, being banned in Belgium but not in France seems a perfect strategy. Fortunately for Rachilde, the threatened commercial interests of French publishers made them the perfect stooges.

Over the course of her life, Rachilde offered several accounts of the genesis of *Monsieur Vénus*. One of the most well-known—precisely perhaps because it conforms to what we might like to believe—is given in the autobiographical preface to *A mort*, but as I have argued elsewhere (see, for example, "1875: The Cultural Injunction to Silence"), this is not a text to be taken too literally. A very different account (one with its own set of reading problems) is embedded in the notes taken by a representative of the Paris police during a meeting with Rachilde concerning her application for permission to cross-dress (a topic taken up in greater detail in the next chapter). The police report offers a glimpse of the way in which Rachilde and her confederates, in this case a Belgian publisher, were quite well aware of the market forces shaping publishing and set out to exploit them profitably.

These two descriptions stress different elements, obviously with different audiences in mind. While the preface to *A mort* contains grains of truth, many of its elements are consciously deployed to present an image of Rachilde that would conform to fin-de-siècle expectations about women writers, and it stresses everything but hardheaded economics. It presents Rachilde as suggestible, as hysterical, as an artist rather than a businesswoman. According to this version of events (written between 1884 and 1886), Rachilde experienced "un transport au cerveau sous le spécieux prétexte que Catulle Mendès était un homme séduisant" that led to a hysterical, two-month-long paralysis of her legs (xvii). She was cured by a doctor and her mother and, after a complete but slow recovery, wrote *Monsieur Vénus* in two weeks on the basis of "un roman qu'elle avait entrevu son transport durant" (xix).

This account no doubt made the right sort of impression on purchasers and readers of *A mort*. She describes herself as living in "paroxysms of chastity," managing to make the claim to chastity sound like a form of perversion by playing on the paradox that something as pure as chastity could express itself in something as pathological as paroxysms. It is difficult to reconcile this account with the version given in the police report, however. In the police report, which shows Rachilde to be much more calculating, there is no mention of Mendès, of transports of the brain, or of hysteria, only of Rachilde's desperate need to earn a living. The police official reports Rachilde's story: "Un jour, un belge, ami d'un éditeur de Bruxelles, lui dit [à Rachilde]: 'Vous mourez de faim. Ecrivez donc des "cochonneries." Vous verrez, c'est un bon métier, on vous éditera à Bruxelles.' On chercha ensemble quelles saletés on pourrait bien trouver nouvelles, imprévues, inédites. Bref, le belge aidant, on trouva *M. Vénus* [*sic*]." The policeman then admits that he did not understand the book and asks for an explanation. He notes Rachilde's answer: "Nous étions très embarrassés pour trouver quelque chose de neuf. Maizeroy, avec les *Deux amies*, avait dépeint l'amour des femmes l'une pour l'autre—le g[omorrhe?]—Bonnetain, dans *Charlot s'amuse*, avait décrit la m[asturbation] et la sodomie. C'était donc fermé de ce côté. Nous avons pensé à une femme qui aimerait les hommes et qui avec des moyens que vous devinez, Monsieur,—l'art mécanique imite tout—les enc[ule]. Voilà *M. Vénus!*" (Auriant, *Souvenirs* 62)

Here, then, is quite a different version of composition, one that emphasizes not the plight of the hysterical woman writer acting alone and inspired only by her imagination but rather a combined effort to make a living by using the vicissitudes of the publishing industry that pitted Belgian against French publishers. It further shows that Rachilde was conscious of imitating other models that claimed naturalist affiliations in order to justify their subject matter, hence the claim "roman matérialiste."

There is a slight problem in putting too much faith in this police report: so far as I have been able to establish, Maizeroy's *Deux amies* did not appear until 1885, so it could not have been an influence on *Monsieur Vénus*, at least not in its book form. Nor could the police report have been written in 1884, presumably before such a title even existed. But, allowing for some slippage (perhaps the report dates from 1885 or later and Rachilde was confusing a recent publication by Maizeroy with an earlier work on a similar theme), the report remains valuable for the perspective that it provides on the business aspects of writing. It was not enough to write something; the writer had to compete for the public's attention.

At the end of the nineteenth century, advertising—or publicity, as it is still called in France (*la publicité*)—was becoming a widespread practice. Rachilde was not impervious to such social shifts. In addition to the titles that Rachilde mentioned as her literary models—*Les Deux amies* and *Charlot s'amuse*—one of her role models, Sarah Bernhardt—whom Ernest Raynaud credits as embodying "l'Empire à la fin de la décadence" and who exercised a strong influence on the development of symbolist expression (Raynaud 1:14–18)—had been involved in a publishing scandal just a few short months before *Monsieur Vénus* appeared. In December 1883, Marie Colombier, formerly an intimate friend and companion of the great actress, published a thinly veiled roman à clef about her friend entitled *Memoirs of Sarah Barnum*. The pseudonym—"Barnum"—could not have been better chosen to underscore the showmanship and circus-like quality of the events that would ensue. Bernhardt, her current lover, Jean Richepin (a friend of Kistemaeckers'), and her son Maurice all showed up at Colombier's apartment and caused a scene (how many of those who flocked to see "des poses plastiques" would have willingly paid to witness that "tableau"!) that ended in Bernhardt's suing Colombier for libel.

While some took these events at face value, others suspected that the whole thing had been orchestrated. Interpretations varied: (1) Bernhardt caused a scene to get publicity purely for herself; (2) Bernhardt and Colombier together staged the scene to stimulate sales of her book (the rupture in their friendship was only for show); (3) the scandal was designed to stimulate interest in Richepin's latest play, which was not doing well at the box office (Gold and Fizdale 207–9). Whatever the motive attributed to the players, the public was becoming too cynical to believe that such theatrical events took place off the stage without some planning, and perhaps Rachilde was among those who derived the message that nothing sells like scandal.

In case the message was not sufficiently evident, it is underscored by Colombier's *Memoirs* themselves, which repeatedly draw attention to Bernhardt's quest for publicity. As a young actress, Sarah received the following advice: "The principal thing in the theatrical profession is publicity. Do like they do with X's chocolate, one reads so often on the walls of Paris that it is the best of all, that we end up buying it" (40). Sarah retains her need for publicity and "was ill when the press remained a day without speaking of her" (79). When she opened her own theater—recounted in chapter XI, "In Which Advertising Reaches Its Highest Limits"—she "promised herself to force a little advertising" (125) in order to keep drawing a crowd.

As if to draw even greater attention to the need to generate publicity, the English translation of Colombier's *Memoirs*, published in the United States in March 1884, has an additional chapter entitled "The Horse-Whipping That This Book Caused," which recounts in lurid detail the series of confrontations between Colombier and Bernhardt that followed publication of the memoirs in France.

It seems only to overdetermine things further to add that Marie Colombier's lover at the time of this scandal was Paul Bonnetain, author of *Charlot s'amuse*, who wrote a preface to Marie's book, defended it in a duel (as Rachilde anticipated Talman would do for her), and was (naturally) reputed to have had a hand in writing it.

That conscious strategy was at work in the publication of *Monsieur Vénus* is further underscored by the fact that, whereas Rachilde's first novel, *Monsieur de la Nouveauté*, first appeared in serial form, the public was not given a foretaste of *Monsieur Vénus*. Once again, it is necessary to know something about fin-de-siècle publishing in order to appreciate some of the possible implications of this decision.

Determining what constituted an "outrage aux bonnes moeurs" was, it was generally agreed, a tricky business, and a series of principles evolved to help guide the representatives of law and order. A decisive criterion was that, in order to be liable to criminal charges, an obscene book had to have been publicized. In practice, this ruling had several ramifications: an appeals court in Paris decided in February 1884, for example, that the premises of a bookstore where the public had free access to books constituted a public space, not a private one, and therefore that the sale, distribution, and display of books there could be considered publicity in the eyes of the law. In addition, the price and the mode of distribution were also factors to be considered. The more cheaply and readily available a publication was, the more likely it was to fall into the "wrong" hands (minors, those easily influenced). Thus, "brochures" and "feuilletons" were more likely to be prosecuted than full-length books (Stora-Lemarre 132–37).

Rachilde may have decided to forgo the revenues of serial publication in order to protect *Monsieur Vénus* from charges of obscenity in France. Booksellers did prudently remove the novel from their displays (as reported in the preface to *A mort*—see above), thereby avoiding any accusation that they were publicizing an obscene book, but they were somewhat protected by the fact that it was a complete *book*.

Rachilde's calculation—if calculation there was—paid off. While she was prosecuted in Belgium, she managed to avoid prosecution in France. Despite the stricter publishing laws, prosecution was in fact more rare in France than in Belgium to begin with: there were only fourteen such trials in France from 1881 to 1910 (Stora-Lemarre 203). While this may at first seem contrary to expectation, it makes sense given the politics just outlined: the Belgian authorities were on the defensive, while the French authorities acted mainly to protect French commercial interests.

Thus, while Belgian police jumped on the book, the Paris police seem to have displayed little interest in prosecuting the author of *Monsieur Vénus*. To begin with, they did not understand it and were not sure exactly what was pornographic about it. Rachilde's article "Le Numéro inconnu" describes a visit from a representative of the *parquet*'s office who enlists her help in figuring out what certain passages of the book mean.[10] While Rachilde satirizes the poor reading skills of the censors, their failure to understand exactly what was pornographic about the novel in fact puts them in good company and makes them seem smarter than the usual stereotype of slow-witted and pedestrian police, all too ready to label the incomprehensible as inherently offensive. Eventually they did investigate, not on their own initiative, but because the *parquet* had received some complaints (letters of denunciation from French publishers, perhaps). The matter was duly and dutifully looked into, and no doubt a report was made out in triplicate, but the end of the story is a matter of historical record (unlike all the paperwork): no legal action was taken against *Monsieur Vénus* in France.

Many of Rachilde's contemporaries were wise to the strategy being employed and were not taken in by the preface to *A mort* and its extravagant claims. Gisèle d'Estoc provides one such contemporary reaction. *La Vierge-Réclame* attacks "Raclife," the author of *L'Homme-Vénus*, a novel in which the heroine, Roberte de Venhanda, "fait embaumer [son mari], non, l'empaille elle-même" (26). One of d'Estoc's main criticisms in this polemic, as the title of the work implies, was that Rachilde was the very personification of *la réclame*, or publicity. D'Estoc's own erotic adventures suggest that her scandalized attitude toward Rachilde's tactics cannot be ascribed to puritanism or moral outrage. Rather, what d'Estoc seems to find most intolerable is Rachilde's crass exploitation of publicity.

La Vierge-Réclame was d'Estoc's attempt to push others out of the limelight and make room there for herself, but it also illustrates the incredulity and skepticism with which other writers greeted some aspects of Rachilde's self-representation, such as those in the preface to *A mort*, one of the texts mocked by d'Estoc. D'Estoc's attack has personal motives that may have been unjustifiable, but the challenge to the innocent image that Rachilde presented to the public offers a useful lesson in skepticism. It serves as a reminder that the outcries that greeted the publication of *Monsieur Vénus* should be read, not entirely as the hypocritical reaction of a repressive society, but also as orchestrated reactions to a disguised form of industrial action. Sometimes, the real motive in getting books banned in France may have been to prevent Belgian competition.

This is not to say that there was nothing pornographic about *Monsieur Vénus*, especially when the text of the *first* first edition is restored. Accounts of exactly what happens in the novel vary, both then and now. Rachilde's own explanation cited in the police report is that Raoule sodomizes Jacques with a dildo (an interpretation also suggested by the restoration of the necrophiliac scene of the animated mannequin spreading its legs). Others read it differently, like the contemporary of Rachilde's "Dr. Luiz." The author of *Les Fellatores* (1888), a roman à clef about a homosexual subculture specializing in fellatio, he was convinced that "le piquant du volume, pour les adeptes, consiste de ce fait: d'une femme devenue par amour la fellatrix d'un pignouf!" (204).

Another contemporary was Oscar Wilde, who was in Paris on his honeymoon at around the time *Monsieur Vénus* was published.[11] It has been suggested that the novel exercised an important influence on him since, in the first draft of *The Picture of Dorian Gray*, the poisonous book given to Dorian is actually named: it is *Le Secret de Raoul* (Ellmann 316). And, if one report at least is accurate—according to André Raffalovich, Wilde was excited about the novel because in it "a lesbian dresses her lover as a man" (Ellmann 282)—Wilde thought that the novel was about lesbianism. While it may seem difficult to defend this particular reading (of all the possible permutations, the lesbian seems the least likely, and, in fact, in a conversation with Raittolbe, Raoule specifically denies that her interests are sapphic), the novel is sufficiently imprecise and vague as to allow many interpretations, including the most innocent.

More recent critics have continued to offer analyses of what makes the novel so scandalous.[12] The late twentieth-century reader who has learned to see sex and gender as social constructions has a renewed appreciation of the transgressive possibilities of *Monsieur Vénus* without needing to reduce the scandal to a particular act of sexual deviance. Indeed, the transgression may be more effective for not being named and for pervading the novel in such as way as to avoid efforts to contain, to isolate, and to quarantine it. On the loose, it can communicate, infect, pervade more effectively.

The lack of definition in *Monsieur Vénus* makes Rachilde's work available for appropriation in many transgressive contexts. Most recently, Rachilde has become a figure of transgender politics. Kate Bornstein's play about transgendering, "Hidden: A Gender," presents a character named Herculine based on Foucault's account of the nineteenth-century French hermaphrodite Herculine Barbin. In Bornstein's play, Herculine reads aloud a letter to her grandfather from his sister "Aunt Carmilla" (a transparent reference to Sheridan Le Fanu's lesbian vampire) in Paris. Aunt Carmilla explains why society sees her as a vampire, refers to the werewolves who haunt the streets of Paris at night, and continues: "Speaking of blood—my anemia is much improved. I stop round the slaughterhouse with other blood-drinkers for my daily cup of ox blood, and that seems to help. Perhaps this medicine only further shows I am a vampire? Dear brother, I am enclosing for your pleasure Rachilde's latest novel, *Mister Venus*. It's a delightful story of a woman who keeps a man as her male mistress in an apartment" (Bornstein 179). The reference to drinking ox blood evokes Rachilde's later novel *La*

Marquise de Sade (1887), and the reference to werewolves requires no further comment here, but the "delightful story" that Aunt Carmilla chooses to send Herculine (via her brother), the novel that circulates in the fictional outsider community of vampires and hermaphrodites at this transgendered fin de siècle, is not Rachilde's first novel but the first one that still counts, *Monsieur Vénus*.

Writing as Cross-Dressing

In which Rachilde applies for permission
to cross-dress and become a writer

That Rachilde cross-dressed is one of the most well-known and often-repeated facts about her life. The precise form of her cross-dressing, along with its meaning for her life and writing, however, is a much more cloudy issue. A gossip item in the first issue of *La Plume* (15 April 1889) noted that, on Wednesday, March 27, 1889, Rachilde had been spotted at the Bal des Incohérents dressed "en petit abbé" (8). In an article in *Le Décadent*, Anatole Baju described Rachilde as "l'auteur qui, on le sait, porte le jupon non sans beaucoup de grâce" (3).

At first, these two reports of Rachilde's sartorial choices seem not incompatible: a woman who dresses up for a costume ball would nevertheless be expected to respect social convention and wear skirts the rest of the time. In Rachilde's case, however, Baju's reassurance that she wears skirts gracefully is offered to a readership who no doubt knew of Rachilde's reputation for cross-dressing, while the disguise of an "abbé" is only one of the many male identities that Rachilde would assume. In pursuing the topic of her disguises, this chapter treats Rachilde as a paradigmatic example of cross-dressing at the fin de siècle in order to suggest that cross-dressing was not a single, monolithic, and univocal phenomenon but rather a more fragmented practice.

For many, it suffices to state that Rachilde cross-dressed. Without pressing the issue further, this simple fact serves to place her in a constellation of figures and categories that are superficially self-explanatory even as they resist deeper analysis. Rachilde joins company with (in no particular order) George Sand, the woman writer par excellence; Mademoiselle de Maupin, the cross-dressing heroine of Gautier's novel; la chevalière d'Eon, a sexually ambiguous eighteenth-century aristocrat and diplomat; Madame Dieulafoy, Rachilde's contemporary and also a novelist, who cross-dressed in order to accompany her archaeologist husband and hence was often invoked as the archetypal bluestocking; the animal painter Rosa Bonheur; and Rachilde's contemporary Colette.[1] Although these figures each represented something slightly different, they all signaled a social challenge through sartorial style. As Marjorie Garber has suggested, cross-dressing is always "a category crisis" looking for a place to happen (16). But in Rachilde's case, as in others, the degree of sartorial nonconformity has been exaggerated in order to represent the degree of perceived nonconformity, and nuances of meaning have been lost in the process.

There is no doubt that cross-dressing conveyed transgressive connotations for both men and women. Codes regulating dress had originated in Europe as sumptuary laws intended to patrol class borders (Garber 21–32; P. Perrot 15–16). In order to preserve visible class differences, the wearing of certain items (such as ermine) was declared the privilege of those who enjoyed a certain status. No matter how much wealth an individual accumulated, and no matter what he or she could afford to buy, wear, or display to advertise that wealth (and here I stress the connection between clothing and advertisement), the old distinctions of rank based on blood line and family were maintained through the regulation of outward appearance. Although such beliefs in class difference were challenged, most notably in France through the Revolution, the class distinction was preserved in vestigial form through the gender system.

In a structure in which maleness confers privilege (suffrage, the right to own and inherit property, the right to enter into legal contracts, in short, full legal personhood), presenting oneself as a man signified a claim to certain rights, just as wearing certain fabrics had done. For a woman to appear as a man was to make claims above her station. Although there is much that goes into self-presentation (including, not only clothing and other fashions such as hairstyles, but also body language and other nonverbal cues), the claim to the privileges of manhood has come down to a metonymy, the wearing of pants. The regulation of dress has often boiled down to proscriptions against women wearing trousers, as in the case of the French decree against cross-dressing of 16 Brumaire IX (November 7, 1800), promulgated (as no one will be surprised to learn) by the misogynistic Napoleon.

This act formed the core of legislation regulating the behavior of women (and men) who contemplated cross-dressing in France in the nineteenth century.[2] Humanely, the law anticipated certain exemptions. Those with a valid medical reason could apply for official permission to cross-dress, a "permis de travestissement." The candidate would apply to the police, presenting a certificate signed by a doctor verifying the medical condition, and, if the application was approved, the applicant received a permit valid for six months, presumably renewable thereafter if the condition persisted.[3] There were those who flouted this law, relying (like George Sand) on their notoriety to shield them from prosecution, as well as those who applied for and received legal permission, such as the animal painter Rosa Bonheur, although even she insisted on wearing "small feminine shoes" with her male attire (Witzling 23). Permission was granted to men as well as women, from very different classes. The law was suspended during periods of carnival, in recognition of the general inversion of the rules that characterized such social safety valves, but otherwise cross-dressing in public spaces and at balls had specifically been forbidden by article 471, section 15, of the Penal Code of 1853 (a stipulation subsequently upheld in 1927 and 1949; see Rosario 193 n. 17; Bard, "Le Dossier").

This, then, was the situation that Rachilde faced at the fin de siècle. Her choice to cross-dress was not without precedent. Indeed, it was the precedents that gave it meaning. Both Rachilde's early biographers (Gaubert and David) mention Rachilde's cross-dressing and tease out of it a number of colorful associations. Gaubert (chronologically the first) frames his discussion with the astute observation that "de Mme Rachilde on retint davantage la légende que les livres," but he proceeds to stimulate the legend with his description of the cross-dressed Rachilde: "Elle était représentée comme une sportwoman [sic] éméritée, une sorte de Mlle de Maupin tirant le poignard espagnol et le pistolet, affiliée de société secrète. Son portrait figurait en tête des journaux sportifs"(Gaubert 14). The reference to Mademoiselle de Maupin clearly evokes the gender ambiguity of the legend, but the references to sport and to wielding swords and pistols may be less transparent to today's readers.

Such references recur in David's description, too: "M. Camescasse, qui était alors préfet de police, donne le signalement de Rachilde en homme, ainsi que celui de madame Dieulafoy, ce qui équivalait, pour l'une et pour l'autre, à l'autorisation de porter le costume masculin, costume sous lequel Rachilde, femme de sport, tirant admirablement l'épée et le pistolet, se trouvait très à son aise et dans un état conforme à son caractère." David makes the parallel with Dieulafoy rather than Maupin, but he also points out Rachilde's sporting accomplishments. He makes it specific, however, that the masculine costume was merely an exteriorization of Rachilde's inner character, a character described as "femme de sport, tirant admirablement." To make the connection even clearer, he goes on: "Enfin, prenant ce travesti au sérieux, elle fait imprimer sur ses cartes de visite: Rachilde, *homme de lettres*" (David, *Rachilde* 20). The appositional syntax of "Rachilde, homme de lettres" echoes the earlier phrase "Rachilde, femme de sport," suggesting a parallel or a near equivalence between the two. For David, then, Rachilde's sporting activities (as a woman) were merely the exterior sign of her inner literariness (which was masculine).

Turn-of-the-century France had witnessed a flowering of interest in athletics, thanks in part to fitness enthusiast Pierre de Coubertin, who revived the Olympic Games as part of his efforts to revirilize the French after their humiliating defeat in the Franco-Prussian War.[4] This new passion for sport (in the modern sense) was mostly a masculine pursuit, however. Such unwomanly interest in physical recreation was a hallmark of the New Woman, both literary and real. The nineteenth century saw the emergence of cycling as a sport, and nontraditional women jumped on such two-wheeled bandwagons (as well as on horseback) as part of their challenge to gender roles.[5] Rachilde portrayed such characters in her fiction, for example, the cycling enthusiast Missy in *La Jongleuse*. It was partly women's participation in sports that led to a relaxation in the laws regulating cross-dressing. Amelia Bloomer's advocacy of appropriate apparel for lady cyclists in the United States was matched by a 1909 law in France, specifying that "la femme tenant à la main une bicyclette ou un cheval [est] officiellement autorisée à sortir en culotte" (Deslandres 244).[6]

Rachilde's cross-dressing thus occurred in a period when the regulation of sartorial manifestations of gender was shifting from state policing to self-policing, from formal to informal regulation. The women of Rachilde's generation were increasingly likely to reject the role of the state in deciding how they would dress. Rachilde, however, chose to go through official channels to sanction her transgression; she applied to the police.

David's account clearly states that Camescasse, the *préfet*, granted Rachilde's request, yet once again a confusing story emerges from a comparison of different sources. Auriant quotes a letter in which Rachilde applied for permission to cross-dress and also provides extensive information about the response. The letter of application is quite long but worth quoting in its entirety:

> Mlle Eymerie [sic]
> dite Rachilde
> Paris, le 12 décembre, 1884
>
> Monsieur le Préfet,
>
> J'ai l'honneur de vous demander l'autorisation de porter le costume d'homme.
>
> Je suis, malheureusement, une femme de lettres et me trouve, cependent, appelée à faire le métier actif de reporter. Cela pour gagner mon pain quotidien, que mes romans ne parviennent pas encore à me fournir.
>
> Dans le journalisme, l'originalité est imposée comme un devoir. Ne me refusez pas le moyen d'être originale puisque

mes directeurs littéraires ne reculent pas, eux, devant ce moyen de réclame.

Veuillez lire l'attestation suivante, je vous en supplie; et ne confondez pas ma demande avec celles de certaines femmes déclassées qui cherchent le scandale sous le costume en question.

Je désire, moi, m'habiller en homme pour dissimuler tous les avantages que je puis avoir, pour qu'il soit bien entendu que je suis un écrivain *quelconque et pour qu'on s'adresse à ma plume et non à ma personne.*

Comme vous ne me connaissez pas, Monsieur le Préfet, permettez-moi de vous dire en deux mots qui je suis.

Je m'appelle Marguerite Eymery dans la vie privée, Rachilde dans la vie des lettres. J'étais émancipée par ma famille à seize ans, j'en ai vingt-quatre aujourd'hui. Je suis dans la publicité littéraire depuis sept ans et j'ai publié dix romans feuilletons. Ma dernière oeuvre, la plus mercenaire, est Monsieur Vénus, *mais c'est à elle que je dois ma célébrité du moment.*

J'ose espérer, Monsieur le Préfet, que vous ne repousserez pas mon humble demande et que vous me permettrez de prendre, pour voyager dans Paris et en province, les vêtements les plus disgrâcieux qui soient au monde.

Recevez, Monsieur le Préfet, mon plus respectueux salut

Rachilde
sociétaire des Gens de Lettres,
ancien rédacteur à l'Estafette,
reporter à l'Opinion
et collaborateur de la Chronique parisienne

> *Mlle Eymery, Marguerite dite Rachilde, se disant âgée de 24 ans et née à Thiviers (Dordogne), femme de lettres, demeurant à Paris, rue des Ecoles, 5.* (Auriant, *Souvenirs* 61)

This letter is both a fount of information and a confoundment of puzzles. To begin with, according to Auriant, the letter is addressed to a Monsieur Puybaraud, not a Monsieur Camescasse (as David had claimed). At first, then, this account appears to contradict the assertion that Rachilde applied to the prefect of police to obtain permission to cross-dress since Antoine Félix Louis Puybaraud (1849–1903) was, not the *préfet de police,* but rather the *chef de cabinet du préfet* (from 1881 to 1887). This office was frequently confused by the layperson with that of the *préfet*, however, and it is possible that Rachilde made a genuine mistake, a common one that adds a note of verisimilitude to the story.[7]

Perhaps Rachilde was also influenced by the fact that Puybaraud was a fellow Périgourdin (he was born in Lezat, in Ariège). She may have calculated that she would receive more favorable treatment by addressing herself to him, and a little flattery through rank inflation might not have hurt either. That Rachilde was anxious to appeal to fellow feeling may be inferred from the fact that she includes such biographical information as her place of birth, but Thiviers? As already noted, her birth certificate records her birth as having taken place at Château-l'Evêque. This aberration occurs in a document notable for its accuracy in other matters. For example, Rachilde here accurately reports her age (not once but twice she gives it as twenty-four); she is disarmingly honest about her desire to cross-dress in order to stand out from the literary crowd and thereby to achieve publicity (she is in "publicité littéraire") and "réclame"; and she is frank about the "mercenary" nature of *Monsieur Vénus*.

So why Thiviers? One possible explanation is simple confusion. Or perhaps it was because her mother was by this time living in Thiviers with her parents, having separated from Joseph Eymery (see "1870: The Ambivalence of the Paternal"). The most likely explanation, however, is that Rachilde was appealing to family connections to help her case. Puybaraud states that, in a follow-up interview, Rachilde was able to mention that she knew people from Thiviers who were "en relations" with Puybaraud's family (Auriant, *Souvenirs* 61). The current deputy, M. Teulier, was also from Thiviers and came up in their conversation. Alas, Auriant gives no source for the letter. As with other books of memoirs, it draws heavily on information supplied by Rachilde in letters and conversations, but there is no further documentation. In quoting from Puybaraud's notes, however, it would seem that Auriant had access to official files (or that Rachilde had somehow obtained a copy).

Before leaving this letter behind, however, let us also note in passing its attractively neat formulation of Rachilde's own understanding of her *dédoublement* (see "1876: Woman as Medium"): "Je m'appelle Marguerite Eymery dans la vie privée, Rachilde dans la vie des lettres." That the private realm was to be increasingly invaded by the literary is something Rachilde was not yet aware of, however.

When Rachilde did not receive a reply to her letter of December 12, Auriant recounts that she followed up in person: "Puybaraud la reçut courtoisement, bien qu'il fût prévenu contre elle pour avoir lu *Monsieur Vénus* et lui expliqua spirituellement les raisons pour lesquelles sa demande serait refusée." After a long conversation, Rachilde left, and Puybaraud proceeded to write a note, dated December 17, 1884, which Auriant reproduces (again without explaining how he came by this document). In it, Puybaraud records his explanation of the refusal: the law provided only for "des raisons de santé, afin de faciliter un traitement ou de dissimuler une infirmité, et non pour aider au reportage" (61). He also notes recollections of what Rachilde told him about her family as well as *Monsieur Vénus* (some of which I have already discussed earlier in connection with the origins of that novel; see "1884: The Politics of Publishing").

It would appear, then, from Puybaraud's notes that Rachilde was *not* granted permission to cross-dress. But perhaps she reapplied, perhaps she dealt directly with Camescasse,[8] perhaps she appealed to the deputy Monsieur Teulier to intervene, perhaps . . . Whatever the means, she received police authorization (the "signalement" from Camescasse referred to by David), which she would produce when she was arrested and marched down to the police station, or so she later claimed to the poet Guillaume Apollinaire: "J'allais parfois au poste pour port d'habit masculin. Au commissariat j'exhibais l'autorisation du préfet de police" (Apollinaire, *Journal intime* 148).

If any official trace remains of Rachilde's dealings with the authorities on this matter, the police archives—located in the same building as the Commissariat de Police in the fifth arrondissement of Paris—would seem the obvious place to begin looking for it, especially in light of the description of the dossier on "le travestissement" by the French feminist sociologist Eveline Sullerot, who claims that "l'on y rencontre quelques excentriques, comme le peintre Rosa Bonheur ou Mme Dieulafoy, la femme de l'explorateur des antiquités assyriennes, les femmes à barbe, et quelques ouvrières désireuses d'être payées au même tarif que les hommes dont elles porteraient le costume, c'est-à-dire, pour le même travail, une somme double du salaire féminin" (Deslandres 244).[9] While, however, the "dossier de travestissement" is a fascinating document, it contains no mention of Rachilde. Indeed, it contains few records, official or otherwise, pertaining to any of the celebrated crossdressers of the century, although it does provide interesting background on the social views of cross-dressing, including newspaper clippings reporting police raids on transvestite hangouts as late as the 1960s (see Bard, "Le Dossier").

One document in the file, dated Paris, December 19, 1882, notes that the *préfet de police* (Camescasse) was about to reissue the law of 16 Brumaire IX, along with other pertinent subsequent legislation. Evidently, the inhabitants of Paris needed to be reminded periodically that there was a law against cross-dressing, and this was duly done. A copy of *Le Moniteur des syndicats* from April 27–May 6, 1886, also preserved in the dossier, states: "Le préfet de police vient de rappeler dans une circulaire qu'il est de vieilles ordonnances interdisant formellement aux femmes de s'habiller en homme, sans une autorisation spéciale, hors le temps du carnaval. Il paraît que depuis quelque temps il était de bon ton, dans un certain monde, que les femmes s'habillassent en homme." A notice in *La Lanterne* (November 9, 1890) claims that there were then ten women in the whole country who had official permission to cross-dress (including a "directrice d'imprimerie"), but, to judge from the prefect's need to keep reminding the populace of the rules, a great many more than ten women were passing themselves off as men, or rather they were not passing since evidently they were coming to the attention of the authorities.

In this sense, while Rachilde was clearly part of a minority, her cross-dressing was not such an unheard-of thing and needs to be situated in the larger context of challenges to dress codes and their sumptuary associations that were taking place. Rachilde was one of a small number of women who challenged the laws, but she was not as eccentric as she might at first appear. She also claimed that she cross-dressed only under pressure from her employer: "Mon directeur m'avait dit: '200 fr. par mois et en homme ou la porte'" (Apollinaire, *Journal intime* 148). Cross-dressing was thus perhaps not even her own idea but one suggested by the business sense of a wily publisher who sought to manipulate the public's perception of cross-dressing women.

If her eccentricity has been exaggerated in this regard, so has the degree and extent of her cross-dressing. Rachilde applied for permission to cross-dress in 1884. According to her own testimony, she had cross-dressed on occasion in the past (when, for example, she would appear as her "brother" to the editor of the Périgueux newspaper; see "1876: Woman as Medium") but not in any systematic way. The official application to cross-dress marks a new departure, a desire to cross-dress on a daily basis in order to pursue her career in journalism. It was not, however, a particularly long-lived desire. Rachilde states that it ended when she married in 1889. Yet David also reports that "son habit de soirée, dont elle faisait changer, selon la mode, les revers de satin, dura dix ans" (*Rachilde* 20). Rachilde also claimed that she cross-dressed for ten years, though elsewhere she claimed that it was only six years (Apollinaire, *Journal intime* 148).[10] Some simple math suggests the following: if she stopped cross-dressing in 1889, and if she had a suit that lasted more than ten years, she began cross-dressing long before she applied for police permission. The application for official permission to cross-dress, then, already signals a modification of her practice since it marks a moment of transition from cross-dressing in opposition to the authorities to an officially sanctioned form of self-advertisement.

For all the critical attention now paid the subject, *cross-dressing* remains an imprecise term. It can refer to aspects of transsexual or transgender practice, cross-dressing with such a degree of accuracy and thoroughness that one passes for the other sex. Or it can mean gender bending, a more playful confounding of categories highlighting the discontinuities between the body beneath the clothes and the surface appearance. One kind of performance aims to avoid attention, the other to attract it. In between lies a spectrum of possibilities. How to characterize Rachilde's performance on this spectrum?

Rachilde stresses somewhat different aspects of her cross-dressing in her own accounts. Like Sand, she claims, she cross-dressed as a man for economic reasons—because it was cheaper. One man's suit could last for ten years, while the rapid shifts in women's fashion entailed continual expense. In addition, there were practical considerations: it meant that she could move around in public anonymously. She could drop in on her publisher without attracting attention. The transgressive form of dress also serves to show that she claims male privilege, in particular the privilege of being an "homme de lettres," as her visiting cards proclaimed.

Yet the intense focus on Rachilde's cross-dressing as a man obscures all the other forms of transvestism and role-playing she engaged in through costume, forms of dressing up that complicate the image of Rachilde as a writer who consistently presented herself to the public as a man.

In some cases, the dressing up was explicitly part of an act. In *Quand j'étais jeune*, for example, Rachilde describes going in 1885 to the "bal des Quat-z-Arts," an annual ball held by students, artists, and models at the Ecole des Beaux Arts.[11] A week before the ball, Jean Lorrain, evidently her "date" for this occasion, called to discuss what they would wear. For Rachilde, the question of an outfit posed a problem: "Moi, je n'ai pas trente-six costumes. Je n'en possède qu'un: mon habit" (24). This was awkward for Lorrain: although his sexual preference for men was hardly a secret, appearing at a public ball with "un petit garçon qui a trop l'air . . . de ce qu'il n'est même pas" was too compromising. Then Rachilde remembered an old dress that she could use: "Je me rappelle, à propos, que j'ai, dans un vieux carton, une certaine tunique de mousseline blanche à pois brodés, un rêve très 1830 qui me vient d'une arrière-grand-mère parfaitement oubliée. En la raccourcissant, la tunique, en mettant des chaussettes, des souliers baby et une grosse ceinture de satin bleu [all of which apparently posed no problem to acquire], le tout surmonté de mes cheveux courts, frisés pour la circonstance . . . " (25).

Rather than cross-dressing as a man, then, here Rachilde proposes to cross-dress as a stereotype of femininity. This outfit, which today might be described as the Shirley Temple look, was the perfect foil to Lorrain's ultramasculine lion-tamer's costume: "un maillot d'un rose violent et un cache-sexe en peau de panthère" (25), the latter item borrowed from a wrestler from Marseille. The body-stocking ("maillot") might be pink, but the color here connotes a manly "violence," while the purpose of the skimpy "cache-sexe" was, despite the name, not to hide the sex of the wearer but to draw attention to it. Thus, both partners agreed to perform their respective genders, suggesting through parody and exaggeration the degree to which such displays of gender are always an act (and hence the rumor that was started to the effect that Rachilde was going to the ball as a wrestler while Lorrain would be wearing a short dress [*QJJ* 26]).

On the night of the ball, Rachilde's concierge, Madame Pierre, ran upstairs to announce that Jean Lorrain was waiting below, "presque tout nu," but that he had been arrested and was accompanied by two policemen who wanted to question Rachilde. When Rachilde went to see for herself, Lorrain was indeed seated in a cab, "son maillot, couleur de vraie chair . . . scandaleusement collant," handcuffed between two policemen. The police, however, also succeed in drawing attention to their performativity: they are "trop déguisé (ou pas assez)" (*QJJ* 27). They are simultaneously too authentic and not authentic enough, both exaggerated and understated. Beneath the disguise (or above it?), Rachilde recognized Oscar Méténier and Alexandre Tanchard. The irony was that Méténier was a *real* policeman, "un véritable secrétaire de commissaire de police" (he had borrowed the handcuffs), but on this occasion he succeeded in impersonating his own self, that is, in appearing only to be dressing up as a policeman.

In their respective costumes, the quartet made "une entrée sensationnelle au bal" (*QJJ* 28). Rachilde and Lorrain made a parody of gender, but their grand entrance also staged a gender performance censured by the police. Rachilde replayed her arrests for dressing as a man and here, in a carnivalesque moment of inversion, presented herself as having been arrested by the police for dressing up as a girl. The irony of the reversal is only heightened by the knowledge that, while one of the "policemen" doing the arresting is only a make-believe agent of the state, the other is a policeman performing a policeman. While discussions of felicitous versus infelicitous speech acts (Austin's term) tend to focus on circumstances in which the speaker lacks the authority to make an utterance (such as "I arrest you") a proper speech act, Méténier's act creates a context in which an otherwise successful speech act must be understood to fail even though it is uttered by a person who in other circumstances has the authority to make it felicitous. Similarly, Rachilde's act "as a girl," which ought to be successful (she *is* "a girl"), draws attention to its failure as a performance.

Something of the same dynamic of an unexpected reversal is at work in another act of self-presentation from around the same time, recorded by Rachilde's future husband, Alfred Vallette, during their courtship. The event was another costume ball, this one given by Léonide Leblanc (an actress whom Rachilde had loudly—and violently—supported in her bid to join the Comédie-Française) in late 1886 or early 1887. In a letter written "lundi, en rentrant chez moi, 5h. du matin," that is, on returning home after the ball, Vallette describes how, on setting out the previous evening, he had imagined that the "paquet de soie blanche" he had helped into the carriage next to him would turn out to be a form of cross-dressing. He had been thinking: "Elle a dû se costumer en page Henri III et le petit bout de plume que je vois dépassant son capuchon, c'est celui du toquet de velours qui est posé sur l'oreille de ce singulier jeune homme. Probablement porte-t-il une dague ou une mignonne épée d'escrime au flanc gauche"(*RHS* 59).

The use of a page or "mignon" (though note the displacement of the adjective *mignon* to the sword) from the reign of Henri III as code for sexual ambiguity was well established. Oscar Wilde, for example, had his picture taken in such a costume, and Rachilde's own heroine Raoule de Vénérande (in *Monsieur Vénus*) appeared in such a costume in a dream.[12] Vallette had thus assumed that Rachilde would merely substitute one form of cross-dressing for another (both her everyday suit and the page costume remaining masculine) but that she would play on the gender ambiguity of the page by dressing as a feminized boy.[13] On arriving at the ball, Vallette was shocked to discover that, when Rachilde removed her cloak, she was instead a ravishing "marquise Louis XV": "Rien n'y manquait, ni le rouge sur les joues, ni les mouches noires, surtout la vraie, du coin de l'oeil droit, et, quant à la perruque poudrée, si bien collante sur les cheveux courts que je vous ai toujours vus, elle semblait faire absolument partie de votre tête" (*RHS* 60). Vallette was evidently enchanted by this unexpected costume, as is clear from the rest of his letter and subsequent ones that begin "Ma chère Marquise" or "Ma petite Marquise" (one of which, a telegram dated January 21, 1887, suggests the approximate date of the ball).

   This would not be the last time that Rachilde would cross-(class-) dress as a marquise, although many of her other performances would be literary, perhaps the most notable being *Madame de Lydone, assassin* (1928). This novel, about a strong aristocratic woman, a throwback to the ancien régime, suggests one of the reasons why the figure of the marquise was so resonant for Rachilde in particular. The eighteenth-century revival was well under way in general: the Goncourt brothers had published their *La Femme au XVIIIe siècle* in 1862, for example, underscoring a vogue for prerevolutionary elegance, in contrast to bourgeois lack of refinement, and suggesting that the eighteenth century had been a time of empowerment for women thanks to the influence they exercised as *salonnières*. The marquise was important in Rachilde's own personal mythology, however, because of the family connection to her reputed paternal grandfather, the marquis d'Ormoy. In *Les Rageac*, "Magui" is shown a portrait of her paternal great-grandmother and told, "C'en était une vraie [marquise], à ce qu'il paraît. On lui a coupé le cou à la Révolution" (243). Jeanne Eymery, her paternal grandmother, had worked for Madame de Lidonne (as discussed above); thus the novel *Madame de Lydone* effects a link between Rachilde's aristocratic ancestor, the marquise, and the Lidonne family. Through the illegitimate branch of the family, Rachilde repeatedly asserted, she was descended from a marquise. She was entitled to the costume.[14]

   Rachilde's performance as a marquise thus alludes to this family history, as Rachilde dresses up as one of her (reputed) ancestors and effects a form of cross-class-dressing that challenges sumptuary regulation. But this particular disguise also presented Rachilde as her own heroine, the product of her own labor. She became the heroine of one of her novels, *La Marquise de Sade*. This novel was published in 1887, but Verlaine admired it as early as 1886 (see the letter of November 12, 1886, van Bever, ed., *Correspondance* 279), and even though neither place nor date is given, the plans and notes for the novel can be dated to 1884.

   While Rachilde was dressing up—as one of her ancestors, as one of her heroines—and as she was effecting a form of cross-dressing that crossed class rather than gender lines, she was also enacting, visibly and through the proliferation of her different costumes (as man, as girl, as marquise), the situation of the woman writer. As Guez de Balzac had written in 1638, women writers "use their minds to cross-dress" (quoted in DeJean 48).

For Vallette, the delight in Rachilde's costume was offset by a certain violence of effect. Mixing his metaphors somewhat, he describes Rachilde emerging from her cloak like a butterfly emerging from a cocoon, but a butterfly that proceeds to slap him in the face: "J'ai reçu votre beauté en pleine figure . . . comme une gifle!" He goes on to state that the image continues to "suffocate" him. Even worse, however, is the total destabilization effected by the surprise costume: "Il y a pire: je me demande, maintenant, *quand* vous êtes travestie?" (*RHS* 60). His question, which forms a complete and separate paragraph of its own and goes unanswered (in part because there is no answer), deconstructs the traditional view of Rachilde's *travestissement*. Rather than being a single, consistent, and recognizable gesture of crossing a clearly demarcated gender boundary, Rachilde's performative transvestism destabilizes that very boundary. By confronting us with the question of how to tell when she is *not* cross-dressing, Vallette's rhetorical comment invites us to acknowledge that there is no unmarked costume, only different forms of dressing up.

Marriage and the Woman Writer

In which Rachilde meets Alfred Vallette and marries him,
despite some second thoughts

Rachilde was once again "en travesti," acting the part of George Sand, when she met her future husband, Alfred Vallette, on a Thursday evening in March 1885. Although their marriage was to be a long and stable one, no one would have predicted this from their first encounter at the Bal Bullier, a popular dance held at the Closerie des Lilas and painted by impressionists such as Renoir. Writing for visitors to the 1889 exhibition, Rodolphe Darzens nostalgically bewailed the way in which in the 1880s the Bal Bullier ceased to be a rendezvous for students: "Les vrais étudiants du bon vieux temps n'existent plus. L'étudiante pas davantage. La femelle actuelle de ces messieurs n'est qu'une poupée articulée et commerçante, sortant des fabriques les plus en progrès de la capitale" (Darzens 210). What he mostly seems to regret is how women changed from naive Mimi Pinson types to "articulated dolls" who look at men with haughtiness ("morgue").

It was precisely on this cusp between bohemian innocence and world-weary scorn that Rachilde was poised when she first met Alfred Vallette. She was still flirting with bohemia, searching for a literary identity, and flouting conventions. Vallette was a "serious man," better equipped to serve literature as an editor and a publisher (as indeed he later became) than as an author (a profession he aspired to in the 1880s). This mismatch came to work almost in spite of Rachilde's orientation as a writer. Juggling the paradoxes necessary to succeed in the literary marketplace required constant effort and ingenuity, and, tired of being the outcast, Rachilde began to search for a place in the established literary family.

Having thrown herself into a muddy pond as an adolescent, Rachilde had thrown herself into a different kind of mire as an adult, that of bohemia, motivated this time by a similar combination of curiosity and an impulse toward self-destruction. Such a lifestyle was dangerous—more so for women than for men. Moreover, most women figured only marginally in bohemia. Few were able to move beyond the role of Mimi, the moribund and self-sacrificing innocent of Mürger's classic novel *Scènes de la vie de bohème*. There was certainly no widely

LES GLOIRES MALSAINES

LA VIERGE
RÉCLAME

VISIBLE POUR LE
HERMAPHRODITES
SEULEMENT

PAR

G. D'ESTOC

Illustrations

PAR

FERNAND FAU

PARIS, A LA LIBRAIRIE RICHELIEU
104, Rue Richelieu, 104

The cover of Gisèle d'Estoc's *La Vierge-Réclame*. Bibliothèque Nationale, Paris.

accepted female analogue to the bohemian man of letters, the position Rachilde aspired to occupy, yet she could learn from male acquaintances such as Willy, a member of the Chat Noir circle and the future husband of Colette, who used publicity so skillfully that he was nicknamed "Monsieur Réclamier" (Castillo 128). Through a manipulation of the conventions, Rachilde learned to market herself by exploiting paradox. In the preface to *A mort*, she described her infatuation with Catulle Mendès prior to writing *Monsieur Vénus* as the problem of "l'hystérie arrivée au paroxysme de la chasteté dans un milieu vicieux" (*AM* xvii). Chastity would be Rachilde's alibi while she lingered in the bohemian dens of vice, but marriage would have upset this delicate balance.

Rachilde's personal appropriation of the bohemian role involved combining social marginality with impeccable personal standards. For example, she would surprise her fellow artists at dinner by putting on white gloves to eat dessert (Colin 17). And she also claimed that she did not drink alcohol, only "pure water," a habit that was much noted at the time and to which she drew attention at every opportunity.

Such self-professed abstention did not, however, prevent her from endorsing Vin Mariani, a "tonic" wine at one time laced with cocaine created by "Angel" François Mariani in his Laboratoires du Vin Mariani—she even served it at her Tuesdays (Auriant, *Souvenirs* 9).[1] As a publicity gimmick, the Mariani company published albums of portraits of those who endorsed their product. Fourteen such *Albums de figures contemporaines* appeared between 1894 and 1925, and Rachilde was featured in the fourth volume, in 1899. Beneath an engraved copy of a portrait by van Bever, she offered a poem reproduced in her own handwriting, entitled "L'Art des vers libres."[2] Although she does not claim to drink Vin Mariani herself in this poem, her endorsement of the product is in interesting contrast to her professed abstinence and creates precisely the kind of paradox that she excelled in exploiting. (Her inclusion in the albums also offers some indication of the extent of her public notoriety at the turn of the century.)

Rachilde also made a point of not dancing. Perhaps in part this was because she was afflicted with a slight limp, the product of having been born with one leg slightly longer than the other. This deformity had affected her mother's view of her as a child, or so Rachilde believed (see "1870: The Ambivalence of the Paternal"), but she had worked hard to overcome it, and as a result it was barely noticeable. At certain moments in her life, her difficulty walking would reassert itself, but for the most part she disguised it well. By *not* dancing, however, Rachilde drew attention to it once again. At first this appears to be a curious choice: she *could* dance, despite infirmity, but did not. The choice makes sense, however, when it is understood that preserving the trace of her limp was also preserving a bodily inscription of the connection to her literary ancestors. Brantôme had pointed out that one of the most famous of French queens—the doubly royal Anne de Bretagne—had "un pied plus court que l'autre," but he went on to suggest that a limp might be read as a sign of sexual passion in women: "Encor dit-on que l'habitation de telles femmes en est fort delicieuse, pour quelque certain mouvement et agitation qui ne se rencontre pas aux autres" (10). Thus, not dancing draws attention to the limp, the sign of otherwise private and hidden attributes, and becomes another paroxysm of chastity.

Rachilde "advertised" the fact that she did not drink or dance. In French, one might say *elle s'affichait,* making her seem a veritable "poster girl" for certain virtues. Yet the virtue is always attenuated by a trace of its opposite (a whiff of cocaine, a hint of sexual passion) that makes the virtue seem perverse. Marriage would have made such ambiguity more difficult to maintain, however, and thus it is partly to preserve her bohemian role, I argue, that Rachilde rejected marriage in the 1880s.

The self-imposed distance from the mores of her fellow bohemians did not, however, prevent Rachilde from serving alcohol and attending dances, and she was an habituée of the Bal Bullier in particular. It was here that Rachilde met Alfred Vallette on that Thursday evening in March 1885. Vallette was in the company of Albert Samain, who, recognizing the famous young author of *Monsieur Vénus* in her man's suit, volunteered to introduce him to her. Rachilde later gave a more detailed version of events to Apollinaire: "La première fois que mon mari m'a vue, j'étais à Bullier ayant au bras une superbe putain. Samain me présente à Vallette qui se détourne en disant: 'Oh non! pas ça!' Je le trouvais godiche" (Apollinaire, *Journal intime* 148).

Clearly, neither party was attracted to the other at that first meeting, as Vallette indicated in a letter of explanation he sent to "Mademoiselle Rachilde" on March 27, 1885:

> *Je ne recule jamais devant une franche explication, devrait-elle me coûter les pires désagréments.*
>
> *Mon ami, Albert Samain, toujours un peu dans les nuages, s'est sans doute mal exprimé. Je n'ai pas refusé de vous être présenté, mais bien:* le contraire.
>
> *Si je ne suis certes pas un mondain, je connais, cependant, le protocole de la bienséance qui ne permet pas de présenter une femme à un homme et malgré la perfection de votre travesti vous en êtes une, Mademoiselle Rachilde.* (RHS 7)

Rachilde immediately characterized Vallette as "un homme sérieux" (9), a label that he willingly accepted in order to distinguish himself from the band of lighthearted and frivolous merrymakers prancing around Rachilde.

In another, later letter he rejected a bohemian identity, describing himself as solidly bourgeois, and offered his own life history:

> *Je suis un parisien de Paris, du vieux centre, je suis né rue Bleue [in the ninth arrondissement]. Ma mère, seule famille qui me reste, est une paysanne venue de Saint-Loup [near Parthenay in the Deux-Sèvres region] pour épouser un parisien, ouvrier typographique qui est mort sans avoir pu réaliser son rêve, bien modeste, de monter une maison ou d'avoir à lui seule un atelier de typographie avec ses pierres, ses ouvriers à demeure. . . . Alors, voilà, moi j'ai réalisé la chose. Je suis le directeur, le correcteur en chef de cet atelier et rien n'est plus fastidieux que la révision, ou la fonction de* collationer *les manuscrits qu'on nous donne à typographier et je fais cela tous les jours avec ma maman, une personne très précise, très volontaire, pleine de bon sens mais d'un caractère, si j'ose dire, encore plus . . . sérieux que le mien.*
>
> *Pour ce métier je demeure, avec elle, rue* Guisarde *[in the sixth arrondissement] et pour mon métier à moi tout seul, je demeure rue* Du Four *[one block away from the rue Guisarde] où j'ai ce que vos amis appellent* une garçonnière, *petit coin haut perché où je domine des toitures, des cheminées et aussi une étendue de ciel presque toujours gris.* (RHS 10 –11)[3]

This was the serious twenty-seven-year-old whom Rachilde met briefly in 1885. It was not the *coup de foudre*, or love at first sight, for either party—far from it. Vallette was leery of women of letters and did not consider himself qualified to pass judgment on literary matters—or so he stated (see RHS 14). Vallette claimed that he believed, not in love at first sight, but instead in what he called "crystallization," or "la magie de l'idée fixe, d'un amour sans aucun désir ordinaire qui vous berce d'un songe sans limite et aussi d'une volupté des plus rares puisqu'on ne se l'explique pas" (RHS 128). The image of crystallization would prove to be an excellent metaphor for the way in which their relationship developed.

Rachilde was not interested in serious young men at first, and, at around the time that she met Vallette (the mid-1880s), there seem to have been at least three people in her life competing for her attention. One was the young Maurice Barrès (1862–1923), destined to become known as a figure of reactionary politics.[4] Barrès had moved to Paris from Nancy on January 12, 1883 (Davanture 1:260), and Rachilde met him around 1884 through the publisher René Brissy, who published both Rachilde's *Histoires bêtes pour amuser les petits enfants d'esprit* (1884) and Barrès's short-lived review *Taches d'encre*.[5] According to her account (in *Portraits d'hommes* 21– 42), Rachilde ran into Barrès as she was doing her "service de presse" and he was waiting for the publisher to arrive. Vallette inquired about him in one of his letters to Rachilde: "Qu'est-ce que ce grand garçon au teint bistré et aux yeux de houri qui se promène avec vous à Bullier? Un modèle d'atelier?" (*RHS* 81). In June 1886, Barrès published a now famous article about Rachilde in which he dubbed her "Mademoiselle Baudelaire" and situated her work in the tradition of *Les Fleurs du mal* and Rachilde herself, somewhat provocatively, in the tradition of bluestockings who "se déshabillèrent par amour de la littérature."

The exact nature of the relationship between Rachilde and Barrès remains a matter of speculation. The sexually flirty tone of Barrès's letters to Rachilde from March 1885 (when Rachilde first met Vallette) is suggestive though certainly not conclusive, and some have had their doubts about whether they were actually lovers.[6] Rachilde did not hesitate to spread rumors about *other* people with whom Barrès was purportedly involved, such as the author Gyp, but she was silent on her own account.[7] If Barrès's letters are any guide, whatever feelings they shared had cooled considerably by the summer of 1885, when Rachilde paid a visit to the Périgord, by which time Barrès was telling her that she was an imbecile.

Later, in 1886, Jean Lorrain responded indirectly to Barrès's "Mademoiselle Baudelaire" with his own "Mademoiselle Salamandre." Lorrain's opening line was a question: "Couche-t-elle?" Although he would go on to explain that this question was only part of a conversation about Rachilde that he had overheard at Tortoni's, his provocative use of it crystallized (although not for the first time) the paradox of Rachilde's pretensions to virginity. Lorrain presented the image of Rachilde that the public had formed on the basis of her novels (that of a very debauched woman), but the rhetorical device of ventriloquism also allowed him to pose the gossipy question about Rachilde herself. The conclusion he draws is that Rachilde merely cultivated a public image of sexual freedom (hence the chameleon-like, cold, and reptilian identity ascribed by Lorrain) and was not nearly as promiscuous as her reputation might lead one to believe. Just as Rachilde's image might lead one to believe that she drank and danced with abandon when in fact she did neither, the public image of promiscuity is false.

While Rachilde may not have been the libertine that her public image suggested, there were also plenty of rumors to deflate the claims to complete chastity. According to some of these rumors, Rachilde was indeed living with someone in the mid-1880s, but the description of this "poet" does not seem to match Barrès. According to Paul Devaux— author (under the pseudonym "Dr. Luiz") of *Les Fellatores* (1888)— Rachilde, "vêtue constamment d'un rouge peignoir," lived in a room decorated all in black with a black cat and "un jeune poète qui compose des vers de cette force et qui les met en action: *Nous, les éphèbes bruns descendus des Sodomes*" (202–3).[8] The text goes on to describe the "bizarre" poet, who corrects the work of the author of *Monsieur Vénus*, "vêtu d'un pantalon effrangé, d'un pardessus presque blanc, le chapeau haut de forme roussi par la lune" (203). Barrès had a reputation as a dandy, so this hardly seems likely to be his style.

A clue to the identity of this poet is supplied by an allusion in a letter from Barrès to Rachilde suggesting that, in 1885, Rachilde was interested in another bohemian, Léo d'Orfer, a mutual acquaintance (Davanture 1:269). This writer, whose real name was Marius Pouget (or Poujet), was also from the Périgord, and his acquaintance with Rachilde dates back to the 1870s. The two had even met before moving to Paris, collaborating on short-lived regional literary reviews, and d'Orfer had reviewed some of Rachilde's earliest publications, such as *Monsieur de la Nouveauté* (1880).[9]

Pommarède refers, somewhat obliquely, to "des traditions familiales" that held that Rachilde fled from her family "en compagnie d'un quadragénaire, M. d'Orfer," speculating that the fugue took place in the 1870s ("Le Sol et le sang" 802 n.75). According to Jean Digot, however, "A. Pouget" was born in Ceyrac on December 5, 1859, making him almost the same age as Rachilde (13). After completing his military service in the colonies, he established himself in Paris, where he became a "spécialiste du lancement de revues" in the 1880s (Davanture 1:302).[10] In addition to launching *Le Scapin* in 1885, he played an important behind-the-scenes role in the founding of *La Vogue* before Gustave Kahn took it over around April 1886 (Digot 15). Pouget/d'Orfer also maintained regional connections: in 1889 he announced an intention to run in the legislative elections as a candidate from Périgueux (Richard 231), the same year saw the first issue of *Le Rouergue* (a weekly paper "de l'arrondissement d'Espalion" that lasted less than a year), and in December 1892 he founded *Paris-Aveyron*, "l'hebdomadaire de la colonie des Aveyronnais du dehors" (Digot 18).

Much later, around the time of World War I, d'Orfer became more interested in Serbian literature and culture,[11] but, in the mid-1880s, d'Orfer was also known as a poet, and his name was publicly linked to that of Rachilde. In addition to *Henri Issanchou* (1885), he paid to have fifteen copies of *Les Enfants morts*, with a preface by Rachilde, published (Digot 20) and published a collection entitled *Les Oeillets* (there are no known surviving copies of these last two).

In the 1886 *Petit Bottin des lettres et des arts* (published anonymously but in fact compiled by Félix Fénéon, Paul Adam, Oscar Méténier, and Jean Moréas), d'Orfer's name was again linked to that of Rachilde in a more coded yet perfectly clear way. In addition to giving her date of birth as 1865 (!), the brief entry for Rachilde (which begins by refer- ring to Catulle Mendès) ends with her "signe particulier:—elle taille ses plumes avec un canif— toujours le même et quand même,—au manche d'or et de fer" (113). To many of Rachilde's contemporaries, the handle of the pocket knife "d'or et de fer" was a transparent reference to d'Orfer.

While the affair with d'Orfer may have lasted a long time (from the 1870s until the mid-1880s), it did not last forever. By the 1890s, Rachilde was married with a child, and d'Orfer, too, had his own "charges de famille" (Digot 18). Although the relationship did not last, their families would become curiously linked in later generations: Geneviève d'Orfer married the poet Paul Fort (Digot 22), and Fort's nephew Robert would marry Rachilde's daughter, Gabrielle.[12]

When Rachilde met Vallette in 1885, however, she was with neither Barrès nor d'Orfer but, as she claimed to Apollinaire, "une superbe putain." Rachilde would later deny any attraction to women,[13] but, as she herself noted in the preface to *A mort*, "On l'accusa d'aimer les hommes, les femmes, les chiens, les chats et les cochers de fiacre" (xxii), and at least one lesbian affair has been attributed to her. This affair, too, took place in the 1880s.

Gisèle d'Estoc is best known, when known at all, as a mysterious lover of Guy de Maupassant's whose existence was revealed only long after Maupassant's death.[14] So little is known about her that, when in the 1930s Pierre Borel, a journalist and "friend of a friend" of Maupassant's, first published his account of d'Estoc's role in Maupassant's life, many suspected a hoax. (Armand Lanoux, the editor of *Les Oeuvres libres*, in which Borel had published one of his articles, later undertook to con- firm Borel's assertions—with mixed results.) Over the years, however, d'Estoc's existence has been accepted, even though the specifics of her life remain murky.

Although little is known for sure about her early life—and I doubt
the proposed identification of d'Estoc as Marie-Elisa Courbe, born
on August 9, 1863—it does seem clear that she was born in Nancy (like
Maurice Barrès). After an adolescent passion for Marie-Edmée Pau, an
artist-writer with whom she shared an interest in Joan of Arc (Borel,
Maupassant et l'androgyne 21),[15] the future d'Estoc left Nancy under a
cloud of opprobrium for Paris, where she exhibited her sculpture, aspired to become a writer,[16] and moved in the same bohemian circles as
Rachilde (she was, for example, involved with the journalist Léo Pillard
d'Arkaï).

Along the way, d'Estoc seems to have acquired several identities. By
1886, she had become "Mme Paule Parent-Desbarres" (Douchin 114),
though no legal evidence has yet been discovered that she was ever really married. Once she became an author in her own right, however,
d'Estoc chose a pseudonym with significant connotations. Her first full-
length work, *Noir sur blanc* (1887), was published under the pseudonym
Gyz-El, a prototype of the name that she would later use.[17] Jacques-
Louis Douchin has offered the beginnings of an analysis of this name:
"'Gyz-El': premier pseudonyme. Je me demande s'il ne faudrait pas
rapprocher 'Gyz' de 'Gyp,' le pseudonyme célèbre de l'arrière-petite-
fille de Mirabeau, Sybille de Martel de Janville, que 'Marie-Paule-Elisa-
Courbe-Parent-Desbarres' admirait beaucoup. Quant à 'El,' c'est la première syllabe de son second prénom, Elisa, le second prénom de l'acte
de naissance" (114).

But Gyp is not the only woman author invoked by this pseudonym.
In particular, the separation of the name into two syllables—the
Oriental-looking *Gyz* and the equally Oriental (if also Spanish) hon-
orific title *El*—highlights the mysterious and exotic aspects of the name,
just as Rachilde's pseudonym evoked such connotations through the invited assimilation to the equally Oriental-sounding Rashid. Unlike its
homonym Gisèle, the name Gyz-El thus also invoked a certain connotation of masculinity lacking in the jaunty monosyllable of Gyp.[18] Gyz-
El evolved into Gisèle d'Estoc, a curious pseudonym that also presents
certain parallels with that of Rachilde. *Estoc*, an old word for "sword,"
announced the interest in fencing that she shared with Rachilde as well
as the piercing invective of her criticism, but the *estoc* is also the attribute of Rachilde's assumed ancestor Aimeri (see "1877: Authority, Authorship, and Authorization").

Literary pretensions were not the only thing that d'Estoc had in common with Rachilde. In addition to liking horseback riding and fencing
(Borel, *Maupassant et l'androgyne* 77) as well as cross-dressing (Réda),

d'Estoc published chronicles (*chroniques*) in *L'Estafette* as well as *Le Vingtième Siècle* (Borel, *Maupassant et l'androgyne* 45), and, like Rachilde, she followed the scandal of Marie Colombier's *Sarah Barnum* (Borel, *Maupassant et l'androgyne* 52). The two women also shared mutual acquaintances: d'Estoc wrote an exposé of Gyp (W. Z. Silverman 51) and feuded with Laurent Tailhade.

One of the more surprising parallels is that, just as Rachilde wrote to Hugo, an author whom she had never met, in December 1880 the young d'Estoc wrote to Guy de Maupassant. Rachilde received a reply and encouragement from Hugo; d'Estoc received a reply and encouragement of a slightly different kind from Maupassant: by January 1881, she had become his mistress (Douchin 114–17). They continued to see each other at least until 1886 (Douchin 124), but the relationship seems never to have been exclusive on either side. In 1885, for example, d'Estoc also became involved with fellow Lorrain journalist Pillard d'Arkaï (Borel 40), a friend of that same Richard O'Monroy the title of whose book *Monsieur Mars et Madame Vénus* Rachilde seems to have borrowed to make her mark with *Monsieur Vénus*.[19] Thus, whether or not the two parties were aware of it, d'Estoc seems to have copied many of Rachilde's examples, just without Rachilde's success, which perhaps explains some of the animosity d'Estoc was later to feel toward Rachilde.[20]

With all that Rachilde and d'Estoc had in common, it was inevitable that they should meet. This, according to Borel, was d'Estoc's style of seduction: "Pour faire la conquête d'une femme qui lui plaisait la tactique de Gisèle d'Estoc était toute simple. Elle lui envoyait une déclaration enflammée et précise tout en l'invitant à venir dîner avec elle" (*Maupassant et l'androgyne* 50–51). Rachilde confided in Apollinaire during one of her salons in 1911 that she had once been duped by such an invitation: "J'avais un habit de soirée. J'y allais. Une fois une dame m'invite à venir chez elle en soirée. Elle était seule et en peignoir. Je lui en ai dit de toutes les couleurs puis je me suis vengée en me faisant faire la cour par son mari" (Apollinaire, *Journal intime* 148).

According to Pierre Borel, in Paris d'Estoc once again fell in love with a woman (her affair with Maupassant notwithstanding), this time a writer:

> *Gisèle est rapidement devenue la maîtresse d'une jeune femme de lettres qui, à cette époque, obtient un très vif succès avec des romans et des nouvelles fantastiques dans le goût d'Edgar Poe et de Barbey d'Aurevilly. Cette fois Gisèle a trouvé son maître dans l'art de la séduction et des caresses. Tous les jours elle écrit à R . . . des let-*

tres de folle passion impossible à reproduire. A côté de ces lettres, les Chansons de Bilitis *sont des litanies. Mais R . . . n'aime que les passades et se fatigue vite de cette amoureuse trop exigeante qu'elle appelle dans l'intimité "La Ventouse." (Borel,* Maupassant et l'androgyne *53)*

Borel names the writer only as R——, but this initial, combined with the reference to the style of writing, is sufficient to suggest that Rachilde was the lucky recipient of d'Estoc's affections.

Lanoux was less hesitant to name names and, writing after Rachilde's death, less reticent: "Après Marie Colombier, une des lionnes de l'époque, la redoutable R. (Rachilde) surnomme Gisèle la Ventouse et la chasse" (378). He thus revealed the identity of the woman writer whom Borel had refrained from naming. Although the affair was short-lived (in June 1888 Pillard d'Arkaï reported that Rachilde had no more "satellites" [9]), its traces are legible in the books each woman would subsequently publish. After "chasing away" d'Estoc, Rachilde would publish *Madame Adonis* (1888), in which she would describe the seduction of one woman (Louise Bartau) by another who cross-dressed as a hunter (d'Estoc would describe herself as "Diana," the Greek hunter-goddess) (Borel, "Une Amie inconnue de Maupassant" 157).[21]

D'Estoc, on the other hand, as the rejected party, would vent her spleen more directly in a publication of 1887. If Rachilde had followed Marie Colombier's example by using scandal to create publicity, d'Estoc had followed Colombier's lead in publishing an attack on a former *intime, La Vierge-Réclame.*[22] Since d'Estoc was herself a failed writer, her attack was probably fueled in part by personal jealousy and envy of the clever way in which Rachilde had manipulated her image to sell her work, but this short book was also in part a disgusted reaction to the self-serving image that Rachilde had presented to the world in the preface to *A mort* (1886). D'Estoc refers specifically to a preface in which "l'héroine . . . clame . . . qu'elle 'n'a pas voulu s'asseoir sur les genoux des vieillards'" (11). D'Estoc was not the only one to criticize Rachilde's self-advertisement. In the *Echo de Paris* of January 28, 1887, Rachilde was described as "Vénus tout entière à la publicité attachée" ("Chronologie" 14).

Despite the venom of d'Estoc's attack, Rachilde seems to have had the last word. Fifty years later, d'Estoc and her work were forgotten, and there were those who maintained that her existence was no more than a literary hoax. The debate took place in part in the pages of the *Mercure de France* in 1939. Rachilde could not have been unaware of it, given her association with the *Mercure* and the fact that one of the participants was her friend and confidant Auriant. She could easily have intervened to settle the matter, but instead she remained silent and allowed d'Estoc's existence to be denied.

In the mid-1880s, meanwhile, Rachilde continued to be attracted to the bohemian lifestyle and its colorful *littérateurs* rather than the safety of the bourgeoisie, but the evolution of her relationship with Vallette during their courtship period of 1885–89 charts a turning point in her life, from rebellion to conformity. In 1885, she was perceived as notorious, a writer who cross-dressed and lived on the margins of society. By 1890, she had become a *bourgeoise rangée*, or married matron: she claimed to have abandoned cross-dressing and let her hair grow, was the mother of a daughter named for her own mother, Gabrielle, and was embarking on the work cycles and responsibilities demanded by the regular publication of a journal, the newly founded *Mercure de France.*

The evolution from bohemian to bourgeoise can be traced in Rachilde's work, particularly in three novels that take literature and marriage as their themes. In *Queue de poisson* (1885), *Nono* (1885), and *A mort* (1886), evidence of the conflicting demands of marriage and a literary career can be discerned. Such attitudes help explain her early diffidence toward Vallette. Later developments in her personal life, however, will cause her to reevaluate the benefits to be gained from marriage, as the rest of this chapter will show.

In 1885, the year she first met Vallette, Rachilde again turned to Brancart in Brussels to publish another "spicy" story, intended to cash in on the popularity of *Monsieur Vénus. Queue de poisson* (dedicated to Léo Trézenik, then one of the editors of *Lutèce*) presents the antihero François Lévincé, who, born prematurely, is destined to amount to nothing for the rest of his life. He acquires the nickname "Queue de Poisson," referring to the way everything associated with him ends disappointingly. François turns to literary bohemia as a place where someone with no talent but grand aspirations can pass for someone important without having to confront his insignificance. The story thus functions as a cautionary tale and as such draws on Rachilde's knowledge of the bohemian context in a satirical manner. It also suggests, however, that while she did not shy away from satire, Rachilde was not yet ready to abandon her own involvement in this milieu, the only one that seemed to offer a place for a woman writer.

Queue de poisson was a short, sparse work in which Rachilde's stylistic talent was well displayed, but her major publication of 1885, the year she first met Vallette, was a return to the long novel format. Despite the length, however, parts of *Nono* represent a carefully plotted murder story, a fact that has not gone unappreciated, as one plot summary comparing the novel to Hitchcock's *The Rope* illustrates ("Bibliographie générale" 123). The drama rests on the irony that the murderer is unable to make her confessions credible and that suspicion therefore instead falls on the man she loves, who is accused—and sentenced—in her place.

That is the manifest level of the novel, but beneath the surface can be found another example of autobiographical self-representation that foregrounds questions of writing and commitment.[23] In this novel, set in 1875, Rachilde is reborn as the heroine Renée, the only daughter of the sixty-six-year-old General Fayor, wounded in 1870.[24] The autobiographical elements are not hard to discern, nor are the accommodations to fantasy and wish fulfillment: Renée is motherless, her mother having died in childbirth.

In addition, the novel contains several examples of *dédoublement* since Rachilde is also reborn as an alter ego, the dark Bruno ("Nono" for short), the antithesis of the son Joseph Eymery would have wanted: docile, afraid of horses, fearful, and—a writer. Bruno's relationship to writing is ambivalent, however, for he is General Fayor's secretary. Writing is thus, not a form of creation or self-expression for him, but just his job, one for which, moreover, he has no particular aptitude or gift (the general is frequently frustrated by his ineptitude). The only personal writing that Bruno undertakes consists of love letters to his childhood sweetheart, letters that are linked to domesticity and femininity by the fact that they are written, not in a flowery style, but on flowery paper (leftover wallpaper). Through the relationship between her alter egos Renée and Bruno, Rachilde thus explores her own relationship to the figure of an ambiguously gendered, struggling writer.

Rachilde's involvement with the bohemian literary world of the 1880s is represented by Renée's relationship with Victorien Barthelme, a personification of bohemia, about whom Renée has mixed feelings: she is attracted to his elegance and charm, but she is also influenced by her father's denunciation of him. Having earlier agreed to marry him, Renée has changed her mind and, in the opening scene of the novel, meets with him and asks him to return her letters. The essence of the intrigue thus encapsulates one of Rachilde's dilemmas: having promised her life to bohemia, and having acted on her commitment by offering *Monsieur Vénus*, she nevertheless remains partially her father's daughter and distrusts such flouting of convention. Having become a woman of letters, she wants her letters back.

Renée's (Rachilde's) dilemma seems to be resolved—and at the end of the first chapter—by a spontaneous act of violence. When the trysting Victorien and Renée are disturbed by a noise, they take refuge under a large rock that has been propped up as part of a construction project, and, acting on impulse, Renée removes the prop and crushes Victorien. The novel goes on to suggest, however, that simply repressing such feelings of attraction is not a long-term solution. Not only has eliminating Victorien not quashed her attraction to bohemia (she readily agrees to marry someone else who looks like Victorien without quite knowing why), but Renée is continually troubled by the conviction that her writerly alter ego Bruno has witnessed her crime.

In the meantime, Renée becomes more involved with professional writing in the person of Bruno, eventually falling in love with him. She vows to redeem her crime through the purity of her love (a commitment to unoriginal but professional writing). Unfortunately, "Nono" proves to be an uninspiring choice and is unable to hold Renée's attention when the temptations of bohemia reenter her life, this time in the person of a dashing duke, a bored, splenetic decadent who bears an uncanny resemblance to the dead Victorien.

Bruno, it should be noted, is at first indifferent to Renée and more concerned with his sweetheart, Amélie ("Lilie"), yet another aspect of Rachilde herself: a naive young girl whose father wants her to marry a stranger, a business associate described as "un homme sérieux" (49). The phrase echoes the words that Rachilde had used to describe Jacques de La Hullière, the fellow officer her father had wanted her to marry, as well as the label that she had applied to Alfred Vallette in the early days of their courtship when she rebuffed his interest in her. In 1885, then, Rachilde's response to marriage was still "just say (No)no." Having avoided a premature attachment to Monsieur de La Hullière, Rachilde was not about to give up such hard-won freedom easily, in fiction any more than in life.

There were many reasons to be wary of committing to marriage in the mid-1880s. Divorce was once again legal (though only since the Naquet law of 1884), but it was far from providing a quick remedy for a hasty decision. Irreconcilable differences, for example, were not considered grounds for divorce, only adultery, grievous injury, and criminal conviction. Moreover, although divorce legally dissolved the links between the marriage partners, the ex-husband continued to have legal rights over his children (for example, he could determine their education and marriage) that could be used to retaliate against his ex-wife.

Marriage was therefore still a major commitment, one that entailed a certain loss of autonomy. The actions of married women were restricted in ways in which those of single women were not: only in 1886 could a married woman open a savings account without her husband's permission, for example. Saving money, it would turn out, was not to be Rachilde's strong point, but marriage imposed other limitations. For example, a married woman had no legal claim to her own income, and it was not until 1897 that she could serve as a legal witness to such civil documents as birth, marriage, and death certificates. In short, the legal doctrine of coverture meant that, once she married, a woman ceased to exist juridically, an erasure to which Rachilde was not about to submit. As Joan DeJean has put it, for a married woman, "the authorial signature seals a contract into which she cannot legally enter" (4). To marry was to cease to be a (legitimate) writer.

Nevertheless, Renée marries the duke, which ultimately proves her undoing. Since all the evidence surrounding Victorien's disappearance conspires to implicate Nono, he is taken into police custody, and Renée's efforts to protect him are in vain. The conflicting emotions of guilt and desire drive Renée mad (just as the unresolvable conflict between desire and duty had affected the adolescent Rachilde). Events move beyond her control, however, and she is spared choosing between the two when the duke tells Bruno that he intends to reveal the truth (that Renée is really the murderer) and Bruno, still in love with her, falsely confesses in order to save her. Uncannily, Renée and Bruno die at the same time— Bruno executed for a crime that he did not commit, Renée following a "crise de folie furieuse"—and thus achieve in death the union that had eluded them in life.

Although certain twists of plot are indeed thriller material, many of the details of this long novel are hackneyed, and the ending exploits romantic cliché to full effect. Nevertheless, *Nono* remains interesting for what it reveals about the paralyzing conflicts that Rachilde perceived between filial duty and self-expression. On the one hand were the twin seductions of bohemianism and decadence; on the other a more mundane and utilitarian form of professional writing offered security. The latter was not without its charms and certainly had some claim on her allegiance, but it lacked dazzle. Having tasted the bohemian delights of notoriety with *Monsieur Vénus*, Rachilde perhaps realized that she could not simply suppress what she knew and return to folktales, safe, businesslike newspaper reports of army maneuvers, and fashion columns. She had also experienced firsthand that competing temptations and desires could lead to immobility and madness. The solution was not clear, as the resolution of *Nono* illustrates, but simply turning her back on bohemia was certainly not the answer. Thus, Rachilde continued to frequent bohemian circles: the Hydropathes, the Chat Noir, the Café de l'Avenir ("Chronologie" 14). She also continued to see the professional writer Vallette. A favorite rendezvous was Chez la Mère Clarisse, the only place in Paris where one could find Strasbourg beer (David, *Rachilde* 34).

The realization that bohemia could not easily be abandoned perhaps accounts for the fact that the relationship between Rachilde and Vallette got off to a slow start, Vallette being more like the serious Bruno than the seductive Barrès. The friendship had started on the wrong foot, and it might have gone nowhere, but Vallette was a diligent correspondent. He was indifferent to Rachilde's cross-dressing, to her desire to shock, and even to her fiction (he read both *Monsieur de la Nouveauté* and *Monsieur Vénus* as attacks on men and found the plot of the latter quite improbable [RHS 15–16]). Perhaps this indifferent acceptance was what Rachilde sought, and she found that the exchanges with Vallette became a welcome distraction (Auriant, *Souvenirs* 34–35). At first she tried to bind him to her by making him part of her bohemian literary crowd, but Vallette resisted, and Rachilde gradually discovered that it was his distance and difference that made him interesting. She found that, with Vallette, she could have the best of both worlds: she could flirt with bohemia and yet go home to the bourgeoisie.

This understanding was slow in dawning, however, and for some time she still found herself drawn to the likes of Barrès. It was to him that she dedicated the 1886 novel *A mort*, another veiled autobiographical novel and example of the "Rachildian triangle" the cold but irresistible aristocrat, the possessive parvenu, and the innocent "wife-doll" ("Bibliographie générale" 124). The hero of the novel is Count Maxime de Bryon,[25] the heroine Berthe Soirès, the naive young wife for whom men kill themselves, empty-headed until Max begins to stimulate her interest in literature. Berthe's husband, the self-made banker Jean Soirès, controls her by convincing her that all men are like him, an assumption that Max challenges. Once again, Rachilde had created a doll-like heroine, a puppet of the men in her life who is forced to choice between the cerebral seductions of decadence and the rewards of bourgeois hard work.

The narrative device exploited by the novel derives from the fact that the husband, Jean, forces the lover, Max, at gunpoint to promise never to see Berthe again. Max keeps his promise faithfully but literally: he continues to meet Berthe, but without looking at/seeing her. The novel thus explores the moral status of an adultery that takes place only in the mind, a typically decadent theme emphasizing the cerebral and ideal over the physical and real. At the same time, however, the mind-body split is the vehicle for expressing competing attractions. Berthe's situation illustrates "the monstrosity of a double love: her body belonging to one, her soul to the other" (128). The situation was not without its parallels for Rachilde, who was perhaps becoming aware of her own divided loyalties.

Just as in *Nono*, events overtake the heroine. Berthe does try to take control of her life. Having been humiliated and raped by her husband, she succumbs to the same temptation as Rachilde once had and attempts to drown herself, choosing, not a safe, shallow pond, but the Seine. Circumstances, however, intervene. She is rescued by a member of Maxime's staff and whisked away to the country to recuperate. At first, Berthe is idyllically happy, but her mood changes when she discovers that she is pregnant. Suddenly inspired with a renewed sense of duty, she repudiates Max's hospitality and renews contact with her family, who believed her dead. This volte-face—her renunciation of independence and return to a subordinate position—is perplexing, but it illustrates the negative view that Rachilde held at that time of motherhood and the constraints that it imposed on women. Berthe believes that pregnancy will bring her close to her mother once again, but she is betrayed because it is her husband who comes to "attend" to her. Instead of reconciling with her, Jean murders her and her unborn child, believing that he has been cuckolded by Max.

In the character of Berthe we have another example of a woman torn between legitimate duty (marriage) and illegitimate attraction (to literature). The text, however, is further doubled: the preface to *A mort* is at once a source of information about Rachilde's life and a tantalizing fictional self-representation, as already discussed. This preface contains, for example, what appears to be the most detailed account of Rachilde's attempted suicide, thereby preparing the reader to see the parallels with Berthe in the novel, yet it undercuts its own veracity by presenting itself as something made up in a hurry to fulfill an obligation.

The preface opens with the arrival of a messenger from the publisher Monnier, who announces that the publisher is ready to begin production but that the manuscript is thirty pages short. Rachilde offers to add a spicy episode to the main narrative, but Monnier demands something new ("du neuf" [*AM ii*]) and suggests that she paint her own verbal portrait. Rachilde proceeds to do so, then closes by assimilating the story to a fictional model: "Barbey d'Aurevilly, c'est en pensant à vous que je viens d'écrire cette histoire" (xxiii). The rhetorical framework of the preface therefore suggests its fictionality; it is literally and figuratively an extension of the main text, a continuation of the act of storytelling. If the novel is fiction with autobiographical overtones, the preface is autobiography with fictional overtones. Rachilde implies that there is little differences between the two.

The preface was one of her first acts of conscious self-representation, but far from the last. The juxtaposition of preface and text serves as a reminder of the need to interpret her autobiographical acts in their context, rather then viewing them as unproblematic statements of pure truth. The example of the preface to *A mort* suggests that Rachilde was beginning to understand how to manipulate her public image in order to create herself as a writer.

While Rachilde continued to produce fiction at an enviable rate, her relationship with Vallette continued to evolve. After their initial meeting in 1885, there appears to have been a hiatus until at least 1886. After a letter dated March 27, 1885, the next is dated September 10, 1886 (there are undated letters that appear in between in *Le Roman d'un homme sérieux*—but, as I have suggested above, at least one is actually from much later, so this order is not necessarily reliable). Vallette's September 10, 1886, letter begins "If I remember you?" (RHS 19), as though in response to a question in a letter from Rachilde. Rachilde's pretext in writing seems to have been to involve Vallette in the Léonide Leblanc affair (Leblanc was seeking support for her bid to enter the Comédie-Française), but Vallette took the opportunity to renew contact for purely personal reasons. He had already tried calling on her concierge: "Cet été [1886], je suis passé chez votre concierge, la nommée Mme Pierre, désirant prendre de vos nouvelles parce qu'on m'avait dit que vous aviez eu des embêtements avec un éditeur ou que vous aviez été souffrante" (20–21). He offered not only advice about the book she was currently trying to get published (it would eventually be issued as *Minette* in 1889) but even a loan so that she could publish it herself (RHS 25). Rachilde showed him the manuscript of another book, *Madame Adonis* (RHS 26–27), and he offered editorial advice on other work, which was not always taken (RHS 45).[26]

Vallette also took the liberty of paying Rachilde's rent when she fell behind, which did not please her (RHS 34). She was too proud to accept such help without protest. But it was true that it was hard to make ends meet, even though she was by now well-known and continued to publish novels regularly (two a year from 1884 to 1889). She also succeeded in placing short stories: "La Fille de neige," for example, later reprinted at the end of *L'Homme roux* in 1888, first appeared in *Le Scapin* in September 1886. Vallette was heavily involved in *Le Scapin*, which had been founded in 1885, but whether it was the renewal of contact with Rachilde that led to her involvement in the review or her connection with the journal that maintained her acquaintance with Vallette is not clear.

By 1886, Rachilde's style was no longer a novelty, and the literary scene was overrun with decadents. There were two decadent reviews founded in 1886 alone—Anatole Baju's *Le Décadent*, which ran from 1886 to 1889, and *La Décadence*, which began as an offshoot of *Le Scapin* and was founded and folded within the first fifteen days of October 1886. Rachilde was herself involved in this proliferation of journals, an involvement that also served to keep her circulating in the same crowd as Vallette.[27]

This was not to say that Vallette and Rachilde did not sometimes find themselves on opposite sides of the literary fence, as an incident from the fall of 1886 illustrates. Rachilde was a contributor to Anatole Baju's *Le Décadent*, which had started as a review open to all. Gustave Kahn, however, orchestrated a coup, and in the September 1886 issue of the review it was announced that, henceforth, the journal would represent "les jeunes" (Richard 85–92). (Rachilde protested Kahn's takeover by writing to *Lutèce*, and her complaints—combined with others—were effective enough that the announced change in editorial policy never took place.) Vallette was one of the editors of *Le Scapin*–revue (as distinct from *Le Scapin*–journal), launched in September 1886 specifically in order to offer an alternative to *Le Décadent* (Richard 102), a choice that seems to place him on the opposite side of the issue from Rachilde.[28]

I do not want to make too much of such differences. Bohemian Paris in the 1880s saw plenty of infighting, as do most literary communities. Decadence was contested, for example, by Jean Moréas's "Manifeste du symbolisme," in which he advocated replacing the term *decadent* with the term *symbolist*. Yet, when they found themselves under attack by the general public, the literati buried their differences and closed ranks against the common enemy.[29]

During this time, Rachilde was living in a small, dark apartment at 5, rue des Ecoles, decorated with Chinese scrolls and a statue of Antinous (*RHS* 41). Vallette visited her here and met her menagerie, which at this time consisted of a cat named Sans-frousse and a canary that perched on the cat's head (40). Vallette began to think of Rachilde as the younger brother he had always wanted (41), a feeling of which Rachilde was skeptical (44), but it was true that he was intrigued by this unusual creature. He described one of his childhood pastimes to explain his interest in terms that were uncannily appropriate: "je ne trouvais rien de plus amusant que de *piéger* des bêtes, non pour les tuer ou les revendre aux marchands d'oiseaux ou au marchand de gibier défendu, mais pour les regarder de près" (50). He could not help but want to get a closer look at Rachilde. And, since he was more at ease expressing himself from a distance in writing than viva voce (33), his letters provide valuable information about the progress of the relationship.

Rachilde continued to rebuff Vallette's friendship when the correspondence resumed in 1886, distrusting his motives: "On n'a jamais d'ami sincère, l'amitié d'un homme pour une femme, ça n'existe pas!" (RHS 44). It is true that Vallette seemed to be wanting more than just friendship, gradually falling in love, making veiled and not-so-veiled declarations in his letters (for example, 68–69). He also realized that Rachilde was not as cold and invincible as she pretended to be (97). But, in early 1887, Rachilde sent a "frank" and "cruel" but "necessary" letter to Vallette that interrupted the relationship once again.[30] What exactly she wrote is not recorded (Vallette returned her letter), and Vallette's answer is suggestive yet tantalizingly vague:

> *Maintenant, voulez-vous vous souvenir de ceci: n'importe à quel moment, dans n'importe quelle situation vous vous trouveriez et malgré vos scrupules ou vos craintes à mon sujet, je me mets à votre entière disposition pour l'avenir.*
>
> *Vous n'aurez qu'à me faire un signe, m'écrire un mot, je viendrai. . . .*
>
> *Je resterai à la même place, moi, je ne m'absente jamais de Paris, et je serai toujours votre ami quoi qu'il puisse vous arriver.*
>
> *J'ai un chagrin fou et je veux croire que si vous avez eu la force de me dire certaines choses c'est que je méritais de les savoir.*
>
> *Non, non, je ne reviendrai pas, mais n'ayez pas peur que je fasse comme l'autre. Le vrai courage consiste à vivre quand même. J'ai charge d'âme. . . .*
>
> *J'attendrai, j'attendrai toujours. . . . On ne se réveille pas d'un rêve comme le mien.* (RHS 100)

Vallette's allusion to someone else who, to judge from the context, committed suicide after being rejected by Rachilde is consistent with the rumor recorded by Gisèle d'Estoc and discussed above. Rachilde's *A mort* (1886) had opened with such an event—a spurned lover committing suicide—and the memory was fresh enough in early 1887 that she needed Vallette's reassurance that he would not behave so foolishly.

But what was the revelation that broke off the relationship, Rachilde's "cruel" but "necessary" confession? Her fear of sexual relations, as has been suggested by Dauphiné (*Rachilde* [1991] 47)? Whatever the secret, it made Vallette agree to keep his distance without ceasing to be a friend.

Vallette apparently kept his word and did not contact Rachilde again, but over a year later, in July 1888, she wrote to him, casually, to invite him to go boating. And he found her changed, no longer like a turbulent schoolboy but a woman. Moreover, he found her hesitant, seemingly afraid of something. She was still role-playing, however. This time she was a working-class girl on a Sunday outing, though she undercut the effect of the working-girl elements of the outfit by adding a man's overcoat and opened-toed sandals more appropriate for evening. Vallette found himself wondering about the reason for the new costume (yet another "travesti") but perhaps received an answer when he discovered that Rachilde's mother was staying with her (*RHS* 102–5). Although Madame Eymery had moved out by September 1888, Rachilde seemed to expect to find her on her doorstep whenever she returned home, and Vallette realized that *this* was the source of Rachilde's fear (*RHS* 131).

He could not, however, understand this fear, given his own close family relations. Rachilde's parents had been leading essentially separate lives ever since she had left home. Le Cros had been sold on November 4, 1883 (without Rachilde being told [*RHS* 132–33]), and Joseph Eymery had bought a château just opposite the old estate, while Gabrielle returned to live with her parents (138). Now she wanted to live in Paris; Rachilde appears to have been terrified at the prospect of having her mother so close, but Vallette (whose mother lived close by) could not understand the problem. Vallette's father had died in January 1888, and perhaps this caused him to place greater value on family connections. For whatever reason, he tried to assure her that her fears were groundless.

It turned out, however, that what Rachilde really feared was, not the simple fact of her mother's proximity, but her madness. Vallette's reassuring tone disappeared immediately after he finally met Madame Eymery: "Ma pauvre Rachilde! Il n'y a, hélas! aucun doute et je ne comprends pas que vous ne puissiez pas vous rendre à la triste évidence. N'importe quel médecin serait au courant de son état après une heure de conversation avec cette femme, amusante, charmante et surtout tellement inquiétante qu'on a envie de lui crier: 'Mais taisez-vous donc et gardez pour vous vos confidences qui vont vous mener bien plus loin que vous ne voudriez aller si vous saviez où l'on peut vous mener avec elles!'" (*RHS* 141). Vallette also realized the strength of Rachilde's opposition to marriage, given that she had refused the arranged marriage to Hullière that would have saved her "de cet enfer" (141–42).

Although he was opposed to marriage himself (RHS 83, 88), Vallette nevertheless proposed to Rachilde to save her from the prospect of being sucked back into her mother's life: "Vous savez que je vous aime *à la folie*. Souffrez que je mette ma folie en face de *l'autre*. Vous ne pouvez pas faire un mariage de raison mais, moi, je vous propose mieux, ou pire: une union libre de raison en ce sens que je vous prie, à genoux, de me laisser devenir votre gardien sans pour cela vous demander ce que vous ne voulez pas donner à personne, pas même à celui que vous aimeriez puisque vous prétendez que . . . l'instinct de la reproduction doit être abandonné aux seuls animaux" (142). It was an odd sort of proposal: Vallette specifically avoided calling it marriage, offering to become not her husband but her guardian. The "union libre" that he had in mind was not even one in which they would live together, for he offered to move in with his mother so that Rachilde could occupy his three-room apartment alone.

Rachilde does not seem to have taken Vallette up on his offer, at least not immediately and not in its original form, but, sometime between late 1888 and 1889, the proposal did in fact turn into an agreement to marry, despite the distaste on both sides for this institution. To retrace the course of events is to recognize the role that Rachilde's mother played in this decision. Rachilde sought to escape her mother's sphere of influence but ended up making choices that only underscored her mother's control over her, choices that reveal the deep ambiguity she felt about her mother. Rachilde may have felt betrayed by her mother, but to feel betrayal one must first feel trust. Rachilde never felt betrayed by her father, despite his rejection of her sex and her literary aspirations, because, while she may have loved him, she never trusted him; his rejection never came as a surprise.

Vallette astutely observed that one of the reasons Rachilde was so threatened by her mother was that they were so alike. With her mother, Rachilde was "en présence d'une égale, d'une artiste qui vous suit de loin, et qui tend à se rapprocher" (RHS 144). It is not surprising, then, to find the traces of that ambiguity in Rachilde's work. Even as she fled in one direction—marrying to escape her mother—she moved closer to her mother in another direction, imitating certain aspects of her mother's life.

Rachilde and Vallette's marriage contract was drawn up by a lawyer in the fifth arrondissement on May 29, 1889. Joseph Eymery was listed as a resident of Chamarat, while Gabrielle's address was given as the Cité aux Fleurs. Rachilde had some furniture and clothing but otherwise brought no property. The marriage was celebrated on June 12, 1889 (Gaubert 16–17; David, *Rachilde* 35–36). Rachilde was twenty-nine. The witnesses were the poet Albert Samain (who had originally introduced them) and Laurent Tailhade for Vallette and Léo Trézenik and an old family friend, the astronomer Camille Flammarion, for Rachilde.

Only a civil ceremony was conducted, which led some, such as Léon Bloy, to view Rachilde as nothing more than a concubine ("Chronologie" 14). Rachilde was no doubt delighted to receive such signs that her racy reputation was alive and well; far more disconcerting must have been the more prevalent assumption that her amazonian life was over. After the wedding dinner, the newlyweds went home (to Vallette's apartment in the rue de l'Echaudé-Saint-Germain) accompanied by Samain, where they talked until four in the morning.

This was no traditional wedding night, and not just because neither party was particularly invested in the institution. There would be no bloody sheets to display the following morning, of course,[31] but, more important, Rachilde would have been about four and a half months pregnant when she married. Her daughter, who would be named Gabrielle, would be born later that year, on October 25. Was Vallette the father, or was Rachilde's "delicate" situation the motivation to accept Vallette's offer of a "union libre" in marriage? In some ways, paternity is not the issue: in the strict sense, Gabrielle was conceived out of wedlock and was thus illegitimate regardless of who her father was (some of the implications of illegitimacy are explored in the next chapter). And it is entirely possible that Vallette was her father (though see Léautaud 1:620): it was not uncommon to view engagement to be married as sanctioning sexual relations, and perhaps this was the case for Rachilde and Vallette.

But Vallette's last letter to Rachilde (noted as such in an editorial comment) alludes to yet another secret. The undated letter begins: "Mon amour, ton secret sera mon secret. Mes deux bras, refermés sur toi, sauront bien te protéger et si tu es ma prisonnière tu n'auras plus rien à craindre de personne" (RHS 146). What is the secret that Vallette will keep? Rachilde could hardly have expected to hide her pregnancy, but she could expect Vallette not to reveal Gabrielle's true paternity. On the other hand, this letter is also notable for being the first time that Vallette addresses Rachilde as *tu*. In novels (and Rachilde presents this collection of letters as a *roman*), such a change in form of address signified that two characters had had sexual relations. Read as part of a novel, then, Vallette's letter may signal that some significant step had been taken toward greater intimacy.[32]

In real life, however, no such convention was strictly observed (Rachilde alternated between *tu* and *vous* in her letters to Barrès—sometimes in the course of a single letter), so, while the change signals a new stage in the relationship, it is impossible to know what prompted it. Whatever the cause, the fact that Rachilde was prepared to admit someone to the state of permanent intimacy signaled by marriage marks a major transition in her career. Rachilde had found a way in which to reconcile what had previously seemed irreconcilable—writing and marriage.

The Photograph Never Lies

In which a front page brings attention to Rachilde's hair

The February 26, 1887, edition of *La Vie moderne* features an engraving of Rachilde on its cover by Ernest Langlois. It appears to depict the head and shoulders of a short-haired Rachilde in three-quarters profile, a man's hat perched on her head, and wearing a tailored man's jacket. This chapter analyzes this image further in order to show how the public image of Rachilde could be "massaged" by both Rachilde herself and others who had an interest in portraying her in a certain way. This analysis requires some comments on the history of gendered clothing and on the legend of Rachilde's short hair.

First, however, it is necessary to say something about Langlois's engraving. In 1887, the routine printing of photographs in newspapers was still in the future (the first photographic image in a French periodical would appear in July 1891, according to Anne-Claude Ambroise-Rendu), but images of people and events could be reproduced in a number of other ways suitable to the mass production of widely circulated publications. Rachilde's appearance on the cover of *La Vie moderne* is both a tribute to her popularity—she was newsworthy—and an example of the ways in which the needs of advertising and the needs of her career reinforced one another. The picture of a well-known, notorious, or otherwise famous person on the cover of a mass-produced journal was not an advertisement in the strict sense. That such attention was given to a writer could be justified by the public demand for information, but, to the extent that such pandering to public tastes increased sales (for both the newspaper itself as well as for the writer), such representations functioned like advertising. In this way, publicity, in the sense of simply making public or attracting public attention, overlaps with advertising, in which the economic interest is more explicit.

The fact that photographs were not yet routinely reproduced in mass publications does not, of course, mean that photography itself was uncommon, at least among the middle class. In fact, there exists an extensive photographic record of Rachilde's life, ranging from formally posed studio portraits extending from her earliest years throughout her professional career to more casual snapshots taken in middle age. (Studio portraits exist of her parents as well.) The more informal photographs

LA VIE MODERNE

PARIS ET DÉPARTEMENTS

Tout Paris

DIRECTEUR : A. LÉBRE

Rédacteurs en chef :

JOURNAL HEBDOMADAIRE ILLUSTRÉ

G. Rodenbach.
G. Lébre.

DIRECTION : 3 bis, RUE LABRUYÈRE

The cover of *La Vie moderne*, February 26, 1887. Reprinted from Dauphiné, *Rachilde* (1985).

begin to proliferate in the 1890s, by which time cameras had become more portable and easier to use and the technology therefore became less the exclusive province of trained professionals and more the pastime of the bourgeoisie. One series of snapshots, for example, shows activities at the collective summer home of the *phalanstère*, with Alfred Jarry and various items of sports equipment—bicycles, boats, fishing rods—and Rachilde posing in a *javanaise* dance (made popular by the 1889 international exhibition's re-creations of exotic street scenes in Paris), as well as indoor dining scenes and pictures of family pets.

In the 1880s, that moment of informality had not yet arrived: it was still easier (that is, cheaper) to reproduce an engraving than a photograph. But it was easier to model an engraving on a photograph (or some other fixed representation) than to model directly from life. To ask the subject to pose for an engraving when a photograph could be made so easily was to waste the subject's time and complicate the life of the engraver. So, even though photographs were not reproduced directly in the mass media, they were being reproduced indirectly (Ambroise-Rendu 7).

To illustrate this phenomenon with reference to Rachilde, one need look no further than the portrait of Rachilde by Marguerite van Bever from 1898 (the date is inscribed in roman numerals on the picture) that was used to illustrate Gaubert's biography in 1907.[1] The description of this work as a "portrait" (Dauphiné, *Rachilde* [1985] between 96 and 97) might be taken to imply that Rachilde actually sat for the engraver, but a glance at the photographic record quickly shows that the engraving was actually based on a Paris studio photograph (also reproduced in Dauphiné, *Rachilde* [1985] between 96 and 97), this one inscribed to Vallette. It is easy to identify the similarities between van Bever's portrait and the photographic original: the pose, with right elbow on the back of the chair and chin resting on hand (the fingers closed except for the index finger, which extends onto the cheek) and the left hand resting half open in the lap; the mysterious half smile; the hairstyle, with center part, bun on top, and spit curls in front of the ear; and the dress, with its distinctive leg-of-mutton sleeves. It is equally easy to see how van Bever embellished this photograph in her portrait, adding a more ornate chair for Rachilde to rest her elbow on (the one in the photo is elegant but straight backed), a decorative screen as background, and a more elaborate dress, with an embroidered bolero and a large bow around her neck (though still with a jeweled stud).

Another photograph, evidently from the same sitting (since Rachilde wears the same outfit and has apparently the same hairstyle, although she is standing and looking off to her left), this time inscribed to Cazals, is described as "vers 1895" (Dauphiné, *Rachilde* [1985] following 96), suggesting the approximate date of the studio portrait session and the date of the original later transformed by van Bever. (An engraving based on van Bever's portrait was later used in the Vin Mariani advertisement mentioned earlier [see "1885: Marriage and the Woman Writer"]. That engraving was thus a copy of a copy.)

Portrait of Rachilde by Marguerite van Bever.
Reprinted from Dauphiné, *Rachilde* (1985).

Photograph of Rachilde inscribed to Vallette. Reprinted
from Dauphiné, *Rachilde* (1985). Courtesy of the Bibliothèque littéraire Jacques Doucet, Paris.

Photograph of Rachilde "vers 1895." Reprinted from
Dauphiné, *Rachilde* (1985). Courtesy of the Bibliothèque
littéraire Jacques Doucet, Paris.

The same process is at work in Langlois's 1887 engraving, though the original is not so easy to identify. Alfred Vallette's commentary on the engraving makes it clear that it is a copy of a portrait, although whether photographic or in some other medium is not specified: "Ce sacré Langlois a *aggravé* le portrait qu'il a copié. Vous êtes, sans flatterie aucune, bien mieux que votre portrait, et le portrait est bien mieux que la gravure Langlois" (RHS 97–98). Vallette's opinion both confirms that the engraving is a copy and alludes to the differences between the engraving and the portrait. The original portrait referred to by Vallette remains unknown, so the "aggravation" (the added seriousness) cannot be measured directly, but the comparison made above between the photographic original and the fanciful embellishments by van Bever suggests that Langlois might have altered a great deal, including details of clothing. Such license in copying was not unusual. To the extent that illustration was expected to convey a moral message, it was understood that "la pose des personnages, l'outrance de certaines grimaces, l'aspect caricatural des visages sont autant de façons de travestir, de défigurer la réalité" (Ambroise-Rendu 12). In order to understand the implications that such changes might have in Langlois's rendition of Rachilde, we must make a digression to talk about Rachilde's hair.

The story that Rachilde wore her hair short is part of the Rachilde legend, along with her cross-dressing. As argued above, however (see "1884: Writing as Cross-Dressing"), cross-dressing was a great deal more complex than most of these legends acknowledge. Similarly, the stories that circulated about Rachilde's hair are symptomatic of the way she exploited the myth of the exceptional.

First and foremost is the story of how Rachilde cut her hair and sold it to a Russian prince, a narrative that has all the elements of a fairy tale. This is another of those anecdotes amplified in the retelling until it has become mythological. Here is David's version: "Elle coupa sa magnifique chevelure et la vendit au prince Romuald Gédroye, grand chambellan de l'empereur Alexandre III de Russie, qui la fit enfermer dans un coffret sculpté par Stanislas Meunier, l'auteur de *La femme à la tortue*" (*Rachilde* 20). That Rachilde should cut her hair and sell it might have had more prosaic meaning, but David's narrative piles on the detail: Rachilde's hair was not ordinary but, as befits a heroine nicknamed "Mademoiselle Baudelaire," "magnifique" (a wonder he did not think to add "et ondulante"). This act of rebellion is compounded by the fact that she sells it, and not just to anyone but to a prince, and not just any prince but one associated with the imperial Russian court, a prince who keeps Rachilde's hair like a fetish object in a box, and not just any (Russian) box but one sculpted by an artist. The narrative leaves the reader breathless, as each successive detail confers a new level of honor on the revered (magnificent) hair.

The exaltation of Rachilde's hair has everything to do with romantic narrative convention and precious little to do with reality. In reality, women did sell their hair, usually to wig makers, and it was no more cause for celebration than resorting to selling one's blood in today's economy. But, in novels, heroines cut their hair for love, or as a grand gesture of sacrifice, not out of financial necessity. (One pertinent example, given Rachilde's repeated invocation of George Sand, is the heroine of Sand's novel *Indiana*.)

Even some of Rachilde's contemporaries were skeptical of the rhetorical inflation that the story had undergone. Gisèle d'Estoc, Rachilde's alienated ex-lover (see "1885: Marriage and the Woman Writer") reserved some of her greatest scorn for this self-serving story, which she clearly presents as a legend: "Faut-il rappeler ici la légende qui représente la belle et susdite jeune fille [Rachilde], faisant couper ses magnifiques cheveux, pour les vendre, (cinq francs) à un *prince*, (si ce n'était un coiffeur, c'était donc un prince!) lequel les fait enfermer dans une châsse (dorée, n'est-ce pas?) dont il porte toujours la clef, (sur son coeur, c'est bien certain), tandis que la châsse (mystère et néant des transitions!) reste en dépôt chez un sculpteur de la rue Notre-Dame-des-Champs"(*La Vierge-Réclame* 9–10). D'Estoc exaggerates each element of the legend (the box containing the hair is golden, the prince keeps the key next to his heart) to emphasize the fairy-tale aspects, implying that it is unbelievable, and, indeed, stretched in this way, the story seems to strain credibility.

Even if the part of the story about the prince is apocryphal, however, there remain the assertions that Rachilde cut her hair short and wore it that way for a number of years. Vallette refers to "les cheveux courts que je vous ai toujours vu" (*RHS* 60). Rachilde herself alluded to her short hair on a number of occasions. In the preface to *Madame Adonis* (1888), for example, she wrote: "Si je porte des chapeaux d'homme, c'est que j'ai les cheveux courts, et si j'ai les cheveux courts, c'est que je porte des chapeaux d'hommes" (xi). She also offered the following self-portrait in which she presents herself in the third person as a passerby: "La dame est certainement une personne originale. Elle porte un feutre d'homme sur des cheveux courts, non pas blonds mais oxygénés, des vêtements discrets, de coupe discrète, et sous son bras un livre" ("Remy de Gourmont" in *Portraits d'hommes* 187).

There is no need to review all the cultural associations with women's hair (its associations with luxuriousness in Baudelaire, for example, in Art Nouveau style, and, indeed, even in the work of Rachilde herself) in order to point out that for a woman to cut her hair short—let alone to alter its color, as Rachilde hints in *Madame Adonis*—was in the 1880s a radical action.[2] Even George Sand, who served as a role model in some ways for the confrontational cross-dressed woman writer, did not go this far. But Rachilde implies that a man's hat and short hair always go together. Part of what the examination of Langlois's engraving will suggest is that a man's hat goes with the *appearance* of short hair, but sometimes this is only because the hat can hide the real length of the hair.

Rachilde got a lot of mileage out of the rumor, to which she herself contributed, that she had cut her hair short and wore it short for a period of time. But how much of this was true and how much exaggeration? In his article "Mademoiselle Salamandre," Rachilde's friend Jean Lorrain refers—somewhat dismissively—to the legend about the prince but attaches a date to the story. Lorrain's version of the prince deflates the romance of the story, presenting Rachilde's haircut as a way of calling the prince's bluff: "Il y a aussi l'histoire des cheveux de Rachilde, vendus vingt-cinq louis à un prince russe, qui la veille à souper, avait côté à ce taux le plaisir de les défaire et de les peigner; le lendemain, Rachilde se faisait tondre à la Titus et envoyait la dépouille au boyard, qui faisait la mine mais s'exécutait, hélas! le cher seigneur" (214).

In Lorrain's narrative, Rachilde is the trickster who gets the better of the prince because she takes him at his word, the offer to pay to play with her hair. She sends the hair—but no longer attached to a body. Lorrain follows this story with a series of descriptions of Rachilde, highlighting her changing, paradoxical nature (she is, for example, more than just a "bas-bleu"; she is a "cordon-bleu expert dans l'art d'accommoder les truffes"), then concludes: "Mlle Salamandre, ma seule amie . . . d'alors c'était il y a deux ans en octobre 1886" (215).

Lorrain does not suggest that Rachilde repeatedly cut her hair, only that she once shocked the prince by calling his bluff. Moreover, if this episode took place around October 1886, as Lorrain suggests, it might explain why the portrait (photograph?) that Langlois copied for publication in early 1887 depicts Rachilde with short hair. The Langlois engraving appears to confirm the short-hair image, then, and this is where the question of how much license Langlois took with the portrait becomes relevant.

The fact that the viewer may be willing to see the head as masculinized (man's hat, short hair) may have something to do with the way the picture as a whole is masculinized, so, in order to "read" Langlois's engraving, we must first examine the costume. The question of Rachilde's cross-dressing was raised earlier, and it was argued that, in some ways, Rachilde was always dressing up, playing a role, using elements of costume to create a public persona. In doing so, she played with elements of masculinity and femininity, manipulating public perception in complex ways rather than simply presenting a consistently masculine exterior.

These elements can similarly be seen in Langlois's engraving. Whether or not he changed details of costume (in the way in which van Bever, for example, added the exoticism of a bolero and the dandyish bow), the clothing in which Rachilde is pictured presents a typically ambiguous image. On the one hand, she appears to be wearing a tailored man's jacket; on the other, the masculinity of the jacket is compromised by a number of elements: the soft folds of a garment draped over the subject's right shoulder (a scarf? a coat or cape?); the decorative stud closing the collar and the large, closely spaced, apparently fabric-covered buttons closing the jacket (three buttons are clearly visible even in the short expanse of upper body included in the engraving); and, finally, a leaf-shaped brooch pinned to the subject's left shoulder. All these elements mitigate and soften the masculine cut of the main garment itself, the man's jacket.

But is it even a man's jacket to begin with? A fashion had sprung up for tailored jackets for women, initiated by Alexandra, Princess of Wales, in England and introduced into haute couture (and eventually everyone's couture) by Redfern in 1885 (Deslandres 151). By the last decade and a half of the twentieth century, this *tailleur* had become a staple item of clothing for well-dressed women as well as men, reinforced by women's increased participation in such outdoor sporting activities as riding and, eventually, driving. Perhaps Rachilde's jacket is merely a fashion statement, not a statement about gender.

Those used to reading the gender semiotics of costume will immediately note, however, that Rachilde's jacket seems to button right over left. While this form of closure is a sure sign to the twentieth-century eye that it is a woman's garment, a reading that seems to foreclose on the gender ambiguity of Langlois's engraving, such clarity was not possible in the context of the late-nineteenth-century French clothing industry. Setting aside the possibility that Langlois was working (carelessly) from a photographic image in which left and right had been accidentally reversed, the practice of distinguishing masculine and feminine clothing

by the way in which the garments close was by no means as widely recognized in late-nineteenth-century France as it is today—for a number
of reasons.[3]

The present gender distinction in how (Western) clothes button up
is quite historically specific. It has been theorized that at one time *all*
garments closed right over left, including men's, but that, for various
reasons, men eventually switched to a left-over-right closure (Lester
and Oerlee 481). Whether there was ever such a rigidly codified standard before the twentieth century is debatable, but, by the nineteenth
century, some generalizations are possible: men's garments, it seems,
generally closed left over right, and women's garments modeled on
them (as the *tailleur* would be) also imitated the left-over-right closure.[4]
So long as clothes were hand tailored, however, inconsistencies persisted, and conventions such as closure were unsystematic.

Two factors, both in play at the end of the nineteenth century, contributed to giving semiotic significance to the way clothes fastened. On
the one hand, as Philippe Perrot has argued, the leveling of social distinctions effected through the increasing uniformity of clothing (such
as men's suits) was offset by the attention paid to otherwise insignificant details, which thus became the bearers of subtle social and cultural
meanings (4, 81). This semiotic system was partly created by a second
factor, the increased mass production of clothing—made possible technically by the industrial revolution (which provided the means) and
socially by the French Revolution (which provided the leveling impulse)—that made the same clothing available to everyone. Mass production required standardization, however, and the randomness of detail that might have reflected individual choice when garments were
hand tailored was eliminated: clothes were all made the same way; to be
different was to mean something.

In the United States, for example, mass production led to increasingly rigid closure codes, as Judith Lopez has shown (77), though the
codes were more rigid for men, not surprisingly, and varied for women
depending on the degree of intimacy of the garment: "public" garments
such as daywear or outerwear conformed more rapidly to the new right-
over-left standard than did such "private" garments as underwear and
sleepwear, suggesting the role of the closure distinction in maintaining
the public observance of gender difference in the face of such conver-
gent fashions as the tailored jacket. (Lopez also found a difference between what fashion plates showed and the practices that extant garments of the period indicate were actually followed.)

The woman's tailored jacket was at the nexus of these social and in-

dustrial changes. On the one hand, women continued to wear individ-
ually tailored garments later than did men; therefore, in late nineteenth-
century France, middle-class women's dresses were still likely to be
custom-made even while the middle-class man bought a ready-to-wear
suit (P. Perrot 69), but the *tailleur* explicitly mimicked *male* fashion and
practice.[5] Moreover, as the "unisex" *tailleur* threatened to collapse the
masculine/feminine clothing distinction in a century of increasing sexual dimorphism in clothing (P. Perrot 34), it evoked the same response
as social leveling had done: an increased attention to detail that would
make difference legible once again. Where gender was being erased by
unisex clothing, it was reinscribed through a new binary that linked closure (left over right for men and right over left for women) more em-
phatically to gender.

In short, then, while a left-over-right closure would for various reasons still be inconclusive on a woman's garment in late-nineteenth-
century France, the right-over-left closure of Rachilde's jacket in the
Langlois engraving does seem significant. If she were adopting male
clothing, we would expect the normal left-over-right closure, and, while
an idiosyncratic deviation cannot be ruled out entirely, the right-over-
left closure carries, as it were, "the mark of difference," feminizing an
otherwise masculine — or unmarked — garment.

Once again, what seems like a straightforward case of cross-dressing
is complicated once the details of the picture are read: Rachilde appears
to be cross-dressing by wearing a woman's version of a masculine garment. In the case of this Langlois engraving, the mixed signals of the tailored jacket must be read alongside the equally mixed signals of the
head. On the one hand, the hat conveys a masculinized connotation.
Rachilde highlights it, for example, in the quotation from the preface to
Madame Adonis cited above. But it is also clear from the photographic
record that Rachilde was perfectly capable of combining the masculine
hat with very feminine elements of self-presentation in a kind of tease
that is gender bending yet stops far short of total cross-dressing.

I am referring once again to the series of photographs from around
1895 that served as the basis for the van Bever portrait. Van Bever's interpretation of one of these studio portraits results in an image of
Rachilde that highlights the feminine through the exaggeration of fabrics (brocades, embroidery, ribbons) as well as the sensuous vegetal
imagery of the screen and the darkening of the eyes as though by
makeup. But another of the studio portraits, the full-length photograph
inscribed to Cazals, presents a more ambiguous image. As in the seated
picture, the restrained (masculine) tailoring of the garment is offset by

its full (feminine) sleeves, and it is evident that the garment is indeed a full-length dress. The conventional femininity of the dress is complicated, however, by the man's hat (absent from the seated picture). The combination of elements in this photograph echoes those of the Langlois engraving—a masculine head on what might be feminine shoulders—and hints at what might be visible if the rest of the engraving were included, the femininity of the main garment. By cutting the portrait off at the shoulders, Langlois preserves more of the ambiguity.

Langlois does more than just preserve ambiguity, however, for, according to Vallette once again, he masculinized the portrait of Rachilde. Writing to Rachilde, Vallette comments (of the engraving): "Vous êtes là trop sérieuse, trop *garçon*" (RHS 97–98; emphasis added). Is it going too far to suggest that the element that effects this transformation from ambiguity to "garçon" is the depiction of Rachilde's hair as short and wavy? It is clear from the photograph, for example, that, while Rachilde's hair could be mistaken for short in that photograph, it is in fact only piled up behind (and under?) the hat. In his engraving, Langlois might have taken the illusion of shortness and made it into what passes for fact.

The conclusion to be drawn from such close reading of the iconographic record, then, is not that Rachilde never, in fact, cut her hair (photographs in private collections seem to attest to the fact that she did). Regardless of actual coiffure, however, Rachilde allowed, and even promoted, the image of herself as a short-haired rebel. The image was created through pictures, such as the one discussed here by Langlois, but also by Rachilde's own words (for example, the preface to *Madame Adonis*), and by numerous subtle representations that go unchallenged.

One final example of the iconographic instability of Rachilde's hair can be gleaned from two sketches from 1888 (that is, just one year after the Langlois engraving appeared), one by Paul Verlaine and one by Cazals, both depicting the same "soirée chez Paul Verlaine" (they are reproduced side by side in Ruchon).[6] The sketches are almost identical in many respects: in the foreground are the rounded backs of two chairs and a table with candles, champagne bottles, and glasses; on the left, a man in a frock coat (Henri d'Argis) stands, leaning slightly forward and holding his top hat behind his back, while, seated just in front of him, Jean Moréas sports a monocle and an outrageously pointed moustache. On the right, another monocled, frock-coated figure, also holding a top hat, is evidently holding forth.

The differences between the two sketches seem minimal, but look again at Rachilde, there in the center, half hidden by that most feminine

"Une soirée chez Paul Verlaine" by Verlaine. Rachilde is circled. Reprinted from Ruchon, *Verlaine.*

"Une soirée chez Paul Verlaine" by Cazals. Rachilde is circled. Reprinted from Ruchon, *Verlaine.*

of accoutrements, a fan. Cazals's drawing clearly shows a leg-of-mutton sleeve, but in Verlaine's drawing the puffiness of the sleeve is reduced and the collar clearly drawn in: is this the Rachilde of Langlois's engraving, in a tailored jacket, or the Rachilde of the photographs, in a fashionable dress? And look again at the head: in Verlaine's drawing, there is a hat at a rakish angle perched atop a head, but is that a hat in Cazals's drawing or hair piled up? No other identifiable figure in these sketches seems to exhibit so much instability in representation, not even the only other female figure present, Sophie Harlay.

A passage in *Portraits d'hommes* (1928) in which Rachilde describes her first meeting with Maurice Barrès suggests that it was not just Langlois who confused the categories but that Rachilde herself liked to mix and match. The details of the story allow the reader to situate it as taking place in around 1884.[7] This is the portrait of herself at that time (in the third person) that Rachilde offers: "La dame a l'air d'une petite institutrice pauvre, très sérieuse malgré son évidente jeunesse; robe de laine noire, veste noire de coupe droite; un feutre masculin cache des cheveux courts, une originalité à cette époque et, anomalie, une voilette blanche, très tirée sur le visage" (22). Here, then, is a verbal equivalent of Langlois's portrait, except for the white veil that even Rachilde concedes is an anomaly. Rachilde juxtaposes a feminine, though businesslike, dress (she suggests that it makes her look like a schoolteacher) with a masculine felt hat and the eccentric short hair and, just to confuse the categories a little more, adds a veil to the hat.

Rachilde's addition of the veil provides an objective correlative to the confusion about her hair. The veil is marked within the fashion system as an unambiguous signifier of the feminine. In this semiotic sense, its function is that of revelation, but the ostensible purpose of wearing a veil is concealment. Thus, the item of clothing that serves to conceal (the face) reveals (the gender). This dual nature of the veil makes it the perfect fashion accessory for Rachilde, whose iconography presents a similar undecidability: the garments that reveal (such as the trilby hat that reveals masculinity) also serve to conceal (the disavowed femininity of the hair). The visual evidence concerning Rachilde's appearance, evidence taken to reveal the truth, is found on closer examination to consist of a series of veils that obscure the record.

The Cultural Legitimacy of the Woman Writer

*In which Rachilde's daughter is born and
questions are raised about legitimacy*

When Rachilde married Vallette, a married woman could not legally enter into a contract. In some senses, then, women writers were all operating illegally to the extent that they entered into writing contracts (both in the strict sense of publishing contracts and in the broader sense of the writer-reader contract). By entering into a marriage contract in 1889, Rachilde underscored the illegitimacy of her writing. The strict legal interpretation only served to highlight a sense of illegitimacy that dogged Rachilde even before the question of marriage arose, however. The decision to marry merely extended Rachilde's sense of illegitimacy into yet another realm (some of the issues around Rachilde's sense of "authority" have already been discussed [see "1877: Authority, Authorship, and Authorization"]).

There would be yet another encounter with questions of legitimacy when Rachilde's daughter was born on October 25, 1889.[1] This event extends the consideration of legitimacy from Rachilde's own sense of authority as a writer to the way in which legitimacy may be expressed and mediated through motherhood. Illegitimate offspring always have a mother, but what they lacked in nineteenth century France was a socially recognized, "legitimate" father. (The right to establish paternity by bringing legal suit was an early feminist demand, but that would not be granted until 1912.)

Despite the ambivalence that Rachilde expressed about her own mother, "the angel Gabrielle," when the time came to name her first child, a daughter, Rachilde nevertheless chose to name her after her mother. The decision was neither obvious nor predetermined. Rachilde's parents had christened her Marie-Marguerite, for example, instead of naming her after one of her grandmothers (Jeanne Eymery and Marie-Etiennette Izaline Desmond). Rachilde, on the other hand, chose to emphasize the maternal connection. Given the commonplace about books being an author's children, Rachilde's choice concerning her real child has implications for her literary offspring as well. In both cases, Rachilde strengthens the maternal link to offset the perceived lack of legitimate paternity. Although this strategy will have hidden costs (some of which are discussed here, others in "1900: Women and Education"), the focus here will be on Rachilde's debt to her mother, a debt that has often gone unacknowledged in accounts of her writing but that is tacitly acknowledged in the naming of the child who would become known as Gabrielle Vallette.

The only picture many readers get of Rachilde's mother is that of the madwoman she came increasingly to represent. This is the side Rachilde often emphasizes, for example, in the memories of her mother's unaffectionate behavior that she shared with Auriant (referred to in "1870: The Ambivalence of the Paternal") and in the accounts of increasing instability that emerge from Vallette's letters (see "1885: Marriage and the Woman Writer"). Such later recriminations have covered up the traces of a sense of debt, and a closer reading suggests that Rachilde's mother was a strong, early influence who helped Rachilde launch her career.

Some of the ways Gabrielle Eymery helped her daughter get her start as a writer have already been discussed. Gabrielle's genealogical connections to writers (mythologized connections to writers such as Brantôme as well as real connections to professional writers such as Rachilde's maternal grandfather) were important to Rachilde in viewing and presenting herself as destined to become a writer as well (see "1860: Women as Outsiders"). Gabrielle may have played an important role in providing her daughter with the enabling fiction of the Swedish gentleman "Rachilde" (see "1876: Woman as Medium"), a role that may well extend to being an ally, a "coconspirator" in Rachilde's early writing.[2] This chapter considers some of the other debts that are acknowledged in the naming of Gabrielle Vallette.

Rachilde's memoirs *Quand j'étais jeune* end with the chapter "Une Dangereuse Explication" in which she recounts a conversation with her father. The two discuss why he had wanted to marry her off, his good intentions in wanting to get his daughter away from what he perceived as the dangerous influence of her mother. These memoirs, then, leave the reader with a sense of Rachilde's reconciliation with her father and their complicity against her mother. The final picture, however, freezes the players in this configuration and obscures the ways in which all had assumed different poses and configurations at earlier moments, some of those moments also being recorded in the memoirs.

One such anecdote records how, when Rachilde first began to establish herself as a writer in Paris, she was chaperoned by her mother and it was her mother, and her world of contacts, who first opened the doors to the offices of editors and publishers. Some of these distinguished people would refuse to help, but others would offer important opportunities. In "Chez Villemessant, le directeur du *Figaro*," Rachilde reveals that it was her mother who encouraged her to set her sights higher than regional journalism and to approach the large-circulation Parisian dailies (*QJJ* 130). Her mother took her to Paris to see Villemessant, the editor in chief of *Le Figaro*, and asked him to print one of Rachilde's stories, "Le Chat jaune," in his paper. The experience was excruciatingly embarrassing for Rachilde, and blame for this falls on Gabrielle Eymery for not realizing the seriousness of what she was asking (133), rather than on the condescension of the editor, who cannot remember the young author's name (he refers to her as "Mademoiselle Rachel" [132]) and who mocks her for aspiring to "replace George Sand" (134). The fact remains that it was Gabrielle who encouraged Rachilde to be more than a regional journalist.

Gabrielle Eymery did not succeed in getting "Le Chat jaune" into *Le Figaro*, but she did succeed in getting it republished in a Parisian publication. The story had first appeared in *L'Echo de la Dordogne* on December 2, 1877, and was reprinted twice more in other regional newspapers (in Nontron and Brittany) before being republished in *L'Ecole des femmes* on November 16, 1879 (Soulignac, "Bibliographie" 198–99). *L'Ecole des femmes* was a review founded with the purpose of promoting a quack beauty product, "l'eau de Brahmas," that was advertised and discussed in the magazine (*QJJ* 104–5). The salient feature of the magazine, however, was that it was edited by Rachilde's cousin Madame Marie de Saverny, "une maîtresse femme" (104) who rubbed herself morning and night with the magical Brahmas water in the vain hope of losing weight and who lived in the center of Paris at 11, avenue de l'Opéra. Marie de Saverny, a member of the Feytaud family (that is, a connection on Rachilde's mother's side of the family), became Rachilde's patron, not only letting her publish in the magazine, but also introducing her to important figures such as Sarah Bernhardt.

At first, Rachilde was unaware of the commercial connections of the magazine with which she was so fortunate to have become associated, but she was fully aware of them by the time she wrote her later memoirs. The memoirs thus also reveal that, in addition to providing a foot in the literary door of Parisian publishing, her association with *L'Ecole des femmes* also provided her with an apprenticeship in the world where publishing and advertising overlapped. If *L'Ecole des femmes* taught Rachilde how literature could be co-opted in the interests of advertising, the connections that she made through this experience—such as Sarah Bernhardt—suggested how advertising could also be co-opted in the interests of literature (see "1884: The Politics of Publishing"). Both lessons can thus be indirectly attributed to the role of Gabrielle Eymery, who provided both the literal, family connection to Marie de Saverny as well as the encouragement to exploit that connection.[3]

The memoirs *Quand j'étais jeune* provide explicit ways to trace Rachilde's early successes as a writer to her mother, but other links are also suggested in allusions that are not as developed. Rachilde tells us, for example, that "il était entendu que j'irais à Paris tous les ans, en attendant ma majorité" (*QJJ* 103), making it clear that her connections to the Parisian world of letters began well before her definitive move to Paris.[4] The statement neglects to mention, however, that she would have been continuously chaperoned by her mother during this time; Gabrielle thus invested considerable time and effort in her daughter's career. The two were a familiar sight, calling on one editor after another. Gabrielle was also supportive in other ways. Rachilde's book of press cuttings shows that, when "Marguerite Eymery" wrote to a newspaper in around 1884 wanting to found a charitable organization for women promising not to leave Paris during the cholera epidemic, the first person to write in and join was a "Mme Gabrielle E . . ." of 23, quai de la Tournelle.

The traces of Rachilde's early reliance on her mother are legible in these details as well as in the note of forgiveness and understanding that characterizes her memoirs. Although the following was written in the context of a chapter on her father ("Un Héros de roman"), it is clearly about "parents" in the plural: "On ne connaît bien ses parents que lorsque, les ayant perdus, on atteint leur âge, et qu'ils vous reviennent à l'esprit comme des remords, des regrets de les avoir mal jugés, ou comme des signes d'une vie antérieure qu'on n'a pas pu comprendre, parce qu'on était sans aucune expérience de la valeur d'une âme toujours fermée à une autre âme" (*QJJ* 66).

In 1889, Rachilde had not yet lost her mother, but she had attained the age of motherhood. Although Rachilde became a mother at an older age than her mother did (Rachilde was twenty-nine, Gabrielle twenty-two), there were similarities in their respective situations: both had a daughter, both would have only one child. In becoming a mother herself, Rachilde perhaps gained some insight into her own mother's problems. It seems more than mere coincidence that it is when she marries and becomes a mother that Rachilde (as she herself notes) stops cross-dressing and settles down ("Chronologie" 14). (And, whether or not this is the moment that she really stops cross-dressing, what matters is that this is the moment that she *identifies* as marking the end of her cross-dressing and short hair.) In a word, when Rachilde became the mother of her daughter, Gabrielle, she became her mother's mother as well. With the birth of Gabrielle (Vallette), it indeed appeared, as Gaubert put it, that "La légende de l'amazone s'éteignait au seuil du foyer. L'histoire de Rachilde n'était plus que celle de ses livres" (17).

The birth of Gabrielle was paralleled by the birth of the literary review *Le Mercure de France*, however, a sign that physical and literary offspring were somehow inseparable for Rachilde in a way that they had not been for her mother. The *Mercure* was born at around the same time as Gabrielle: the first issue appeared on December 25, 1889 (two months to the day after Gabrielle's arrival). The founders were Albert Aurier, Jean Court, Louis Denise, Edouard Dubus, Louis Dumur, Remy de Gourmont, Julien Leclerq, Ernest Raynaud, Jules Renard, Albert Samain, and Alfred Vallette. The journal was so successful that, within four years, and at a time of retrenchment in the publishing industry, it became a publishing house that survives today: "En mars 1894, M. Vallette transformait sa revue en société anonyme et lui adjoignait une maison d'éditions qui faisait aussi de la commission. Vers la fin de cette année, un roman de Pierre Louÿs, *L'Esclavage*, refusé par la *Revue blanche* fut publié par le *Mercure de France*. Sur le conseil de M. Vallette, quand le roman parut en librairie, Louÿs en changea le titre en celui d'*Aphrodite*" (Auriant, *Souvenirs* 40). According to Lesage, Oriol, and Soulignac: "*Aphrodite* . . . extraordinairement vendu—plus de 68 éditions (au moins 34,000 volumes) à la fin de 1896—permettra à la Société du Mercure de France de se lancer véritablement. *Aphrodite*, sous son titre primitif de *L'Esclavage*, parut en livraisons dans les numéros 68 à 72 août-décembre 1895, de la revue" (Lesage and Soulignac, eds., *Lettres à A.-Ferdinand Herold* 26).

The date actually printed on the first issue of the *Mercure* was fudged, however. The review in fact made its appearance in late 1889, but the cover bore the date January 1890. Partly, this was to make it coincide with the new decade, the 1890s, which seemed to promise new developments, but, given the pairing of offspring (journal and child), the delay in the date of the review also carried over to the child. Thus, although Gabrielle was in fact born in 1889, the delay situates the moment of her birth in the more socially acceptable year of 1890. Gaubert, for example, correctly states that Rachilde married Vallette in 1889, but he then adds (in the same sentence) that "the next year" Vallette founded the *Mercure de France*. When Gaubert writes in the following paragraph "La même année naissait leur fille Gabrielle," it then seems as though he is referring to the "same year" as the founding of the journal (1890) rather than the "same year" as the wedding (Gaubert 16–17).

The traces of the help that Gabrielle Eymery may have tried to provide for her daughter can be difficult to discern. The reader of Rachilde's fiction is more often aware of the erasure of mothers and maternal figures. While military fathers abound, mothers are either entirely absent or else killed off in the course of the narrative, as though Rachilde were taking revenge through her fiction and erasing all traces of Gabrielle (Eymery). Some of the reasons for Rachilde's anger at her mother are not hard to understand. While Gabrielle provided an important symbolic connection to writing and may have offered tangible help in the early years of Rachilde's career, these advantages were overshadowed by the madness that would overtake her in later years and that undid all the good she had tried to do. Other aspects of Gabrielle Eymery's mental illness will be explored later (see "1900: Women and Education"), but one anecdote will suffice to show here the ways in which Gabrielle also undercut her daughter's writing career.

It was noted earlier that Rachilde's discovery of the empowering fiction of the position of the medium would come back to haunt her. Once again, this is a story that she tells in *Quand j'étais jeune*. Immediately after describing her mother's embarrassing intervention in taking her to see Villemessant, the editor of *Le Figaro*, Rachilde recounts another visit to a publisher, this time Dentu, who had published her first novel, *Monsieur de la Nouveauté*, and whom she regarded as a father figure. As benevolent adviser, Dentu felt obliged to tell her that rumors were circulating to the effect that her work was plagiarized, that she was not the real author of the novels she was selling. Dentu himself had received a visit from the lady who had started the rumors, who seemed perfectly credible.

Rachilde racked her brains trying to think of who might betray her in this way (she immediately thought of rival writers such as Georges de Peyrebrune, Camille Delaville, and Marc de Montifaud), but when Dentu mentioned that the lady was very well connected and had been a schoolgirl friend of the wife of the astronomer Camille Flammarion, the truth began to dawn. Rachilde pressed the publisher for a description of the person and recognized in his verbal portrait her own mother. All too quickly, Rachilde realized that her mother had come to believe only too well the story that "Rachilde" was really a Swedish gentleman from the spirit world who dictated stories to "Marguerite." Whether "the angel Gabrielle" was motivated by jealousy of her daughter, or troubled by a guilty conscience, or motivated by some entirely different concern, the effect was a direct threat to Rachilde's literary success in these early days of her career.

In 1886, Rachilde had been hesitating between two possible futures, like her heroine in *A mort*. Seductive bohemian aristocrats like Bryon/Barrès symbolized one set of possibilities—passion, notoriety, marginality—while steady bourgeois companions like Vallette seemed to offer a safer route: a steady, respectable future, without glamour. Wrestling with these choices, Rachilde had had to confront the question of literary legitimacy. She wanted to belong to the literary family of writers, a family composed largely of men, but she did not want to be related to them merely by marriage. In this desire, she came up against culturally imposed assumptions that intellectual activity was inherently male. Even her mother, it turned out, believed that only men could write and that her daughter was only a passive medium. That her mother should have tried to undermine her early writing career seems predictable when read in the light of these stereotypes. Although it was through her mother's side of the family that Rachilde traced her literary heritage, then, women themselves could do nothing to legitimize her career since they had been traditionally excluded from the literary family. Rachilde had been led to think that a legitimate connection to writing could pass through the maternal line, but it turned out that legitimacy was conferred only by the father.

Rachilde had imitated some of her literary foremothers. She had cross-dressed like George Sand, for example, but she also shared more with Sand than she perhaps realized. In a chapter devoted to Sand's self-representation in the autobiographical *Histoire de ma vie*, Béatrice Didier notes how, for Sand, "Des le depart, l'identite etait ebranlee par un conflit violent entre la branche paternelle et la branche maternelle" (190). Marie Maclean considers the way in which women writers, particularly French women writers of the nineteenth century such as Flora Tristan and Louise Michel, embraced illegitimacy, symbolized by the name of the mother, as a way of claiming a public voice. Maclean devotes an entire chapter to Sand, whose expressed relationship to her mother anticipates so many of the elements already noted in Rachilde's representation of the family constellation (see also Didier 190–91, 205).

Perhaps by the time Gabrielle Vallette was born in 1889 Rachilde believed that her mother's mental illness could be controlled. Perhaps the gesture of naming her daughter after her mother was intended as appeasement or to effect a reconciliation. If so, the gesture would fail: Gabrielle Eymery's condition would continue to worsen until medical intervention was necessary. But, whatever the intent, the birth of Gabrielle Vallette marks an important moment. Part of what Rachilde found frightening about her mother, part of what made Rachilde want to reject her mother, was that she was so much like her. Like her, then, she too might go mad, and Rachilde often wrote of this fear (both directly and through allusions to the curse of the werewolf and her "lunatic" disposition). Rachilde's entry into the state of motherhood echoed some of the similarities: Rachilde settled into the role of what Simone de Beauvoir would later describe as "une jeune fille rangée." At the same time, however, Rachilde took charge by reversing the mother-daughter role. Rachilde was now the mother and Gabrielle the daughter.

Gabrielle Vallette's birth also signaled Rachilde's continued commitment to writing. I have stressed throughout how writing was conceived of as an illegitimate activity in a number of ways by Rachilde, and this chapter has shown in particular how the deliberate obscuring of dates created a parallel between the birth of Gabrielle and the literary offspring of the Vallette-Eymery marriage, *Le Mercure de France*. The confusion about dates can be read as making Gabrielle legitimate, but it can also be read as making *Le Mercure* somehow illegitimate. Biographers stress that Gabrielle's birth and the birth of the review took place in the same year but displace the event to 1890, thereby masking the illegitimacy. Recovering the illegitimacy of the birth of Gabrielle, conceived out of wedlock, raises the question of what it would mean for Rachilde's role in the *Mercure de France* to be viewed as "conceived out of wedlock" also.

In *Tender Geographies*, Joan DeJean offers an answer, noting: "At least from the time of the widow Sévigné to that of the divorcée George Sand [whose role as a model for Rachilde has already been suggested] French women's writing has most often been conceived out of wedlock" (109). Entering into a married state, Rachilde reasserted the fundamental illegitimacy of women's writing by giving birth to a child conceived out of wedlock and linking the birth of that child to the foundational moment of a literary review. DeJean points to the fact that marriage often impeded women's writing (most women wrote outside marriage), but Rachilde's situation highlights the inescapability of illegitimacy for women writers.

Illegitimacy (works "born" out of wedlock) was a powerful metaphor for women writers, as Maclean suggests in *The Name of the Mother*, but in part the metaphor was socially imposed since legitimacy (through marriage) was unattainable: the married woman ceased legally to exist; a woman could not (legally) sign a contract such as a book contract; she could not sign her married name to a book without her husband's permission (Juliette Adam's husband had brought suit to have "his" named removed from the cover of a book). In short, it was impossible to be both a married woman and a *legitimate* woman writer. Despite the fact that Rachilde was entering into what appeared to be a state of social legitimation, the birth of Gabrielle Vallette and its link to the literary activity represented by the *Mercure*, then, merely serve to underscore the continued illegitimacy of Rachilde's (literary) situation.

Imagining the Self

In which Rachilde's first play is performed
and some mirrors are looked into

In addition to being at the forefront of movements such as decadence, Rachilde was at the forefront of symbolist theater in France, and some have gone so far as to suggest that she was the only "domestic" symbolist playwright. Moreover, the symbolist movement of the 1890s is credited with the creation of an avant-garde in France, both in the sense of an avant-garde movement in the arts in general (leading to such international and interdisciplinary phenomena as surrealism and abstract art) and in the more specific sense of the theatrical avant-garde movements that would flourish in the twentieth century such as Antoine Artaud's theater of cruelty and the theater of the absurd. As one of the principal figures of the symbolist movement, then, Rachilde is also one of the founding members of the French avant-garde.

Theater was the most popular form of mass entertainment throughout the nineteenth century, and it flourished in Paris, especially in the 1880s and 1890s, as developments in mass transportation brought more and more people to the city in search of distractions. In addition to such established theaters as the Comédie-Française, the 1890s saw the beginning of a fringe movement that changed the direction of theater history. This avant-garde introduced new Scandinavian dramatists such as Strindberg and Ibsen to French audiences as well as new staging techniques. Through their innovations, they influenced not just the content of plays but the entire theatrical experience: a night at the theater changed from being a social event to an art performance.

One of the first innovators and developers of fringe theater was André Antoine, an amateur producer. After gaining experience in this capacity, he decided to begin producing new plays and founded the Théâtre libre, which gave its first performance on March 30, 1887, and flourished until 1893. Because it functioned as a private club (seats were by subscription), Antoine was not always consistently regulated by the censor, and he was therefore able to mount productions of quite controversial plays. Antoine challenged the conventions that predominated in mainstream theater and proposed the injection of realism into set design, acting, language, and subject matter.

Antoine's Théâtre libre was primarily identified with naturalism, however, while symbolism had been headed in a less and less realist direction for over a decade. Paul Fort, for example, had started the Théâtre mixte, another amateur company, which gave its first production in the rue Condorcet in 1890, followed by another varied program at the Théâtre Beaumarchais later that year. Fort had been working with Louis Germain, founder of Théâtre idéaliste, but when Germain dropped out (in November 1890), Fort changed the name to the Théâtre d'art and stayed on as its director. On Wednesday, November 10, 1890, the company staged Rachilde's one-act play *La Voix du sang* (Robichez, *Symbolisme au théâtre* 86–92).

Rachilde's role in symbolist theater begins with this play and with Paul Fort's Théâtre d'art. Along with its successor, Lugné-Poe's Théâtre de l'oeuvre, the Théâtre d'art was responsible for changing the face of theater in France. Between them, these two troupes promoted Scandinavian drama (principally Ibsen, but also Strindberg); they transformed theatergoing from a form of entertainment to an aesthetic experience; they pioneered techniques of synaesthesia by combining music, lighting, and perfume as part of the performance; they involved painters whose work would transform art theory (such as Gauguin, Toulouse-Lautrec, and Munch); they brought important and influential works such as Maeterlinck's *Pelléas and Mélisande* and Wilde's *Salomé* to the stage for the first time; and last but not least they acted as midwife for the birth of one of the most important figures in the pantheon of the grotesque, Alfred Jarry's Ubu. The symbolist theater movement was one of the most innovative in theater history, and Rachilde was at the center of the ferment, offering vehicles to further the experiment and advising those who made it happen.

Although Antoine's Théâtre libre had opened the door to innovation, Paul Fort's Théâtre d'art had almost no precedent. The troupe broke with tradition and reinvented theatrical practice. Theater historian Jacques Robichez would summarize the value of this short-lived theater as "une expérience manquée mais féconde" (*Symbolisme au théâtre* 141). Fort was barely out of high school. Rachilde knew him from the literary circles of the 1880s; they had both worked on *Le Décadent*, for example, and frequented the same literary *cénacles*, and he would later become family (Rachilde's daughter would marry his nephew). This last development was still a long way off in 1890, but it takes little effort to imagine how Rachilde's literary connections extended naturally into an intimate involvement in the Théâtre d'art.

The short *La Voix du sang* was only a one-act play (dedicated to Paul

Fort when it was published the following year), but it was by a writer who by then enjoyed notorious popularity and who would serve as a drawing card for the new theater. The troupe operated on a shoestring budget at the best of times, but its mode of financing performances made it especially dependent on reputation. Like Antoine's theater, it ran on subscription rather than receipts collected at the door, meaning that most patrons bought a season ticket ahead of time on the basis of what the theater promised to offer.[1] There were usually only two performances of each program, so, no matter how outstanding the play or the performance, there was almost no opportunity to profit from it by long runs to sold-out houses as in more commercial ventures. In this context, Rachilde's involvement gave important assistance to the new theater (the free *coupe-papier* [letter opener] offered to critics who attended the first performance could be expected to exert only moderate influence).

La Voix du sang obviously could not fill an entire evening. As was typical of symbolist theater, it formed part of a program of varied events that included poetry readings as well as plays. On the inaugural evening of Wednesday, November 10, 1890, there were five items on the program. The opening and closing events were dramatic scenes—"Sur la lisière d'un bois" and "Les Gueux"—adapted from *Théâtre en liberté* by Victor Hugo (of course). In between were three plays: Jules Méry's *Morized* (a Breton-inspired "mystère en deux tableaux"), Alexis Martin's *Le Débat du coeur et de l'estomac* (a medievalistic farce), and *La Voix du sang*. There was also a recital of Mallarmé's poem "Le Guignon" by Georgette Camée, who would go on to become one of the principal interpreters of symbolist drama (until she married Paul Pottecher and left Paris to join him in running a provincial theater troupe).

The members of the Théâtre d'art did not expect to be hailed by the establishment critics, and in this they were not disappointed, but they were sufficiently encouraged by the reception of the first program to continue their efforts.[2] In January 1891, both Rachilde and Vallette joined the play selection committee of the theater, along with a number of other *confrères* (including Jules Méry, whose play had shared the bill with *La Voix du sang*, Saint-Pol-Roux, and Jules Renard), committing themselves further to its success. The theater's next offering was a French translation of Shelley's *The Cenci* on January 16 (which lasted for six hours, according to Rachilde).

The Cenci was not a success, but it captured the attention of the critics all the same. Among those whose interest was aroused was Aurélien Lugné-Poe, then a young actor in Antoine's company who shared a studio with a group of artists that included Paul Gauguin (grandson of the socialist feminist writer Flora Tristan, another woman who struggled with issues of illegitimacy [see Maclean]). Thanks to this connection, Fort was able to announce in January 1891 that, starting in March, each of the performances of the Théâtre d'art would end with the display of a painting representing the work of the new school. The curtains would be raised for three minutes, and the display would be accompanied by occasional music and the release of perfume corresponding to the subject of the painting.[3] These intentions were never realized, but they serve as an early signal of the ambitious changes in aesthetics that the theater sought to implement (Robichez, *Symbolisme au théâtre* 112–13).

By February, Fort had moved further into the avant-garde and away from the theater's *mixte*— or eclectic— origins, pronouncing that, henceforth, the Théâtre d'art would become "resolutely symbolist." The next production was announced as the last of the nonsymbolist programs, but in fact it already showed symbolist influences (Robichez, *Symbolisme au théâtre* 113). It ran from Thursday, March 19, to Friday, March 20, 1891, on the rented stage of the Théâtre moderne. Friday's program included Rachilde's "cerebral drama in 3 acts," *Madame la Mort* (a work later admired by Franz Kafka [see Dauphiné, *Rachilde* [1991] 156).

The spring of 1891 has been referred to as the "heure privilégiée" by one historian of symbolism (quoted in Robichez, *Symbolisme au théâtre* 19), and, in his memoirs of the symbolist period, Ernest Raynaud described 1891 as the "date heureuse" of symbolism, as its "phase héroïque," analogous to the early days of Romanticism: "L'air est chargé d'une odeur de poudre et d'une rumeur de bataille comme à la veille d'*Hernani*" (2:5). The evening of March 20, when *Madame la Mort* premiered, was that kind of evening, the kind of spectacle associated with theatrical innovation, characterized by upheaval and dissension in the audience. Also on the program was a Mallarmean "passion play" by Pierre Quillard entitled *La Fille aux mains coupés*, a somewhat bizarre presentation (the poem was recited slowly and monotonously behind a muslin screen), but one well received by the critics for its novelty; Paul Gabillard's *Les Veilleuses*, which made little impression at all; and Chirac's *La Prostituée*, about a woman selling herself to feed her children, a work that was intended as a satire on realist theater but that ended up stimulating support for Zola and the naturalists (it also led to a quarrel between Fort and his reading committee, including Rachilde and Vallette). In other words, the evening contained both successes and failures, but even the failures provoked debate, strong reactions for and against, the stuff drama history is made of, and ensured that the evening would be memorable (Robichez, *Symbolisme au théâtre* 113–17).

The program for these performances was designed by Paul Gauguin and Paul Sérusier.[4] The former, still relatively unknown, worked very closely with the Théâtre d'art until his departure for Tahiti in April 1891, designing sets as well as programs, and was one of the conduits through which ideas flowed back and forth between the "Nabis" and those working on developing symbolist theater. While the most famous of the Nabis would be Gauguin, the group also included a number of major postimpressionist painters who shaped the direction of twentieth-century art, such as Edouard Vuillard and Paul Bonnard.

Another member of the group, Maurice Denis, had been at school with Lugné-Poe and had shared rooms with both Lugné-Poe and Sérusier. In 1890, under the pseudonym Pierre Louis, Denis had published articles about painting in the new art review *Art et critique* in which he advocated thinking about a painting as a flat, two-dimensional surface with color rather than primarily as a representation of three-dimensional reality (see Robichez, *Symbolisme au théâtre* 105–9). This was a revolutionary concept in painting, the full importance of which can perhaps be appreciated only in retrospect, given the knowledge of how painting would develop as a nonrepresentational medium in the twentieth century.

Gauguin was not quite as involved in the theater as some of his friends were—partly because of his departure for Tahiti—but he was nevertheless part of the milieu. On May 21, the Théâtre d'art gave a performance to benefit him and Verlaine jointly in the Théâtre du vaudeville, during which his paintings were on display in the lobby of the theater. The profits were small, and in the end Gauguin got nothing and Verlaine only two hundred francs, but the exposure of his work was no small service. Gauguin's stature as a painter is so well established today that it is hard to remember that, in 1891, the Théâtre d'art was doing him a favor by being associated with him, rather than the other way around.[5] Again, however, the point is also to note that Rachilde was quietly involved in shaping events that would transform the arts in dramatic ways.

In the meantime, Fort's innovations continued. December 11, 1891, saw the performance of the biblical *Cantique des cantiques* by Paul-Napoléon Roinard, with music and perfume, a pinnacle of symbolist experimentation. Fort did not have a good head for finances, however, and the Théâtre d'art could not keep going.[6] Its last performance was given on March 30, 1892. After ambitiously beginning rehearsals of

Maeterlinck's *Pelléas and Mélisande*, Fort was forced to abandon his work. Fortunately, his replacement, Aurélien Lugné-Poe, was ready to take over the leadership of symbolist theater and inaugurate a new theater—the Théâtre de l'oeuvre—with Maeterlinck's masterpiece.

Once again, Rachilde's hand was at work shaping events. On February 15, 1893, she wrote to Lugné-Poe, expressing her support for his decision in language akin to Hugo's: "J'apprends, Monsieur Lugné-Poe, par Paul Fort, que vous avez bien compris que la représentation de *Pelléas et Mélisande* était, même si la réalisation n'atteignait pas à la perfection, pour le *Théâtre d'Art* la porte de la gloire et que vous êtes décidé à nous l'ouvrir tout entière avec le plus absolu dévouement littéraire. Soyez remercié par le plus fervent admirateur de Maurice Maeterlinck et maintenant adoptons la devise de notre courageuse directrice: En avant!" (Lugné-Poe 1:225–26). This is not the last time that Rachilde would steer Lugné-Poe's decisions (she would do so again, most notably in the case of the staging of Jarry's *Ubu roi*, but that case is so well documented that I need not dwell on it here). Rachilde was also among those whose subscriptions made the play possible, and *Pelléas et Mélisande* was duly offered on May 17, 1893.[7]

Lugné-Poe carried on the work begun by Paul Fort and founded his own professional group, the Théâtre de l'oeuvre. Rachilde had played her part as playwright and reviewer in helping establish symbolist theater,[8] theater that familiarized the public with names such as Strindberg and Ibsen, theater that brought *Ubu roi* and laid the foundations for modern developments, theater that changed how the audience watches.

This last factor is worth dwelling on. The twin changes of dimming the house lights and changing the design of the stage brought theater closer to the twentieth-century experience of viewing films. Symbolist plays were among the first mass art forms where the audience sat in the dark and all directed their attention not to each other but to something resembling a screen. If film activates the scopic pleasures of voyeurism, this mode of viewing had its origins in symbolist theater.[9] The philosophical idealism of symbolism made it more introspective than melodrama or classical drama. This kind of introspection is evident in Rachilde's plays, such as *Madame la Mort*, *La Voix du sang*, and *Le Vendeur du soleil*, and, in the following analysis of her work, in particular of *L'Araignée de cristal* (first performed in 1894), I am suggesting that Rachilde used symbolist drama as a vehicle for the exploration of psychic issues in the same way that cinematographers would later use the medium of film.

Rachilde became as involved in Lugné-Poe's Théâtre de l'oeuvre as she had been in Fort's Théâtre d'art, and, as she had done earlier, she continued to have her work performed by the symbolists. This was the case for the one-act play *L'Araignée de cristal*, adapted from a short story in dialogue that had been published in the *Mercure de France* in June 1892 (and subsequently collected in *Le Démon de l'absurde* in 1894), which was performed by the Théâtre de l'oeuvre at the Bouffes du nord on February 13, 1894, with Lugné-Poe himself in the lead role of the terror-stricken Sylvius.[10]

This short, one-act play (dedicated to Jules Renard) is symbolist in being virtually nonnarrative (symbolist theater was nonnarrative in a way that paralleled the nonrepresentational aspects of avant-garde painting). It consists entirely of a dialogue between a young man of twenty and his mother (her age is given as forty-five). The young man is referred to in stage directions throughout the play as *l'épouvanté*, which is usually translated as "terror stricken," although the connotations of the French also suggest the abjecting power of horror, but his mother consistently calls him by his name, Sylvius. This given name resonates with that of other Rachildian heroes and antiheroes, such as Sylvain de Hauterac (*La Sanglante Ironie*), Jacques Silvert (*Monsieur Vénus*), and Silvie de Givray (*L'Autre crime*), suggesting links between Sylvius and other characters in the Rachildian universe. Several other works by Rachilde open with characters looking in mirrors (*Les Hors-Nature*, for example, and *La Jongleuse*), but, in *L'Araignée de cristal*, the mirror becomes the main focus of the work.

The use of the mirror as a device in decadent and symbolist work has already been noted (see, for example, Winn 72–76). The motif illustrates the narcissism of the hero and can also be used as a device to create a double, an evil twin through whom the darker, irrational side of the self that Freud was just beginning to expose could be explored. (Freud had come to Paris to study with Charcot in October 1885, and his publications in the 1890s would begin to give form to intellectuals' lack of confidence in positivism.)[11] Rachilde's use of the mirror in her fiction is consistent with these patterns, but it also genders the problems of identity represented in and by the mirror, as an analysis of *L'Araignée de cristal* will show.

The play begins with a demand on the part of the mother for access to the psyche of her child: "Voyons, petit fils, à quoi penses-tu?" Sylvius, clearly in the grip of some melancholy, is thin and wasted, with a fixed stare and a morbid disposition, which seems to prompt his mother's concern. She presses him for an explanation (Does he have a migraine? Is he in love? Is he worried about debts?), and he finally confesses that the cause of his dis-ease is a fear of mirrors.

On the one hand, then, in this play Rachilde extends her decadent preoccupation with pathology, exploring yet another phobia. Yet symbolism consistently uses the power of suggestion in order to access that which cannot be expressed in normal language, the fear of mirrors therefore also standing for something more complicated and indirect, as indeed proves to be the case with Sylvius. His fear is, among other things, gendered: for his mother and other "intelligent women," the reflections in a mirror are a "chose simple" in the sense of not complicated but also in the sense of singular, not plural (20).[12]

For Sylvius, this is not the case. He explains that his fear goes back to an incident of childhood trauma that, in a postmodern psychoanalytic interpretation, reveals the fragmentation at the core of his identity. In a long speech, he reveals how, when he was ten years old, he had been locked in a summerhouse to do his homework. His mind wandered, however, and he found himself staring at a mirror that hung on the wall. At first, the mirror was like a lake, and an extended comparison ensues.

The water imagery here might seem to suggest that Rachilde is evoking the mythological figure of Narcissus, who fell in love with his own reflection in water and has come to stand in modern psychology for self-love and egocentrism, but, though there is a later reference to Narcissus, Sylvius does not fall in love with his reflection; rather, it scares him to death. Rachilde is evoking a female, not a male, figure, then, that of Psyche, who represents the soul or inner being and for whom the whole enterprise of psychology is named. Psyche also gives her name in French to a full-length mirror, the object to which one looks to see one's "real" (or inner) self and that forms the centerpiece of the play's set: "Au centre de cette demi-obscurité, une haute glace psyché de style empire, maintenue de chaque côté par de longs cols de cygnes à becs de cuivre" (13).

The special property of water, then, is that, like a mirror, it reveals the self. The watery surface of the mirror Sylvius saw in childhood reflected "specters" and reminded him that he was trapped, locked in a small room as though locked in his own mind ("On m'avait enfermé à clé" [22]). Forced to contemplate himself, he sees at first "un point brillant au milieu de ces brumes" (22), but, as he watches, he begins to see lines that radiate out from this point and gradually come to look like a spider, a crab, an octopus. The vision becomes a nightmare in which the creature reaches out to him and sucks out his brain.

Just at the point when the terror becomes unbearable, the mirror shatters, and Sylvius faints. When he comes to, the gardener explains the prosaic cause of the traumatic vision: he had been hammering a nail into the wall of the garden shed on the other side of the summerhouse.

The nail had accidentally gone right through both walls and shattered the mirror, hence the image of the cracks in the mirror like the legs of a huge spider (which gives its name to the play) and Sylvius's shattered nerves.

Despite the logical (if far-fetched) explanation, Sylvius continues to see the experience as an encounter with inner identity and has been frightened of mirrors ever since. He is convinced that his mother has put reflective surfaces all over the apartment just to persecute him. He sees mirrors everywhere—in oceans, rivers, and streams, even in drinking glasses—all of which conspire to torment him. The mother-child confrontation ends in violence as the dark psychic forces put into play continue to obsess the mind of the unfortunate Sylvius. When his mother insists on having light and orders Sylvius to fetch a lamp, he smashes (into) the mirror (the "psyche") in the middle of the room and slits his throat (the text does not specify whether this is intentional or accidental) with or on the broken glass.

The eight-legged spider of the play's title is a displacement of another eight-legged beast, the octopus, and the mirror is only one example of a series of reflective surfaces that includes water. In certain ways, then, the story of Sylvius and the mirror turns out to be another version of the childhood nightmare of the pond and the *noyé*: a watery male figure upsets the mental stability of the self and threatens silence. Yet, at the same time that the play evokes a familiar set of associations, it also adds another layer to the story. Rachilde's use of the striking and original image of a broken mirror as a spider to convey the sense of terror adds to the network of images already in play and underscores the centrality of the play in her career. The threat here comes, not from external sources (such as patriarchy), but from a version of the self, and the threat is mediated, not through the figure of the father, but through the that of the mother.

L'Araignée de cristal represents what happens when the (female) writer internalizes the threat of the *noyé*. Rachilde comments on the role of the mirror in her "coming to writing" in *Quand j'étais jeune*. If the vision of a coherent self as glimpsed in a mirror is what gives the subject an image—albeit illusory—of an identity, as Lacan has suggested, then the sudden and unexpected fragmentation of that image such as Sylvius experiences could destabilize that image just as easily. Once the coherent identity is split apart and replaced by an image of fragmentation, Sylvius cannot function as a subject. Where modern psychoanalysts such as Lacan see the mirror as that which consolidates an image of identity, in *L'Araignée de cristal* Rachilde makes the mirror the instrument that undoes identity, that reveals, rather than disguises, fragmentation. Mirrors show monsters characterized by multiplicity and proliferation (spiders, crabs, octopuses with their many legs); mirrors frighten because they show that what should be "simple" (easy and singular) in the psyche is really complex (complicated and plural).

To understand more fully the terrifying implications of this breakdown, we must read Sylvius as yet another aspect of Rachilde's self-representation. It is in this context that Sylvius's gender anxiety associated with mirrors makes sense. Mirrors reveal to him, not only that he is fragmented, not whole, but also that parts of him are not male at all. One of the ways in which Sylvius is plural in this text is that he has a female cousin (double), Sylvia. For Sylvius, the mirror represents (shows him) "la délation personnifiée" (28), the very personification of betrayal, a female allegory.

I shall argue later (see "1900: Women and Education") that part of what was discomforting about mirrors for the woman *writer* (as opposed to women in general, or "mothers and other intelligent women." as this play calls them) was that they insistently revealed the reality of a female self after the writer had taken such pains to establish a male authorial persona. For now, let me again note the gendered fear of mirrors in this play: it is only men who are troubled by them, while women *become* them: "Des femmes, des jeunes filles, des créatures qui ont toutes au fond des yeux des reflets de miroirs" (18).

In a chapter on Virginia Woolf (a woman writer who would succumb to the injunction to silence herself and who would succeed in the suicide by drowning that Rachilde merely rehearsed) in *L'Écriture-Femme*, Béatrice Didier notes the symbolically weighted recurrence of mirrors in Woolf's work, particularly of moments where looking in the mirror is associated with guilt, which is in turn linked to autobiography or self-presentation and a dream in which Woolf looked in the mirror and saw an animal's face looking back over her shoulder: "Lorsque la femme se regarde dans le miroir, elle ne parvient pas à se voir seule. Lui apparaît l'Autre: monstre, ennemi, animal—en tout cas terreur" (228). Didier speculates that the search for identity represented by the mirror may be more complicated for women than for men "dans la mesure précisément où la situation de son identité par rapport à la société et par rapport à son propre corps n'est pas la même que s'il s'agissait d'un homme" (229).

To be sure, such trouble with mirrors is not exclusive to women writers. The scene in Guy de Maupassant's short story "Le Horla" in which the first-person narrator is shocked to look in the mirror and see no reflection at all is an excellent example of a writer's fear of becoming invisible, both personally and as a writer in the world.[13] Yet Maupassant's hero attributes his problem to external vampiristic forces, making his work part of the fin-de-siècle literature that projects fear onto the figure of the foreigner or stranger rather than the internal workings of the writer's psyche. (Rachilde's post–World War I contribution to vampire literature, in contrast, will turn out to involve the domestic forces of traditional gender roles.)

For the woman writer at the turn of the century, on the other hand, the threat need not come from outside; one need look no further than the values of domestic culture, the values internalized to some degree by all members of the society, to perceive the potential conflicts in combining the aspirations of a writer with the social roles prescribed for women. It is not surprising, then, that mirrors figure so frequently in Rachilde's work. From *L'Araignée de cristal* to *La Tour d'amour* (discussed in "1900: Women and Education") to the motherless Eliante Donalger, who checks herself confidently and publicly (though discreetly) in the mirror at the beginning of *La Jongleuse*, the mirror is an important source of information, either disruptive or reassuring but always relevant.[14] The mirror tells the writer how she appears to the outside world. In the fin-de-siècle world of incipient advertising where appearance would come to play such a dominant role, the woman writer was coming to terms with the disjunctions between her public and her private images of self.

The problem of the mirror also involves gender by staging the mother-daughter relationship. Here, however, the problem is one of sexual sameness, not sexual difference. As Marianne Hirsch puts it, "The heroine who wants to write, or who wants in any way to be productive or creative . . . must break from her mother, so as not to be identified with maternal silence" (45). Sylvius's problems all derive somehow from his *mother*. It is the mother's initial interrogation that triggers Sylvius's narrative and her order to fetch lamps that leads to his death. In some senses, then, it would appear that the mother is to blame. At one point, what Sylvius sees in the mirror is his mother, so, if the mirror reveals to us our inner self, then part of Sylvius's fear is that his inner self is his mother.

In the context of Rachilde's fear of inheriting her mother's madness, sharing an identity with the mother is no small threat and, in Rachilde's case, entails more than just the fear of the invisibility described by Hirsch. When Rachilde wrote the original short story, she had just become a mother herself. Furthermore, Rachilde's father would die on

April 6, 1892, shortly before the publication of the story in June of that year, leaving her both totally responsible for her mother and without a parent figure of a different sex to disrupt the identification (see "1900: Women and Education").

Rachilde's entry into the bourgeois world of marriage and motherhood was concomitant with her foray into the world of theater. In her personal life, Rachilde may have appeared to become *une bourgeoise rangée*, but the contrast between the apparent conformity of her life (the marriage and motherhood plot) and the continued experimentation of her work at this period suggests that this conformity was only superficial. Rather than embarking on any fundamental change, Rachilde continued to exploit the "paroxysms of chastity" paradigm with which she had become so familiar.

Male Anxiety at the Fin de Siècle

In which Rachilde, cupbearer to the symbolist gods,
meets Alfred Jarry

Rachilde opens her book of memoirs devoted to Jarry, *Alfred Jarry;*
ou, Le Surmâle de lettres (1928), with her recollections of her first meeting with him: "La première fois que je vis cet étrange personnage, qui
se jouait à lui-même la comédie d'une existence littéraire poussée jusqu'à l'absurde, ce fut dans le salon du *Mercure de France* de la rue de
l'Echaudé-Saint-Germain" (11).[1]

What emerges from Rachilde's account of this first acquaintance in
1894 is Jarry's anxious masculinity and his role as gender enforcer. After
the announcement that the meeting took place in the private yet public
sphere of the Mercure's salon, Rachilde proceeds to stress the accuracy
of her memory of this meeting, some forty years earlier—"La scène est
encore présente à mon imagination, laquelle imagination enregistre à la
façon photographique les moindres détails d'un incident qui l'a frap-
pée" (11)—before outlining the gender politics of the salon and her split
consciousness of what went on there: "Recevant déjà, tous les mardis,
des hommes de lettres, les uns très bohèmes, les autres arrivés ou ar-
rivistes, de pauvres gens de génie ou des amateurs trop riches pour
avoir du talent, je m'étais résignée, ne voyant presque pas de femmes,
au rôle de la simple verseuse de thé, parlant peu, écoutant beaucoup,
m'amusant toujours, ne comprenant jamais que ce que je voulais bien
comprendre" (12). This general description of the salon makes a clear
distinction between the roles of men and women, a distribution in
which men are gods and women merely cupbearers ("verseuse de thé"),
roles that Rachilde simultaneously upholds and challenges through her
presence.

But, on the day of Jarry's first visit, the question of gendered behavior is further accentuated: "Ce mardi-là, de bonne heure, devant que
les chandelles fussent allumées, j'avais posé, sur les poignets d'un très
jeune poète de province, un écheveau de soie que je dévidais, car je bro-
dais souvent, durant les discussions âprement techniques, sur un autre
canevas que celui des controverses de ces Messieurs du Symbole" (12–
13). This was the scene that greeted Jarry on his arrival. Rachilde continues: "J'eus tout juste le temps d'entendre mon mari me dire: 'Alfred

Jarry' et de répondre par une salutation plus ou moins banale qu'Alfred Jarry, d'un geste violent, arrachait l'écheveau de soie des poignets du jeune poète et le jetait par terre en grondant, d'un bizarre accent, martelant les syllabes comme les dents d'un engrenage rouillé: 'Idiot! Pourquoi pas filer au rouet?'" (13–14). Rachilde offers no further comment on this anecdote, but it leaves a clear impression of Jarry's protest against perceived emasculation. The young poet from the provinces is never identified by name, and his anonymity allows him to stand as a reflection of Jarry himself, also newly arrived from the provinces at this time, whose first words are, not those of a conventional greeting, but an act of gender policing.

At first, then, Jarry's concern with enforcing gender boundaries might have seemed offputting to someone like Rachilde who played with androgynous markers. Moreover, Jarry's appearance hardly compensated for his rude behavior. Apollinaire described him as "l'air d'un noyé, ichtyophage, monstre." Given Rachilde's fear of the figure of the *noyé* who threatened her writing voice, Jarry's appearance as a drowned man who intervenes to maintain gender roles must have indeed made a strong impression in order for her to recall it so vividly years later.[2] But Jarry's anxiety about gender was related to his sexual ambivalence, and this, in turn, is what made him the ideal companion (in some ways) for Rachilde. An exploration of Jarry's sexuality, therefore, will also raise some questions about Rachilde's.

On the one hand, Jarry's work is full of examples of heterosexuality, but they are pushed to such a pathological degree that they become unsettling. In *Le Surmâle*, for example, "une petite fille" is found in André's chateau "violée à mort," and André's new world record for sex leads to the apparent death of his partner, Ellen Elson (Jarry 2:235). In such examples, heterosexual forms of expression are both extreme and lethal (for women).

It has been suggested that, if Jarry expressed himself sexually at all, it was in homoerotic ways. Some of this is based on what little is known about his life, in which close male friendships figure more prominently than sustained attachments to women. The theatrical director Lugné-Poe, founder of the Théâtre de l'oeuvre, which staged Jarry's *Ubu roi*, recalls in his memoirs, for example, that Jarry was often seen in the company of Alfred Douglas at the theater,[3] and Noël Arnaud recounts that they were sometimes seen together at the Chat Noir. Toward the end of 1896, they participated in a competition of artistic nudes, a tantalizing tidbit of gossip (Arnaud 191).[4] (Douglas was also included in Jarry's *Les Jours et les nuits* as the character Bondroit.)[5]

Lugné-Poe also recorded Jarry's suggestion regarding who should play the role of Bougrelas (a name that is seldom translated but that puns on the word for *bugger*) in the first performance of *Ubu*. This is Jarry's idea: "J'ai confiance dans cette idée d'un gosse dans le rôle de Bougrelas: j'en connais un à Montmartre qui est très beau, avec des yeux étonnants et des cheveux bruns bouclés jusqu'aux reins. Il a treize ans et est assez intelligent pourvu qu'on s'en occupe. Ce serait peut-être un clou pour *Ubu*, cela exciterait des vieilles dames et ferait crier au scandale certaines" (2:166–67). Jarry's idea of who should represent "ce Bougrelas," then, was an androgynous adolescent who would be sure to incite scandal.

Other evidence of Jarry's ambiguous sexuality may be derived from his writing. Noël Arnaud offers several examples of Jarry's work that contain a homoerotic subtext, such as "Haldernablou" (first published in the *Mercure de France* in July 1894, the year Jarry met Rachilde) in which Duke Haldern seeks a love who is neither man, woman, nor monster and finds it in his page Ablou.[6] Arnaud suggests that Haldern represents Jarry himself, Ablou his friend Léon-Paul Fargue (96–98).[7] Arnaud also argues that *Les Jours et les nuits*, based on Jarry's experience of military service and begun in 1895 (though not published until 1897), contains similar echoes of former lovers in the character of Valens, the younger brother of the main protagonist, Sengle (the army deserter).

Since these arguments have already been made, this chapter will merely add another example, one that depends less on a biographical decoding of Jarry's work and more on Jarry's use of language to create a distinctly gay subtext. This is the play *Jef*, based on the Belgian folk hero Jef Van Coppernol, and written in the early years of the twentieth century, perhaps intended as an operetta. This play concerns three characters who meet one night in an alpine club inn, and one of the sources of humor is their difficulty communicating. Although they all speak French, each has a different accent: one is from Brussels, one from Marseille, and one from England. To complicate matters, the last is not a man but a cross-dressed woman passing as a man who struggles with appropriate gender agreements in first-person speech. The temptation to read this character as an example of the sexologists' "third sex"—a woman's soul trapped inside a man's body—stems, not only from the plot structure of a character who struggles to maintain a masculine exterior in the face of a sense of feminine inner identity, but also from the character's names: Nelly (her real name) chooses John Dick as her male pseudonym.

The three settle in, resigned to spending a night under the same roof. The two *real* men, Jef and Marius, make themselves at home by taking off their boots and eating various masculine delicacies, such as herring and garlic, while Nelly complains in asides of their smelliness and reaches for her lavender salts. The men then discuss their girlfriends and ask John Dick about his. When "he" declares that he has none, they tease him: "Vous n'êtes pas un de la chapelle Sixtine, n'est-ce pas?" (Jarry 3:38).

Having dined, they set about whiling away the evening. Since they have no cards or dominoes, Marius proposes a game of "trou commun," a version of "Simon Says." Here are the rules, as explained by Marius: "Un des joueurs dirige, par exemple moi. Les autres ferment la main gauche comme ça, de façon qu'on puisse y glisser un doigt. On met sur son genou gauche le poing ainsi disposé. . . . Rapprochons-nous! . . . Le trou commun, c'est le vide qui existe entre nous. . . . Le trou du voisin, c'est celui du voisin, dans sa main. . . . Et le propre trou, c'est le sien. . . . Vous avez compris?" (3:40) The leader then calls out "trou commun! trou du voisin! propre trou!" and the others put their fingers as directed, but the leader attempts to mislead them by doing something different than what he orders. If they do as he does instead of as he says, they must pay a forfeit. After this explanation, the game begins in earnest.

Nelly is the first to pay a forfeit since she pulls her hand away when Marius calls "trou du voisin," eliciting a double entendre in rebuke: "Vous n'avez pas le droit de refuser votre trou à monsieur Van Coppernol" (3:41). Jef is next, but he protests in a similarly suggestive fashion: "J'aïe été dans le trou de John!" Precisely, replies Marius, "J'ai dit: trou propre!" As forfeit, Jef offers his joke tie pin, a miniature of the famous Belgian Manneken-Pis statue complete with attached hose and bulb used for squirting one's neighbor.

After the extended play with gender-role stereotypes and sexual innuendo, the plot returns to that of a conventional heterosexual marriage narrative. When it is Nelly's turn to choose a game, her uninspiring (feminine) efforts put the two men to sleep, so she leaves them on the floor and climbs into the bed. When the cold awakens them, they, too, seek refuge in the bed, where they finally realize Nelly's true sex. They both declare that they have fallen in love with her and want to marry her. She agrees to marry the first one who brings her an edelweiss flower, and, while they are off looking for one, she slips away, bringing the play to a close. *Jef* is not one of Jarry's most well-known works, but its linguistic playfulness is characteristic of all his work, and, like his other works, a sexually charged subtext is never far away, as the game of (finger in the) "hole" illustrates.

Rachilde's depictions of alternative sexuality in her work also often led people to assume that her own affective life was similarly deviant. A recent example (from Eugen Weber) illustrates how people tend to think of her: "Many transvestites—male, like Major du Paty de Clam who played an ambiguous role in the Dreyfus Affair, or female, like Mathilde de Morny, or Nathalie [*sic*] Clifford Barney, or Rachilde, co-founder of the important literary *Mercure de France* and purveyor of some daring soft porn—were probably or notoriously homosexual" (37). In addition to the popular inference that all transvestites are homosexual, this passage captures the lingering suspicion that clings to Rachilde's scandalous persona. While it appears that Rachilde did indeed have at least one lesbian relationship (see "1885: Marriage and the Woman Writer"), I have also argued that her cross-dressing was far more complex than simple male impersonation. Similarly, questions about her sexual expression will evade simple categorization, as this chapter will show.

Beyond the affair with d'Estoc (and some rumored flirtations discussed in "1928: Gender Anxiety in French Modernism"), Rachilde's sexual interest seems to have been consistently directed toward men. Moreover, her life was superficially at least one of conventionality: she married Alfred Vallette in 1889 and remained in an apparently monogamous marriage until Vallette's death from a perforated ulcer on September 28, 1935. In his diaries, the sometimes sharp-tongued Paul Léautaud, who wrote under the name Maurice Boissard as drama critic for the *Mercure de France*, offered the following evaluation of their relationship in 1928, one based on over three decades of observation: "Il doit vraiment y avoir entre eux deux une grande amitié. Ils doivent et ont dû faire toujours un ménage parfait, après avoir sans doute connu tous les deux un grand amour réciproque. Cette idée qu'elle a eue de commencer sa série de *Portraits [d'hommes]* par le sien, et de montrer tous les mérites qu'il a eus et auxquels on ne pense peut-être pas? Cela ne peut venir certainement que d'un grand sentiment d'affection conjugale" (2:117).

While there may be some reason to doubt that the marriage was based on a "grand amour réciproque" (see "1885: Marriage and the Woman Writer"), for it to endure for over forty years there was clearly a very strong bond of some sort. In the introduction to *Le Roman d'un homme sérieux*, her collection of letters written to her by Vallette and published in 1944, Rachilde confirms that there was indeed passion on Vallette's side but hints that she herself did not always return the sentiment when she describes the collection as "tout palpitant de tendresse et de rude sincérité, aussi plein de reproches mérités par celle qui ne comprenait pas" (6).[8]

Yet, in between the misprision that Rachilde's life resembled that of her decadent heroes and heroines and the banal facts of her *état civil,* there was indeed something queer about her. The question of her friendships with gay men in the 1920s will form the subject of a later chapter, but here the focus will be on her relationships with gay men from the early years of decadence in the 1880s and especially on her friendship with Jarry, which began in the 1890s and lasted until his death in 1907.

Rachilde formed friendships and alliances with gay men from her earliest years in Paris in the 1880s. As the "queen of decadence," she affiliated with decadent queens. She sheltered Verlaine in her apartment for a while in 1886, for example; she was received by the aging dandy Barbey d'Aurevilly; and Oscar Wilde frequented her salon in addition to being influenced by her work. She was also a lifelong friend of Jean Lorrain, who once described her as "délicieusement pédéraste" ("Deux appréciations" 75).

One of the earliest sources of rumor about Rachilde's adoption by the gay male community comes from *Les Fellatores* (1888) by "Dr. Luiz" (Paul Devaux). The author claims that Rachilde followed the success of *Monsieur Vénus* by writing about "toutes les sensations du tribadisme" (204) and goes on to cite from an article by Rachilde on the front page of *L'Etudiant* (Saturday, December 4, 1886): "Décidément, dans une horreur de la femme, je me consacre à l'amour contre nature de tous les hommes braves" (205). Despite the fact that the author refers to Rachilde as "une tribade" (205) and that the newspaper *L'Etudiant* contains advertisements for "brasseries à femmes" (206), Rachilde's declaration of nothing but horror for women (neither her first nor her last such comment) suggests that she resisted recognizing her own sexual attraction as being primarily directed toward women. In fact, her stated preference for "l'amour contre nature," along with the popularity of *Monsieur Vénus* among men in the gay subculture, leads Dr. Luiz to describe her as a "femme-tapette" (205). Gay men's admiration for her only increases when they learn that "cette fausse femelle pratiquait leur vice" and that "la romancière de *Monsieur Vénus* avait *vécu* son livre" (206). Another example comes from an unpublished but widely repeated ballad by Jean Tinan about Robert de Souza's gift for using the "e muet." The poem enumerates God's gifts and contains the line "Il [Dieu] a donné Rachilde aux Uranistes" (quoted in Goujon 103).

Luiz's claim that *Monsieur Vénus* was based on personal experience is supported by remarks made by Rachilde herself in a recently redis-covered letter from September 17, 1896 (see Soulignac, "Ecrits de jeun-esse" 193–96). In this letter (to the symbolist poet Robert de Souza men-tioned above), Rachilde offers a defense of Alfred Douglas. The French press had rallied behind Oscar Wilde when he went on trial in 1895, and the *Mercure de France*, along with a number of other literary and cur-rent affairs journals, had published articles denouncing the hypocrisy of the English courts in condemning Wilde (Ellmann 482–83). By 1896, when Wilde was serving his prison sentence, the context had changed slightly, however, and the French press, including the *Mercure*, unwit-tingly became the forum for Alfred Douglas to betray Wilde, who could communicate from prison only through friends such as Robert Sherard and Robbie Ross.

To begin with, perhaps abusing the sympathy of the *Mercure* for Wilde's cause, Douglas planned to publish an article on Wilde in the journal in 1895 in which he would quote from love letters written to him by Wilde. The letters, "fervently and brazenly homosexual" (Ellmann 488), could be construed as evidence that Wilde had indeed perjured himself during the trials and threatened to disrupt Wilde's plans for a reconciliation with his estranged wife: "What it came down to was a brag that it was Wilde's love for him that had brought him down, and a candid admission that this love was on both sides homosexual" (Ell-mann 489). When, through Robert Sherard, who had a friend at the *Mercure* (Ellmann 488), Wilde learned of Douglas's intentions, he in-structed Sherard to intervene by writing to the *Mercure* and Douglas.

In response to Sherard's letter, Vallette evidently wrote in turn to Douglas, asking him his intentions. Douglas replied in September 1895 that, since his plans had become known, he "would rather that the ar-ticle should not be published," but he nevertheless did not abandon the idea entirely and revived it with the *Mercure* the following year (Ell-mann 489–90). According to Ellmann, "the *Mercure de France* episode provided evidence of Douglas's 'hideous rashness' and incapacity to enter imaginatively into anyone else's feelings" and showed that "the Queensberry family consisted not of two totally different beings, but of two very similar ones, both determined to expose [Wilde], one out of purported love and one out of evident hate" (490).

In 1896 this became even clearer. In May, during a visit from Sherard and Ross, Wilde learned that Douglas was again on the verge of publication, this time a book of poems in English (with French translations by Eugène Tardieu) to be published by the Mercure and dedicated to Wilde. Wilde objected to the dedication, and in June Douglas agreed to withdraw the book even though it "was to have appeared in three or four days, and is practically ready" (quoted in Ellmann 501). But on June 1, 1896, Douglas published an article, "Introduction to My Poems with Some Remarks on the Oscar Wilde Case," in *La Revue blanche*. It was substantially the same tenor as the article he had withdrawn from the *Mercure* but minus the letters.

This, then, is the rather complicated background to Rachilde's letter to Robert de Souza. The *Mercure* had been "burned" by Douglas, who had agreed to publish things, only to withdraw at the last minute and then compound the fault by turning around and publishing in a rival review. Rachilde's defense of Douglas in this letter could be read as excusing his behavior toward the journal and the press in 1895–96.[9]

By defending Douglas, Rachilde is also being drawn into taking sides in the widening gulf between Wilde and Douglas, although she was probably not aware of this. In general, Rachilde was not obviously hostile toward Wilde and probably thought that, in defending Douglas, she was also defending Wilde. After all, Wilde and Rachilde were personally acquainted, they had many mutual friends, and Wilde had greatly admired *Monsieur Vénus* (see "1884: The Politics of Publishing"). Rachilde had recently weighed in on the question of homosexuality in her own article in *La Revue blanche*, "Questions brûlantes," in which she had defended Douglas's "manifesto" and concluded that "lord Alfred Douglas devait crier son amour" (200) (see Ploye).

In the course of defending homosexual love, Rachilde sets out her ideas about sexuality in general, and her comments on this subject form an interesting backdrop to the letter to de Souza as well as to the discussion of her attraction to gay men at the heart of this chapter. She compared love to a god who marks its "victims" before their birth, which in today's terms might be read as a belief that sexual orientation is innate and not a choice. But, while she seems to come down on the side of essentialism in the question of cause, she is provocatively antibiological in her privileging of the intellectual over the physical side of sex: "Placez deux amoureux, intellectuellement sincères, à quarante pas de distance l'un de l'autre, liez-leur les mains derrière le dos et défendez-leur de se regarder; je vous parie un oeuf de colombe contre un crâne de libertin qu'avant une heure, rien qu'en levant sournoisement les paupières pour se contempler malgré vous, ils auront tous les spasmes qu'il leur plaira d'avoir!" ("Questions" 199).

In addition to anticipating the scene in Martin Sherman's play *Bent* (1979), in which two gay interns in a Nazi concentration camp succeed in having sexual relations despite the fact that they cannot touch or even look at each other, this description of sexual attraction is clearly flexible enough to encompass many models of affective expression. It can be read as a defense of homosexual love, but it can also be read as a defense of love that finds expression, not in any physical sense, but in a more intellectual form. Cerebral passion was especially dear to the hearts of the decadents, but Rachilde's description also finds an echo in contemporary social constructionism, for example, in Carole Vance's formulation that the most important sexual organ is located between the ears (see Alderfer 72).

Rachilde's letter to Robert de Souza reveals a personal dimension to the topic missing from her "Questions." In it, her defense of Douglas rests both on principle—"la culture des mauvaises passions . . . est une belle chose car elle produit les mêmes résultats que la vertu ou l'honneur bourgeois"—and on personal feelings, identifying strongly as she does with Douglas, whom she describes as her double: "Personne ne sait ce qu'il y a au fond de Lord Alfred . . . or, je le sais, moi" (194). To defend him, she claims, is to defend herself, for "Lord Queenberry [*sic*] c'est mon père, absolument et sa femme c'est le type de ma mère." She goes on to describe the horrors of a childhood marred by sadism and brutality: "J'ai entendu les cris de ma mère retentir d'une colline à l'autre colline, sans pouvoir faire autre chose que recevoir les coups pour elle" (195). It borders on understatement to suggest that the result of this upbringing was a very troubled adolescent: "Redoutant les mâles, ayant horreur des faiblesses intellectuelles des femmes . . . je m'épris . . . d'un garçon de vingt ans, le secrétaire de notre député, un paysan perverti devenu mignon genre Henri III qui portait des bracelets d'or et à partir de ce jour le mythe Monsieur Vénus fut mon histoire!" (196).

From this description, then, Rachilde suggests that her adolescent experiences made her distrust traditional gender roles (macho men and intellectually feeble women), with the result that, although she herself was heterosexual, she was attracted to those men who did not display traditional masculine characteristics associated with dominance. She specifies that she was "remis[e] debout" by "un hétérosexuel bon et vraiment mâle," Alfred Vallette, which suggests that she viewed her behavior as an aberration or at least some sort of "fall" or stumble, but, at the end of the letter, it is apparent that she believes that such situations call for sympathy and understanding, not condemnation. What her letter does not say, perhaps because she did not know it yet, is that, although she considered herself to have been put back on track ("remise debout") by Vallette, she would continue to have important relationships with gay men.

One of the most interesting details about this letter is Rachilde's use of the term *heterosexual*. It must be one of the earliest usages of the word in French outside a medical (sexological) context. Although the *Oxford English Dictionary Supplement* traces it back to 1868 (Katz 10), the word did not catch on in French or English until Krafft-Ebing's *Psychopathia sexualis* introduced it to medical experts and sexologists in the early 1890s. As Jonathan Katz has recently shown, the exact meaning of the word remained unstable during this time. In some contexts, heterosexuality was a form of perversion, a pathology, but Krafft-Ebing's work was one of the texts that helped stabilize the word, leaving it with more or less its modern meaning.

The French translation of *Psychopathia sexualis*, which helped fix the term in its modern sense of "one who is attracted to the opposite sex" (the way in which Rachilde appears to be using it here), was published in 1895, just one year before Rachilde's letter was written. The translation proved popular, and this letter is perhaps evidence of how quickly the word was picked up and disseminated generally, but it also suggests the high level of interest in medical sexology felt by Rachilde in particular, an interest piqued by the fact that, although she was eventually "rescued" by a heterosexual, her first inclination was toward a gay man.[10] This early attraction, combined with her lifelong commitment to gay men, suggests that the identity that best describes Rachilde's sexual orientation is that of the *fag hag*.

This label can have strong negative connotations, but it is intended here, not as a derogatory term, but rather as an affirmative way of referring to primarily heterosexual women who find themselves attracted to primarily gay men or who form their most intense emotional attachments with them.

A more specific definition is difficult because fag hag remains an undertheorized identity. Very little has been written describing or theorizing this affective preference, but, in what literature does exist on the subject, much of it superficial and anecdotal pop psychology, two somewhat different models are collapsed under the same heading.[11] It has been suggested that women find such relationships with gay men attractive because they allow them to form close friendships with men in a "safety zone" in which sexual pressures are minimized and that women have more in common emotionally with gay men. This model represents a form of heterosexuality but one in which the woman chooses a sex object who is less likely to reciprocate her feelings. This choice can have several advantages: it allows women to explore friendships with men without the risk that the friendship will be "spoiled" by sex; or it allows women to explore their sexual attraction to men as a more general form of desire, not one that necessarily takes the form of a sexual relationship. The man's homosexuality is supposed to act as an inhibitor to sexual expression, and thus the woman can explore her desire "safely."

The other model of what motivates the fag hag emphasizes not attraction, but identification. The woman does not *want* the gay man; she wants, in some sense, to *be* the gay man. The woman identifies with the gay man's sexual attraction to men but also aspires to his social status *as a man*. This is the perspective put forward by Camilla Decarnin, who suggests that "women whose primary erotic objects are gay men have consciously or otherwise recognized men's valued position in society and desired to be valued as men are valued" (10). The suggestion of "false consciousness" or "male identification" aside, Decarnin's argument usefully makes a separation between (sexual) attraction to and identification with. In Decarnin's analysis, the gay man occupies a social position that the woman herself aspires to attain, "as the recognized peer *and* the lover of a male" (10).

This proves to be a useful description of Rachilde's situation. There is little evidence that she strayed very far from heterosexual inclination, yet she masculinized herself by cross-dressing, by adopting her ambiguously gendered pseudonym, and by writing about herself in the masculine form. Many of her peers described her talents as "virile," a compliment that she never rejected, and her feminism is complicated precisely by her failure at times to identify with women.

Rachilde aspired to be the equal of a man and distanced herself from women and from feminism, which led her to identify with gay men. Rachilde as fag hag then reminds us that, in turn-of-the-century France, men enjoyed a level of social prestige that women envied. Even—perhaps especially—the men who stepped outside the prescribed gender roles (see the comments on Marinetti, Apollinaire, and Jarry in "1925: Women and Surrealism") were not anxious to give up this social privilege and policed the gender boundaries assiduously, as has already been illustrated in the case of Jarry. A return to Rachilde's description of her first meeting with Jarry will show how Rachilde encodes her identification with gay men there.

In the account of Rachilde's birth ("1860: Women as Outsiders"), it was noted that all three biographers—Gaubert, David, and Dauphiné—mention that Rachilde was born under the sign of Aquarius. But not all three situate this information in the same way. Rachilde's first biographer, Gaubert, mentions it only in a note ("sous le signe zodiacal du Verseau"), while, for the most recent biographer, Dauphiné, it is a synonym of the adjective *Saturnian*, given in apposition as the key to Rachilde's character. André David's mention is much more extensive and allusive. For David, the gay man with whom Rachilde will collaborate in the 1920s (when his biography of her was written), Aquarius is the sign of Ganymede, beloved cupbearer of Jupiter and a coded figure for male homosexuality from the Renaissance on.[12] For David, Rachilde was born under a gay male sign. As if this astrological predetermination were not enough, David also notes that Ganymede (he of the sign of Aquarius) was chosen to replace Hebe, the female cupbearer and daughter of Zeus/Jupiter and Hera/Juno. The allusion thus situates Rachilde in the rather ambiguous position of a woman born under the sign of a man (Ganymede) who usurps the place of a woman (Hebe), a fitting emblem for a woman who identified with gay men, and who sensed an opportunity to rise above her station as cupbearer to the symbolist gods, but who found that social gender norms placed severe constraints on her desire to be a woman writer. Her very birth sign predicted her role as *verseuse* (*de thé*), the role that she was playing in the salon when Jarry made his first appearance.

There has often been speculation as to whether, in addition to enjoying a particularly close friendship with Jarry, Rachilde ever had an affair with him.[13] In the light of Rachilde's theories about love and her self-presentation as a cupbearer to the gods, it seems unlikely that they ever consummated their relationship in anything resembling a sexual fashion. Rachilde was prepared to play Ganymede to the antigod Ubu, but not only were both perhaps afraid of sex, Rachilde's theories of love made sexual contact unnecessary. They needed only to be "intellectually sincere" in order to experience "tous les spasmes" ("Questions" 199).

Jarry could have joined Rachilde in her rejection of such conventional gender roles, but his preoccupation with gender-appropriate behavior (men work not, neither do they spin) suggests that, despite the sexually charged themes of his work, he was not interested in exploring alternatives in real life. It is too easy to assume that all aspects of the sex/gender system shifted together at the turn of the century while the norms presented a united front that resisted change, that so-called deviant sexualities and newly emergent identities were accompanied by gender nonconformity in a mutually reinforcing challenge to some monolithic bourgeois system. But the friendship of Rachilde and Jarry suggests, rather, that sexuality and gender could be mobilized in contradictory ways. A pattern of lifelong heterosexuality reveals a queer underside, while decadent queers did not necessarily threaten to displace the two-tier gender hierarchy.

Women and Education

*In which Rachilde's mother is admitted to
the asylum of Charenton and some deficiencies
in Rachilde's education become apparent*

On July 27, 1900, Doctor Albert Prieur was called to the side of Gabrielle Eymery. In his report, the doctor later declared "que cette dame est atteinte d'idées délirantes manifestes entretenues par des hallucinations auditives presque constantes pendant lesquelles elle se croit en communication directe avec une foule de personnages absolument inconnus d'elle qui lui donnent de cette façon des conseils et des ordres auxquels elle obéit avec une scrupuleuse exactitude." The report is dated October 25; it was the eleventh birthday of Gabrielle Eymery's granddaughter, Gabrielle Vallette.

In his next report, on December 8, the doctor confirmed not only that Gabrielle Eymery's state had not improved, but that it was in fact deteriorating. Her hallucinations had become more or less constant, leaving her no free will, and putting her "à la merci de telle ou telle suggestion délirante qu'on ne saurait prévenir et contre laquelle on ne peut protéger la malade et son entourage qu'en la mettant en observation dans un établissement spécial."[1]

The "special establishment" turned out to be the asylum at Charenton, made famous by its most infamous inmate, the marquis de Sade. The irony could not have been lost on Rachilde. She had already claimed her allegiance to this almost mythical figure in *La Marquise de Sade*, published thirteen years earlier, and she had also adopted his coat of arms as her *justification de tirage* at the Mercure,[2] but that she should literally be the daughter of one who shared the address of the mad marquis must have seemed both completely inevitable and totally unforeseeable.

Gabrielle Eymery was admitted to the asylum on December 10, 1900, according to the hospital records. Her profession was given as "rentière" and her address as 14 rue du Presbytère, Thiviers (Dordogne). Perhaps the most significant detail of this part of her record, however, is the name of the person who requested the admission: M. Alfred Vallette, director of the "Mercure Français," of 15 rue de l'Echaudé-St.-Germain, Paris, son-in-law. Whatever Rachilde's difficulties in coping with her mother's madness, she was not the one officially to initiate her confinement, voluntary though it was.

Once admitted, Gabrielle Eymery was treated by the asylum's director, Doctor Antoine Ritti, who composed his initial diagnosis the following day (December 11): Madame Eymery "paraît atteinte d'une aliénation mentale caractérisée par du délire de persécution des hallucinations multiples, de fausses interprétations, etc." She is described as a "malade réticente, dissimulée."

Except for her husband, Rachilde was alone in confronting this chapter of her mother's life. Her parents had been leading separate lives for many years, and Joseph Eymery had died on April 6, 1892, in his country home of Chamarat. Gabrielle Feytaud Eymery had been dividing her time between Thiviers and Paris.[3]

In any case, Joseph Eymery's influence had waned long before his death (Rachilde claimed that she was not even notified about his funeral [*QJJ* 170]). While Chamarat was just "une gentilhommière qui tombe en ruine, et qu'il faudrait faire réparer" (*QJJ* 168), Rachilde later learned that Gabrielle had taken even this small residence back, despite the fact that she already had "le *Cros*, le vieil hôtel de *Thiviers* et un somptueux mobilier qui aurait suffi à combler tous les salons de la préfecture" (169). Joseph, meanwhile, had only his army pension to live on, just enough to support himself and his hunting dogs. But, no matter how small his sphere of influence, when he died, Rachilde's last family ally against her increasingly mad mother was gone. Joseph had tried to protect Rachilde from her mother. While his attempt to marry her off had been misguided, it had been motivated by the desire to "[l]'éloigner d'une famille un peu *originale*" (166). And Joseph's attitudes toward his daughter's writing softened over the years so that, despite his hatred of "plumitifs," when Rachilde finally went off to make a name for herself in Paris, father and daughter parted on good terms: he sold his hunting pack to raise money for her (170; see also "1870: The Ambivalence of the Paternal").

With Joseph Eymery's death, there was no one left to protect Rachilde from her eccentric family, which now comprised only her increasingly unstable mother. Gabrielle Eymery even moved in with her daughter and son-in-law for a time, sharing their apartment on the rue de l'Echaudé (Léautaud 2:491–92). As already discussed above, it did not take long for new acquaintances to perceive that all was not right. Even before marrying Rachilde in 1889, Vallette was convinced that it would take a doctor only an hour of conversation to arrive at a diagnosis (*RHS* 141), a judgement that Dr. Antoine Ritti's testimony a decade later seems to bear out.

The debt that Rachilde owed her mother has already been discussed. This debt has gone unacknowledged for so long that it is important to recognize it, but acknowledging that Rachilde received help from her mother does not mean that their relationship was an idyllic one. This chapter, then, explores in greater detail the other side of the coin, the sources and expressions of Rachilde's anger at her mother.

This anger had various motivations. To begin with, Gabrielle committed specific acts of betrayal, some of which have already been recounted (for example, when she denounced Rachilde as not the author of her own work). There is anger when Rachilde describes how there would be no female presence to protect the young Magui from her father's ire at a hunters' dinner because her mother had retired "with a migraine" (*PM* 237–38). But some of Rachilde's resentment toward her mother was also culturally determined. Just as her father was bound up with a cultural model of the patriarchal, so her mother in part represented cultural expectations about femininity and the place of women. In rejecting her mother, Rachilde was rejecting some of these cultural expectations as much as she was rejecting her mother herself. For, if Rachilde traced her connection to writing and writers through her mother and her mother's side of the family, so too she was able to trace her disconnection from the patriarchal family of writers, her alienation from the centers of power, her marginalization from the literary mainstream.

Some of the anger at mother figures in Rachilde's novels can be traced to specific resentments having to do with her own family. This is clearly the case, for example, in *La Marquise de Sade* (1887). This novel is often read as a kind of fictional pathography, one of Rachilde's favorite genres, a biography that emphasized the pathology of its subject. Such fictional case studies provide a veritable portrait gallery of types of perversion, combining the decadent interest in perversity as a rejection of bourgeois complacency with the burgeoning interest in disorders of the mind in the scientific community of psychologists and sexologists.[4]

Rachilde had already begun this portrait gallery with *Monsieur Vénus*, which might be read as depicting the pathography of heterosexual love between inverts, followed by *A mort* and *La Marquise de Sade*. She continued the theme over the next few years, for example, in *Madame Adonis* (1888)—frequently called the companion piece to *Monsieur Vénus*—*Minette* (1889), and other novels that would appear in the 1890s. She also found a market for older works such as *L'Homme roux*, published in 1888 but begun (so Rachilde would claim) "the last day I was seventeen and finished on February 27, 1878" (quoted in "Bibliographie générale" 126).[5] And she continued to write about writing itself, using, for example, the roman à clef formula, as in *Le Mordu* (1890).

The allusion to Sade in *La Marquise de Sade* can be misleading today since, in 1887 (when the novel was first published), the concept of sadism had not yet taken on its contemporary definition, which can be attributed to Krafft-Ebing's formulation of sadism and masochism in the 1890 publication of *Psychopathia sexualis*.[6] Sade had always exercised an important influence on Rachilde's writing: she claimed to have read his works as a teenager and later imprinted her publications with his emblem by using it as her *justification de tirage*. In the 1880s, Sade's novels had also enjoyed renewed public vogue and were much discussed, and no doubt Rachilde intended *La Marquise de Sade* as her contribution to this debate (see Rosario 148 – 49; Birkett 19 – 20). When Krafft-Ebing acknowledged the role of novelists in drawing his attention to the pleasures of cruelty, it was writers such as Rachilde whom he had in mind, but it is anachronistic to expect the analysis of sadism presented in *La Marquise de Sade* to conform to the profile of sadism later derived from the work of turn-of-the-century sexologists. The novel's heroine, Mary Barbe, represents but a very faint version of that kind of sadism. As Claude Dauphiné notes, if Rachilde's novel owes anything to the marquis, it is only in some of its philosophical underpinnings.[7]

La Marquise de Sade offers both an autobiographical representation and a revenge fantasy. It presents the story of Mary Barbe, the unwanted child of a military family who grows up to become an unusually independent woman whose sexual gratification is linked to bloodshed through childhood trauma. The novel focuses on the childhood of the heroine rather than on her adult adventures, which are for the most part rather sketchily described. This emphasis on childhood and adolescent formation depicts the etiology of her perversion, showing how she comes to associate love with suffering. Her adult sadism is expressed only in mild form (mild, that is, in comparison to the works of the marquis de Sade), and murder is mostly anticipated rather than actualized in the text. The novel ends with Mary returning from a slaughterhouse bar, dreaming of "la joie prochaine du meurtre, fait devant tous, si l'envie la prenait trop forte" (297).

The novel's main theme, then, is not sadism but maternal betrayal. Mary is neglected as a child by her mother, whose frail health and selfish disposition take priority. As a result, Mary is often left in the care of relatives and surrogate mothers (as was Rachilde), constantly reminded that her parents had wanted a boy (as was Rachilde). The autobiographical elements could hardly be more obvious. The maternal betrayal is fully brought out through Mary's gradual realization that it is not milk—a fluid associated with innocence and maternity—that her mother drinks every day but fresh blood, the food of vampires. Her mother is not a victim but a monster, a monstrousness underscored by Mary's (and Rachilde's) identification with animals, the bloodsucker's victims. When the young Mary accompanies her aunt to the slaughterhouse and witnesses the agony of the bull, sacrificed to her mother's ghoulish need for fresh blood, the narrative presents the action through Mary's eyes as a scene of primal trauma.

Rachilde uses her own experience as a starting point (it was noted above, for example, that the movement of the regiment in the novel follows the itinerary of Captain Eymery's postings) but rapidly transforms the text into a wish-fulfillment fantasy. Her parents are granted their wish and given the son they so much desire, but it costs Mary's mother her life; Madame Barbe is punished by dying in childbirth. That's what you get, implies Rachilde, for not being satisfied with the child you already have. This price is viewed ambivalently by Mary: on the one hand it seems perhaps a fitting punishment, but on the other it also deprives her entirely of her mother, and she can never forgive her uncle, the doctor who made the choice to save the baby at the cost of the mother. To complete the revenge fantasy, Mary's brother also dies in infancy, and Mary has the satisfaction of watching him suffocate accidentally without lifting a finger to save him. She thus contributes to his death but without assuming the responsibility for it: a crime of omission rather than commission.

In this novel, then, Rachilde explores the fate of the child who is unmothered, who, like Victor Frankenstein's monster, turns to antisocial behavior out of rage and frustration at not being provided for. Rachilde expresses her rage at her parents' unreasonable rejection of her because she was not a boy and also explores the consequences for a woman of exceptional sensitivity who must find her way in the world without the protection and support of a mother. Mary identifies with men as a self-defense strategy. At the same time as she is infuriated by her mother's behavior, she is unable to prevent herself from repeating it, becoming a blood drinker like her mother, unconsciously identifying with her only role model.[8]

La Marquise de Sade thus links two stereotypes that recur throughout Rachilde's fiction: the absent mother and the evil man of science. It is remarkable how few of Rachilde's many novels present a heroine who even has a mother, let alone a good one. In addition to Mary Barbe, raised in part by her cousin Tulotte, there is Raoule de Vénérande (*Monsieur Vénus*, 1884), who is "mothered" by an aunt who treats her like a boy, Eliante Donalger (*La Jongleuse*, 1900), who was raised by a Creole nurse and who lives with an elderly uncle while herself "mothering" her niece Missie (also masculinized), and Hermine de Messiange, whose mother dies in the opening pages of *Minette* (1889), to mention just a few examples. In *L'Amazone rouge* (1932), the mother is simply eliminated by "une maladie de langueur" that no one is allowed to mention (19–20), and Rachilde's mother's name is reassigned by the author to the father (Jean-Gabriel). Rachilde's feelings about maternity are summed up in a photograph of her reproduced in the *Organographes du cymbalum pataphysicum* (19–20 [1983]:76). This photograph, the property of her daughter, Gabrielle, was entitled—by Gabrielle—"maternity," yet Rachilde is holding, not a child, but a cat. Gabrielle thought her mother's maternal instincts best captured by her relationship with animals.

The evil man of science/doctor is another recurrent figure. Scientists and doctors are attractive because they are powerful. There were certainly men of science among her acquaintances. The astronomer Camille Flammarion, for example, was a family friend and served as a witness at her wedding. In Rachilde's fiction, however, scientists or doctors are associated with sexual knowledge that is both unwelcome and yet empowering, the sort of knowledge that makes a young girl's hair stand on end (*MS* 187). This horripilating experience is unwelcome, because it comes in the form of unwanted sexual advances at a time when the heroine is still innocent, but ultimately empowering, because it frees the heroine from any further vulnerability to seduction and gives her power over men. (In this sense, Rachilde's heroines are Sadeian: they undergo a painful initiation into sexual matters, but such "dangerous liaisons" ultimately turn them into libertines themselves with the ability to manipulate others.) There may be an autobiographical basis for this: in *Face à la peur*, Rachilde recounts that a well-known man of science tried to seduce her.

Moreover, scientists are doubly evil because they practice vivisection. As Rachilde explains, again in *Face à la peur*, she became an antivivisectionist and animal rights activist after seeing experiments performed on laboratory mice as a young lab assistant. Since she also experienced sexual harrassment in the lab, her dislike of men of science and lifelong distrust of doctors therefore seem doubly determined. Men of scientific learning are consistently presented as evil in Rachilde's fiction, like Mary Barbe's uncle Célestin Barbe in *La Marquise de Sade*. Even medical students are suspect: Léon Reille (in *La Jongleuse*) is slightly dangerous because of the knowledge, as well as the outlook, that he is acquiring from his studies.

That the mother is absent means that the daughter is not protected from such men, one of the sources of the daughter's anger. In some cases, however—for example, *La Tour d'amour*—the anger is less focused and therefore harder to locate. *La Tour d'amour* once again displays femicidal fury, with women—and especially mothers—the target of revenge. As an analysis of the novel will suggest, however, although still linked to the mother, the anger arises for somewhat different reasons.

La Tour d'amour was first published in 1899.[9] The narrative, a story of apprenticeship in a lighthouse, describes a process of integration into a pseudofamily that suggests simultaneously the personal issues faced by Rachilde in her biological family of origin and also the larger problems of a woman writer seeking adoption into a patriarchal family as an author with authority. It has been suggested that, in general, "les écrivains décadents se cherchent des paternités littéraires" (Dufief 16), but, in Rachilde's case, the search for paternal authority is a matter, not just of literary anxiety, but of an anxiety that saturates all realms. The novel pits phallic power against "the eternal feminine" and describes the misfortune, or "malheur," of Jean Maleux, who is appointed as second lighthouse keeper to assist, and eventually succeed, the head keeper, Mathurin Barnabas.

The novel has a first-person narrator who speaks in the masculine, just as Rachilde herself spoke and wrote of herself in the masculine. Although she was no longer cross-dressing, Rachilde continued to identify with aspects of male roles, especially as a writer who, like many of her female precursors in France, had adopted a male literary pseudonym but who had carried this identity beyond her public persona and into her personal life. Moreover, given her father's desire for a male child and his disappointment that his only offspring turned out to be a girl, Rachilde's assumption of a male identity as part of her life-long quest for her father's approval appears overdetermined. Rachilde's search for her father's approval was simultaneously a quest for acceptance as a daughter (a girl), as a writer (a "plumitif"), and as a daughter who writes (a woman writer). Rachilde's description of her father as "un héros de roman" reveals the extent to which she recognized the overlap between the "family romance" and its fictional reworkings.[10]

The narrative voice of *La Tour d'amour* therefore has autobiographical overtones and appears to weave biographical facts into a story of literary identity. At the opening of the novel, Jean accepts a posting to the lonely lighthouse because it represents "une maison" (10, 16, 17). He further assumes that the placement will make him master in his own home: "On était casé, son maître dans une propriété de l'état, un endroit respectable où qu'on serait tranquille" (3). In assuming his "position" in life, Jean expects to attain a mastery sanctioned by the laws of the state, a placement that will bring respect, the destiny of both the paterfamilias and the male literary master.

The lighthouse is an exclusively male environment, and the two lighthouse keepers form bonds in a stereotypically bachelor atmosphere. They eat out of cans because there is no woman to cook for them: "Point de soupe, puisque point de cuisinière dans la maison," observes Jean (24). Jean's first gesture of appropriation of this new space is to place a girlie pinup above his bed. His companion, Mathurin, has the disgusting habits of throwing garbage on the floor and urinating on the door; he sleeps with his boots on and does not wash his clothes.

The adoption process that takes place in this environment repeats the process that Rachilde underwent both in earning her father's approval and in asserting her place in the literary tradition. As Jean sets off to take up his post, he is reminded of his new responsibilities and responds: "Bien, quoi, on sera un homme" (8). The response, with the emphasis not on being but becoming, not on a present but a future state, is the same response as was acted out by Rachilde. To please her father, she let herself be raised as a boy, let herself become a man; to please her literary peers, she became an "homme de lettres" (as her visiting cards proclaimed).

Like both the female child Marguerite and the apprentice writer Rachilde, however, Jean Maleux, the "malheureux," finds that earning approval will not be the matter of course that he had assumed. Having nearly drowned in reaching the lighthouse, Jean feels that he has earned a warm reception: "Rapport à mon entrée dans cette maison, la mienne un peu, je me croyais des droits à une bienvenue plus cordiale" (27). Instead, he faces the cold indifference of Mathurin, who goes to bed without offering either a glass of rum or a word of advice, leaving the exhausted Jean the first night shift. Mathurin's indifference extends so far that he duplicates Jean's work as though he were not even there. Jean thinks Mathurin a brute, but he no more renounces his intentions of overcoming the initial rejection together with Mathurin's more explicit "anxiety of influence" that Jean will betray him than Rachilde abandoned her plans to earn her father's approval and become a writer.

Lest there be any doubt, the masculinity of this "home" is underscored by the obviously phallic symbolism of the lighthouse itself. On first catching sight of it, Jean is impressed by its size: "Juché sur une roche où on ne devait pas pouvoir mettre les pieds, jadis, il tenait par miracle, si gros, si long, qu'on se sentait de l'orgueil pour la force de l'homme qui l'avait conçu" (13–14). Its aspirations to transcendent signification lead to divine rivalry: "Le phare se dressait, énorme, tendu comme une menace vers les cieux, s'érigeait, colossal, dans la direction de cette gueule d'ombre, de cette noire fêlure de la clarté céleste, car il y était attiré par le suprême devoir d'être aussi grand que Dieu" (198). This lighthouse, standing on a rock abandoned by God , is named Ar-Men (Breton for "on the rock"), its very name hinting at the incantation ("amen": so be it) that the ur-men Jean and Mathurin implicitly intone as they reaffirm its power.

If the lighthouse is "Lui" (198), its counterpart, "Elle," is the sea, the eternal feminine, the dangerous, engulfing female element kept in check by "MM. les ingénieurs" (31) and the massive power of the lighthouse. The sea, source of darkness and death, is constantly compared to female figures. The waves are whores with green thighs in undulating waves of silk teasing the men imprisoned in the lighthouse, furies screaming and frothing at the mouth and biting at the lighthouse, and, most especially, suffocating mothers: "On leur confie sa destinée, et elles vous noient entre leurs seins mouvants" (250).

Along with the valorization of the paternal, then, there is a corresponding rejection of the maternal. Rachilde bitterly acknowledged the disappointment that she experienced in maternal relationships in *Pourquoi je ne suis pas féministe*: "Je n'ai jamais eu confiance dans les femmes, l'éternel féminin m'ayant trompé d'abord sous le masque maternel et je n'ai pas plus confiance en moi. J'ai toujours regretté de ne pas être un homme, non point que je prise davantage l'autre moitié de l'humanité mais parce qu'obligé, par devoir ou par goût, de vivre comme un homme, de porter seule tout le plus lourd du fardeau de la vie pendant ma jeunesse, il eût été préférable d'en avoir au moins les privilèges sinon les apparences" (6). This account of maternal failure, written with hindsight when Rachilde was sixty-eight years old, disingenuously fuses two situations from her youth: her childhood, when the burden was not that of material security but of psychic survival in the face of a distant father and a mentally unstable mother who left her "with no confidence" in herself, and her early writing career, when the burden was to survive as a writer in spite of the lack of literary foremothers, who, like her own biological mother, failed to provide for her, leaving her to "live like a man," a male author seeking the approval of a patriarchal male tradition.

Choosing not to take shore leaves, Jean rejects the sea and the feminine in order to earn Mathurin's respect and become a man. Jean is unable completely to repress the feminine, however. Just as the saltwater seeps into every crevice of the lighthouse, Jean is haunted by images of women, from the ghostly feminine appearance of Mathurin and the eerie voice of a siren, to dreams of a former companion, Zuléma, that prove dangerous distractions from his duty. His relationships with women become the stuff of nostalgia and dream. Particularly in his fantasized recollections of Zuléma, the repressed feminine returns with uncanny echoes in the refrain to a series of comparisons: "comme les chats!" The slang meaning reinscribes the repressed knowledge of the mother's genitals, echoed in the other uncanny manifestations of the feminine in the lighthouse.

Jean attempts to control these troubling irruptions by seeking a legitimate wife, but, after a brief and disappointing affair with a young girl named Marie, who has the maternal promise of a Madonna but the sexual nature of a Magdalene, Jean begins to share Mathurin's perspective that the only good woman is a dead one. These are the only ones who will not deceive, *tromper*, the very word that Rachilde used to describe the failure of the eternal feminine behind the maternal mask.

Jean's disappointment at his own failure to control the dangerous feminine element by taming it through marriage fuels his hostility toward women. His disappointment turns to rage when his precarious sense of masculine identity, so carefully constructed, is challenged by a confrontation with a corpse. Mathurin has fetishistically preserved the head of a drowned woman, which Jean finally discovers hidden in the lighthouse. Jean sees the head floating in a jar as though looking at an "étroit miroir de verre" (223). When he looks in this mirror, he is horrified to discover, not the illusory but satisfying image of a coherent— and male—identity, but "une autre tête que la [s]ienne qui [l]e regardait!" (223). Expecting to see a man in the mirror, he instead sees a woman, "un jeune visage de femme contemplant la mer de ses yeux pleins de larmes" (224).

The role of the mirror was touched on earlier (see "1890: Imagining the Self"), and here the constellation of meanings recurs, resonating with all the symbolic associations already noted. First, the mirror fails to reassure the viewer that he has a stable identity (it is a man who looks in the "mirror," but he sees a woman's face). The reflection also speaks specifically to Rachilde's sense of failure. She thought she had become "un homme de lettres," but the mirror shows instead a woman. Moreover, this *noyé(e)* (the woman had drowned in a shipwreck) silently recalls the very interdiction uttered by the drowned *revenant* of Rachilde's childhood: "Tu ne parleras pas."

For Jean, this confrontation with unacceptable reality culminates during his next shore leave in an act of violence. Drunk, and still burning from Marie's rejection, Jean is leaving a bar in a dark alley when a woman accosts him, calling him "petit homme," and throwing herself on him in an octopus-like embrace (the image recalls *L'Araignée de cristal* as well as Rachilde's nickname for Gisèle d'Estoc). Jean stabs her, then declares, "Ben, quoi? J'ai tué la mer" (237). He claims to have killed the sea, but, both through the symbolic associations of the sea itself and through the homonym, in French, of *mer* (sea) and *mère* (mother), his rage and apparent triumph are also over that other feminine element, the maternal.[11]

This cathartic act of erasure is not the end of the story, however, either literally or figuratively. Mathurin eventually dies, and Jean takes over as head keeper of the lighthouse, carrying on the tradition set by his adopted father and vowing never to set foot on land again. But there is one important digression from Mathurin's path. The older man's identification with the phallic lighthouse had led to cultural sterility and loss of cultural memory: Mathurin had *forgotten* how to read and write. Fearing the same fate, Jean has written his own account of events, creating the book that the reader holds. The act is one of disloyalty, as it reveals the sordid details of a story that Jean was resolved never to tell, but it remains the only protection against losing access to the symbolic code of language.

Rachilde, too, is "disloyal to civilization," inscribing the story of her paternal identification, her rage at the disappointment of the feminine, and her struggle as a woman to become part of a literary family.[12] Like Jean, who "knows neither mother nor grandmother" (20), Rachilde knew of no accepted literary foremothers, and, thus, in order to reconcile herself to a father who neglected his "métier de père" (166) and a male literary tradition that excluded her, she rejects the disappointing feminine and forges an adoptive identification with the phallic in an attempt to speak against her culturally prescribed silence. Like Jean, who wants Mathurin to "authorize" his marriage (165), Rachilde seeks an impossible reconciliation as a woman writer between the "madwoman" of female identity in the sea and the "*père*-version" that she must confront in her adopted family in the lighthouse.

Rachilde had sought adoption into the national family of male writers because she knew no literary foremothers of her own. Although her mother provided a connection to writing in general, it was to men, not women. Had Rachilde had the education that was shortly to become available to all French girls through the reforms of the Third Republic, she might have been exposed to examples of such female predecessors, but she was one generation too early to benefit from these changes.

The Third Republic would legislate (in 1879) that primary school teachers actually had to be *qualified* to teach and that every *département* had to provide an *école normale* to train women teachers (the *institutrices*), but implementation was slow. In Rachilde's hometown of Périgueux—part of the "France du retard" (Chartier and Martin 18)—a building that had served as (among other things) a Jesuit college and a barracks was finally turned into an *école normale de filles* in 1883 (Pommarède, *Périgueux oublié* n.p.). According to the law, these *écoles normales* were to be staffed by graduates of the famous (or infamous) Ecole Normale Supérieure de Sèvres, founded in 1881.[13] The Ferry government would also institute mandatory lay secondary education (*lycées*) for girls through the loi Camille Sée of 1880. The following year, the government legislated free secular education for girls and boys and followed up in 1882 by mandating compulsory attendance from ages six through thirteen. Admittedly, there were problems with compliance and enforcement, but the point is moot in the case of Rachilde. When, for example, the *lycées* were (legally) created, she was already twenty years old, just a few years too old to attend the French equivalent of a state high school, even had one opened up the day the law passed.

By 1900, when *La Tour d'amour* was published, enough time (twenty years) had elapsed for the effects of the educational reforms to be felt—an entire generation had come of age in a world where education for girls was a state-sanctioned fact of life—enough time, perhaps, for Rachilde to become aware, however unconsciously, of what she had so narrowly missed. She might have blamed the patriarchal state for this omission, but, instead, it seems that she blamed her mother: as Rachilde saw it, Gabrielle had failed both to provide female role models and to provide an education that would teach her daughter about the existence of such a prior tradition.

Instead, Rachilde's education had been haphazard and uninspiring. When Rachilde was growing up, secondary education for girls was neither required nor standardized. The loi Falloux of 1850 mandated an

école de filles in every commune of eight hundred or more people (reduced to five hundred or more in 1867), but funding was left up to the
individual municipalities, with the result that nearly all primary education for girls was still provided by the Catholic church. Also, while the
law required primary education, it ignored secondary education and
thereby even retarded the development of secondary education (Margadant 21). Of course, there were some private girls' schools in France,
though mostly in Paris and other large urban areas. Reforms did begin
under the Second Empire: in 1867, the minister of education, Victor Du-
ruy, had introduced municipal secondary courses for girls in an effort
to wrest education away from the church and inculcate basic civic values into girls of impressionable age. The *cours* had several advantages,
the main ones being financial: all that was required was a rented lecture
hall and lecture fees for (male) teachers from the boys' schools who
wanted to moonlight. In an effort to retain control, the church argued
that men teaching girls would lead to immorality, an argument that later
paved the way for the creation of a female teaching corps, but, meanwhile, the *cours* were a failure. By 1879, they survived in only five towns
(backward Périgueux probably not being one of them [McMillan 49]).

Thus, it was not until the reforms of the Third Republic in the 1880s
that the face of education changed significantly for French girls. Within
a short time, primary education became both free and compulsory,
while, at the secondary level, secular *lycées* were created for girls along
with female teacher-training schools. But all these reforms came too late
to affect Rachilde's education. By the 1880s, Rachilde was an adult, no
longer subject to the shaping influences of the state school system. If
the male writer is, as Harold Bloom has argued, always prone to "the
anxiety of influence," the need to assert one's difference from one's literary predecessors, what anxiety besets the woman writer who knows of
no predecessors or knows of them only anecdotally or as the butt of
jokes and disparagement? Of course, she may choose to view herself in
relation to male writers, but, if she feels that her sex sets her apart from
men in important ways, with whom does she identify in such agonistic
struggles? And to what extent is the school system responsible for making young writers aware of their predecessors and of what sets them
apart? Rachilde's anxiety, then, may have been an anxiety of originality
(rather than of influence), an ignorance of previous accepted women
writers made possible in part by her lack of formal education.

While future generations of women might benefit from the opportunities afforded by formal public instruction, Rachilde was stuck
with the advantages and disadvantages of her class, sex, and generation.

What education she did receive took place mostly at home (and later in a convent), was unsystematic, and was administered by priests or other representatives of the church.

Like most girls of the middle class at this time, Rachilde received only what little education was thought appropriate for her future needs. As a child, she attended a small private school in the village of Gorse run by Mademoiselle Eugénie Sauvinet (Pommarède, "Le Sol et le sang" 796). The schoolteacher in *Les Rageac*, who seems to be based on Sauvinet, is described as a "vieille demoiselle très pieuse regrettant amèrement que sa personnelle santé lui défendit de se consacrer à Dieu" who taught for five years "avec une remarquable timidité" (198). Thanks to this minimal and unchallenging instruction, Rachilde could sum up her educational achievements in a mock school report as follows: "Instruction religieuse? . . . néant! (comme on le voit sur les notes des écoliers) Histoire de France: quelques faits d'armes. . . . Géographie, ignore la position de l'Allemagne sur la carte. Morale: si on te donne une tape rends-en deux et ne joue jamais avec les petits garçons, parce qu'ils te prendraient tous les bonbons, ni avec les petites filles, parce qu'elles voudraient partager avec toi. . . . Talents d'agrément: dessin, musique, fables de La Fontaine et les contes incohérents de Lala" (*AM* vi).

This changed when Rachilde's education was taken in hand by a Jesuit priest. Rachilde claimed that this was her grandmother Izaline's idea and that taking the priest—a distant relative in disgrace—into the household would also fulfill vague family obligations. Rachilde's parents were slightly reluctant to comply because, "en ce temps-là, on avait peur d'être mal vus en protégeant des persécutés" (*Pourquoi* 36). According to Pierre Pommarède, this Jesuit named Raoul de Lambertere was actually part of the household of the countess de Lamenuse, who lived in the chateau of Château-l'Evêque and had an altar built for the abbé there so that he could celebrate mass. After the decrees of 1880 concerning the separation of church and state, a number of priests were taken in by the nobility in this way ("Le Sol et le sang" 797).

Whatever scruples the Eymerys may have had about this education, they eventually overcame them, and the severe and demanding "abbé Raoul" (as Rachilde refers to him) took over Rachilde's education, a task that proved harder than he had anticipated. He at first disclaimed responsibility, stating coldly that it was not within his powers to train a squirrel, but, with some humorous cajoling from Izaline, he set about his task by bribing his pupil with "les pralines à la rose des nouvelles découvertes instructives et relativement agréables" (*Pourquoi* 37). Rachilde also depicted the abbé Raoul in more disturbing terms in *La Souris japonaise* (1921).

Such informal arrangements had at least two consequences. First, Rachilde could remain ignorant of the fact that some women had succeeded in becoming nationally recognized as writers of canonical literature. Had Rachilde been one generation younger, she might have been subject to the national curriculum set forth for girls' secondary education. Here she would have received a mixed message. On the one hand, it is true that she would have encountered institutionalized messages about the expectations of women's silence. She might have encountered the opinions of Dupanloup (bishop of Orleans, 1849–78), for example, who firmly believed that the woman writer was an aberration of nature. The bishop, who helped shape the curriculum, stated that women should write only "à la condition qu'elle n'écrive que pour ses enfants et qu'elle ne soit jamais publiée" (quoted in Bricard 98).

Yet it is often the case that what one is supposed to learn in school and what one actually learns are two different things. Thus, Linda Clark has shown, specifically with reference to nineteenth-century French education for girls, that the curriculum offered an image of the bourgeois wife who stayed home and looked after the house even as the economic reality kept moving women out of the home and into the labor force. While the explicit content of education told girls that they should not be writers, the educational system itself offered a different message. The literary curriculum, for example, emphasized French literature over Latin for girls (Mayeur 211), with a predilection for the golden age of the seventeenth century (Bricard 96), which meant that girls had a chance to encounter the work of Madame de Sévigné and Madame de Maintenon (Bricard 96; Mayeur 214). They also learned — by example if not by design — that sometimes it was acceptable to disobey Bishop Dupanloup if one were publishing school manuals. A number of women were very successful authors in this genre: the famous reader *Tour de la France par deux enfants* (1877) was by a woman, Madame Alfred Fouillée (though she used the pseudonym G. Bruno); Madame Henry Gréville, also the author of numerous adventure novels, penned a textbook, *Instruction morale et civique des jeunes filles*, in 1882; and Clark identifies twenty-two other such women authors of textbooks (176 n.23).

In addition to suggesting that there was a role that women could play in the world of publishing, the reform of girls' secondary education required the creation of a teaching corps of women. Much has been written about the professionalization of teaching (see, for example, Gemie;

Margadant), but the point here is that, whether girls dreamed of becoming teachers, writers, or something else, the example of the secondary school teacher had the (no doubt unintended) effect of legitimizing
all girls's professional aspirations (see also McMillan 51). Despite the
fact that education in the last two decades of the nineteenth century
could be experienced by girls as confining, the effects of these reforms
were dramatic and offered new narratives for women's lives in the future.[14] By the dawn of the twentieth century, the experience of schooling itself was well enough established that it could generate a literary
subgenre, starting with Colette's *Claudine à l'école* (1901) at the beginning of the century. The professional role of the schoolmistress was well
enough defined that, as Gemie points out, Rachilde's contemporary
Paul Adam could write in his novel *Stéphanie* in 1913 that the heroine
was "too ignorant for the demanding role of the schoolmistress" without further comment (78).

Rachilde barely missed all this; her education followed almost the
opposite of what would become the state-recommended curriculum.
While the girls's curriculum in French focused on the seventeenth century, for example, Rachilde's literary education would be primarily in
eighteenth-century literature, the period most avoided by the official
curriculum (Bricard 96). She would read Voltaire and Sade where a generation later her younger sisters would encounter Madame de Sévigné.
Of course, for Rachilde, such reading took place outside the institutional context altogether. She found such works in her grandfather's library, in which she was allowed to browse, and the institutional side of
her educational experience provided different lessons.

Rather than attending a secular, state school with a standardized curriculum, Rachilde was sent to a convent as a teenager. To begin with,
this "education" was a punishment, not a privilege. Rachilde was "sentenced" to convent life because she had refused to marry Jacques de La
Hullière, and what she learned principally was to mortify her body
rather than improve her mind. In her description of these convent years
in *Face à la peur*, intellectual development plays no role at all; rather,
Rachilde learns *not* to mind—not to mind cold, not to mind hunger,
not to mind solitude (see "1953: On Minding").

Rachilde would fill the lacunae in her knowledge of women writers
later. Thus, she eventually learned about the existence of such popular
novelists as George Sand, although Sand's reputation at this time was
not that of an officially sanctioned literary figure. Still, Rachilde modeled herself fairly consciously on such examples, following the scandalous things that were known about Sand, such as her cross-dressing.

Rachilde did not know about such cases at a time in her education when it mattered, however, and she certainly did not know (at a time when it mattered) about socially accepted women writers, ones who were so acceptable that they were deemed suitable to be taught to children.

The second effect of her haphazard education was that Rachilde did learn about a whole lot of things that she was not ready for. Since she had free access to her grandfather's library and read things like Sade and Voltaire rather than the solicitous letters of Madame de Sévigné, what she learned about women's roles was somewhat different. The scariness of such premature knowledge is preserved in the sexual knowledge that Mary Barbe acquired from her uncle the doctor in *La Marquise de Sade*.

One of the dimensions, then, of Rachilde's anger at her mother comes from her mother's failure to provide for her in a literary sense as well as in an interpersonal sense. The parent to whom she looked for support in her literary endeavors failed to tell her that she was not alone in wanting to be a woman writer and that social acceptance as a women writer might be possible.

Even more alarming, while for many years her mother was Rachilde's only connection to the literary world and therefore the parent with whom she identified in many ways, Gabrielle became increasingly insane. If, as Gilbert and Gubar have suggested in *The Madwoman in the Attic*, nineteenth-century women writers often felt that their desire to write was a sign of madness and monstrosity, how much more intense must this fear have been for Rachilde when confronted with her mother's very real signs of madness. The desire to kill the mother, the *mer/mère*, must for Rachilde have been overwhelmingly powerful at times, especially when compounded with the terrifying fear that, since madness can be inherited, she was destined to become mad, too. She expresses this fear on a number of occasions, and the desire to kill her mother seems both punitive and prophylactic.

Time brought little reassurance. Although Rachilde came to know popular and indubitable success as an author, her mother became indubitably what is popularly known as "mad." Gabrielle Eymery was in some ways her daughter's mirror image, her alter ego, her portrait. Just as Dorian Gray's portrait took on the outward signs of age and vice, so Rachilde's mother took on the madness of the woman writer. While Rachilde started out pretending to hear voices in a story that her mother may have written, over the years her mother replaced her as the prisoner of these hallucinations, enabling Rachilde to escape them. The ventriloquist becomes the dummy, while the dummy learns to speak for itself.

Gabrielle stayed at Charenton (now renamed the Hôpital Esquirol after the doctor who formulated the concept of monomania in 1810) for less than a year. In December, Dr. Ritti noted her symptoms: "Délire de persécution. Hallucinations de l'ouïe. Troubles de la sensibilité générale. Idées de grandeur." His monthly reports from 1901 changed little. In January and February, he merely noted "même état." By March, the only change was that now the patient was trying to hide her symptoms—"Dissimule son délire. Nie ses hallucinations"—which continued throughout April and May. In June, she gave up pretending: "Reparle de ses communications occultes avec de grands personnages." Gabrielle Eymery was finally released in September 1901. The last comment written by Dr. Ritti before signing his name: "Non guérie."

Just as the spirit voices dictated their words to "Magui," who became a writer by following their instructions, the voices in Gabrielle's head made a writer of her, too, although not one who would present her writing as fiction. Gabrielle became a writer of letters. Pierre Pommarède cites police files in both national and regional archives containing "des lettres extravagantes à des personnalités en vue dont [Gabrielle Eymery] se sent conseillée dans des 'hallucinations auditives'" ("Le Sol et le sang" 816). Rachilde had stopped writing to strangers like Victor Hugo, but her mother carried on the work of writing madness.

Gabrielle Eymery would not die until September 15, 1910, at which point Rachilde inherited her furniture. Rachilde no doubt hoped that she would never inherit the furnishings of her mother's mind.

Women and Surrealism

In which Rachilde gets into a bun fight

A number of witnesses and critics have described the banquet Saint-Pol-Roux, that memorable encounter on Thursday, July 2, 1925, that started out as a dinner organized by the *Mercure* to honor the poet and ended by deteriorating into a bun fight that staged a literary and literal confrontation between what was perceived as the old guard and the new avant-garde, represented by the surrealists. For Shattuck, for example, the event marked the end of "the banquet years," that period of innovation and ferment that broke with both realism and finally even symbolism and led to modernism (359–60).

And many people remember or repeat that, as the banquet came to an end, Rachilde was one of the people still fighting. According to Dauphiné (*Rachilde* [1991] 72), she came to blows with Max Ernst, for example. For Shattuck, the events unfolded as follows:

> Along with all the young bloods of surrealism, such venerable figures as Lugné-Poe and Rachilde were present. These former collaborators of Jarry's were now considered reactionary. When, in the middle of the meal, Rachilde stoutly affirmed the patriotic sentiment that "a French-woman must never marry a German," sufficient provocation had been provided for the start of hostilities. André Breton rose to defend the insulted nationality of Max Ernst, the German surrealist painter, present at the banquet. It is said Breton went so far as to fling his napkin in Madame Rachilde's face and call her a fille à soldats. While shouts of Vive l'Allemagne resounded through the building, the tumult centered around the figure of Philippe Soupault, who was swinging from the chandelier capsizing glasses and dishes with his feet. The traditional pieces of overripe fruit found their mark among dignitaries of the banquet. An irate crowd formed outside, ready to attack the sales artistes who were now yelling out the window "Down with France." There was considerable damage inside the restaurant, and the police could barely prevent a lynching as the banqueters emerged. The affair ended violently with several arrests and injuries. (359–60)[1]

In accounts such as these, Rachilde gets represented as beleaguered and victimized. She also consistently gets lined up with the old guard by virtue of her attack on the surrealists. Rachilde had not always been at odds with the surrealists, however. She had corresponded sympathetically with André Breton, and Cocteau had been a supporter in 1917, crowing, "Vive la France et Rachilde" (quoted in "Rachilde et la France" 45). This chapter reexamines Rachilde's reactionary tendencies and argues that, while she certainly had many allegiances with fellow writers from the symbolist days, her hostility toward surrealism marked a resistance to a specific literary movement in which she felt she had no place rather than an attack on modernist tendencies in general. While in some senses she had no place because the movement valued innovative literary values that threatened to displace her own (innovative in their own day but now passé), the lack of place for her was not only about literary rivalry and old versus new. It was also about the displacement of women as writers and a certain view of what would be considered innovation (and hence modernism).

At least one person, for example, thought that Rachilde had actually gone to the banquet looking for a fight. Her colleague at the *Mercure de France* Paul Léautaud noted in his diary the day after the banquet that she had gone to the dinner armed with a revolver (1:1618–21). Later in July, Léautaud also heard surrealist Louis Aragon's version of events. According to him, no one had even touched Rachilde (1:1626).[2] Léautaud frequently displays no small amount of animus toward Rachilde in his diary, so he was predisposed to believe that she was acting in bad faith and looking for trouble, but his observation is consistent with the way in which Rachilde liked to present herself. Rachilde's pose as target, rather than attacker, was yet another example of her self-presentation as victim. On the one hand, this was typical of her consistent need to present herself as the underdog and her search for self-promotion and publicity through scandal, but the confusion about the real role that Rachilde played in this event is also a story about the way in which surrealism comes to dominate French modernism and the consequences of that dominance for women writers.

In part, the rise of surrealism was a natural literary phenomenon: those who were once the avant-garde (in this case, the symbolists) come to represent the old guard and are in turn challenged by newcomers (in this case, the surrealists). But this time there are several inflections that need to be noted: the misogyny of surrealism, which marginalized women writers and artists; the dominance of surrealism, which rendered other forms of modernism invisible; the perceived foreignness of surrealism, which activated certain reactionary nationalist tendencies and alienated Rachilde.

It is true that, even before the banquet, Rachilde had become politically quite conservative. On the eve of World War I, Léautaud reflected on the increasingly bourgeois values of Vallette: "L'héritage de Rachilde, son auto, sa Légion d'honneur, ses nouvelles relations, tout cela a bien changé Vallette. Il faut l'entendre parler du peuple, des ouvriers, lui, l'ancien ouvrier mécanicien, et de la rigueur, de la poigne avec lesquelles on devrait mener les gens" (1:953). The war only intensified this trend in the Vallette-Rachilde household. For one thing, it revived all the fears of 1870, the patriotism, xenophobia, and germanophobia, only this time Rachilde and her immediate family were much closer to the action. Rather than being tucked away in the Périgord, they were in Paris, where fears of another German invasion were all too vivid. In September 1914, just after the war broke out, Rachilde and Vallette fled to Charité-sur-Loire (in the Nivernais). While they visited Paris occasionally—they both attended the banquet for Apollinaire at the Palais d'Orléans on December 31, 1916, for example (Léautaud (1:1008)—they returned permanently to Paris only in 1917 after the Marne victory (Léautaud (2:913–17). Even then, they kept their bags packed ready to flee again at a moment's notice.

Rachilde alternated between aggression and pacifism, depending on the moment. Léautaud caught her in a bad moment: "Tout chez elle est revêtement, attitude, artificiel. Elle parle, sans qu'on puisse rien rattacher de ses paroles à quelque chose de vraiment senti ou pensé. Aujourd'hui elle est dans les pacifistes, fait partie des réunions avec Séverine. Il y a un an, elle demandait qu'on lui donnât un 'Boche' entre les mains pour lui écrabouiller la tête contre le mur" (1:1033). It did not help that Rachilde's son-in-law, Robert Fort, was injured in battle. Now Rachilde had a specific grievance against the Germans, a personal as well as a patriotic justification for whichever side of the fence she happened to be on.

World War I also changed the climate of gender politics, as Mary Louise Roberts has recently shown. Feminism and calls for women's rights suddenly seemed selfish coming from a segment of society that had not been called on to make any personal sacrifice in the war (or so it was perceived). The symbols of female emancipation—childlessness, short hair—were viewed with mixed feelings. While the 1920s was thus the era of the liberated flapper, it was also a moment of growing conservatism, a trend that carried Rachilde along with it. Thus, both personal experience and the broader cultural climate pushed Rachilde in more conservative directions. By the end of the decade, she would join the chorus of voices denouncing feminism with the publication of *Pourquoi je ne suis pas féministe* in 1928. While this pamphlet is in fact more about personal history than about feminism or politics, the title plays into a certain public perception of feminism, and, in some ways, the content of the book is secondary to the proclamation made in the title.

In the case of broader political sympathies, Rachilde's hatred of German fascism was determined by her general opposition to everything German, but it does not follow that she opposed fascism in general, and her germanophobia should not be mistaken for a left-wing critique of fascist ideology. On the contrary, throughout the 1920s and 1930s, Rachilde sympathized with a number of reactionaries. She no longer fraternized with such right-wing figures as Barrès, who had by now evolved into one of France's most important neofascist thinkers. Indeed, in 1921, Rachilde participated in the mock trial of Barrès, along with many of the surrealists—but then, of course, so did Pierre Drieu la Rochelle, who would later become a Nazi collaborator (see Marguerite Bonnet). While Rachilde shunned Barrès, however, she collaborated with other figures on the Right such as the futurist F. T. Marinetti and Francisco de Homem-Christo, with whom she wrote two books in the 1920s: the epistolary *Le Parc du mystère* (1923) and the short story collection *Au seuil de l'enfer* (1924).

Some of the details of Rachilde's friendship with and influence on Marinetti have already been described (see my "(En)Gendering Fascism"). The point to be emphasized here is that, if it is true that Marinetti's thinking was influenced by Rachilde, and if it is also true that Marinetti's futurism was a precursor of Italian fascism (though both these suppositions are open to debate), then it follows that Rachilde played a role in shaping the cultural roots of fascism, at least in its Italian manifestations.

Sympathy for Mussolini also colors Rachilde's friendship and collaboration with Francisco de Homem-Christo. Originally from Portugal, Homem-Christo had made a name for himself as a firebrand by refusing to take the religious oath when admitted to the University of Coimbra, defending himself with force, then converting to Catholicism anyway. He died prematurely in a car accident in 1928 (anticipated in *Le Parc du mystère*)—thus the way in which his politics would have developed remains forever unknown, but he was said to have been driving to meet Mussolini when he met his death instead. When Vallette showed Rachilde the report of Homem-Christo's death in *Débats*, she responded: "Il devait être en route pour Rome. . . . Il était à la solde de Mussolini. Il me l'avait dit" (quoted in Léautaud 1:2273).

After this accident, Rachilde even put it about that she suspected Homem-Christo of having been a spy, and Vallette liked to repeat that there was some sort of mystery in his background. He came from a "good" Portuguese family and had undertaken some vague missions in South America during World War I. Vallette thought it odd that Homem-Christo got people like Poincaré to attend dinners but that, when Rachilde wanted to get him awarded a decoration, it was always out of the question. (Rachilde and Vallette would later attribute this to the fact that Joé de Chogas, a Portuguese diplomat, was having an affair with Homem-Christo's wife.) According to Vallette, Homem-Christo's appearance contained many elements: "A la fois du sbire, de l'espion, de l'escroc" (Léautaud 1:1680–84; 2:86).

Despite Rachilde's patriotism when it came to people such as Apollinaire, these shady associations do not seem to have been reasons to shun Homem-Christo; on the contrary, she cultivated his acquaintance. Rachilde's politics seem always to have been determined by what would be most annoying to whatever she believed to be the establishment position. Thus, when it was popular among the symbolists to support Dreyfus, Rachilde was the gadfly antidreyfusard (arguably even an overt anti-Semite). If the majority worried about one of Mussolini's spies being in their midst, she would defend the individual in question instead. Her impulse to defend the underdog and brave ignominy and unpopularity would be laudable were it not for the fact that she so often chose her causes unwisely and so often exploited the occasion for self-promotion.

Further evidence of Rachilde's own conservative political thinking comes from her writing both at this time and later. Her antifeminism has already been alluded to in *Pourquoi je ne suis pas féministe*. In *Face à la peur*, her book of World War II memoirs, she makes her political sympathies clearer: she despised the Front Populaire and thought that the country needed a strong leader. After telling an anecdote about a handyman to whom she paid a deposit for some work that he never returned to complete, she concludes: "Le meneur de foule, député ou ministre, qui eut le triste honneur d'inventer *le front populaire* et dont le front personnel aura à rougir, dans l'histoire, d'avoir encouragé le peuple français à trouver naturel d'être payé pour se croiser les bras, n'a-t-il donc pas songé que la paresse est la mère de tous les vices et qu'il allait créer des voleurs et des assassins parmi de braves imbéciles qui s'embêtaient de ne pas mieux employer leur force?" (78). Whatever sympathies Rachilde held for the underdog as worker when she associated with bohemians, socialists, and anarchists in the 1880s and 1890s, these sympathies had long since evaporated.

During World War II, when her books were placed on the Otto list of proscribed authors because her name was mistakenly thought to indicate Jewish ethnicity (through confusion with the name Rachel), Rachilde protested (see Auriant, *Souvenirs* 1989; and "Rachilde et la France" 57). This could be seen as a desire to distance herself from any association with Jewish identity, but it is not necessarily evidence of anti-Semitism.[3] By then, Rachilde was dependent on her books for her income. Vallette had died in 1935, and she had no savings. (Her financial difficulties have been described elsewhere [see Dauphiné, *Rachilde* (1991) 142–57].) So to have her books banned represented a severe economic threat.

Antisemitism was also probably irrelevant to Rachilde's hatred of the Germans, which was already well established after the 1870 war and was only intensified by World War I. She came to hate everything that she identified as of German origin. She repeatedly referred to Apollinaire, for example, as a German, a foreigner, even a "Russian," and was often later heard by Léautaud to say things like, "En voilà un qui a bien fait de mourir" (Léautaud 1:1846). She and Vallette refused to contribute to a monument for Apollinaire on the grounds that there were too many foreigners on the organizing committee: "des métèques, des cubistes, des bolchevistes, des dadaïstes et autres sortes de Boches" (Léautaud 1:1154). In an exchange with Picabia in *Comoedia* in 1920, Rachilde also explained her view of dadaism: "Le mouvement *Dada* n'est pas français: il est né en Suisse, de parents *allemands* quoique neutres" (quoted in "Rachilde et la France" 51; see also Sanouillet). Called to account by Picabia, she elaborated in a later article: "C'est un mouvement suisse bien français hautement approuvé par les Allemands. Vous êtes roumains, en outre, par M. Tristan Tzara" (quoted in "Rachilde et la France" 51). Although Rachilde was reconciled with Picabia by the end of the year and he subsequently attended her salon, the exchange reveals something of the way in which Rachilde used nationalism to express a sense of belonging or alienation.

It is only logical, then, that, if she identified surrealism as of German origin, she would hate this movement and all that it represented, too. Although the surrealists counted Jarry as one of their influences, the movement indeed had important international connections—which

was one of its appeals, at least to others—but the German and Rumanian origins of Ernst and Tzara gave Rachilde reason enough to get up on
the table and hurl stale bread at them.[4]

Rachilde was thus a politically reactionary figure, but this is a trait
that she shared with numerous other contemporary women who have
nevertheless been linked literarily to modernism, such as Natalie Barney, Colette, and Gertrude Stein. The distinction between German,
Nazi ideology and the less racially motivated example of Italian fascism
is also relevant to a number of these cases, too. Because some of these
writers opposed Nazism, it has been all too easy to assume that they all
opposed fascism *tout court*, but such is not the case. Barney, along with
Romaine Brooks, may have opposed Hitler, but both took refuge in fascist Italy during World War II, and I have argued elsewhere that Colette's work betrays certain reactionary tendencies (see "'C'est si simple,
c'est si difficile'"). In the case of Stein, recent revelations about her
Vichy sympathies have raised troubling questions about her politics (see
Van Dusen). Reactionary politics do not preclude an assessment of
Rachilde's role as a modernist.[5]

The perception that Rachilde was a literary reactionary (as opposed
to merely a political one) stems from her perceived role in the banquet
Saint-Pol-Roux and her legendary opposition to the surrealists, but
it must be recalled that surrealism was generally inhospitable to all
women, especially those who dared to escape their role as muse and
claim a role as artist, an old and familiar attitude that Rachilde would
have known from her days as a bohemian. While, in recent years, there
have been attempts to document the participation of women in surrealism (and Rachilde was acquainted with women such as Valentine de
Saint Point), it is also widely accepted that the movement had significant misogynistic tendencies.[6] Rachilde's resistance to the surrealists—
her reaction to this particular expression of gender anxiety—can thus
be read, not merely as reaction or xenophobia, although those factors
also play a part, but as indeed the very expression of her modernism.

For it has become increasingly clear that modernism is characterized, not only by experimentation in form, but by its expression in both
theme and form of reactions to the new gender configurations that re-
sulted from nineteenth-century reforms (legal, educational, and elec-
toral) as well as the social upheavals wrought by the Great War. Part of
the misogyny of surrealism, then, stemmed from the gender anxiety
that marks modernism in general, as critics such as Sandra Gilbert and
Susan Gubar (in the three-volume *No Man's Land*) and Bonnie Kime

Scott (in *Refiguring Modernism*) have shown. Surrealism resonates with sexual insecurity and gender anxiety, both in general and in the specifically French context.

This can be seen already in the work of some of the precursors of surrealism: the unique work of Jarry, whom the surrealists hailed as a model; the work of futurists such as Marinetti; and the work of early modernists such as Apollinaire (who also coined the term *surrealism*). All these men register a certain gender anxiety in their work; all were also friends to various degrees with Rachilde. This is not to say that Rachilde is *responsible* for their anxiety (though she might be, at least in part), but rather that she is representative of a certain kind of woman, of a certain generation of women, who made inroads into areas of male privilege—in the arts, in education, in the media, and even to some extent already in politics—and began to unsettle the previously unchallenged sense of secure superiority.

In each case, the anxiety expresses itself in the form of overcompensation. Alfred Jarry, for example, one of Rachilde's closest friends, wrote a novel with the prophetic and highly compensatory title of *Le Surmâle* (The superman) in 1902. In this precursor of modernism, the hero, André Marcueil, sets a new world record for the number of times he is able to have intercourse in a day. The irony here, of course, is that, while André shares a number of characteristics with Jarry himself (for example, his passion for cycling), André is primarily a sexual superman and Jarry was, by all accounts, somewhat asexual. Not that he was unattractive or undesirable. He apparently seduced Boni de Castellane's mistress—but in order to play a trick on Castellane, not because he was attracted to her. But it is widely accepted that Jarry's inclinations were more toward men, as I have argued above (see "1894: Male Anxiety at the Fin de Siècle"). André's heterosexuality, then, is more a veiled expression of hostility toward women than an expression of attraction, as his performance as a lover of women suggests: he fucks his lover to death.

Rachilde was one of the first to praise the work of the Italian futurist F. T. Marinetti (the admiration was mutual), particularly his novel *Mafarka, le futuriste* (1910). This novel (written in French) is considered one of Marinetti's most important contributions to the development of futurism and hence modernism. Like the work of Jarry, it is misogynistic, not only a fantasy of male parthenogenesis that gives men power over reproduction and makes women redundant, but also a compensation fantasy in which the hero, Mafarka, narratively endows himself with a penis eleven cubits long (five and a half meters). Like André, Ma-farka's need to rape, dominate, and sexually torture women masks homoerotic elements,[7] and the fantasy of superhuman sexual prowess is not to bring pleasure to women but to punish them. Marinetti's own predatory heterosexuality—the literary manifestations of which have recently been complemented by translations from his own diaries documenting his need to perform sexually (see "Selections from the Unpublished Diaries")—thus takes on almost a pathological quality. Karen Pinkus has recently suggested that "Mafarka the futurist is a repository for bourgeois fears" (41), and I would add that these are often bourgeois *male* fears, including the kind of male fears of women analyzed in the work of German fascists by Klaus Theweleit.

Guillaume Apollinaire was well enough acquainted with Rachilde that she confided in him, as shown by anecdotes recorded in his diary that have already been cited, even though she professed on numerous occasions (though mostly *after* World War I) that she disliked him. Apollinaire was also one of the few men who published under a female pseudonym (in the history of literature, it has mostly been the other way round). Perhaps because female sensibility was perceived as an advantage in the domain of art criticism, Apollinaire used the pseudonym "Louise Lalanne" to pen the rubric "littérature féminine" in *Les Marges* from 1909 to 1910.

On the surface, Apollinaire seems to have found easy success with a series of women—Annie, Marie, Lou, Madeleine, and Jacqueline—but neither identifying with women nor being a great lover of women quite masks the underlying sexual anxiety expressed in both his life and his work. His relationships with women suggest that, while he could be quite charming (when he was in the army, Lou went to a lot of trouble to track him down without knowing his address or even his full name), there was a troubling underside. Annie was so afraid of his possessiveness and sexual jealousy that, in Steegmuller's words, "she feared for her life" (71). At least in Annie's mind, it would appear that Apollinaire was capable of enacting a form of André Marcueil's fatal heterosexuality; she emigrated to America to get away from him. In another troubling episode, Apollinaire proposed marriage to Madeleine even though their entire acquaintance was limited to a train ride from Nice to Marseilles and a subsequent exchange of letters.

Did Apollinaire love women or a certain image of women? The author of incomparably beautiful lyric love poetry, this *mal aimé* also wrote a considerable amount of violent pornography. One such novel has the title *Les Onze Mille Verges* (Eleven thousand pricks). Where Jarry compensates with frequency and Marinetti with size, Apollinaire compensates with sheer numbers.

Apollinaire, too, seems to emphasize heterosexuality to disguise a fascination with homosexuality. His *Journal intime* reveals a concentrated predilection for gay anecdote and gossip. On one page, he returns home from an encounter with "Léa" who "dit aimer aussi les femmes" (115). On the next, we meet Jeanne, who eloped with an Englishman to Calcutta, where "elle tribadise avec une soeur de la Recouvrance" (116). The next page offers an anecdote overheard at a performance of *Claudine*: "J'ai dû renvoyer mes domestiques, ma femme me trompait," says one man. His companion inquires, "Avec le valet de chambre?" but the first man replies, "Non, avec la femme de chambre" (117). Some pages later, Apollinaire notes that Max Jacob, Bernouard, and Doury are "tous tantes" (142) and that "Salmon est devenu très tante" (145). And, a few pages later, he notes, "Fauré couche avec Debussy" with no further comment or explanation (149).

Thus Apollinaire displays the same constellation of factors noted in the work of Jarry and Marinetti: homosexual panic, misogyny, compensatory sexual fantasies. If these figures are representative of the avant-garde in early twentieth-century France, Rachilde's resistance becomes somewhat clearer.

It is still true that Rachilde was part of the old guard. Perhaps she had lived too long. It was inevitable that she would see her reputation decline when she survived symbolism, but the superficially radical break of surrealism and its dominance of the avant-garde also obscured ways in which Rachilde's writing did evolve in the postwar period.

This is not to say that Rachilde's writing changed radically—her fiction is full of examples of ambivalence toward modern life, and not all aspects of modernity were greeted with enthusiasm. Her depictions of jazz clubs and the café atmosphere of cubist, postwar Paris present yet another negative view of the modern era. *Les Voluptés imprévues* (1931) echoes *Le Prisonnier* (discussed in "1928: Gender Anxiety in French Modernism") in its focus on the feelings of an older man, François de Valerne, for the younger Lucien Girard, but it presents François as somewhat more self-deluded about his feelings, confusing his desire with paternal protectiveness.

Lucien is a war refugee and a latter-day dandy: "Fatigué (depuis sa naissance) [il] représentait le monde nouveau, sinon le meilleur, et il était naturellement artificiel" (11). François accompanies Lucien to various shady—in both senses of the word—nightclubs, for example, one where a "feminist" is to speak and there are "tables cubistes" (37). The clubs represent a synecdoche of modern society, encompassing a babel of different languages, loose morals, lascivious modern dances, jazz, cocktails, politics, and what would now perhaps be called *gender bending*: "On n'est jamais sûr du sexe de l'individu qui vient prendre place en face de vous" (25).

Such changes represent, not freedom, however, but a lowering of standards, at least as far as the main protagonists are concerned. That such modernity is vulgar is clear, not only from the judgmental descriptions and from the satirical presentation of characters such as the boorish Communist deputy, but also in a concisely revealing scene in which, seeing another man caress Lucien's neck, Valerne responds by throwing his gloves right in the mouth of a black jazz singer performing at the club.

On the other hand, some of Rachilde's fiction from the interwar years indeed offers some "unexpected pleasures" (to borrow the title of her novel), and Rachilde herself continued to challenge the status quo, as an analysis of one of her novels of this period, *Le Grand Saigneur* (1922), will show. Before we consider this novel, however, her work from this period must be set within the larger context of the role of gender anxiety in the evolution of modernism.

In her fiction from the interwar years, it is possible to discern without doubt a pattern that links Rachilde's work to that of other women writers of this period. Her heroes are often typical of the shell-shocked figures that have been noted in Anglophone modernist fiction of the post–World War I period (noted, for example, in Gilbert and Gubar, *No Man's Land*, esp. vol. 2, chap. 7), reflecting the intersection of the moral and intellectual crisis following the war coupled with gender anxiety caused by women's greater claims to and presence in the public world. Thus, the brother of the heroine of *Le Grand Saigneur* is a neurasthenic version of the Archangel Michael, while the angst-ridden hero of *Madame de Lydone, assassin* (1928), the wolfish Gaston Louveteau, is a pilot unable to find a place in postwar society.

An even more extended treatment of the theme is offered in *L'Homme aux bras de feu* (1930), whose hero has been marked indelibly by his wartime experiences. Rachilde explains the general effects of the war on French society: "Après la guerre, la bonne société française fut saisie d'une indicible angoisse dont le vrai nom est *la peur*, mot qui n'est pas français, mais qui s'introduisit dans le langage courant sous différents pseudonymes tels que: neurasthénies, phobies, névroses, intoxications, folies de tous genres, monomanies de la persécution, des gran-

deurs, des petitesses, du ridicule, vices de toutes les sortes, vertiges per-
mettant l'oubli momentané du grand vertige de la mort" (77). The hero,
Gilles de Kerao, has been particularly affected by a narrow escape from
death. He recounts how the commander of the submarine on which he
was serving, his uncle, had run out of torpedoes and consequently decided to use the submarine itself to ram a German ship. Gilles was the
only survivor, which led him to vow, on the bodies of his comrades,
never to marry and never to have children. That such treachery should
have been perpetrated by a blood relative no doubt played no small role
in the decision not to continue the family name, but Gilles is also symbolically committed to not reproducing a certain social order, and his
decision has more than personal implications.

Rachilde's female counterparts to these unmanned males do not represent the corresponding models of emancipation one might expect,
however, on the basis of the observations of heroines who populate
other modernist texts, women empowered by their wartime experiences. In *Le Château des deux amants* (1923), for example, it is a woman,
not a man, who is paralyzed. A more extended counterexample can be
found in *Madame de Lydone, assassin* (1928), where the eponymous
heroine, an eccentric countess, regrets the past rather than welcoming
the new freedoms for women. As the novel opens, readers find themselves in a Paris neighborhood "où l'on peut se croire très loin du siècle" (5). Madame de Lydone lives in a Napoleon III–style building,
carefully protected from "progress," which she continually bemoans:
standards of justice and education have declined, vandalism has increased, she does not like new technology, and she refuses the offer of a
plane ride, although she is reconciled to motorcars.

Lest it seem that this "petite fille de Voltaire" (112) is totally reactionary, however, it should be noted that she is a true libertine when it
comes to freedom of thought and that, in this sense, she is indeed "hors
du temps, des conventions et de l'existence normale" (18). She does not
agree with Gaston's mother, a "bourgeoise rangée," that her nephew
Gaston should be in a hurry to settle down and get married, for example. Indeed, she ends up falling in love with him herself, despite the
difference in their ages, creating a love triangle that will prove fatal.

While Rachilde's heroes experience a decline in their influence or
power, an impotence that speaks to both their sexual and their social
loss, her heroines do not seem to experience a concomitant emancipation. The heroine of *Le Grand Saigneur*, Marie Faneau, for example,
indirectly owes her freedom to the war but feels guilty about it. A successful artist, many of her commissions come from soldiers' relatives:

"Quand elle avait eu l'occasion de faire un portrait de *soldat* elle s'était sentie comme coupable . . . parce qu'elle aussi *profitait* de la guerre! Que de pauvres mères ou de pauvres veuves étaient venues la trouver avec une très mauvaise photographie en la suppliant de faire revivre les traits à jamais effacés sous une terre inconnue!" (53). Although Marie thus owes her economic independence to the war, her experience of this freedom remains tied to the cost, although, interestingly, the cost is expressed, not in terms of men's lives, but in terms of the unhappiness caused to their mothers and widows, other women.

Marie's independence is threatened by her attraction to the marquis de Pontcroix, the *grand saigneur* reputed to be a vampire (hence the pun in the title on *seigneur/saigneur*). He is a *revenant*, the play on words here combining the literal meaning (he has returned from—that is, survived—the war) with the more figurative meaning of a ghost. Marie's marriage is threatening, not just because the narrative contrives to suggest the bloody fate that awaits her on her wedding night, but because, once she is the "legitimate property" of the marquis, she loses her economic independence. Asked whether she thinks that the marquis will stop her from working, she responds: "De travailler, non. De gagner de l'argent, oui" (206). Her reply pointedly shows that the growing opposition to women's work in the post–World War I period was based, not on a desire to spare women from hard work, but simply on a resentment of their economic independence.

That the social, political, and economic situation of French women had improved during Rachilde's lifetime is undeniable: divorce had been legal once again since 1884; in 1907, married working women had finally gained legal control over their own income; and, in 1912, all women earned the right to bring paternity suits. While the war itself did not directly affect legal rights per se, it nevertheless offered new experiences of social and economic freedom and meaningful work. In the twentieth century, war has frequently been an incentive for women to acquire new abilities, such as learning to drive in World War I, thus giving more women more control over their mobility and hence their lives, and no doubt such incentives were at work in France earlier in the century. The interwar period is, after all, often remembered as the era of the flapper, a climate reflected in fiction, for example, in Victor Margueritte's *La Garçonne* (1922) as well as in Colette's *La Fin de Chéri* (to cite another woman author of the period) (see Bard, *Les Garçonnes*).

Rachilde's connections to the Left Bank would seem to place her in an environment where, even if she chose not to indulge in such freedoms herself, she would have been aware of their existence and growing importance. The antipathy with which the modern is presented in her fiction thus seems to call for comment. It is difficult to generalize about women's situation from one country to another. Thus, the patterns noted in British and American women's fiction may not apply to the French context, given the differences in French historical background, such as the French experience of occupation and the history of conflict dating back to the Franco-Prussian War of 1870.

The period following World War I was also a period of reaction in France (see Bard, *Les Filles de Marianne*; M. Perrot). To mention only one obvious but nevertheless telling fact, the suffrage movement made much slower progress in France: French women did not receive the vote after the Great War, as did their American and British counterparts; they had to wait until after World War II to gain that right. Nevertheless, Rachilde's fiction of the interwar years makes her more of a modernist than has previously been recognized. While her reactionary political sympathies are not to be underestimated, they do not necessarily preclude greater recognition of some of the ways in which her work registered and responded to the crisis in gender that lies at the root of modernism. As the retrospective dust settles on the banquet Saint-Pol-Roux and all that it represents for the battle to dominate the perception of modernism, it becomes possible to see that Rachilde was one of the people fighting for a different outcome.

Gender Anxiety in French Modernism

In which Le Prisonnier *is published and Rachilde acts rather queerly*

"On or about October 11, 1928, the character of the woman writer changed," asserts Bonnie Kime Scott, paraphrasing Virginia Woolf's famous formulation in order to pinpoint a later moment in modernist history (*Refiguring Modernism* 1:183). In a practical application of what Kristeva calls "women's time," and in recognition of Joan Kelly's insight that women's history might require different chronologies, Scott argues that, for women, modernism peaked, not in 1914 (as for men), but instead in 1928: "The women of modernism had come into a sense of their own strength by the late twenties, by which time many of the male modernists were feeling a loss of vitality" (1:109). She chooses 1928, not only because of historical factors (British women finally earned the right to vote on an equal basis with men), but also—and principally—because of the extraordinary list of publications by women that year: Djuna Barnes's *Ladies' Almanack* and *Ryder*; Radclyffe Hall's *The Well of Loneliness*; Rebecca West's *The Strange Necessity*; Nella Larsen's *Passing*; and of course Woolf's *Orlando* (its publication providing the date "on or about" which things changed for women so dramatically) as well as the lectures that would become *A Room of One's Own*. To this list of 1928 publications we might also add Margaret Mead's *The Coming of Age in Samoa*, not only because it made women and women's sexual experience the center of a major work of anthropology, but because, as Torgovnick notes, it is one of the first serious treatments of cross-cultural lesbian experience (even though it is buried in the appendices).

While this sea change is most evident in Anglophone literature, the French connections of the "women of 1928" cannot be ignored. Djuna Barnes's roman à clef *Ladies' Almanack* may have been written in English, but it was written, printed, and distributed in France (Herring 151–53), and it depicted the circle of writers and *salonnières* who surrounded Natalie Barney in Paris as well as Radclyffe Hall and her partner, Una Troubridge. The publication of Radclyffe Hall's *The Well of Loneliness*, parts of which were composed in Paris and which also depicted Natalie Barney's coterie, initiated an obscenity trial that created international ripples. As soon as the publisher, Cape, was forced to withdraw the book in England, it was to France that he turned. The

American edition of Hall's novel appeared the following year, 1929, and the publisher, Covici Friede, cashed in on the novel's notoriety by bringing out other risqué literary works, including the first English translation of Rachilde's *Monsieur Vénus*, published that same year, thereby placing Radclyffe (Hall) and Rachilde (whose name, as we saw earlier, was sometimes assimilated to that of [Ann] Radcliffe) in a kind of international juxtaposition.

At first glance, Rachilde would seem to be the antithesis of these modernist "women of 1928" (as Scott calls them, in comparison to the "men of 1914"), at least given her own publications in that year. After all, *Pourquoi je ne suis pas féministe* fares poorly when compared to *A Room of One's Own*. Yet 1928 was nevertheless a prolific year for Rachilde, and mid-October was significant for her in other ways. *Refaire l'amour* appeared early in 1928 (despite having been given a publication date of 1927), as did her memoirs of Jarry (in Carco's series on "la vie de Bohème"). She finished *Madame de Lydone, assassin* in September; she would spend the month of October correcting the proofs of that novel; on October 17, she attended a commemoration of the Hydropathes Club at the Sorbonne; and, most important, she would (again) defend *Le Prisonnier* at the October meeting of the Faubourg Club, a popular literary club (organized by Léo Poldès) at which Rachilde had been one of the regular subjects of discussion since early in the decade (*Refaire l'amour*, for example, had been discussed in March 1928 [Léautaud 1:2165, 2209; see in general 1:1189ff.).

The previous chapter presented the argument that the dominance of surrealism eclipsed Rachilde's contributions to literary developments of the interwar years. This chapter offers a counterpart to that argument, suggesting that Rachilde should be considered one of what Shari Benstock calls the "women of the Left Bank" and perhaps even one of the "women of 1928." The modernist aspects of her work have been underrated and neglected, but they exist nevertheless.[1]

If the publications of Anglophone women writers in 1928 highlight gender—a definitive element of modernism, as Gilbert and Gubar (in *No Man's Land*) along with others have argued—French publications of this period highlight sexuality, a culmination of almost a decade of publication and debate on homosexuality in particular.

The post–World War I period saw a relaxation of attitudes in France and a flourishing of gay male culture, especially in Paris (Barbedette). Perhaps, in the same way that the groundwork for post–World War II homophile societies in the United States was laid by the experience of what Allan Bérubé has called "coming out under fire," this tolerance re-

sulted in part from the homosociality of wartime experiences, which
had thrown men and women together (men in the trenches, women in
the land army or auxiliary services), experiences that were not simply
forgotten after the war. In such periods of crisis, the usual social re-
straints were removed, and the trials of war led to close bonding that
sometimes found sexual expression.

Whatever the causes of this sexually permissive mood in France,
the first gay periodical—the short-lived *Inversions*, founded in 1924—
appeared during this time (Robinson 21). On the level of public dis-
course, Gide defended homosexuality in *Corydon* (also 1924) and also
revealed his homosexual experiences in *Si le grain ne meurt* (1926).
Other writers described the homosexual subculture of that period in
later memoirs: Julien Green's *Jeunesse* (1974) "shows the ease with which
an inexperienced young man could pick up partners for casual sex,"
while Daniel Guérin's *Son testament* (1979) "claims that from his own
experience working-class boys in the period 1925–30 were relatively re-
laxed about taking part in recreational sex with another male of their
own age" (Robinson 20). In the literary realm, François Porché's study
of homosexual themes in literature, *L'Amour qui n'ose pas dire son nom*,
appeared in 1927. Although it was not a particularly sympathetic survey,
portraying homosexuality as a vice unrelated to love, it gave validity to
the subject.

In 1928, several new works took their place in gay literary history.
Cocteau published *Le Livre blanc*, one of his few explicitly homoerotic
works. True, it appeared anonymously, but that it was the work of Cocteau was an open secret (Robinson 50). This same year saw the publication of Francis Carco's *Dialogues des courtisanes* about drag queens
(Carco had commissioned Rachilde's book on Jarry) and of Maryse
Choisy's *Un Mois chez les filles*, one in a series of "reportages vécus" that
was followed in 1930 by her *L'Amour dans les prisons*. While *Un Mois
chez les filles* was concerned primarily with prostitution, *L'Amour dans
les prisons* dealt more explicitly with same-sex love among women.
"J'ai fait le voyage de Mytilène. J'ai fréquenté les lesbiennes les plus
célèbres de Paris, de Londres, de New York, d'Athènes," declared Choisy
(*L'Amour dans les prisons* 144). Such qualifications earned her an invitation to contribute to a special issue of the satirical journal *Le Rire* in 1932
on the topic of "Dames seules" (reprinted as *Cahiers Gai Kitsch Camp*
23 [1993]).

Some of Choisy's experience was obtained at Natalie Barney's salon (*L'Amour dans les prisons* 144), some in the company of Rachilde.
Choisy had "flirted" (her word) with surrealism but was also submitting

verse to the *Mercure de France* in part because, as she put it, "A cette époque [1925] le salon du Mercure était la première forteresse littéraire de Paris" (*Sur le chemin* 102). By frequenting the Mercure's salon, Choisy became intimate friends with Rachilde, who called her "rahat loukoum" ("Turkish delight"), and the two planned to collaborate on a book to be called *La Vie amoureuse de la vierge* ("Rachilde et la France" 46).

In early 1925, after Choisy had heard Rachilde's story about her de-frocked great-grandfather and the curse of the werewolf, she invited Rachilde to spend Candlemas (February 2, when the werewolves would appear) with her in her apartment to test the story. The evening was marked by some typically Rachildian gender play expressed through cross-dressing. Declaring, "Moi, je suis un homme," Rachilde arrived wearing a veil: "En 1925 elle est la seule à porter une voilette 1900" notes Choisy. This appearance "in drag," as it were (declaring herself a "man" but wearing a retro veil), once again draws attention to Rachilde's insistence on playful self-representation that stresses the conscious challenges to the boundaries of sex, class, and fashionable taste. Rachilde's transgressive behavior did not end with transvestism on this occasion, however. Late in the evening, after a dinner of crepes and champagne, and after sprinkling Rachilde with holy water to hasten the transformation into a werewolf, Choisy notices a change—"Son visage rond de chatte s'allonge en pointe de loup"—and, the next thing she knows, Rachilde is indeed transformed: "Elle brise une coupe, déchire ma jupe, hurle: 'je te veux!'" (*Sur le chemin* 106). Choisy deflects the attention by getting Rachilde to tell the story of how she rescued a hunted wolf, which makes her eventually drift off to sleep. The long-awaited werewolf never appears more manifestly than this, and Choisy astutely concludes: "Ce n'était pas un loup. C'était une femme comme les autres, qui voulait se faire illusion. Une romancière, quoi!" (108).

This anecdote sheds further light on Rachilde's sexual curiosity in the 1920s. In "1894: Male Anxiety at the Fin de Siècle," it was argued that, in some ways, her identity might be construed as that of the fag hag, but Choisy's experience suggests that Rachilde's identification with a male persona was more complicated still. Despite tactical denials of attraction to women, the same feelings that may have drawn her into a relationship with Gisèle d'Estoc forty years earlier persisted, perhaps requiring only too much champagne (or holy water) to manifest themselves.[2]

Rachilde's curiosity also led her to attend the *générale* of Edouard Bourdet's controversial play *La Prisonnière* (translated as *The Captive*) in 1926 at the Théâtre fémina. She took with her Maryse Choisy, about

whom she had become "possessive" (*Sur le chemin* 112). This play, a suc-
cès de scandale like much of Rachilde's work, would enjoy an international reputation, playing in cities such as New York, and was obviously
one of the references that Rachilde intended to evoke in *Le Prisonnier*. It
generated a "prisoner craze" with, among other things, a sartorial style
for women consisting of a severe black tailored suit worn with a high-
collared white blouse, a man's tie, and very short hair (as illustrated in
some of the cartoons reprinted in *Cahiers Gai Kitsch Camp* 23 [1993]).

Rachilde professed disdain and outrage in reaction to the play:
"Quelle époque! L'esprit parisien se dégrade. D'ailleurs Lesbos . . . je
suis contre. Je suis un homme, moi!" (Choisy, *Sur le chemin* 112). It is a
typical reaction for Rachilde, who often appears actively hostile toward
lesbians. Along with mothers, they always seem to come to a bad end in
her fiction, as though the author herself is punishing them. In *Madame
Adonis*, Marcelle is stabbed to death, for example, while, in *La Marquise
de Sade*, Mary Barbe sadistically brands the woman who makes sexual
advances. This fictional hostility has its counterpart in nonfictional
contexts, too. As already noted, Rachilde boasted to Apollinaire that she
punished a woman who tried to seduce her by flirting with the woman's
husband instead.

Rachilde's disparagement of lesbians is often taken at face value, but
Choisy insightfully sees beyond the superficial, asking rhetorically:
"Voulait-elle se cacher à elle-même qu'elle s'identifiait à la femme forte
de *La Prisonnière*?" (*Sur le chemin* 112). In some ways, then, Rachilde
seems a perfect example of the sexologists' definition of an invert—a
man trapped in a woman's body—except that this invert openly em-
braces a male identity but represses all feelings of attraction to women.
In the taxonomy of the sexologists, Rachilde is more like a gay man
trapped in a woman's body (of course the sexologists did not recognize
such a category).

In the light of her apparent bad faith or self-deception when it comes
to her own homoerotic tendencies, Rachilde's exploration of one man's
attraction to another in *Le Prisonnier* takes on added significance.[3] Although the work was coauthored with André David and therefore can
be seen as not necessarily reflecting Rachilde's own preoccupations, it
can be seen as an apologia for homoeroticism in general. Certainly, the
title invokes the lesbian themes, not only of Bourdet's play, but also of
Proust's *La Prisonnière*, an exploration of the narrator's attraction to the
lesbian Albertine.[4]

Rachilde and David's *Le Prisonnier* should be situated in the general
context of the sexually liberal 1920s as well as the more specifically liter-

ary debate swirling around the exploration of sexual themes in publications of the period. By taking advantage both of the popularity of the
gay theme and of the notoriety of scandal, the novel can be seen merely
as exploitation, but at the same time it nevertheless boldly demands to
be seen as a plea for homosexual tolerance, as a defense, particularly, of
the French literature on pederasty.[5]

The novel was published in June and immediately became the topic
of discussion: it was mentioned at the Faubourg Club before the month
was up. The novel presents the experience of a first-person narrator,
"un simple professeur d'histoires inutiles" (10), who acts as tutor and
guide to a young man of good family, with whom he falls in love. In the
process of struggling to balance impulse and intellect, the narrator also
attempts to articulate some theory of love that borrows from tribadism
but escapes reductive gender categories. Love is "électricité sentimen-
tale," he claims (42), and he continues: "Tous les corps sont électrisables
par frottement, à la seule condition que les deux surfaces frottées l'une
contre l'autre soient de nature différente. Mais est-il nécessaire pour
cela que le sexe soit différent?" (44). The relationship ends when a government scandal implicates the narrator by association, and he returns
to a seminary. While he has lost his faith, the cloistered life holds other
attractions: it allows him to continue to idolize a young male figure
while seeming to worship a crucifix.

A second debate at the Faubourg Club in October, at which Rachilde
defended the work, prolonged interest in the novel throughout the fall.[6]
Once again, there was talk of police involvement and censorship, and,
for a moment, it seemed like *Monsieur Vénus* all over again. Despite the
fact that Rachilde had repudiated that book earlier in the year (Léautaud
1:2209), she still had a reputation for writing pornography, and some of
her novels, such as *L'Heure sexuelle* (1898), could not be sold to women
or minors by the increasingly lucrative franchises of railway station
booksellers (Stora-Lamarre 186).

While Rachilde was exploiting the vogue of gay eroticism in *Le Prisonnier*, her interest in the topic was no doubt genuine. Rachilde continued to seek out the company of gay men, and, in the post–World
War I period especially, she drew attention to herself through her association with a group of gay men of a much younger generation. In 1930
(at the age of seventy), she was still going to parties and staying out late,
as Léautaud censoriously noted in his journal: "L'effarant c'est de voir
Vallette la laisser traîner partout, et la nuit jusqu'à 4 heures du matin,
avec tous ces jeunes gens d'allures assez équivoques. Jolis garçons pour
la plupart, d'ailleurs. Elle-même le répète à chaque instant, parlant de

l'un et de l'autre: 'il est si beau.' Elle-même dit qu'elle se doute bien de tout ce qu'on dit: 'C'est encore un petit jeune homme à Rachilde'" (2:575). Rachilde's energy for such an active nightlife would not desert her for years. In 1936 (six months after Vallette's death), she laughingly boasted, "Je cours les boîtes de nuit jusqu'à trois heures du matin" (Léautaud 2:1621). Rachilde chose to work closely with some of these "jeunes gens," such as André David, writing a preface for his *L'Escalier de velours* (1922) as well as collaborating with him on *Le Prisonnier*.

At the same time, Rachilde had ambivalent feelings about the life-style that these young men represented. At times, she was unsympathetic to public statements about gay male sexuality. Léautaud recorded a comment that Rachilde made to the effect that the current open discussions of sexuality were "à vomir" (2:116–19). In *L'Autre Crime* (1937), her alter ego protagonist, the countess Silvie de Givray, condones what today would be called a "homosexual panic" murder with the words, "Vous avez bien fait" (84). Rachilde's reactions were not only the result of postwar patriotism. In 1909, Jacques d'Adelswärd-Fersen wrote and invited her to contribute to a new review that he had founded, *Akademos: Revue mensuelle d'art et de critique* (the first issue appeared January 15, 1909). Rachilde had reviewed some of Adelswärd's work favorably in the past, including *Le Baiser* (1907), which was bound to find favor with her given its plot (the hero drowns in his own mirror image), and *Une Jeunesse* (also 1907), which Rachilde thought worthy of the Prix Goncourt (Ogrinc 44).[7] Rachilde seems to have followed the advice that Vallette scribbled on the letter of invitation, however: she declined to contribute and become publicly associated with this ostracized figure who had been convicted in 1903 of corrupting the morals of Parisian schoolboys (Ogrinc 31).[8] Perhaps some of Rachilde's reluctance came from the fact that pedophilia was viewed more severely than homosexuality, but other pronouncements show that, at times, she viewed merely the expression of support for homosexuality quite negatively.

In the March–April 1926 issue, the review *Les Marges* published an "enquête" on "l'homosexualité en littérature" in response to Gide's *Corydon* (republished in *Cahiers Gai Kitsch Camp* 19 [1993]:19–59). Rachilde was one of the respondents whose opinions were included (49–50). On the one hand, she stated that there was no point being coy or modest about such things, and she castigated hypocrisy, just as she had done in her defense of Wilde, but the latter part of her comments concern the spectacle of the flapper, the "insexué féminin," whose "mauvaises habitudes" would counter the tendency toward (male) homosexuality (50). This early defense of Gide is a fine example of damning with faint praise. Later, when Rachilde received a copy of *Latinité*'s "enquête" on Gide, she dashed off a "terrible" response and "est tout de suite tombée sur le pédéraste" (Léautaud 2:553). When François Porché's book appeared in 1933, she went on a tirade against it and "le goût de l'époque et des gens pour l'ordure, pour le fumier" (Léautaud 2:1298–99). In short, she was supportive of homosexuality mainly when it offered her the occasion to denounce hypocrisy and defend the underdog, when it provided her with the chance to play "Aimeri" getting the better of his peers (see "1877: Authority, Authorship, and Authorization"), but, when the issue of homosexuality threatened to eclipse her, she was quick to criticize.

But works such as *Le Prisonnier* and *Au seuil de l'enfer* (which was coauthored with Francisco de Homem-Christo and published in 1924, and which contains a discussion of transvestism)—works in which Rachilde explores theories about sexuality and love—are related in both form and content to other examples of modernist experimentation.[9] Like the other modernist "women of 1928," Rachilde was questioning the nature of love and gender, and the predilections of *Le Prisonnier* echo those of *Orlando, Ladies' Almanack,* and *The Well of Loneliness.*

In her exploration of gender and sexuality, Rachilde is clearly linked to a group of mainly expatriate Anglophone writers but more generally to a generation of modernist women writers. Just as the traditional paradigms of Anglophone literature have failed at times to perceive and capture the particular qualities of modernist women writers because they did not fit the paradigm of the "men of 1914," so the traditional French paradigms have underestimated the contributions of Rachilde's twentieth-century fiction. In Rachilde's case, this is not simply because she was being read against a male definition of modernism but because modernism has been more fragmented in the French context. While the origins of modernism in the nineteenth century have been explored (see, for example, Chambers), twentieth-century modernism is fragmented: surrealism dominates, and such figures as Gide and Proust are seen as following their own lights. The alternative paradigm of women's modernism helps show that we must think in terms of modernisms, rather than a single, one-size-fits-all paradigm in French as well as in English. In such a pluralistic view of literary history, it is easier to see the role that Rachilde played.

Recent discussions of the "women of the Left Bank" have revived interest in women writers of this interwar period and initiated a reappraisal of their work.[10] Rachilde is all too often given only brief consideration in these reevaluations,[11] yet it is known that Rachilde was part of

Natalie Clifford Barney's circle and was thus connected to an important social and literary network that linked her to many other modernist writers. The acquaintance between Rachilde and Barney dates at least to 1917 (Causse 239), when Rachilde attended feminist antiwar meetings held at the Temple de l'amitié, and continued through World War II, when Barney had her housekeeper, Berthe Cleyrergue, take food round to Rachilde to help her through the shortages (Causse 144).

Rachilde was clearly a member of what Cleyrergue dubbed "the French clan" rather than the American (see Orenstein; Causse). The two clans often had little interaction, but Barney organized a series of salons with the explicit intention of introducing the French to the Anglophone personalities, in the belief that their mutual influence would be a source of cross-fertilization in the arts. A card sent out in 1927, for example, announced the following program for June 3: "Rachilde, then Ford Madox Ford will discuss American women of letters, including Djuna Barnes" (Wickes 188). (It is far from clear that Rachilde accepted the invitation to Barney's, however.) [12] Other writers featured at the Friday salons that year included Colette (playing a scene from *La Vagabonde*), Lucie Delarue-Mardrus, Gertrude Stein, and a retrospective of the works of Renée Vivien. Thus, Barney played a pivotal role in bringing Anglophone and French traditions together, particularly around the time of 1928, when so many modernist women's texts appeared.

Rachilde also continued to be connected to a wide circle of French writers through her work for the *Mercure de France*. Although her involvement in the review began to diminish from the 1920s on (her last book review for the review appeared on April 15, 1924), she remained closely associated with it and continued to live on the premises at 26, rue de Condé. If that metonymy of modernism the rue de l'Odéon—which contained both Sylvia Beach's Shakespeare and Company (for the Anglophones) and, almost opposite, Adrienne Monnier's Maison des amis des livres (for the Francophones)—was the intellectual center of Paris in the interwar period, it should not be forgotten that the rue de Condé runs nearly parallel and eventually joins it.

The connection was more than merely geographic, however. Adrienne Monnier described the role of the *Mercure de France* in introducing her to literature in an article she wrote in 1946 ("*Le Mercure* vu par un enfant"). Monnier discovered the review when she was only ten years old, and, later, a visit to Rachilde in 1913 cemented her intentions to commit herself to a literary career on the Left Bank. Monnier was so impressed by the meeting with Rachilde that she believed that she "would have accepted sweeping the offices of the *Mercure*" (Monnier,

The Very Rich Hours 11). She was not called on to undertake such work, but, shortly afterward, when a sum of money became available to her, she was sufficiently inspired by her contacts with the literary world to use the money to open her own bookstore, and the Maison des amis des livres was born.

In addition to reminding us of the existence of these writers and of the extraordinary literary atmosphere that flourished in Paris at this time, however, recent scholarship has called, not just for literary history, but for theories and frameworks with which to reappraise these works. One fertile area of discussion already touched on has been the question of the role of expressions of gender and gendered anxiety in modernist fiction. Rachilde's work suggests that another productive theme was the modernist view of time. If in *Orlando* Woolf experimented with a protagonist who lives through five hundred years of history, and if in *Ladies' Almanack* Barnes adopts a deliberately archaic style, Rachilde can be said to explore the empowerment of women through a deployment of nostalgia in such novels as *Madame de Lydone*.

This work foregrounds one of Rachilde's favorite stock characters, that of the marquise. Her fiction is full of such figures, from the aristocratic Raoule de Vénérande of *Monsieur Vénus* (1884) and of course the eponymous marquise de Sade (1887), to Louise de Valrasse of *La Femme Dieu* (1934) and "Madame Bathilde" of *Duvet d'ange* (1943)—the latter positioned as a marquise through her marriage to "Edmond Dormoy," whose name inscribes the nobility of Rachilde's elusive ancestor the marquis d'Ormoy, but Madame de Lydone is one of the best examples of the genre. The character draws on autobiographical elements in typically Rachildian fashion: her paternal grandmother Jeanne Eymery's employer, Madame de Lidonne, loans her name to one of Rachilde's more mythical ancestors, the marquise, "une vraie," as Gabrielle says in *Les Rageac* (243), who was beheaded during the Revolution.

Rachilde uses the nostalgia for such anachronistic figures to explore sexual politics in the present. On the one hand, the nostalgia seems to be for a past era that does not necessarily entail the subordination of women. Like the Goncourts, Rachilde seems to suggest that such a highly regulated society actually gave women certain freedoms. For example, the class structure affected the definition of *modesty* for women, and Mme de Lydone borrows a class distinction to explain her gender philosophy: "[Les hommes] ne comptent pas plus à mes yeux les uns que les autres. Je suis de l'avis de cette grande dame du XVIIIe siècle qui se déshabillait devant ses laquais parce que ça n'avait aucune importance. Le cas échéant, l'on peut même se déshabiller devant n'importe qui si l'on a la force morale de réduire les témoins au rôle d'obéissants serviteurs" (*Madame de Lydone* 78). Idealistic it may be, but such an attitude presents an interesting feminist challenge to the importance of the male gaze and suggests a powerful, if problematic, reassertion of female subjectivity. Rachilde here reflects concern about gender relations and dominance, not by drawing on contemporary reality (men's perceived relative loss of status, women's emancipation, and the ensuing reaction), but by portraying strong women in terms of past paradigms, particularly as aristocrats.

While such figures appear to represent a form of desire to return to a powerful past, it must be remembered that this vision of the female-dominated past is itself a fiction. In fact, most women probably never had the kind of socially recognized authority that Rachilde claims for her heroines. Their regret must be read, therefore, as a form of nostalgia, implying, as that term does, a regret for something lost that was never fully present in the first place, a distorted and imperfect form of recollection. Rachilde's fiction participates in a rewriting of history, using nostalgia as a way to avoid simple dichotomous views about progress. As one of her earlier heroines, Eliante Donalger, remarks, "Comme on sent que je ne suis pas coquette, je peux aller très loin" (*La Jongleuse* 79)—the woman who appears to follow certain social rules can break others with impunity.[13] Rachilde's fiction of the interwar years thus suggests the existence of a previously ignored dimension of women's writing, one that offers a way in which to reread fiction that appears, superficially, to carry a reactionary message, but one that perhaps encodes different forms of female resistance.

On Minding

In which Rachilde is reunited with Lison

Rachilde was a master of not minding. This is just as well because there was much to mind in her final years. The deprivations of World War II were hard to bear: in addition to immediate material shortages (food, heat, clothing), the fact that her work was placed on the Otto list affected her ability to earn an income, her only source of revenue since she was a notoriously poor financial planner who had made no provision for old age.

Fortunately, Rachilde enjoyed good health for most of her life, which was also just as well: like Jarry, she distrusted "les merdecins," as her fiction shows (for example, Célestin in *La Marquise de Sade*), and consulted them as little as possible. The minor health problems that she endured (her limp, eye trouble, depression) did not prevent her from writing, at least not for long. After Vallette's death in September 1935, Rachilde depended entirely on what she could earn (either by writing or by selling books, manuscripts, and letters). Her post-1935 literary production shows her career taking new turns.

Notably, but not surprisingly, given Vallette's death, there are no publications at all in 1936. Then, in 1937, things pick up again, and Rachilde publishes a mystery, *L'Autre Crime*, and her first volume of poetry, *Les Accords perdus*, the elegiac title evoking her recent loss. The year 1938 would see *La Fille inconnue*, a throwback to the romans à clef featuring Barrès (here the hero is named Dormes) combined with the influence of Nel Haroun, who had inspired a number of earlier novels. In 1939 came another novel, *L'Anneau de Saturne*, but her literary production was slowing down. The next novel, her last, would not appear until 1943: *Duvet d'ange*, another roman à clef, this time starring Madame Bathilde, wife of Edmond Dormoy (read D'Ormoy), editor of the *Revue mauve*. Meanwhile, Rachilde published memoirs (*Face à la peur* [1942], a rehash of *Dans le puits*), more poetry (*Survie* [1945]), and yet more memoirs, *Quand j'étais jeune*.

Quand j'étais jeune would be her last publication, appearing in 1947, but she would live another six years before dying at the age of ninety-three, after a fall at her apartment at the Mercure in April 1953. The relative inattention to her work in later life was another thing that she

Rachilde's grave. Courtesy of the author.

might have minded had she thought about it. Used to being courted by young writers for her literary influence, the neglect was a sign that she had outlived even her usefulness to them, that her triumphant declaration, "Plus moyen de m'enterrer," when she signed a breakthrough deal with Flammarion in 1921 (Léautaud 1:1157) was not only literally false but also figuratively false even before she was dead. When she died, many people thought that she had already been in her grave for some years. She might also have minded that the leading daily paper, *Le Monde*, got some of the facts wrong in her obituary (although her own obfuscations about her date of birth are also partly to blame). Still, at least she did not live to see the public mourning and outpouring of grief that followed the death of Colette the following year. This she would have minded a lot more, always having felt a certain rivalry with Colette, whom she once characterized as a "putain" and an "immonde fripouille" (Léautaud 1:1534, 2:574–75).

Minding is a complicated business. On the one hand, *minding* can mean "to pay attention to, to give one's mind or consciousness to something." This is complicated enough: *minding the step* can be as simple as paying attention so as not to fall, whereas *minding children* can be a complicated process with a whole host of possibilities to consider rather than one specific pitfall to avoid. The minded step does not require that we do anything on its behalf, but minded children often do. *Minding one's own business* means *not* minding someone else's, and *what one does not mind* is even more complicated. It can mean a kind of indifference rather than simple inattention ("I don't mind where we go" does not mean "I don't pay attention to the process, but I feel a certain indifference to the outcome").

There is also a third context of *minding*, one in which *giving one's mind to something* entails acknowledging pain or discomfort. "Do you mind if I smoke?" means more than just "Will you pay attention?" or "Do you have an opinion one way or the other?" It is a question about the degree of discomfort or suffering. In this context, *not minding* can mean more than indifference; it can mean a studied refusal to give one's attention to things that might hurt. It was because she minded (hurt) that Rachilde learned not to mind (pay attention to) certain things.

Pain is a recurrent theme in Rachilde's work, as it was in her life, but there are striking asymmetries in the presentation of pain. There is much violence done to people, but it is frequently perfunctory. There is also much violence done to animals, but it is recounted in more painful detail (see, for example, Frappier-Mazur, "Rachilde"). Compare the description of the bull slaughtered at the beginning of *La Marquise de Sade* with the scenes of sadism in which Mary Barbe makes her lovers bleed. Rachilde was clearly more invested in the fate of the bull than in the fate of Mary's lovers (in 1930, she would let herself be arrested for protesting a bullfight [*corrida*] in Melun).

Rachilde liked to think of herself and present herself as an animal lover (even though some others, such as Léautaud, doubted whether her commitment to animals was sincere). From her early sentimental fiction (mother animals mutely mourning the loss of their murdered offspring), to such decadent works as the story of the mistreated and vengeful panther that many saw as an autobiographical representation, to recurrent motifs (such as the wolf) that run throughout her entire oeuvre, animals are a constant presence in Rachilde's work, sometimes as the central characters, and always significant. And it is a typical Rachildian paradox that, while her sadism is often tame, it is her sentimentalism that is painful. Rachilde's animal stories are the ones that cause me to flinch and turn away. I have trouble finishing *Le Théâtre des bêtes*, and there are many chapters of other works that I would rather not read again. In her need to master the pain caused by cruelty to animals, Rachilde repeats such scenes obsessively in a Freudian game of fort/da, insistently rehearsing an episode of loss in order to deaden the pain, learning to not mind.

On the one hand, this sentimentality is frequently viewed as a typical feminine trait that made her assimilable to other writers (such as Colette [see Gadala]). Her opposition to vivisection linked her to female political activism and an ideology of women's moral superiority. But her love of animals is more complicated than can be explained by sentimentalism or politics. While she loved animals, she was accustomed to seeing them suffer and often accepted that she could do nothing about it. The description of all Magui's pets being killed in *Les Rageac* when her room is cleaned in preparation for her (unwanted) marriage seems to draw on autobiographical sources echoed throughout Rachilde's work.

In *Les Rageac*, Magui has pilfered little treats for each member of her menagerie (cats, birds, fowl, mice, goldfish, even an owl and a snake)—"les enfants"—so that they may share in celebrating her engagement and takes the tidbits back to her room after a day of preparations: "Mais elle fut saisie d'une atroce douleur, d'une douleur vraiment physique qui lui coupa les flancs, comme si elle avait été touchée jusqu'aux entrailles par une lame et pliée sur elle-même, le souffle court, elle demeura prostrée dans le silence qui régnait là" (211). It turns out that everyone in the household was complicit in the need to "clean" (*balayer*) her room, from her father, who gave the initial order to get rid of the animals, to the servant who actually put them all in a sack and threw them in the pond, to her mother and the cook, who try to console her by rationalizing the action. But, rather than blame those who execute and condone the decision, Magui blames herself: "C'était de sa faute. Depuis le matin qu'on nettoyait partout. . . . Elle aurait dû se douter"

(212). From those who minded the order (that is, those who obeyed it) to those who did not mind it (that is, those who were indifferent to its effect), the incident serves as a paradigm for all Rachilde's complicated minding: minding (caring for) animals meant not minding (disobeying) her father and learning not to mind (care) when others did mind (obey) orders.

Like Mary Barbe, whose bed was decorated with the motto "aimer c'est souffrir" (*La Marquise de Sade* 84), and Magui Rageac, whose motto is "aimer c'est savoir" (*Les Rageac* 175), a major part of the "éducation d'une jeune fille au début de la Troisième République" (as it is called in *Les Rageac*) was learning not to mind such mindless killing. It was not an easy lesson for Rachilde. In *Les Rageac*, it even becomes the reason why Magui attempts suicide: on learning that the servant Anille threw all the animals in the pond, "Elle [Magui] alla se jeter elle même dans l'étang" (216). The protest against marriage here is also a protest against loss, but it is not a gesture of suicide: "Ce n'était pas pour se suicider. Instinctivement, elle voulait les rejoindre, rejoindre ses petits" (217), and Rachilde likens her heroine to a medieval witch put to the test. In addition to defying parental authority, resisting marriage, asserting her desire to write, joining the *noyé*, and seeking her mother, then, in throwing herself in the pond Rachilde was also following, rescuing, identifying with her pets, and asserting her family ties to animals ("ses petits").

Rachilde minded terribly the treatment of animals because, in addition to being childhood friends, alter egos, and fellow outsiders, animals were her sibling substitutes: "N'ayant eu ni frère ni soeur, j'ai peuplé la solitude glaciale de mes premières années, celles que l'on appelle, je ne sais pourquoi, les belles années, par un nombre incalculable d'adoptions de petits frères inférieurs qui me tenaient chaud, physiquement ou moralement" (*PM* 182). These family members always got killed. As sheer survival mechanism, Rachilde had to learn not to mind. Not minding is what makes it possible for her to tell the wrenching stories that she tells.

It was from animals that Rachilde learned not to mind a great variety of things, from personal loss to cultural illegitimacy. When, as an adolescent, she was sent to a convent, she was punished for infractions of the discipline by being locked in a cell (*cachot*) under the stairs and placed on a diet of bread, corn soup, and water. Rachilde learned not to mind the punishment by befriending a mouse that came to nibble her bread (*Face à la peur* 51–52). Paying attention to the mouse distracted her from her deprivations, enabled her not to mind her surroundings. Thanks to her convent experience, Rachilde learned to be stoic:

> *J'ai appris à mépriser le froid, la chaleur, les menues souffrances que l'on doit offrir en sacrifice à celui qui endura le supplice de la croix:*
>   *On ne devait pas soigner un rhume.*
>   *Il n'était pas permis d'avoir mal aux dents.*
>   *On ne pouvait pas refuser un mets qui ne plaisait pas ou qui se présentait sous un aspect malpropre.*
>   *On ne pouvait pas rire quand on en avait envie.*
>   *On ne devait pas parler en des circonstances où l'on pouvait avoir raison.*
>   *Et l'on devait, surtout,* supporter d'être accusée quand il était de la dernière evidence qu'on n'était pas coupable. (*Face à la peur 56*)

These were some of the things that Rachilde learned not to mind, thanks to animals. In *L'Amazone rouge*, the ironically named Félicia de Tressac receives a lesson in sacrifice that becomes a lesson in not minding. Her brother covertly brings her a treat from the bakery in defiance of their father's disapproval of luxury. When their father discovers the pastry among the bread rolls and assumes that it was sent mistakenly by the baker (no one in the household would have purchased it deliberately), he throws it to a hound, who gulps it down without even tasting it (*AR* 68). In order not to betray her brother, Félicia must pretend not to mind her father's decision, his thoughtless denial of her pleasure. Whether she loses pastries or pets, the Rachildian heroine first learns to pretend not to mind in order to protect others or to deny those who cause the pain the satisfaction of seeing her display vulnerability. But it becomes increasingly difficult for the heroine, as well as the reader, to distinguish between feigned and real indifference.

In addition to the deliberate destruction of her pets, Rachilde also minded the accidental loss as an adolescent of her horse Lison, who minded her rider, jumped, and impaled herself on a fallen branch, all because her rider, Rachilde, failed to mind where she was going. I shall spare the reader the details of these events since, unlike Rachilde, I find that I do mind them, but the episode is recounted repeatedly (see, for example, *TB* 63). Although Rachilde's mortal remains were placed with those of Vallette and his family when she died in 1953, something leads me to hope that some other part of her would find peace among her childhood animal companions. I would like to think that Rachilde finally found respite from her visions of childhood (and sometimes adult) loss and that, finally, she did not need either to mind or not to mind.

Rachilde's remains were interred with those of "ami Vallette" and his parents in the cemetery of Bagneux, just outside central Paris. When I visited the grave in 1992 to see what kind of wolf trap had finally claimed her, I found an abandoned, crumbling site. Virginia Woolf suggests that "all women together ought to let flowers fall upon the tomb of Aphra Behn" (69), Behn being one of the first (British) women to make a living by the pen and open the way for others. Rachilde cannot quite claim the distinction of being the first such French woman, but she was among the first female professional writers in France, and her struggles in an age that gave us some of the most strident expressions of misogyny deserve recognition. I left some purple flowers (the closest to Rachilde's favorite color, mauve, that I could find). I think Rachilde would not have minded.

NOTES

Introduction

1. The poem was part of the collection *Alcools*.
2. For the complete narrative, see Steegmuller 345–53.
3. Annie married at twenty-seven and remained married until her husband's death twenty-five years later. She then had a "position" with a Mr. and Mrs. Jackson of Santa Barbara for another twenty-five years (Steegmuller 348). She thus worked at least until the age of seventy-seven. At the time of Steegmuller's interview, she claimed to be eighty-three.
4. For more on the role of the blush as rhetorical disclosure, see O'Farrell.
5. For an overview of the new challenges of biography, especially feminist biography, see Wagner-Martin and Heilbrun. On dealing with estates, see Hamilton, *In Search of J. D. Salinger* and *Keepers of the Flame*; Rose; and Malcolm. On the use of sensitive information in biography, see Bair; Cook; DeSalvo; Fitch; Middlebrook, *Suits Me*; and O'Brien. On unconventional sources of information, see Middlebrook, *Anne Sexton*; and Toth.

1860, February 11

1. There are technically two biographies by Claude Dauphiné—*Rachilde: Femme de lettres 1900* (1985) and *Rachilde* (1991)—I am counting them as one since the second is a substantially revised version of the first (although only the 1985 edition contains illustrations).
2. At one point, Rachilde even claimed to have been born in Thiviers, not Château-l'Evêque or even Périgueux. The claim is made in a letter to a fellow countryman, the policeman Puybaraud in 1884 (Auriant, *Souvenirs* 61), as discussed below in "1884: Writing as Cross-Dressing."
3. In this and subsequent discussions of Rachilde's family, I rely heavily on Pierre Pommarède's authoritative "Le Sol et le sang de Rachilde."
4. According to Pommarède, "La vérité est plus modeste. Les Feytaud sont des marchands de Biras" ("Le Sol et le sang" 808).
5. As Pommarède confirms. For this and a more accurate account of the life and religious and civil career of Urbain-François Feytaud (1759–1845), see Pommarède, "Le Sol et le sang" 808–10.

6. Although Rachilde's only known child, Gabrielle Vallette Fort, experienced at least one pregnancy, probably around 1920, either she miscarried, or the child was stillborn, for no birth was recorded (*PM* 185).

7. The publisher no doubt wanted to capitalize on the author's scandalous reputation to increase sales, and the suggestive *Minette* perhaps accomplishes this better than the merely supernatural *The Werewolf* would have. To a reading public alive to slang and double meanings, *Minette* evokes the whiff of perversity evident in such titles as *Monsieur Vénus* and *Madame Adonis*: *minette* (the common French diminutive name for a cat) could be used both as a reference to the female genitals and as a euphemism for cunnilingus (see Lagail; and Sautman 179). In Vallette's letter to Rachilde in which he discusses this novel, he brings this suggestive meaning to her attention, urging her not to accept the offer of a disreputable publisher: "Si vous donnez un livre sous un . . . *diminutif* pareil c'est que l'homme qui vous l'achète sait bien ce qu'il fait" (*RHS* 25).

1870, October 29

1. Urbain-François married Charlotte, a seventeen-year-old surgeon's daughter, in a civil ceremony on December 29, 1793. A few years later, he was studying law in Bordeaux, and, by 1806, a year before Urbain Raymond's birth, he was a practicing lawyer (Pommarède, "Le Sol et le sang" 809). The date of Urbain Raymond Feytaud's birth is given as July 3, 1807, in the Acte de naissance, Commune de Périgueux, Archives départementales de la Dordogne, EC O TD44. Later that same month, on July 31, 1807, Urbain-François's marriage to Charlotte was celebrated in a religious ceremony in the Cathedral of Saint-Front in Périgueux. Charlotte died in 1816.

2. Urbain Raymond's two older brothers also left the provinces to became professionals in large cities. When their father, Urbain-François, divided his estate between his three sons in 1827, Victor Feytaud was a doctor in Bordeaux, Joseph Feytaud a lawyer in Paris (Pommarède, "Le Sol et le sang" 809–10).

3. The spelling of the name varies, as is often the case in historical records. Dauphiné (*Rachilde* [1991]) uses the spelling *Isoline*, Rachilde (in *Pourquoi*) *Isaline*. The birth certificate and the marriage contract of her daughter Gabrielle (Rachilde's mother) gives her full name as Marie-Etiennette-Izaline Desmond, but, since these documents are handwritten, it is sometimes difficult to distinguish *o* from *a*, Also, clerks themselves were sometimes unsure of a spelling and used sev-

eral different variations. Thus, *Raymond* also appears as *Raimond* and *Reymond*.

4. Acte de naissance, Marie-Gabrielle Feytaud, Archives départementales de la Dordogne, EC 5 E 306/18, no. 52.

5. There remains some confusion on this point. Dauphiné claims that it was "Mademoiselle de Lidonne" herself who was seduced (*Rachilde* [1985] 10), but other evidence comes from "Chronologie" 7; and Pommarède, "Le Sol et le sang."

6. "Mon père était donc bien un enfant naturel et il avait volontairement renoncé au titre du beau séducteur qui voulait le reconnaître lorsqu'il eut dix-huit ans, mais refusait d'épouser sa mère, coupable seulement d'avoir été jolie, quoique sans dot" (*QJJ* 69).

7. Rachilde is careful to remind the reader of her memoirs on more than one occasion of the interchangeability of these two names (see also *QJJ* 69, 127). I discuss the significance of this in "1877: Authority, Authorship, and Authorization" below.

8. Acte de naissance, Joseph Eymery, Archives départementales de la Dordogne, DEP O E DEP 6258.

9. Pommarède adds some details on Joseph's early life: when found, he was wearing "un bourrassou de cadis brun et coiffé d'une bonnette d'indienne bleue à fleurs jaunes, garnie de dentelle noire." A yellow ribbon was later tied around his arm to identify him. The next day he was baptized and given to Marie Vergnias, the wife of Pierre Dessoudy of Maison-Neuve, to look after ("Le Sol et le sang" 803–4).

10. Research by Pierre Pommarède has, however, established a number of facts about her (see "Le Sol et le sang" 803–5). Jeanne Eymery is also referred to by Madame de Lidonne as her cook.

11. Rachilde refers to the "place du *Couderc*" in her memoirs (*QJJ* 68), presumably either a variant spelling or an error.

12. The property in question is probably the property that Rachilde claims she would have inherited: "Un jour, quand j'étais à Paris, en train de gagner péniblement ma vie, de femme ou d'homme de lettres, on m'ordonna *péremptoirement* de renoncer à un héritage, l'héritage d'une maison ayant appartenu à la nommée Jeanne Eymery ou Aimeri, parce qu'il n'était pas décent d'hériter d'une personne qui n'avait pas été mariée" (*QJJ* 68–89). The fact that this took place when Rachilde was still earning her living "péniblement" as a writer in Paris suggests that Jeanne Eymery died in the early 1880s. Rachilde obeyed the order to renounce her claim to the property.

13. Izaline's date of birth is unknown (Gabrielle's birth certificate notes the father's, but not the mother's, age).

14. The date of the marriage has always been given as 1859, but records show that the marriage contract was signed on November 15, 1858, and that the ceremony took place on November 17, 1858.

15. This and other quotations from *La Marquise de Sade* are from the 1981 edition published by Mercure de France.

16. Rachilde claimed at different times that she learned to ride at only four years of age (David, *Rachilde* 13) and that she had her first lessons at seven (Auriant, *Souvenirs* 27). In *La Marquise de Sade*, which contains a number of autobiographical elements, "Ce fut à Haguenau que Mary débuta dans les exercices équestres" (150).

17. For accounts of the role of dueling in the performance of nineteenth-century French masculinity, see Berenson; and Nye.

18. In *Les Rageac*, the duel is delayed until after Joseph Eymery is released from prison, but it must still be fought (without official sanction). He loses and returns to the family home on reserve status.

19. He was, however, not without opinions (see *Les Rageac* 138).

20. According to Dupuy, who gives a detailed account of the campaign of 1870–71. Rachilde obviously knew Dupuy's *Historique du 12e régiment de chasseurs*—she uses it in *Les Rageac*—but she also seems to have owned a copy (see Auriant, *Souvenirs* 58), testimony to the interest that she took in her father's career.

21. Without editorial commentary, the journal gives an eyewitness view of the war, the lack of supplies being overshadowed by the lack of information about what was going on.

22. According to the "liste des officiers qui ont appartenu au Régiment depuis 1860," Eymery had arrived with the rank of captain on August 8, 1869, and was placed on reserve status, still a captain, on June 11, 1872 (Dupuy 391).

23. That the couple were never legally separated, despite maintaining separate households, is demonstrated by Gabrielle's application as surviving widow for Joseph's military pension following his death in 1892, which is preserved as part of Joseph Eymery's military records. As part of her dossier, Gabrielle included declarations from neighbors in the avenue d'Orléans (one from a baker and one from a wine merchant) testifying that Gabrielle was entitled to the benefits since she was neither divorced nor legally separated.

24. For references to Joseph Eymery's physically abusive behavior, see the notes of Puybaraud quoted in Auriant, *Souvenirs* 61; and

Rachilde's letter to Robert de Souza of September 17, 1896, published in Soulignac, "Ecrits de jeunesse."

25. Rachilde states that he gave her "deux billets de mille francs" (*QJJ* 170). This sum represented about a year's income. According to Hahn, a captain under Napoleon III (as Eymery had been) earned an average of 2,000–2,400 francs a year (138).

1875, January or Early February

1. Auriant recalls that, in her old age, Rachilde had a crucifix above her bed in her apartment at the Mercure de France but attributes its presence to a memory of her innocent childhood: "Ce n'était là qu'un souvenir du temps lointain où elle était une petite fille innocente, mais déjà volontaire, qu'elle conservait sentimentalement" (*Souvenirs* 51). In *Face à la peur* (1942), Rachilde declares categorically, "Non, je ne crois pas en Dieu" (53), and goes on to explain that her atheism was the result, not of reason, but of instinct.

2. The exact date of Rachilde's confirmation is unknown. According to "Chronologie" (8), it took place in 1872. Pommarède describes Rachilde in the photograph commemorating her first communion: "Elle représente un ange veillant l'enfant-Jésus couronné d'épines et porte en devise: 'Je veux laisser mon coeur auprès du saint berceau'" ("Le Sol et le sang" 801).

3. A footnote at this point directs the reader to *Les Rageac*, which had appeared in 1921, three years before David's biography was published.

4. Rachilde describes the two years (from age sixteen to age eighteen) that she spent in a convent (a former fortress belonging to the Montfort family) in *Face à la peur* 51–52.

5. I have found no trace of Jacques de La Hullière, however. The *Annuaire de l'armée française*, a register in the Archives de l'Armée, which lists all army officers, shows no one of this name (or any similar name) for the years 1873–75. Other sources suggest that the fiancé's name was Edouard (but no last name is given): the adolescent Rachilde kept a portrait of an Edouard in her bedroom (*PM* 157), and a series of (fictional?) letters dated 1875 to Edouard, a captain in the military, is preserved in her *cahier de style* in the Fonds Doucet.

6. This photograph is also described by Frazer Lively in her introduction to *Madame la Mort and Other Plays* (6).

7. For a discussion of some of the problems in obtaining accurate statistics on suicide rates, see O. Anderson. A historian, Anderson fo-

cuses on the British context, but much of what she says can be applied, mutatis mutandis, to France as well. The association between the fin de siècle and suicide is not limited to the nineteenth century. For an account of the perception that suicide is once again on the rise at this fin de siècle, see H. Schwartz.

8. Pierre Spivakoff's 1987 stage adaptation of Rachilde's *Monsieur Vénus* gave, as the play's subtitle, "Le rêve fou de Louis II de Bavière."

9. Four years later, that event formed the basis of Jules Lemaître's *Les Rois*, the first play to be performed at Sarah Bernhardt's new Théâtre de la Renaissance, which opened in Paris on November 6, 1893 (Gold and Fizdale 248). For a story that also speaks to the cultural preoccupation with suicide, see Robert Louis Stevenson's "The Suicide Club" (1896).

10. Weber sets out the perceived gender differential quite simply: "Men hanged, women drowned themselves" (49). O. Anderson goes into the question more thoroughly in her historical study of suicide but repeatedly notes the same fact. In some cases, of course, the perception was borne out by the facts.

11. Gates devotes a chapter to suicidal women.

12. The topos was apparently not confined to French and British contexts. In her autobiography, Emma Goldman recounts a similar anecdote about growing up in St. Petersburg. She wanted to persuade her father to let her emigrate to America with her sister, but he would not consent. "I pleaded, begged, wept. Finally I threatened to jump into the Neva, whereupon he yielded" (1:11). Goldman left St. Petersburg in December 1885. See also Paperno.

13. Since both Rachilde's parents were apparently only children (if Joseph had siblings, no record of them has survived), Rachilde had no first cousins. Marie was perhaps the granddaughter of Urbain Feytaud's older brother Joseph, who had become a lawyer in Paris.

14. Rachilde would thus have met Bernhardt in the 1870s, when Bernhardt was becoming known as the leading actress of the Comédie-Française and when she was having her house built in the fashionable Monceau area, made famous in, for example, Zola's *La Curée*.

15. Bernhardt was older than Rachilde but wrote and published her memoirs only after Rachilde had produced autobiographical texts such as *A mort*.

16. I visited le Cros in June, 1999. Although there is now a shallow creek in front of the house, there is nothing resembling a pond, and the current occupants of the house have no recollection of one. The best that they could suggest, when asked about the pond, was that,

when it rains in the winter, the creek sometimes floods. For more on le Cros, see Chèvre 3–6; Pommarède, "Le Sol et le sang."

17. This and other quotations from *La Sanglante Ironie* are from the 1923 Mercure de France edition.

1876, March 1

1. See, for example, Gelfand, who equates writing with indecent exposure for women in the nineteenth century. As Remy de Gourmont puts it, "La littérature des femmes, c'est ma chère amie [Rachilde], leur façon polie de faire l'amour en public" (qtd. in David, *Rachilde* 49).

2. The copy of the "reconnaissance d'enfant" in Joseph Eymery's military records shows that, when he was legally recognized by Jeanne Eymery in 1839, he was, ironically, a lithographer (*écrivain lithographe*), which is to say an engraver in stone, working for a Monsieur Dupont, "imprimeur" in Périgueux. He would not join the army until three years later (1842), so it is tempting to speculate that it was partly his early apprenticeship in this technical aspect of the publishing world that gave him his later distaste for "des plumitifs."

3. The source of this anecdote, like the rest of David's book, is presumably Rachilde herself, but the story is also mentioned in an article about Rachilde by Christian Seignol that appeared in a regional newspaper.

4. A contemporary review (see Dumur) gives the title as *Le Spiritisme devant la conscience,* published by Chamuel, but Pommarède ("Le Sol et le sang" 814, 820 n.78) gives the following publication information: *Le Spiritisme devant la science* (Thiviers: Imprimerie Fargeot, 1893, 1894).

5. Spiritualism had been associated with Sweden for some time. The dabblings of King Gustavus III, for example, had been the subject of rumors in the postrevolutionary and Napoleonic periods, and in the latter part of the nineteenth century France was once again subject to a strong wave of Scandinavian influence.

6. I rely in this section on information in P. Lewis. Among the sources of information about Queen Christina that might have been available to Rachilde were Queen Christina's published aphorisms and autobiography, the diary published by her companion Mathilde von Echner, and memoirs by contemporary French friends of hers such as Mademoiselle de Montpensier ("La Grande Mademoiselle," herself a figure of Amazonian and literary ambitions) and Françoise de Motteville. Works that appeared in the nineteenth century include

d'Abrantès; Barine; Catteau-Calleville; Cousin; Jubinal; and Marin. She was also the subject of an 1829 play by Louis Brault, and publications with suggestive titles continue well into the twentieth century (see, for example, Princess Murat's *La Vie amoureuse de Christine de Suède, la reine androgyne.*

7. There is much more that could be said about the figure of Queen Christina as a signifier of female deviance, from Greta Garbo's erotically charged performance in the 1933 film (see, for example, White's analysis), to Pam Gems's *Queen Christina*, the first play by a woman to be performed (in 1977) by Britain's Royal Shakespeare Company. Diane Middlebrook has recently speculated, for example, that it may have been Garbo's incarnation of Christina that prompted jazz musician Billy Tipton to start cross-dressing and passing as a man in order to succeed in her chosen profession, arguably as closed to American women in the 1930s as was that of writer to French women in the 1870s (*Suits Me* 59–60).

8. Antoine Ritti, the director of the Charenton asylum, who cared for Gabrielle, told Rachilde that it was because she could write that she avoided madness (*PM* 187).

9. Pierre Pommarède reports finding the death record of a child named Rachilde in diocesan archives ("Le Sol et le sang" 802 n.75). As a French name, it could perhaps be a corruption of Ragnahilda, a queen who ruled an area including the modern Périgord as wife of the Visigoth king Euric (r. A.D. 466–85) referred to in the letters of Sidonius Apollinaris, bishop of Auvergne (2:90). (Ragnahilda was later the subject of a poem by Auguste Fourès dedicated to Laurent Tailhade in *Le Décadent* in July 1888.) Perhaps Marguerite misremembered the name of Richilde (d. 1091), an only child who became queen of Hainaut as the wife of Baudouin VI of Flanders, particularly since Richilde is referred to by Brantôme in the context of princesses and ladies who took up arms (699).

10. Rachel's biographer Rachel Brownstein notes the doubling that characterizes her subject's life and focuses on "the paradoxes she presented" (x). Brownstein also notes that women artists have been known by their first name only since Madame de Staël's famous creation, Corinne (50–51).

11. See also W. Silverman's discussion of the name Gyp.

12. For further discussion of the differences between these novels, see M. J. Anderson.

13. This is not to deny the self-destructive impulses to which Marcelle is subject (and in this context I would note in particular Marcelle's

impulse to drown [292], which echoes Rachilde's suicide attempt discussed above).

1877, June 23

1. As already noted—see "1860: Women as Outsiders"—the reference to the full moon is also a reminder of her werewolf status. Rachilde is the apparently ordinary girl who turns into a monster—a writer!— under a full moon.

2. See Goudeau 147–54; Auriant's preface to Rachilde's play *A l'auberge de l'aigle*, the composition of which was inspired by the celebration of the fiftieth anniversary of the founding of the Hydropathes held at the Sorbonne in 1928; Seigel; Cate and Shaw.

3. Lugné-Poe describes the (somewhat later) soirées of *La Plume* in his memoirs, for example. Numerous descriptions of the Chat Noir have also been recorded, perhaps because it was more colorful than most (for example, Salis's tradition of greeting guests with insults, the events such as the shadow puppet theater). Such a gathering is the sort of event depicted in some of the pictures of Rachilde to be discussed later (see "1887: The Photograph Never Lies").

4. The book bears the date 1880, but, according to Christian Soulignac, it in fact appeared some time between September and December 1879 ("Bibliographie" 200).

1884, May–July

1. All the subsequent omissions were recently republished under Talman's name—that is, as "*Monsieur Vénus* by Francis Talman" rather than as "*Monsieur Vénus* by Rachilde"—as a curious literary document.

2. For more on the role of duels in the literary community of Paris in the 1880s, see Lefrère, esp. chaps. 14 and 15.

3. Joris-Karl Huysmans's *A rebours* appeared a few months before *Monsieur Vénus*, in mid-May, but, contrary to some assertions, there is nothing to suggest that Rachilde was influenced by this novel or that she knew of it when she wrote *Monsieur Vénus*.

4. Printings usually ranged from five hundred to one thousand copies. Thus, three *éditions* would have run from fifteen hundred to three thousand copies, depending on the size of the printings.

5. So far as I have been able to determine, there are three copies of this edition in the United States: one can be found in the Library of Congress; one is in the special collections of the University Park Libraries at the University of Houston Library (I am grateful to Tony Snider

for bringing this copy to my attention); and one resides in the rare books collection of Vanderbilt University (I am grateful to Wendi Arant for helping verify this).

6. An edition dated 1885 with the publisher's address given as 30, rue d'Aremberg and with the anonymous preface thought to be by Houssaye can be found in Harvard's Widener Library. For information about some of the differences between the 1884 editions and the 1889 Brossier edition (the one that has been used in most modern editions and also as the basis for both English-language translations), for example, the name changes, see the introduction to Talman.

7. The wax mannequin is one probable source of the title. As Elaine Showalter has recently reminded us, sexually suggestive wax models were used as anatomical teaching aids in nineteenth-century Europe. These models, made of wax but sometimes incorporating real body parts (such as hair), were known as *anatomical venuses.* The wax mannequin of Jacques Silvert is thus a *venus*—a sexually suggestive wax model—but also a *monsieur.* Rachilde was certainly aware of these devices—Dr. Célestin Barbe has one in his study in *La Marquise de Sade* (180). Vanessa Schwartz reports that "scientific collections [of wax figures] used for teaching by anatomists were fairly common" and notes that at least one such collection (the Musée Hartkoff, opened by a Swedish phrenologist in the passage de l'Opéra in 1865—would Rachilde have been aware of this Swedish collection not far from cousin Marie de Saverny's offices?) was open only to men (97). In addition, interest in wax models had been revived by the recent opening of the waxworks museum, the Musée Grévin, on June 5, 1882. In settling on a title, Rachilde (or Brancart) may also have been aware of the novel by Richard O'Monroy (pseudonym of the vicomte de Saint-Geniès) entitled *Monsieur Mars et Madame Vénus.*

8. Of course, I am speculating somewhat about Brancart's reputation, but not without justification. Brancart was investigated in connection with another publisher in 1895, and the dossier of that investigation provides some information about him. He was born in Saint-Quentin on July 21, 1851, married a woman from Brussels, and moved to Antwerp on August 3, 1894. By the time of the police inquiry the following year, the couple had four children. The *Petit Bottin des lettres et des arts* of 1886 refers to him reaching "la Néerlande hospitalière" (Fénéon et al. 12), perhaps a flight from prosecution. He was already known to police authorities as early as 1885, having published

Paul Adam's *Chair molle*, which was prosecuted that year for "outrage aux bonnes moeurs" (Archives de Paris D 2U8, 188). He also appeared before a judge in Brabant in May 1886 and April 1888 (Stora-Lamarre 165–66).

9. Much of the recent criticism of *Monsieur Vénus* focuses on the extent to which Rachilde succeeded in escaping the constraints of misogynist, decadent views of women. Some, such as Dominique Fisher, Dorothy Kelly, and Nathalie Buchet Rogers, emphasize the transgressive aspects of the novel. For Margaret Bruzelius, Rachilde was "able to write within the decadent tradition by taking the image of the vampiric fatal woman and using [it] to create a parodic written persona" (52). Others, such as Jennifer Birkett and Diana Holmes (*French Women's Writing*), conclude that Rachilde did not transcend the limited perspectives of her time.

10. This "souvenir" was published in *Pélagie* in 1889 (see Soulignac, "Bibliographie"). According to Soulignac, "cette revue au format de journal ne connut qu'un seul numéro" ("Bibliographie" 217). The (a?) manuscript version of "Le Numéro inconnu" may be found in the Harry Ransom Humanities Research Center.

11. Wilde was married on May 29, 1884, and returned from his honeymoon on June 24, 1884 (see Ellmann 249–54).

12. For Dorothy Kelly, for example, the scandal lies in the way in which Rachilde deconstructs gender, while Janet Beizer asserts that the novel offers "much less a reversal than a dispersal of convention" (228). Rae Beth Gordon reads the novel as encoding the "perverse phantasies that a woman of the fin de siècle was allowed only under the guise of hysteria" (230), while Rita Felski argues that "Rachilde's heroines [are] not hysterical but perverse" (184). The focus on Rachilde's invocation of gender in this novel underlines the extent to which *Monsieur Vénus* is the forerunner of David Henry Hwang's play *M. Butterfly*. The paradox of *M. Butterfly*, articulated by the character Song—"only a man knows how a woman is supposed to act" (63)—could be said to apply equally well to *Monsieur Vénus*. For further comparison between these two texts, see my "'Du Du That Voodoo.'"

1884, December 12

1. On Sand and Colette, see, for example, Freadman; on d'Eon, see Kates; on Bonheur, see van Slyke.

2. Rosario points out that an earlier version of this—the decree of 8 Brumaire II (October 29, 1793) was, ironically, democratic in inten-

tion: it abolished class distinction by granting each citizen the right to wearing *any* clothing "of his [or her] sex" (193 n.17).

3. Eugen Weber cites examples drawn from court records, of women who, since women's pay was still only half that of men's for the same work, cross-dressed to earn a better wage (36).

4. See MacAloon; Rearick; and Weber, esp. chap. 10 on the fashion for bicycles and chap. 11 on sports in general. On swimming (the first swimming championships held in France took place in 1899), see Leeuwen.

5. For a study of how advertising, cycling, and reading merged in the popular press of the 1890s in the United States and suggested new strategies for reading in general, see Garvey.

6. Philippe Perrot maintains that "this ordinance [of 16 Brumaire IX] has never been abrogated, so that today any woman who wears pants does so in violation of the law" (20), but see the discussion in Bard, "Le Dossier."

7. Rachilde, her mother, and the publisher Dentu all seem to have been under the impression that Puybaraud was the prefect (see *QJJ* 141), and Alfred Vallette would make the same mistake, referring to "Puybaraud, notre sympathique préfet" (*RHS* 94).

8. Camescasse was *préfet* from July 18, 1881, to April 26, 1885, when he was succeeded by Gragnon (who served in the position from April 26, 1885, to November 17, 1887).

9. The dossier is cataloged as no. DB/58. A more extensive treatment of the contents of this dossier is given by Gretchen van Slyke. I am grateful to her for generously sharing her research. See also the extensive description and discussion of the dossier in Bard, "Le Dossier."

10. That she cross-dressed for ten years is implied by a passing comment at the beginning of "On va au bal" in *QJJ*, although her language is more circumspect here: she states that one suit *could* be made to last ten years simply by reversing the lapels (*QJJ* 24). See also the letter to Jean-Joë Lauzach (Jacques Bossard) of February 6, 1927 (in the collection of the Harry Ransom Humanities Research Center, University of Texas at Austin).

11. Rachilde does not mention the date explicitly but gives her age at the time as twenty-five (*QJJ* 26). When reporting her age in this text, however, she is notoriously unreliable.

12. See my "Comment peut-on être homosexuel" and Poirier. The photo of Wilde is reproduced in Holland.

13. On the gender ambiguity of the page, see Vicinus and also my "The Seduction of Terror."

14. Vallette also alludes to a marquise "qui voulait vous adopter ou vous annexer pour vous soustraire à un mariage calamiteux" who had left Rachilde a watch (*RHS* 76–77).

1885, A Thursday in March

1. Mariani's laboratories were founded in 1875 (see "Bibliographie générale" 148). On the use of cocaine in Vin Mariani and other medicinal products during the nineteenth century, see Weber 32.
2. The text of the poem is as follows:

   Les Décadents
   N'ont pas d'talent
   Me dit-on!
   Oh! que nenni!
   Moi, je dis
   Qu'ils ont du génie
   Dans le fond
   Car les plus épuisés
   Se sont refaits
   (Et nous refont)
   Avec un flacon
   De vin Mariani.

3. Rachilde placed this undated letter second in *Le Roman d'un homme sérieux*, her collection of Vallette's correspondence, but the reference to the death of his father means that it must, in fact, have been written sometime after January 1888, several years after his first meeting with Rachilde. The misleading position that it occupies in the published correspondence is symptomatic of the many problems encountered when attempting to establish an accurate chronology for the items contained in this collection.
4. Rachilde would not remain close to him and in fact participated in the "Affaire Barrès," an orchestrated attack on him in 1921 (see Marguerite Bonnet).
5. "René Brissy (R.A.M.S.C.) imprimeur, rue de la Fidelité 9," would go bankrupt on January 14, 1885 (see the *Dictionnaire des faillites pour l'année 1885* in the Archives de Paris).
6. Paul Léautaud, for example, noted in his diary that his "amie" thought that Rachilde had been the mistress, not only of Barrès, but also of Paul Adam and Jean Lorrain, but that he himself thought that there was no basis to the rumors (2:262, April 20, 1929).
7. On Rachilde on Barrès and Gyp, see Mugnier 482.
8. See also Vallette's description of Rachilde's apartment (*RHS* 38–42).
9. See Rachilde's book of press clippings (Fonds Doucet).

10. Among the reviews were *La Jeunesse*, *Le Molière*, and *Le Capitan* (a "journal hebdomadaire illustré" founded in 1883). He became the "secrétaire de rédaction" of *La Revue critique* in January 1883. He also founded a "journal," *Le Zig-Zag*, that later became *Gil-Blague* (a parody of *Gil-Blas*). He owned and operated a publishing company, Pouget et Vidal, that published a weekly newspaper for children, *Paris-Bébé*, and that acted as distributor and administrator for Barrès's *Taches d'encre* (see "Au Temps des *Taches d'encre*"). In March 1887, d'Orfer launched the *Revue de Paris* and served as its business manager (*gérant*) and administrator but managed only one issue (Davanture 1:302 and catalog of the Bibliothèque Nationale). Finally, "M. A. Pouget" is listed as the business manager of *La Décadence*.

11. The Bibliothèque Nationale catalog includes his *Chants de guerre de la Serbie* and *L'Épopée serbe*.

12. Moreover, since the marriage of Gabrielle Vallette and Robert Fort would be without surviving issue, the descendants of Léo d'Orfer would inherit Rachilde's literary estate through another branch of the Fort family.

13. Suggestions of of lesbianism are repudiated in *Monsieur Vénus* and later in a letter to Jean-Joë Lauzach (Harry Ransom Humanities Research Center, University of Texas at Austin).

14. For many years, Maupassant's reputation was protected from scrutiny, with the result that, when rumors about his active love life began to emerge, many people found them incredible. Paul Ignotus reviews the way in which the existence of Gisèle d'Estoc was gradually revealed by Maupassant's biographer Pierre Borel beginning in 1927. At first, she was referred to only as "Mlle X——," and some doubted her existence, but further enquiries by Armand Lanoux gave credibility to the claims. See Borel, *Maupassant et l'androgyne*; Lanoux; Maupassant, *Correspondance*; Maupassant, *A la feuille de rose*; Douchin; and d'Estoc, *Cahiers d'amour*.

15. Borel identifies this first love interest only as "Marie-Edmée X" (*Maupassant et l'androgyne* 21) but leaves sufficient clues scattered throughout his text (her work on Joan of Arc, the publication of her journal, the fact that her last name is the same as that of a World War I general) that it is possible to establish that her last name is Pau. (I am grateful to Pamela Matthews for helping me make this identification.) Among other things, Marie-Edmée Pau published a children's book about Joan of Arc, lavishly illustrated with her own engravings. (Since it was intended for the moral instruction of chil-

dren, it was published modestly under the name "Marie-Edmée" only.) The book serves as a reminder that the Franco-Prussian War had revived interest in Joan of Arc as a national heroine and a role model for girls. It would be tempting to speculate about the role of such pedagogical literature in shaping the expression of Rachilde's adolescent aspirations, which emerged in the immediate postwar period. Like Joan of Arc, Rachilde heard voices and received instruction from supernatural sources, and of course both cross-dressed.

16. In addition to those discussed here, d'Estoc's works include the following: She wrote stories entitled "Mortel Courage," "Adultère préhistorique," "Le Trouvère," and "Contes d'amour" that appeared in such literary reviews as *Vingtième Siècle* and *L'Estafette* (Borel, *Maupassant et l'androgyne* 44–45). She wrote at least one installment of a work about androgyny in the life of Joan of Arc, *Psychologie de Jeanne d'Arc*. She was the editor of the *Revue caudine* published in Paris in the winter of 1887–88. Borel attributes to her a work about intersexuality in art, *Le Secret de Michel-Ange*, which he claims was translated into several languages (Borel, *Maupassant et l'androgyne* 38–39), though I have never been able to verify this. And the catalog of the Bibliothèque Nationale in Paris also attributes to her *Ad maximam Dei gloriam: Comme quoi les Jésuites pourraient bien ne pas descendre du singe* (Paris: Librairie anti-cléricale, 1880), although Jacques-Louis Douchin suggests that this is in fact a misattribution and is more likely the work of Martial d'Estoc (115).

17. Lanoux located a copy of the work in the Bibliothèque Municipale de Nancy. Although it carried the pseudonym Gyz-El, it was cataloged under the name "Mme Desbarres née Courbe."

18. El is also a homonym of Hél, one of d'Estoc's lovers (Douchin 118).

19. See d'Arkaï's description of his visit to her in 1885, quoted in Lanoux 378.

20. When, for example, d'Estoc had her "aventure épistolaire" with an officer in the African army (Borel, *Maupassant et l'androgyne* 48), was she aware that Rachilde's father had belonged to this unit? Did she cultivate her intimacy with Catulle Mendès in order to make Rachilde jealous? Maupassant undertook on several occasions to procure female lovers for d'Estoc, usually including both himself and the woman's male escort in the action, as d'Estoc's *Cahiers d'amour* makes clear. She describes, for example, a dinner attended by Suzanne L——: "Durant tout le repas, elle a été follement gaie. Tantôt, elle donnait à mon voisin ses belles lèvres rouges et char-

nues. Tantôt, à moitié nue, elle s'offrait à mes caresses" (quoted in Douchin 121). Maupassant's correspondence is equally explicit: "Ma chère amie, il faut absolument que vous veniez dîner chez moi vendredi. Vous y trouverez Catulle Mendès, plus une jeune et jolie femme, son amie, ravagée par des désirs féminins" (quoted in Douchin 118). How would Rachilde have reacted had she known that d'Estoc enjoyed such intimacy with Catulle Mendès, one of her own former heartthrobs?

21. Borel also asserts that the androgynous d'Estoc looked like an "Adonis" (*Maupassant et l'androgyne* 37). The names of Rachilde's protagonists, Louis and Louise, evoke, through both the symmetry and the initial, Maupassant's illegitimate children Lucien (born 1883) and Lucienne (born 1884).

22. *La Vierge-Réclame* was published in 1887, in a series entitled "Les Gloires malsaines" by the Librairie Richelieu in Paris, and appeared as the work of "G. d'Estoc," with illustrations by Fernand Fau.

23. I am not suggesting that Rachilde wrote *Nono* specifically to represent her ambivalence toward Vallette since the origins of the novel antedate her first meeting with him. The manuscript of the first draft, entitled "La Fille au coeur noir," is dated at the beginning "Le Cros, 13 juillet 1882," but the manuscript is spread over four notebooks, or *cahiers*, each with a stationer's sticker on the front inside cover showing where each notebook was purchased. While the first two were purchased at "Librairie nouvelle Dubessé, Périgueux" (for seventy centimes), the third was purchased in Paris at "V[ict]or Radiguer, rue du Cardinal Lemoine, 43" (for only sixty centimes!). Rue du Cardinal Lemoine was just around the corner from the rue des Ecoles, where Rachilde lived in an apartment at no. 5. The draft of "La Fille au coeur noir" ends in the fourth notebook and is followed by a manuscript begun in 1884. (The notebooks are held by the Fonds Doucet.) References are to the 1889 Piaget edition.

24. Note the similarity of the name Fayor and Rachilde's maternal family name Feytaud (originally Faytos).

25. The name Bryon is an obvious anagram of Byron, but Rachilde later admitted that the character was also based on Barrès ("Bibliographie générale" 127). Both Byron and Barrès typify the type of Romantic hero to which Rachilde was attracted. Maxime de Bryon also makes a brief appearance in the later roman à clef *Le Mordu* (1889).

26. In a letter dated December 1, 1886, for example, Vallette offers editorial comments on a "nouvelle" (*RHS* 28–29). To judge from the

context that he supplies, the story in question is "Le Trésor," which had already been published in the *Courrier de Bretagne* 58 (July 20, 1878) (Soulignac, "Bibliographie" 200). The nine-page manuscript can be read at the Harry Ransom Humanities Research Center, University of Texas at Austin. The pages appear to have been torn out of a notebook, and the first page of the story is numbered 46.

27. According to Dauphiné, "Elle essaya donc de lancer une revue concurrente qui ne dépassa pas le troisième numéro" (*Rachilde* [1991] 49). No evidence of such a journal founded by Rachilde in the fall of 1886 has been discovered, but she is listed as a collaborator in *La Décadence*.

28. D'Orfer also contributed to *Le Scapin* under the pseudonym VIR (Richard 102).

29. For example, writers came together at an open forum intended to explain symbolism to a rather confused general public in October 1886. Not only was this meeting organized primarily by anarchists, but during at least one meeting Vallette shared the floor with contributors to *Le Décadent* (see Richard 107–8; and Shryock, "Anarchism at the Dawn of the Symbolist Movement").

30. This dating assumes that the letters appear in the correct order in *Le Roman d'un homme sérieux* (though this is not always the case). The undated response from Vallette, headed simply "dimanche soir," is positioned between a letter dated February 1887 and one dated July 18, 1888 that carries Rachilde's editorial comment "un an après" (101).

31. For a suggestive connection of the theme of the staining of sheets to the problems of female authorship, see Isak Dineson's short story "The Blank Page" and Susan Gubar's analysis of it.

32. We should be careful about what implications to draw from this form of address. On the front page of *Le Décadent* of September 11, 1886, Léo d'Orfer published a sonnet entitled "Testament" dedicated to Rachilde in which he used the *tu* form of address. Some members of the review's editorial staff evidently felt that d'Orfer thereby compromised Rachilde's reputation and warned her. She provided a stern rebuke, which followed the poem on the front page: "Je saisis l'occasion pour affirmer, une fois de plus, et hautement, le droit que possède tout poète de tutoyer dans ses vers Dieu, le roi, et les *femmes*" (Richard 88–89). Noël Richard speculates that the "imbécile" who made such inferences might have been Baju himself and that this may account for d'Orfer's break with *Le Décadent* (105).

1887, February 26 (A Saturday)

1. Adolphe van Bever preceded Jarry as secretary to the Théâtre de l'oeuvre, later joined the *Mercure de France*, and authored a number of works of literary criticism.
2. As a girl, Mary Barbe, in *La Marquise de Sade* (one of Rachilde's most autobiographical novels), has "magnificent" hair that is admired by her father's regiment (75–76).
3. Examples of left-right reversal are known to have occurred: a 1920 studio photograph of Rachilde by Martinie-Viollet, for example, is reversed as it appears in Dauphiné's *Rachilde* (1985). The mistake is easily recognized: the distinctive mole just below Rachilde's right eye, so evident in van Bever's portrait and the photographs on which the portrait is based, appears to be below Rachilde's *left* eye in this picture. No such reversal can be seen in Langlois's engraving.
4. See, for example, fashion plate 53 from 1876 in Waugh, in which the "Ladies double breasted Alexandra Pelisse" closes left over right, just like a man's coat.
5. Rachilde refers to her seamstress, "une vieille couturière" who came to the house for fittings and brought her barley sugar, in *QJJ* 137.
6. See also the description of Verlaine's sketch in Raynaud 2:16.
7. Their meeting takes place as both are waiting to meet with a publisher who is responsible for "une revue et ça va fort mal" for Barrès and a book of "histoires pour les enfants" for Rachilde (*Portraits d'hommes* 23). The publisher in question would seem to be René Brissy (see "1885: Marriage and the Woman Writer").

1889, October 25

1. The information about her date of birth comes from her death certificate.
2. In *Quand j'étais jeune*, Rachilde denies that her mother was an "ally" but adds: "Chose étrange: je ne devenais vraiment sa fille que lorsque le capitaine Eymery se montrait en opposition complète avec mes inutiles rêveries littéraires" (13).
3. Saverny was not the only important acquaintance to whom Gabrielle Eymery introduced her daughter. Rachilde also claims to have met Barrès at her mother's salon (*QJJ* 32).
4. According to Puybaraud's recollections, Gabrielle Eymery separated from her husband in 1878, moved to Paris with her daughter, and gave piano lessons to make a living (Auriant, *Souvenirs* 61).

1890, November 10

1. Making the theater into a "private" enterprise in this way also avoided—in theory at least—the legal requirement that scripts be submitted to authorities (see Goldstein). In practice, such supervision could not always be circumvented. The Théâtre libre was required to submit its plays to the censor just like other public theaters (Lefrère 131).

2. For a more detailed assessment of the reception of this play, see Frazer Lively's introduction to *Madame la Mort and Other Plays*.

3. "A partir du mois de mars les représentations du Théâtre d'art seront terminées par la mise en scène d'un tableau inconnu du public ou seulement en projet d'un peintre de la nouvelle école. Le rideau restera levé sur le tableau pendant une durée de trois minutes . . . . Une musique de scène et des parfums combinés s'adaptant au sujet du tableau représenté viendront en préparer, puis parfaire l'impression" (*L'Echo de Paris* Jan. 30, 1891). According to Robichez, "Ce projet sensationnel devait rester sans lendemain" (*Symbolisme au théâtre* 113).

4. See the reproduction of Gauguin's drawing of Madame la Mort in Lively's introduction to *Madame la Mort and Other Plays* 24.

5. In February 1891, Gauguin wrote to Rachilde in connection with the frontispiece that he supplied for *Théâtre* (the original is now in the Louvre). While the tone of respect and even awe might be disingenuous (he dared not write before, how could he do justice to *Madame la Mort* in a single drawing, and so on), it is nevertheless testimony to the fact that, for better or worse, Rachilde was a figure to be reckoned with. (See Gauguin 208–9.)

6. Publicly, however, Rachilde maintained that Fort's theater had died owing to a dearth of plays to produce (her opinion from 1893 is quoted in Jasper 244).

7. See also Geat, who cites extensively from twelve letters from Rachilde, preserved by the Société des auteurs et compositeurs dramatiques, to illustrate her role in supporting symbolist theater.

8. She published five theatrical reviews in the *Mercure de France* between 1891 (after her debut as playwright) and 1896.

9. The practice of dimming the house lights was facilitated by technical advances such as gas lighting, which made such modulations possible. Wagner was the first to implement this practice so that audiences would focus on the performance rather than treating a visit to the theater as a social opportunity. Such practices were slower to

catch on in France, however, than in Germany. For more on the emergence of increasingly cinematic conventions of fin-de-siècle visual culture, see V. R. Schwartz; and Charney and Schwartz.

10. Gerould. Also on the bill was Björnsterne Björnson's *Beyond Human Power*. Rachilde was the first *French* author to be performed by the Théâtre de l'oeuvre (Jasper 135; Lugné-Poe 2:65).

11. On his arrival in Paris in 1885, Freud was struck by the culture of advertisement and display that he found there. He wrote to his sister-in-law Minna Bernays about, among other things, "the ghastly posters in the streets announcing a new novel" (quoted in V. R. Schwartz 43–44).

12. This and other quotations from *L'Araignée de cristal* are from *Le Démon de l'absurde*.

13. Gisele d'Estoc reported in the *Cahiers d'amour* (reprinted in Borel, *Maupassant et l'androgyne*) that Maupassant claimed to have lived the experience that he gives to the hero of "Le Horla" and was also frequently troubled by mirrors and vision disorders in which he would see doubles of himself. For further discussion of the role of mirrors in Maupassant's work, see Gicquel and Williams.

14. Some other examples of mirrors can be found in the plays *Volupté* and *La Femme peinte*. In *Volupté* (first performed in 1896), two adolescents (a boy and a girl) discuss their fears next to a mysterious pond in the woods. The girl sees a corpse in the pond; the boy does not. In *La Femme peinte* (published in *Le Mercure de France* on 1 August 1, 1921) a mirror once again forms an essential part of the décor. The play concerns a soldier and his mistress. She puts on makeup in her bedroom, but her face cannot yet be seen. In the dramatic climax, the soldier confesses his complicity in the execution of a prostitute during World War I. When the woman shows her face finally, she has made herself up to look like the grotesque face described by the soldier.

1894, A Tuesday

1. According to Arnaud 87. Jarry alternated attending Rachilde's Tuesdays with those of Mallarmé. Jarry first came to Rachilde's attention when he published a description of a poetry reading that he had attended on December 6, 1893, in *L'Art littéraire* in January 1894. Rachilde wrote to him in response to this article: "Vous n'aimez pas les vers de Samain" (Arnaud 69). On March 4, 1894, he wrote to Vallette proposing his translation of Coleridge's "Rime of the Ancient

Mariner" for inclusion in the *Mercure* (Jarry 1:1036). Two days later, having evidently received a response from Vallette in the meantime, Jarry wrote again, indicating that he would be interested in becoming a stockholder in the new Mercure publishing house that was being formed (1:1306–7). On April 3, 1894, he purchased four shares at one hundred francs each, making the first payment of one hundred francs. Although the Coleridge translation was rejected, his dramatic poem "Haldernablou" was accepted, and, by May, Jarry was writing to Vallette to change some details of the manuscript (which would appear in July). After a conversation with Remy de Gourmont, Jarry decided to change both the title of the piece and the names of the characters—from Henrik and Cameleo to Haldern and Ablou. The title would become simply "Haldernablou" "en un seul mot de l'horreur de la bête double accouplée" (1:1037).

2. On Jarry and drowning, see also Bordillon.

3. Lugné-Poe describes the period when Jarry worked as the theater's secretary: "Il y vint même accompagné de lord Douglas et de deux autres jeunes bonshommes, ce que j'appris plus tard. Cela me contraria bien un peu, mais n'était-il pas de la maison?" (2:163). He mentions it again when describing the gatherings at the "Nouvelles Athènes": "On y voyait aussi Douglas et Jarry ainsi que molle et gourmande Fanny Zessinger" (3:27). Fanny Zessinger (or Zaessinger) was said to frequent "les tapettes de la Nouvelle-Athènes" (quoted in Lefrère 511).

4. Arnaud suggests, however, that Jarry did not meet Oscar Wilde until May 19, 1898, when he was introduced to the exiled writer by Henry D. Davray (418).

5. Douglas claimed to find Jarry repulsive, however. When Rachilde sent him a copy of *Les Hors-Nature*, he thanked her in a letter (July 26, 1897) rather than in person because "vous vous plaisez à ne vous montrer que les mardis où je risque de rencontrer des Raffalovitch [*sic*], des Jarry et d'autres personnes qui me font un effet de répulsion physique" (quoted in "Géométries perverses" 73n).

6. Note that the adolescent figure of the page has often been a vehicle for expressing same-sex love. Vicinus offers other examples, such as Vernon Lee's "Prince Alberic and the Snake Lady."

7. Jarry and Fargue had been schoolmates, and their closeness had caused sufficient concern that Fargue's parents had removed their son from Jarry's influence. Questions about their intimacy arose again in 1893 (Arnaud 38–45).

8. It would seem that Vallette's passion quickly dissipated, however. Rachilde wrote to Mademoiselle Blaizot that "M. Vallette m'a épousée. Aussitôt après il a épousé les livres" (quoted in Léautaud 2:1670).

9. Douglas wrote to her, for example, that he was not "a monster" (the letter is quoted in Ellmann 512, but the date is not given).

10. Perhaps Rachilde's interest in medical sexology was stimulated by Jarry, who was acquainted with Krafft-Ebing (see "Géométries perverses" 73). In any case, Rachilde's work can be seen as a literary correlative of sexological study, offering a series of case studies. See, for example, "Géométries perverses," which matches her works to the pathological categories described by Krafft-Ebing.

   Jarry would play on the word *heterosexual* in his personal dedication to Rachilde of a copy of his *L'Amour en visites* (1898). Addressing the dedication to "Jean de Chilra," another of Rachilde's pseudonymous alter egos, though this one even more clearly male than Rachilde, Jarry offered "ces XI moments hétéro . . . doxes de l'heure autosexuelle de M. Ubu" (*Organographes du cymbalum pataphysicum* 18 [1982]: 44).

11. Among the more serious works are Nahas and Turley, a mostly anecdotal survey of straight women involved in a variety of ways with gay men; Goodwin, a study that applies the methodology of folklore to an analysis of gay acculturation but dismisses the stereotype of the fag hag as only derogatory (19); and Moon, which focuses on how gay men perceive fag hags. For an example of superficial and anecdotal pop psychology, see Rauch and Fessler, a lighthearted series of cartoons comparing gay and straight men.

12. See, for example, Barkan; Boswell; Fernandez; Saslow.

13. See, for example, Lennon 33. Rachilde maintained that she was faithful to Vallette, but, given some of her unconventional notions of adultery and sexuality, what this meant is not clear. For example, in her fiction, adultery could be committed mentally as well as physically.

1900, December 10

1. The records on Gabrielle Eymery cited throughout this chapter form entry 5230 in vol. 4x563 ("Admises du 26 février 1898 au 30 août 1905") of the records of the Hôpital Esquîrol held in the Archives départementales du Val de Marne.

2. Christian Soulignac explains the use of this symbol: "Les marques de justification de tirage se trouvent sur les pages où sont annoncés

les différents papiers utilisés pour les exemplaires de tête ou de luxe de l'édition. Elles remplacent, pour les exemplaires ordinaires, la numérotation, ou même une absence totale de numérotation" (*Justifications de tirage du Mercure* preface [unpaginated]). Only two publishers used this device at the turn of the century, the Mercure de France and the *Revue blanche*.

3. Note that this is not the only Paris address that we have for Gabrielle Eymery. In her memoirs, Rachilde claimed that, while she lived at 5, rue des Ecoles, her mother lived at 12, quai Bourbon (*QJJ* 33). Quai Bourbon is on the île Saint-Louis, but the location of no. 12 remains unclear: today the numbers skip from 10 to 14. Other addresses known include 102 avenue d'Orléans, where Gabrielle was residing in 1892 when she applied for her military widow's pension (Archives Château de Vincennes); 23 quai de la Tournelle, the address of the "Mme Gabrielle E." who responded to Rachilde's appeal concerning the cholera epidemic (see the "coupures de presse," Fonds Doucet); and the cité aux Fleurs.

4. See, for example, Clive Thomson's work on Rachilde's incorporation of medical literature on criminality in novels such as *La Marquise de Sade*.

5. In other words, the novel was begun on February 10, 1877—the day before her eighteenth birthday (it appears that she was acknowledging here that her year of birth was 1860)—and finished on February 27, just over two weeks later. Rachilde admitted that, once she had begun drafting a novel, she wrote very fast. It will be recalled that *Monsieur Vénus*, too, was supposedly written quickly.

6. Later editions of *Psychopathia sexualis* even mention *La Marquise de Sade* specifically. See Felski's analysis of female sadism in *La Marquise de Sade* and *La Jongleuse* (174–206).

7. In "Sade, Rachilde, et Freud," Dauphiné points out that Mary has more in common with the real marquis de Sade than the real marquise de Sade (55) but that there is little trace of his style in Rachilde's novel: "Rares sont, dans ce récit, les éléments du réalisme figuratif de Sade. Et lorsqu'ils apparaissent, ils prêtent à sourire." Furthermore, an examination of the manuscript of *La Marquise de Sade* "ne contient aucune allusion à Sade, aux ouvrages de Sade" (56). The comments are developed in Dauphiné, *Rachilde* (1991) 64–68.

8. For a Freudian reading of this identification, see Lukacher, "Mademoiselle Baudelaire."

9. All citations in the text are to the 1980 edition published by Le Tout sur le Tout, a facsimile version of the 1916 Crès edition.

10. "Un Héros de roman" is the title of the first in a series of chapters devoted to recollections of her father in *Quand j'étais jeune.*

11. Frazer Lively reports that, when Rachilde's play *L'Araignée de cristal*, discussed above, toured in Denmark, the ending of the play was changed so that Silvius killed his mother before killing himself (introduction to *Madame la Mort* 30). As Lively notes, it remains unknown whether Rachilde even knew about this change, but, in the light of the matricidal subtext of *La Tour d'amour*, the change would merely seem to make explicit what was already implicit in some of Rachilde's work.

12. The phrase "disloyal to civilization" was coined by Adrienne Rich to describe women's need to break with tradition in order to write themselves into history and society.

13. On nineteenth-century French education for girls, see Bricard; Clark; Gemie; Margadant; Mayeur; McMillan.

14. On images of confinement, see Gemie. Some of these accounts offer an uncanny echo of Charlotte Perkins Gilman's story "The Yellow Wallpaper."

1925, July 2

1. Shattuck's is but one summary of events. See also the description in "Rachilde et la France" 52–53, which also makes available a hitherto unpublished poetic rendition of events by Breton.

2. An article in *Les Nouvelles littéraires* (July 10, 1925) also accused Rachilde of exaggeration, and Georges Ribemont-Dessaignes, a surrealist sympathizer, remembers Rachilde as one of the provoking "personnalités déplaisantes, qui d'ailleurs se livrèrent à des propos stupides" (125). On the other hand, support also poured in for Rachilde (see "Rachilde et la France" 54–56).

3. For evidence of Rachilde's anti-Semitism, see "Rachilde et la France" 56 n.5.

4. Paradoxically, though not entirely surprisingly, Rachilde viewed the Rumanian origins of others, such as Nel Haroun (who inspired some of her later work such as *L'Homme aux bras de feu*), as an asset that gave a certain exoticized appeal.

5. For an example of the challenges posed by such a task, see Friedman.

6. See, for example, Caws and, more recently, Brandon. For more on surrealist women, see Caws, Kuenzli, and Raaberg. Conley argues that surrealism was not "unremittingly misogynist" (3), but her argument rests on seeing surrealism as a movement that extends well into the twentieth century and merges into *écriture féminine*. The women surrealists whom she examines in order to show

the ways in which surrealism has been hospitable to female self-expression produced their most significant work at a much later period than the one under consideration here.

7. Mafarka's primary homoerotic relationship is with his brother Magamal. See also Spackman's analysis of the novel's "homosexual panic" (49–76).

1928, June

1. For some of the few discussions of Rachilde and modernism, see Felski; Stillman (esp. n.4); and Dauphiné, *Rachilde* (1991).

2. An example of such a denial can be found in a letter to Bossard now held by the Harry Ransom Humanities Research Center, University of Texas at Austin.

3. Rachilde was unforgiving when it came to allegations of same-sex attraction. A veiled reference to Rachilde and their "shared tastes" in women by Joseph Delteil cost Maryse Choisy (whom Rachilde apparently held responsible for the indiscretion) the Prix Fémina for her novel *Mon coeur dans une formule* in 1927, or so Choisy believed (*Sur le chemin* 138–39). Perhaps, however, the novel was doomed from the start since Choisy describes it as "le drame actuel de le femme qui ne veut pas devenir homme" (138).

4. Despite the hommage implicit in such intertextuality, Rachilde was not sympathetic to Proust. In 1909, Proust had written to Alfred Vallette about a book he was finishing in which "un des principaux personnages est un homosexuel" (9:155), asking Vallette to keep the fact confidential. As Philip Kolb states in his note, "Proust sait que la femme du destinataire est l'auteur de romans bien équivoques, qu'elle signait du pseudonyme Rachilde, notamment *Madame Adonis* (1888), *Monsieur Vénus* (1884), *Les Hors-Nature* (1897)" (Proust 9:158). The *Mercure de France* declined to publish his work. While Rachilde was not personally responsible for this decision, she might have intervened on his behalf but declined to do so. She also wrote negative reviews of *Du côté de chez Swann*, which she found soporific, and of *A l'ombre des jeunes filles en fleurs*. I am indebted to Michael Finn for drawing my attention to these facts.

5. For an overview of the theme of pederasty in gay male French literature, see Robinson.

6. Rachilde's notes for her speech are preserved at the Harry Ransom Humanities Research Center, University of Texas at Austin.

7. Critics have also interpreted Rachilde's naming of the Fertzen brothers in *Les Hors-Nature* (1897) as evidence of Adelswärd's influence on her, but, as Ogrinc points out, the relatively early date of this

novel makes this interpretation highly unlikely. Moreover, Fertzen was a common enough name (with variant spellings) for there to be other possible models (see Ogrinc 53 n.51). One example that might have appealed to Rachilde, given her predilection for aristocratic figures, is the Count Fersen said to have had an affair with Marie-Antoinette.

8. The letter of invitation is held today by the Harry Ransom Humanities Research Center, University of Texas at Austin.

9. For Rachilde's explorations of theories about sexuality and love, see, for example, her "Questions brûlantes" and *Pourquoi je ne suis pas féministe.*

10. See esp. Benstock, *Women of the Left Bank*; and Hanscombe and Smyers. The 1980s saw the publication of many works of biography and criticism devoted to individual figures in this constellation (Natalie Clifford Barney, Janet Flanner, H. D., Djuna Barnes, Renée Vivien, Gertrude Stein); among the most recent publications that testify to the vigor of this reappraisal, see Broe and Ingram; Broe; and Scott, *The Gender of Modernism* and *Refiguring Modernism.*

11. In Benstock's *Women of the Left Bank*, for example, Rachilde is mentioned only three times in a text of some 450 pages.

12. Berthe Cleyrergue, the source of much firsthand information about Barney's salon, had previously worked for Djuna Barnes (Herring 149). She was first interviewed for her position by Barney on June 5, 1927, and entered her service on June 8. She would not, therefore, have been present at the June 3 salon (and therefore able to verify Rachilde's presence), but she recounted memories of Rachilde's visits on other occasions: "Rachilde, par exemple, venait toujours avec des jeunes gens, un Turc en particulier [probably Nel Haroun, actually of Rumanian origin], et comme elle s'habillait très mal, en fée Carabosse, je ne pouvais m'empêcher de rire" (Causse 118).

13. This citation is to the 1982 edition published by Des Femmes in Paris.

BIBLIOGRAPHY

Principal Works by Rachilde

This is not an exhaustive list of Rachilde's work but simply an inventory of her principal publications (it does not include journalism, criticism, re-editions, or posthumous publications). For a detailed bibliography of her juvenilia, see Christian Soulignac, "Bibliographie des oeuvres de jeunesse de Rachilde, 1877–1889 (édition revue et corrigée)," *Revue Frontenac* 10–11 (1993–94): 198–218, which supersedes "Eléments d'approche d'une bibliographie périgourdine de Rachilde," *Organographes du cymbalum pataphysicum* 19–20 (1983): 109–20. See also the "Bibliographie générale," *Organographes du cymbalum pataphysicum* 19–20 (1983): 121–48, which gives more detailed (though inevitably still incomplete) bibliographic information on Rachilde's works as well as comments on plots. (Note, however, that the date of publication of *Mon étrange plaisir* has been corrected in the listing below.)

1880. *Monsieur de la Nouveauté*. Paris: Dentu.

1884. *Histoires bêtes pour amuser les petits enfants d'esprit*. Paris: Brissy.

1884. *Monsieur Vénus*. Brussels: Brancart.

1885. *Queue de poisson*. Brussels: Brancart.

1885. *Nono*. Paris: Monnier.

1886. *A mort*. Paris: Monnier.

1887. *La Marquise de Sade*. Paris: Monnier.

1887. *Le Tiroir de Mimi-Corail*. Paris: Monnier.

1888. *Madame Adonis*. Paris: Monnier.

1889. *L'Homme roux*. Paris: Librairie Illustrée.

1889. *Minette*. Paris: Librairie Française et Internationale.

1889. *Le Mordu*. Paris: Genonceaux.

1891. *La Sanglante Ironie*. Paris: Genonceaux.

1891. *Théâtre (Madame la Mort, Le Vendeur de soleil, La Voix du sang)*. Paris: Savine.

1893. *L'Animale*. Paris: Simonis Empis.

1894. *Le Démon de l'absurde*. Paris: Mercure de France.

1896. *La Princesse des ténèbres*. Paris: Calmann Lévy.

1897. *Les Hors-Nature*. Paris: Mercure de France.

1898. *L'Heure sexuelle*. Paris: Mercure de France.

1899. *La Tour d'amour*. Paris: Mercure de France.

1900. *Contes et nouvelles, suivis du Théâtre*. Paris: Mercure de France.

1900. *La Jongleuse*. Paris: Mercure de France.

1903. *L'Imitation de la mort*. Paris: Mercure de France.

1904. *Le Dessous*. Paris: Mercure de France.

1905. *Le Meneur de louves*. Paris: Mercure de France.

1912. *Son printemps*. Paris: Mercure de France.

1915. *La Délivrance*. Paris: Mercure de France.

1917. *La Terre qui rit*. Paris: Maison du livre.

1918. *Dans le puits, ou la vie inférieure, 1915–1917*. Paris: Mercure de France.

1919. *La Découverte de l'Amérique*. Geneva: Kundig.

1920. *La Maison vierge*. Paris: Ferenczi.

1921. *Les Rageac*. Paris: Flammarion.

1921. *La Souris japonaise*. Paris: Flammarion.

1922. *Le Grand Saigneur*. Paris: Flammarion.

1922. *L'Hôtel du grand veneur*. Paris: Ferenczi.

1923. *Le Château des deux amants*. Paris: Flammarion.

1923. *Le Parc du mystère*. Paris: Flammarion. With Homem-Christo.

1924. *Au seuil de l'enfer*. Paris: Flammarion. With Homem-Christo.

1924. *La Haine amoureuse*. Paris: Flammarion.

1926. *Le Théâtre des bêtes*. Paris: Les Arts et le Livre.

1927. *Refaire l'amour*. Paris: Ferenczi.

1928. *Alfred Jarry; ou, Le Surmâle de lettres*. Paris: Grasset.

1928. *Madame de Lydone, assassin*. Paris: Ferenczi.

1928. *Pourquoi je ne suis pas féministe*. Paris: Editions de France.

1928. *Le Prisonnier*. Paris: Editions de France. With André David.

1929. *La Femme aux mains d'ivoire*. Paris: Editions des Portiques.

1929. *Portraits d'hommes*. Paris: Mornay.

1929. *Le Val sans retour*. Paris: Fayard. With Jean-Joë Lauzach.

1930. *L'Homme aux bras de feu*. Paris: Ferenczi.

1931. *Notre-Dame des rats*. Paris: Querelle.

1931. *Les Voluptés imprévues*. Paris: Ferenczi.

1932. *L'Amazone rouge*. Paris: Lemerre.

1932. *Jeux d'artifices*. Paris: Ferenczi.

1934. *La Femme Dieu*. Paris: Ferenczi.

1934. *Mon étrange plaisir*. Paris: Baudinière.

1935. *L'Aérophage*. Paris: Les Ecrivains Associés. With Jean-Joë Lauzach.

1937. *Les Accords perdus*. Paris: Editions Corymbes.

1937. *L'Autre Crime*. Paris: Mercure de France.

1938. *La Fille inconnue*. Paris: Imprimerie la Technique de Livre.

1938. *Pour la lumière*. Brussels: Edition de la Nouvelle Revue de Belgique.

1939. *L'Anneau de Saturne*. Paris: Ferenczi.

1942. *Face à la peur*. Paris: Mercure de France.

1943. *Duvet d'ange*. Paris: Messein.

1944. *Le Roman d'un homme sérieux*. Paris: Mercure de France.

1945. *Survie*. Paris: Messein.

1947. *Quand j'étais jeune*. Paris: Mercure de France.

Archives and Libraries Consulted

Archives de la Préfecture de Police, Paris

Archives de l'Armée, Service Historique, Vincennes

Archives de Paris

Archives Départementales de la Dordogne

Archives Départementales du Val de Marne

Bibliothèque Municipale de Périgueux

Bibliothèque Nationale de France, Paris

Fonds Doucet, Bibliothèque Littéraire Jacques Doucet, Paris

Harry Ransom Humanities Research Center, University of Texas at Austin

Lilly Library, Indiana University

Musée d'Orsay, Paris

Books and Articles

d'Abrantès, duchesse. *Les Femmes célèbres de tous les pays*. Paris: Lachevardière, 1834.

Ageorges, Joseph. "Rachilde." *Critique de sympathie: Portraits littéraires*. Lyon: E. Vitte, 1909. 126–28.

Alderfer, Hannah, et al., eds. *Diary of a Conference on Sexuality*. New York: Barnard College Women's Center, 1982.

Ambroise-Rendu, Anne-Claude. "Du dessin de presse à la photographie (1878–1914): Histoire d'une mutation technique et culturelle." *Revue d'histoire moderne et contemporaine* 39 (Jan. / Mar. 1992): 6–28.

Anderson, M. Jean. "Writing the Non-Conforming Body: Rachilde's *Monsieur Vénus* (1884) and *Madame Adonis* (1888)." *New Zealand Journal of French Studies* 21.1 (2000): 5–17.

Anderson, Olive. *Suicide in Victorian and Edwardian England*. Oxford: Clarendon, 1987.

Angenot, Marc. *Le Cru et le faisandé: Sexe, littérature, et discours social à la Belle Epoque*. Brussels: Editions Labor, 1986.

Apollinaire, Guillaume. *Journal intime, 1898–1918*. [Montpellier]: Editions du Limon, 1991.

————. *Oeuvres poétiques*. Paris: Gallimard, 1965.

Arban, Dominique. "Un Entretien avec Rachilde." *Opéra* Dec. 25, 1946.

Arnaud, Noël. *Alfred Jarry: D'Ubu roi au Docteur Faustroll*. Paris: La Table Ronde, 1974.

Aron, Jean-Paul, and Roger Kempf. *Le Pénis et la démoralisation de l'Occident*. Paris: Grasset, 1978.

Audinet, Pierre. "Une Visite à Rachilde." *Les Nouvelles littéraires* 2593 (July 13, 1977): 5.

Audoin-Rouzeau, Stéphane. *1870: La France dans la guerre*. Paris: A. Colin, 1989.

Auriant. "9 lettres inédites de Rachilde au Père Ubu." *Le Bayou* 20 (1956): 42–51.

————. *Souvenirs sur Madame Rachilde*. [Reims]: A l'Ecart, 1989.

Austin, J. L. *Philosophical Papers*. Oxford: Clarendon, 1961.

"Au temps des *Taches d'encre*: Lettres inédites de Barrès." *Les Nouvelles littéraires* Oct. 6, 1960: 1, 7.

Bachelin, Henri. "Rachilde." *Vient de paraître* Mar. 1924: 142–45.

Bair, Deirdre. *Simone de Beauvoir: A Biography*. New York: Summit, 1990.

Baju, Anatole. "Les Décadents et la vie." *Le Décadent* Feb. 15–29, 1888: 1–4.

Baldick, Robert. *The Life of J.-K. Huysmans*. Oxford: Clarendon, 1955.

Barbedette, Gilles. *Paris gay 1925*. Paris: Presses de la Renaissance, 1981.

Barbey d'Aurevilly, Jules. *Les Bas-Bleus*. Paris: Société Générale de Librairie Catholique, 1876.

Bard, Christine. "Le Dossier D/B 58 aux Archives de la Préfecture de Police de Paris." *Clio* 10 (1999): 155–67.

————. *Les Filles de Marianne: Histoire des féminismes, 1914–1940*. Paris: Fayard, 1995.

————. *Les Garçonnes: Modes et fantasmes des années folles*. Paris: Flammarion, 1998.

Bard, Christine, ed. *Un Siècle d'antiféminisme*. Paris: Fayard, 1999.

Barine, Arvède. *Princesses et grandes dames*. Paris: Hachette, 1893.

Barkan, Leonard. *Transuming Passion: Ganymede and the Erotics of Humanism*. Stanford: Stanford University Press, 1991.

Barney, Natalie Clifford. *Aventures de l'esprit*. 1929. Rpt. With a preface by Katy Barsac. Paris: Editions Persona, 1982.

————. *Traits et portraits*. Paris: Mercure de France, 1963.

Baronian, Jean-Baptiste. "Rachilde ou l'amour monstre." *Magazine littéraire* 288 (May 1991): 42–46.

Barrès, Maurice. "Mademoiselle Baudelaire." *Le Voltaire* June 24, 1886. Rpt. *Les Chroniques* (Feb. 1887): 77–79.

Barrès, Maurice. Preface. *Monsieur Vénus*. By Rachilde. Paris: Brossier, 1889.

————. *Les Taches d'encre*. Nov. 1884–Jan. 1885. The entire run of the journal, all Barrès's own work.

Baudet, Colette. *Grandeur et misères d'un éditeur belge: Henry Kistemaeckers (1851–1934)*. Brussels: Editions Labor, 1986.

Beaumont, Keith. *Alfred Jarry: A Critical and Biographical Study*. New York: St. Martin's, 1984.

Beaunier, André. Rev. of *Contes et nouvelles*, by Rachilde. *Revue bleue* 15.7 (Feb. 16, 1901): 219–20.

Beizer, Janet. *Ventriloquized Bodies: Narratives of Hysteria in Nineteenth-Century France*. Ithaca: Cornell University Press, 1994.

Benstock, Shari. "Paris Lesbianism and the Politics of Reaction, 1900–1940." *Hidden from History: Reclaiming the Gay and Lesbian Past*. Ed. Martin Bauml Duberman, Martha Vicinus, and George Chauncey Jr. New York: NAL, 1989. 332–46.

————. *Women of the Left Bank: Paris, 1900–1940*. Austin: University of Texas Press, 1986.

Berenson, Edward. *The Trial of Madame Caillaux*. Berkeley: University of California Press, 1992.

Bernhardt, Sarah. *Ma double vie: Mémoires*. Paris: Charpentier & Fasquelle, 1907.

Bernier, Georges. *"La Revue blanche," ses amis, ses artistes*. Paris: Hazan, 1991.

Bertaut, Jules. *La Littérature féminine d'aujourd'hui*. Paris: Librairie des Annales Politiques et Littéraires, [1909].

Bérubé, Allan. *Coming Out under Fire: The History of Gay Men and Women in World War Two*. New York: Free Press, 1990.

Besnard-Coursodon, Micheline. "'Monsieur Vénus,' 'Madame Adonis': Sexe et discours." *Littérature* 54 (May 1984): 121–27.

Bettega, Victor. *John Grand-Carteret (1850–1927)*. Grenoble: Editions des Cahiers de l'Alpe, 1991.

"Bibliographie générale." *Organographes du cymbalum pataphysicum* 19–20 (1983): 121–48.

Birkett, Jennifer. *The Sins of the Fathers: Decadence in France, 1870–1914*. London: Quartet, 1986.

Blin, Georges, ed. *Autour de Natalie Clifford Barney*. Paris: Université de Paris; Bibliothèque Littéraire Jacques Doucet, 1976.

Bloom, Harold. *The Anxiety of Influence: A Theory of Poetry*. New York: Oxford University Press, 1973.

Bonnefon, Jean de. *La Corbeille des roses, ou les dames de lettres*. Paris: Société d'Editions de Bouville, 1909.

Bonnet, Marguerite. *L'Affaire Barrès*. Paris: José Corti, 1987.

Bonnet, Marie-Jo. *Un Choix sans équivoque*. Paris: Denoël, 1981.

Bonnetain, Paul. *Charlot s'amuse*. Brussels: Kistemaeckers, 1884.

Bordillon, Henri. "Jarry, Rachilde, et les noyés." *Organographes du cymbalum pataphysicum* 19–20 (1983): 99–100.

Borel, Pierre. "Une Amie inconnue de Maupassant." *Le Mois suisse* 32 (1941): 142–68.

———. *Maupassant et l'androgyne*. [Paris]: Les Editions du Livre Moderne, 1944.

———. *Le Vrai Maupassant*. Geneva: Cailler, 1951.

Bornstein, Kate. *Gender Outlaw: On Men, Women, and the Rest of Us*. New York: Routledge, 1994.

Boschian-Campaner, Catherine. *Barbey D'Aurevilly: Biographie*. Paris: Séguier, 1989.

Boswell, John. *Christianity, Social Tolerance, and Homosexuality: Gay People in Western Europe from the Beginning of the Christian Era to the Fourteenth Century*. Chicago: University of Chicago Press, 1980.

Bourdet, Edouard. *La Prisonnière*. Paris: Librairie Théâtrale, 1925.

Bowlby, Rachel. *Just Looking: Consumer Culture in Dreiser, Gissing, and Zola*. New York: Methuen, 1985.

Brandon, Ruth. *Surreal Lives: The Surrealists, 1917–1945*. New York: Grove, 1999.

Brantôme, Pierre de Bourdeille, seigneur de. *Recueil des dames, poésies, et tombeaux*. Paris: Gallimard, 1991.

Brault, Louis. *Christine de Suède: Drame historique, en cinq actes et en vers*. Brussels: Ode & Wodon, 1829.

Bricard, Isabelle. *Saintes ou pouliches: L'Education des jeunes filles au XIXe siècle*. Paris: A. Michel, 1985.

Broca, Henri. *"T'en fais pas! Viens à Montparnasse!" Enquête sur le Montparnasse actuel*. Paris: n.p., [1928].

Broe, Mary Lynne, ed. *Silence and Power: A Reevaluation of Djuna Barnes*. Carbondale: Southern Illinois University Press, 1991.

Broe, Mary Lynne, and Angela Ingram, eds. *Women's Writing in Exile*. Chapel Hill: University of North Carolina Press, 1989.

Brownstein, Rachel M. *Tragic Muse: Rachel of the Comédie-Française*. New York: Knopf, 1993.

Bruzelius, Margaret. "'En el profundo espejo del deseo': Delmira Agustini, Rachilde, and the Vampire." *Revista hispanica moderna* 46.1 (1993): 51–63.

Butler, Judith. *Gender Trouble: Feminism and the Subversion of Identity*. New York: Routledge, 1990.

Cachin, Françoise. "'Monsieur Vénus' et l'ange de sodome: L'Androgyne au temps de Gustave Moreau." *Nouvelle Revue de psychanalyse* 7 (spring 1973): 63–69.

Cahiers Gai Kitsch Camp. Number 23 (1993) reprints a special issue of the satirical journal *Le Rire* from 1932 on the topic of "Dames seules."

Callu, Florence, and Marie-Odile Germani, eds. *Correspondance de Maurice Barrès: Inventaire des lettres reçues, 1874–1923.* Paris: Bibliothèque Nationale, 1992.

Caradec, [François]. "Mademoiselle Eymery, écrivain mineur." *Organographes du cymbalum pataphysicum* 19–20 (1983) 90–96.

Carassus, Emilien. *Le Snobisme et les lettres françaises: De Paul Bourget à Marcel Proust.* Paris: Armand Colin, 1966.

Carter, A. E. *The Idea of Decadence in French Literature, 1830–1900.* Toronto: University of Toronto Press, 1958.

Castillo, Michel del. *Colette, une certaine France.* Paris: Stock, 1999.

Cate, Phillip Dennis, and Mary Shaw, eds. *The Spirit of Montmartre: Cabarets, Humor, and the Avant-Garde, 1875–1905.* New Brunswick NJ: Rutgers University Press, 1996.

Catteau-Calleville, Jean-Pierre. *Histoire de Christine, reine de Suède.* Paris: Pillet, 1815.

Causse, Michele. *Berthe ou un demi-siècle auprès de l'Amazone: Souvenirs recueillis et précédés d'une étude sur Natalie C. Barney par Michele Causse.* Paris: Editions Tierce, 1980.

Caws, Mary Ann. *The Surrealist Look: An Erotics of Encounter.* Cambridge: MIT Press, 1997.

Caws, Mary Ann, Rudolf Kuenzli, and Gwen Raaberg, eds. *Surrealism and Women.* Cambridge: MIT Press, 1991.

Chambers, Ross. *Mélancolie et opposition: Les Débuts du modernisme en France.* Paris: José Corti, 1987.

Champion, Pierre. *Mon vieux quartier.* Paris: Grasset, 1932.

Charasson, Henriette. "Rachilde." *Revue de Hollande* 4 (1917): 977–85.

Charney, Leo, and Vanessa R. Schwartz, eds. *Cinema and the Invention of Modern Life.* Berkeley: University of California Press, 1995.

Chartier, Roger, and Henri-Jean Martin, eds. *Histoire de l'édition française.* Vol. 3, *Le Temps des éditeurs: Du romantisme à la Belle Epoque.* Paris: Fayard, 1990.

Chèvre, Jean. "Rachilde et le Cros." *Corymbe* 18 (May–June 1934): 3–6.

Choisy, Maryse. *L'Amour dans les prisons.* Paris: Montaigne, 1930.

———. *Un Mois chez les filles.* Paris: Montaigne, 1928.

———. *Sur le chemin de Dieu on rencontre d'abord le diable: Mémoires, 1925–1939.* Paris: Emile-Paul, 1977.

"Chronologie." *Organographes du cymbalum pataphysicum* 19–20 (1983): 5–18.

Citti, Pierre. *Contre la décadence: Histoire de l'imagination française dans le roman, 1890–1914*. Paris: PUF, 1987.

Citti, Pierre, ed. *Fins de siècle: Colloque de Tours, 4–6 juin, 1985*. Bordeaux: Presses Universitaires de Bordeaux, 1990.

Cixous, Hélène. *La Venue à l'écriture*. Paris: Union Générale d'Editions, 1977.

Clark, Linda L. *Schooling the Daughters of Marianne: Textbooks and the Socialization of Girls in Modern French Primary Schools*. Albany: State University of New York Press, 1984.

Cody, Morrill, with Hugh Ford. *The Women of Montparnasse*. New York: Cornwall, 1984.

Colette. *Lettres à ses pairs*. Paris: Flammarion, 1973.

"Colette à Rachilde: Le Mystère des Claudine enfin éclairci." *Le Figaro littéraire* 1392 (Jan. 20, 1973): 15.

Colin, René-Pierre. "La Vie d'un homme de lettres: Souvenirs d'Henry Fèvre." *Histoires littéraires* 1.2 (Apr.–May–June 2000): 15–21.

Colombier, Marie. *Memoirs of Sarah Barnum. Munro's Library of Popular Novels* 1.123 (Mar. 5, 1884).

Compagnon, Antoine. *La Troisième République des lettres, de Flaubert à Proust*. Paris: Seuil, 1983.

Conley, Katharine. *Automatic Woman: The Representation of Woman in Surrealism*. Lincoln: University of Nebraska Press, 1996.

Conrad, Barnaby, III. *Absinthe: History in a Bottle*. San Francisco: Chronicle, 1988.

Cook, Blanche Wiesen. *Eleanor Roosevelt*. 2 vols. New York: Viking, 1992.

Corymbe: Hommage à Rachilde, écrivain du Périgord. 18 (May–June 1934). Special issue of the journal *Corymbe* devoted to Rachilde.

Coulon, Marcel. "L'Imagination de Rachilde." *Mercure de France* 142 (Aug. 15–Sept. 15, 1920): 545–69.

Cousin, Victor. *La Société française au XVII siècle d'après le Grand Cyrus de Mlle de Scudéry*. Paris: Didier, 1858.

Crecelius, Kathryn J. *Family Romances: George Sand's Early Novels*. Bloomington: Indiana University Press, 1987.

Cutshall, J. A. "'Excuses Madame Rachilde': The Failure of Alfred Jarry's Novels." *Forum for Modern Language Studies* 24.4 (1988): 359–74.

Darío, Rubén. *Los Raros*. Buenos Aires: Tip. La Vasconia, 1896.

d'Arkaï, Léo Pillard. "Fantaisie littéraire." *Le Décadent* 3.13 (June 15–30, 1888): 9–12.

Darzens, Rodolphe. *Les Nuits à Paris*. Paris: Dentu, 1889.

Datta, Venita. *Birth of a National Icon: The Literary Avant-Garde and the Origins of the Intellectual in France.* Albany: State University of New York Press, 1999.

Dauphiné, Claude. *Rachilde.* Paris: Mercure de France, 1991.

———. "Rachilde et Colette: De l'animal aux belles lettres." *Bulletin de l'Association Guillaume Budé* 2 (1989): 204–10.

———. *Rachilde: Femme de lettres, 1900.* Périgueux: Pierre Fanlac, 1985.

———. "Rachilde ou de l'acrobatie critique." *Bulletin de l'Association Guillaume Budé* 3 (Oct. 1992): 275–88.

———. "Sade, Rachilde, et Freud: Lecture de *La Marquise de Sade.*" *Bulletin de l'Association des Professeurs de Lettres* 17 (1981): 55–59.

———. "La Vision médiévale de Rachilde dans 'Le Meneur de louves.'" *Mélanges Jean Larmat: Regards sur le Moyen-Age et la Renaissance.* Ed. Maurice Accarie. Paris: Les Belles-Lettres, 1982. 489–92.

Davanture, Maurice. *La Jeunesse de Maurice Barrès (1862–1888).* 2 vols. Lille: Atelier Reproduction des Thèses, 1975.

David, André. *Compte à rebours avec Dieu.* Paris: Bibliothèque Historique de la Ville de Paris, 1986.

———. "Femmes de lettres 1900." *Revue de Paris* 71.10 (Oct. 1964): 94–97.

———. "Les 80 ans de Rachilde." *Marianne* Feb. 21, 1940: 7.

———. "Le Mercure de France entre les deux guerres." *La Revue des deux mondes* Aug. 1971: 290–301.

———. *Rachilde, homme de lettres.* Paris: Editions de la Nouvelle Revue Critique, 1924.

———. *Soixante-quinze années de jeunesse.* Paris: A. Bonne, 1974.

Deak, Frantisek. *Symbolist Theater: The Formation of an Avant-Garde.* Baltimore: Johns Hopkins University Press, 1993.

Decarnin, Camilla. "Interviews with Five Faghagging Women." *Heresies* 12 (1981): 10–14.

De Gramont, Elisabeth. *Mémoires.* 4 vols. Paris: Grasset, 1928–35.

DeJean, Joan. *Tender Geographies: Women and the Origins of the Novel in France.* New York: Columbia University Press, 1991.

Delpech, Jeanine. "Les Muses à l'Odéon." *Les Nouvelles littéraires* 1068 (Feb. 19, 1948): 1, 6.

Demaison, Louis. *Aymeri de Narbonne: Chanson de geste.* 2 vols. Paris: Société des Anciens Textes Français, 1887.

DeSalvo, Louise A. *Virginia Woolf: The Impact of Childhood Sexual Abuse on Her Life and Work.* Boston: Beacon, 1989.

Deslandres, Yvonne. *Le Costume, image de l'homme.* Paris: A. Michel, 1976.

d'Estoc, Gisèle. *Cahiers d'amour*. Paris: Arléa, 1993.

———. *Noir sur blanc: Récits lorrains*. [Nancy:] Voirin, 1887.

———. *Psychologie de Jeanne d'Arc*. Paris: J. Strauss, 1891.

———. *La Vierge-Réclame*. Paris: Librairie Richelieu, 1887.

Didier, Béatrice. *L'Ecriture-Femme*. Paris: PUF, 1981.

Digot, Jean. *Trois du Rouergue: Jean Clary, Roger Frène, Léo d'Orfer*. Remoulins sur Gardon: J. Brémond, 1995.

Dijkstra, Bram. *Idols of Perversity: Fantasies of Feminine Evil in Fin-de-Siècle Culture*. New York: Oxford University Press, 1986.

d'Orfer, Léo. *Chants de guerre de la Serbie, étude, traductions, commentaires*. Paris: Payot, 1916.

———. *Les Enfants morts*. N.p., n.d.

———. *L'Épopée serbe*. Paris: F. Rouff, 1918.

———. *Henri Issanchou*. Paris: Bibliothèque Européenne, 1885.

———. *Les Oeillets*. N.p., n.d.

Douchin, Jacques-Louis. *La Vie érotique de Maupassant*. [Paris]: Suger, 1986.

Douglas, Alfred. "Introduction to My Poems with Some Remarks on the Oscar Wilde Case." *La Revue blanche* 10.72 (June 1, 1896): 484–90.

———. *Oscar Wilde and Myself*. New York: Duffield, 1914.

Dubreuilh, Léon. "Lettres de Maurice Barrès à Charles le Goffic: La Revue *Les Chroniques*." *Annales de Bretagne* 58 (1951): 19–88.

Duckers-Ward, H. *L'Ame ardente des livres*. St. Raphael: Les Tablettes, 1922.

Ducrey, Guy. Introduction. *Romans fin-de-siècles: 1890–1900*. Paris: Robert Laffont, 1999.

Dufief, Pierre-Jean. "Les Goncourt Précurseurs de la décadence." *Cahiers Goncourt* 3 (1994): 13–22.

Duhamel, Georges. "Adieu à Rachilde." *Mercure de France* 1078 (June 1, 1953): 193–94.

———. "Souvenir de Rachilde." *Le Figaro* Apr. 6, 1953: 1.

Dumur, Louis. Review of *Le Spiritisme devant la conscience*, by Urbain Feytaud. *Mercure de France* July 1893: 260–62.

Dupuy, Raoul. *Historique du 12e régiment de chasseurs, de 1788 à 1891, d'après les archives du corps, celles du dépôt de la guerre et autres documents originaux*. Paris: E. Person, 1891.

Durkheim, Emile. *Le Suicide: Etude de sociologie*. Paris: F. Alcan, 1897.

Dutourd, Jean. "Un Bibleot de style Grévy." *Le Point* 256 (Aug. 15, 1977): 62.

Ellmann, Richard. *Oscar Wilde*. New York: Knopf, 1988.

Faderman, Lillian. *Odd Girls and Twilight Lovers: A History of Lesbian*

Life in Twentieth-Century America. New York: Columbia University Press, 1991.

―――. *Surpassing the Love of Men: Romantic Friendship and Love between Women from the Renaissance to the Present.* New York: Morrow, 1981.

Faludi, Susan. *Backlash: The Undeclared War against American Women.* New York: Crown, 1991.

Felski, Rita. *The Gender of Modernity.* Cambridge: Harvard University Press, 1995.

[Fénéon, Félix, Paul Adam, Oscar Méténier, and Jean Moréas]. *Petit Bottin des lettres et des arts.* Paris: Giraud, 1886.

Fernandez, Dominique. *Le Rapt de Ganymède.* Paris: Grasset, 1989.

Fisher, Ben. "The Companion and the Dream: Delirium in Rachilde and Jarry." *Romance Studies* 18 (summer 1991): 33–41.

Fisher, Dominique D. "Du corps travesti à l'enveloppe transparente: *Monsieur Vénus* ou la politique du leurre." *L'Esprit créateur* 37.4 (winter 1997): 46–57.

Fitch, Noel Riley. *Anaïs: The Erotic Life of Anaïs Nin.* Boston: Little, Brown, 1993.

Foster, Jeanette H. *Sex Variant Women in Literature.* 1956. Rpt. N.p.: Naiad, 1985.

Fourès, Auguste. "Ranahilde." *Le Décadent* July 1–15, 1888: 4–5.

Frappier-Mazur, Lucienne. "Marginal Canons: Rewriting the Erotic." *Yale French Studies* 75 (1988): 112–28.

―――. "Rachilde: Allégories de la guerre." *Romantisme* 85 (1994): 7–18.

Freadman, Anne. "Of Cats, and Companions, and the Name of George Sand." *Grafts: Feminist Cultural Criticism.* Ed. Susan Sheridan. London: Verso, 1988. 125–56.

Freeman, William. *The Life of Lord Alfred Douglas: Spoilt Child of Genius.* London: Herbert Joseph, 1948.

Friedman, Susan Stanford. "Modernism of the 'Scattered Remnant': Race and Politics in H. D.'s Development." *Feminist Issues in Literary Scholarship.* Ed. Shari Benstock. Bloomington: Indiana University Press, 1987. 208–31.

Gadala, Marie-Thérèse. "Nos amies les bêtes: De Colette à Rachilde." *Ceux que j'aime . . . : De Maurice Barrès à Paul Morand.* Paris: Figuière, 1927. 160–67.

Garber, Marjorie. *Vested Interests: Cross-Dressing and Cultural Anxiety.* New York: Routledge, 1991.

Garvey, Ellen Gruber. *The Adman in the Parlor: Magazines and the Gen-*

dering of Consumer Culture, 1880s-1910s. New York: Oxford University Press, 1996.

Gates, Barbara T. *Victorian Suicide: Mad Crimes and Sad Histories*. Princeton: Princeton University Press, 1988.

Gaubert, Ernest. *Rachilde*. Paris: Sansot, 1907.

Gauguin, Paul. *Lettres de Gauguin à sa femme et à ses amis*. Ed. Maurice Malingue. Paris: Grasset, 1946.

Geat, Marina. "Rachilde et il teatro 'simbolista': Per una poetica dell'ir-rappresentabilità." *Micromégas* 13.1 (Jan.–Apr. 1986): 27–46.

Gelfand, Elissa D. *Imagination in Confinement: Women's Writings from French Prisons*. Ithaca: Cornell University Press, 1983.

Gemie, Sharif. *Women and Schooling in France, 1815–1914: Gender, Authority, and Identity in the Female Schooling Sector*. Keele: Keele University Press, 1995.

"Géométries perverses." *Organographes du cymbalum pataphysicum* 19–20 (1983): 71–76.

Gerould, Daniel, ed. *Doubles, Demons, and Dreamers: An International Collection of Symbolist Drama*. New York: PAJ, 1985.

Gicquel, Alain-Claude. "Jeux de miroirs." *Magazine littéraire* 310 (May 1993): 57–58.

Gide, André. "Le Groupement littéraire qu'abritait le 'Mercure de France.'" *Mercure de France* 999-1000 (1946): 168–70.

Gilbert, Sandra M., and Susan Gubar. Introduction. *The Female Imagination and the Modernist Aesthetic*. New York: Gordon & Breach, 1986. 1–10.

———. *The Madwoman in the Attic: The Woman Writer and the Nineteenth-Century Literary Imagination*. New Haven: Yale University Press, 1979.

———. *No Man's Land: The Place of the Woman Writer in the Twentieth Century*. Vol. 1, *The War of the Words*. Vol. 2, *Sexchanges*. Vol. 3, *Letters from the Front*. New Haven: Yale University Press, 1988–94.

Gilman, Richard. *Decadence: The Strange Life of an Epithet*. New York: Farrar Straus Giroux, 1979.

Girard, René. *Deceit, Desire, and the Novel: Self and Other in Literary Structure*. Baltimore: Johns Hopkins University Press, 1965.

———. *To Double Business Bound: Essays on Literature, Mimesis, and Anthropology*. Baltimore: Johns Hopkins University Press, 1978.

Gold, Arthur, and Robert Fizdale. *The Divine Sarah: A Life of Sarah Bernhardt*. New York: Knopf, 1991.

Goldman, Emma. *Living My Life*. 1931. Rpt. New York: Dover, 1970.

Goldstein, Robert Justin. "Fighting French Censorship, 1815–1881." *French Review* 71.5 (1998): 785–96.

Goncourt, Edmond de, and Jules de Goncourt. *La Femme au dix-huitième siècle*. Paris: Firmin Didot, 1862.

Goodwin, Joseph P. *More Man Than You'll Ever Be*. Bloomington: Indiana University Press, 1989.

Gordon, Rae Beth. *Ornament, Fantasy, and Desire in Nineteenth-Century French Literature*. Princeton: Princeton University Press, 1992.

Goudeau, Emile. *Dix ans de Bohème*. Paris: Librairie Illustrée, 1888.

Gougy-François, Marie. "Le Salon de Rachilde." *Les Grands Salons féminins*. Paris: Nouvelles Éditions Debresse, 1965. 183–86.

Goujon, Jean-Paul. "Rachilde et Tinan." *Organographes du cymbalum pataphysicum* 19–20 (1983): 101–3.

Gourmont, Remy de. "Rachilde." *Le Livre des masques*. 1895. Rpt. Paris: Mercure de France, 1963. 109–11.

Grivel, Charles. "Rachilde. Envers de deux. Enfer de deux. Réponses." *Du féminin*. Ed. Mireille Calle. [Sainte-Foy, Québec]: Le Griffon d'argile, 1992. 185–202.

Gubar, Susan. "'The Blank Page' and the Issues of Female Creativity." *Critical Inquiry* 8.2 (winter 1981): 243–63.

Guilbert, Yvette. *Autres temps, autres chants*. Paris: Robert Laffont, 1946.

Hahn, Pierre. *Nos ancêtres les pervers: La Vie des homosexuels sous le Second Empire*. Paris: Orban, 1979.

Hamilton, Ian. *In Search of J. D. Salinger*. New York: Random House, 1988.

———. *Keepers of the Flame: Literary Estates and the Rise of Biography from Shakespeare to Plath*. Boston: Faber & Faber, 1994.

Hanscombe, Gillian, and Virginia L. Smyers. *Writing for Their Lives: The Modernist Women, 1910–1940*. London: Women's Press, 1987.

Hawthorne, Melanie. "'C'est si simple . . . c'est si difficile': Colette's Cattiness in *La Chatte*." *Australian Journal of French Studies* 35.3 (1998): 360–68.

———. "'Comment peut-on etre homosexuel': Oscar Wilde's *Salomé* and Multinational (In)Corporation." *Perennial Decay: The Aesthetics and Politics of Decadence in the Modern Era*. Ed. Liz Constable, Dennis Denisoff, and Matthew Potolsky. University Park: Pennsylvania State University Press, 1998. 159–82.

———. "'Du Du That Voodoo': *M. Vénus* and *M. Butterfly*." *L'Esprit créateur* 37.4 (winter 1997): 58–66.

———. "(En)Gendering Fascism: Rachilde's 'Les Vendanges de Sodome' and *Les Hors-Nature*." *Gender and Fascism in Modern France*.

Ed. Melanie Hawthorne and Richard J. Golsan. Hanover NH: Univerity Press of New England, 1997. 27–48.

——. "'Monsieur Vénus': A Critique of Gender Roles." *Nineteenth-Century French Studies* 16.1–2 (fall/winter 1987–88): 162–79.

——. "The Seduction of Terror: Annhine's Annihilation in Liane de Pougy's *Idylle saphique*." *Articulations of Difference: Gender Studies and Writing in French*. Ed. Dominique D. Fisher and Lawrence R. Schehr. Stanford: Stanford University Press, 1997. 136–54.

——. "The Social Construction of Sexuality in Three Novels by Rachilde." *Michigan Romance Studies* 9 (1989): 49–59.

Heilbrun, Carolyn G. *Writing a Woman's Life*. New York: Norton, 1988.

Hemmings, F. W. J. *Culture and Society in France, 1848–1898: Dissidents and Philistines*. New York: Scribner's, 1971.

Herring, Phillip. *Djuna: The Life and Work of Djuna Barnes*. New York: Viking, 1995.

Hirsch, Marianne. *The Mother/Daughter Plot: Narrative, Psychoanalysis, Feminism*. Bloomington: Indiana University Press, 1989.

"Historique du 5ᵉ Régiment de chasseurs de 1673 à 1887." Archives de l'Armée, Service Historique, Vincennes.

Holland, Merlin. *The Wilde Album*. New York: Henry Holt, 1997.

Holmes, Diana. *French Women's Writing, 1848–1994*. London: Athlone, 1996.

——. "Monstrous Women: Rachilde's Erotic Fiction." *Desiring Writing: Twentieth Century French Erotic Fiction by Women*. Ed. Kate Ince and Alex Hughes. London: Berg, 1996. 27–48.

hooks, bell. *Wounds of Passion: A Writing Life*. New York: Henry Holt, 1997.

Howard, Michael. *The Franco-Prussian War: The German Invasion of France, 1870–1871*. London: Rupert Hart-Davis, 1961.

Huddleston, Sisley. *Bohemian Literary and Social Life in Paris: Salons, Cafés, Studios*. London: Harrap, 1928.

Hugo, Victor. "Aymerillot." *La Légende des siècles*. Paris: Garnier, 1964. 161–69.

Ignotus, Paul. *The Paradox of Maupassant*. London: University of London Press, 1966.

Jackson, Arthur B. *La Revue blanche (1889–1903): Origine, influence, bibliographie*. Paris: Lettres Modernes, 1960.

Jarry, Alfred. *Oeuvres complètes*. 3 vols. Paris: Gallimard, 1974–87.

Jasper, Gertrude R. *Adventure in the Theatre: Lugné-Poe and the Théâtre de l'Oeuvre to 1899*. New Brunswick NJ: Rutgers University Press, 1947.

Jay, Karla. *The Amazon and the Page: Natalie Clifford Barney and Renée Vivien.* Bloomington: Indiana University Press, 1988.

Jordanova, Ludmilla. *Sexual Visions: Images of Gender in Science and Medicine between the Eighteenth and Twentieth Centuries.* Madison: University of Wisconsin Press, 1989.

Jouve, Séverine. *Les Décadents: Bréviaire fin de siècle.* Paris: Plon, 1989.

Jozé, Victor. "Le Féminisme et le bon sens." *La Plume* 154 (Sept. 1895): 391–92.

Jubinal, Achille. *Mémoire sur les manuscrits de la bibliothèque de l'Ecole de médecine de Montepellier contenant la correspondance de Christine de Suède.* Paris: n.p., 1849.

Jullien, Phillipe. *Jean Lorrain ou Le Satiricon 1900.* Paris: Fayard, 1974.

Kahn, Gustave. *Symbolistes et décadents.* Paris: L. Vanier, 1902.

Kamuf, Peggy. *Signature Pieces: On the Institution of Authorship.* Ithaca: Cornell University Press, 1988.

Kates, Gary. *Monsieur d'Eon Is a Woman: A Tale of Political Intrigue and Sexual Masquerade.* New York: Basic, 1995.

Katz, Jonathan Ned. *The Invention of Heterosexuality.* New York: Dutton, 1995.

Kelly, Dorothy. *Fictional Genders: Role and Representation in Nineteenth-Century French Narrative.* Lincoln: University of Nebraska Press, 1989.

Kelly, Joan. "Did Women Have a Renaissance?" *Women, History, and Theory: The Essays of Joan Kelly.* Chicago: University of Chicago Press, 1984. 19–50.

Kiebuzinska, Christine. "Behind the Mirror: Madame Rachilde's *The Crystal Spider.*" *Modern Language Studies* 24.3 (summer 1994): 28–43.

Kingcaid, Renée A. *Neurosis and Narrative: The Decadent Short Fiction of Proust, Lorrain, and Rachilde.* Carbondale: Southern Illinois University Press, 1992.

Kistemaeckers, Henry. "Mes procès littéraires, souvenirs d'un éditeur." *Mercure de France* Sept. 15, 1923: 670–92.

Kolney, Fernand. *Le Salon de Madame Truphot: Mœurs littéraires.* Paris: A. Michel, 1904.

Kristeva, Julia. "Women's Time." *The Kristeva Reader.* Ed. Toril Moi. New York: Columbia University Press, 1986. 187–213.

Lacombe, François. *Lettres secrètes de Christine, reine de Suède.* Geneva: Frères Cramer, 1761.

Lagail, Dr. A. S. [Alphonse Gallais]. *Les Mémoires du Baron Jacques: Lubricités infernales de la noblesse décadente.* 1904. Rpt. *Cahiers Gai-Kitsch-Camp* 21 (1993): 87–131.

Lake, Carlton. *Confessions of a Literary Archaeologist.* New York: New Directions, 1990.

Lambert, Pierre. "3 lettres de Rachilde à J.-K. Huysmans." *Bulletin de la Société J.-K. Huysmans* 41 (1961): 250–54.

Lang, André. *Déplacements et villégiatures littéraires.* Paris: La Renaissance du Livre, 1923.

Lanoux, Armand. *Maupassant le bel-ami.* Paris: A. Fayard, 1967.

Larnac, Jean. *Histoire de la littérature féminine en France.* Paris: Kra, 1929.

———. Rev. of *Quand j'étais jeune*, by Rachilde. *Europe* 30 (June 1948): 118–19.

Latour, Antoine de. Introduction. *Le Journal de Marie-Edmée.* By Marie-Edmée Pau. Paris: Plon, 1876. v–xxxi.

Léautaud, Paul. *Journal littéraire.* 4 vols. Paris: Mercure de France, 1986.

Leblond, Marius-Ary. *La Société Française sous la 3e République d'après les romanciers contemporains.* Paris: Alcan, 1905.

Le Cardonnel, Georges, and Charles Velley. "Madame Rachilde." *La Littérature contemporaine.* Paris: Mercure de France, 1905. 118–21.

Leeuwen, Thomas A. P. van. *The Springboard in the Pond: An Intimate History of the Swimming Pool.* Cambridge: MIT Press, 1998.

Lefrère, Jean-Jacques. *Les Saisons littéraires de Rodolphe Darzens.* Paris: Fayard, 1998.

Lennon, Nigey. *Alfred Jarry: The Man with the Axe.* Los Angeles: Panjandrum, 1984.

Lesage, Claire, Philippe Oriol, and Christian Soulignac, eds. *Lettres à A.-Ferninand Herold (1891–1935) et quelques-unes à son épouse.* Paris: Editions du Fourneau, 1992.

Lester, Katherine Morris, and Bess Viola Oerlee. *Accessories of Dress.* Peoria IL: Charles A. Bennett, 1940.

Lewis, H. D. "The Legal Status of Women in Nineteenth-Century France." *European Studies* 10 (1980): 178–88.

Lewis, Paul. *Queen of Caprice: A Biography of Kristina of Sweden.* New York: Holt, Rinehart & Winston, 1962.

Lively, Frazer. Introduction. *Madame la Mort and Other Plays.* By Rachilde. Baltimore: Johns Hopkins University Press, 1998. 3–53.

———. "Rachilde, the Actor's Spectre, and Symbolist Dramaturgy: The Staging of *Madame la Mort.*" *Nineteenth Century Theatre* 231–32 (summer/winter 1995): 33–66.

Lombroso, Cesare. *L'Homme de génie.* Paris: F. Alcan, 1889.

Lopez, Judith. "Buttonholes: Some Differences in Gender-Related Front Closures." *Dress: The Annual Journal of the Costume Society of America* 20 (1993): 74–78.

Lorrain, Jean. "La Débutante." *Une Femme par jour*. Ed. Michel Desbruères. Paris: Christian Pirot, 1983. 190–92.

———. "Deux appréciations de Jean Lorrain concernant Rachilde." *Organographes du cymbalum pataphysicum* 19–20 (1983): 75. Footer in middle of "Géométries perverse."

———. "Mademoiselle Salamandre." *Le Courrier français* Dec. 12, 1886. Rpt. *Dans l'oratoire*. Paris: C. Dalou, 1888. 204–15.

Louÿs, Pierre. *La Femme et le pantin*. Paris: Mercure de France, 1898.

Lugné-Poe, Aurélien. *La Parade: Souvenirs et impressions de théâtre*. 4 vols. Paris: Gallimard, [1930–35].

Luiz, Dr. [Paul Devaux]. *Les Fellatores: Moeurs de la décadence*. Paris: Union des Bibliophiles, 1888.

Lukacher, Maryline. "Mademoiselle Baudelaire: Rachilde ou le féminin au masculin." *Nineteenth-Century French Studies* 20.3–4 (spring/summer 1992): 452–65.

——— *Maternal Fictions: Stendhal, Sand, Rachilde, and Bataille*. Durham: Duke University Press, 1994.

MacAloon, John J. *This Great Symbol: Pierre de Coubertin and the Origins of the Modern Olympic Games*. Chicago: University of Chicago Press, 1981.

Maclean, Marie. *The Name of the Mother: Writing Illegitimacy*. London: Routledge, 1994.

Maizeroy, René. *Les Deux amies*. Paris: Victor-Havard, 1885.

Malcolm, Janet. *The Silent Woman: Sylvia Plath and Ted Hughes*. New York: Knopf, 1994.

Margadant, Jo Burr. *Madame le Professeur: Women Educators in the Third Republic*. Princeton: Princeton University Press, 1990.

Mariani, Angelo. "Madame Rachilde." *Figures contemporaines tirées de l'album Mariani*. Vol. 4. Paris: Librairie Henri Floury, 1899. N. pag.

Marin, Scipion. *Mémoires de Christine, reine de Suède*. Paris: Dehay, 1830.

Marinetti, F. T. *Mafarka le futuriste*. Paris: Sansot, 1910.

———. *Selected Writings*. Ed. R. W. Flint. Trans. R. W. Flint and Arthur A. Coppotelli. New York: Farrar Straus Giroux, 1972.

———. "Selections from the Unpublished Diaries." *Modernism/Modernity* 1.3 (1994): 1–44.

Martin du Gard, Maurice. *Impertinences: Portraits contemporains*. Paris: Bloch, 1924. 133–39.

Martinoir, Francine de. Rev. of *La Jongleuse*, by Rachilde. *Europe* 662–63 (June–July 1984): 212–13.

Mauclair, Camille. "Eloge de la luxure." *Mercure de France* 8.41 (1893): 43–50.

Maugue, Annelise. *L'Identité masculine en crise au tournant du siècle, 1871–1914*. Paris: Rivages, 1987.

Maupassant, Guy de. *A la feuille de rose: Maison turque*. Paris: Encre, 1984.

———. *Correspondance*. Ed. Jacques Suffel. 3 vols. Geneva: Edito-Service, 1973.

Mayeur, Françoise. *L'Enseignement secondaire des jeunes filles sous la Troisième République*. Paris: Presses de la Fondation Nationale des Sciences Politiques, 1977.

McLendon, Will L. "Autour d'une lettre inédite de Rachilde à Huysmans." *Bulletin de la Société J.-K. Huysmans* 20.75 (1983): 21–24.

———. "Huysmans, Rachilde, et le roman de 'moeurs parisiennes.'" *Bulletin de la Société J.-K. Huysmans* 77 (1985): 21–24.

———. "Rachilde: *Fin-de-Siècle* Perspective on Perversities." *Modernity and Revolution in Late Nineteenth-Century France*. Ed. Barbara T. Cooper and Mary Donaldson-Evans. Newark: University of Delaware Press, 1992. 52–61.

McMillan, James F. *Housewife or Harlot: The Place of Women in French Society, 1870–1940*. New York: St. Martin's, 1981.

"*Le Mercure de France* et la littérature en 1890." *Revue d'histoire littéraire de la France* 92.1 (Jan.–Feb. 1992). Special issue on Rachilde.

Merrick, Jeffrey, and Bryant T. Ragan Jr., eds. *Homosexuality in Modern France*. New York: Oxford University Press, 1996.

Middlebrook, Diane Wood. *Anne Sexton: A Biography*. Boston: Houghton Mifflin, 1991.

———. *Suits Me: The Double Life of Billy Tipton*. Boston: Houghton Mifflin, 1998.

Miller, Nancy K. *Subject to Change: Reading Feminist Writing*. New York: Columbia University Press, 1988.

Miomandre, Francis de. "Rachilde, princesse des ténèbres." *Art Moderne* 13 (Mar. 29, 1903): 117–19; 14 (Apr. 5, 1903): 125–27.

Monnier, Adrienne. "*Le Mercure* vu par un enfant." *Mercure de France* 999–100 (1946): 188–91.

———. *The Very Rich Hours of Adrienne Monnier: An Intimate Portrait of the Literary and Artistic Life in Paris between the Wars*. Trans. Richard McDougall. New York: Scribner's, 1976.

Moon, Dawn. "Insult and Inclusion: The Term Fag Hag and the Gay Male 'Community.'" *Social Forces* 74.2 (Dec. 1995): 487–510.

Moréas, Jean. "Manifeste du symbolisme." *Le Figaro* September 1886.

Morlant, Jacques. "Mme Rachilde." *Enquête sur l'influence allemande*. Paris: Mercure de France, 1903. 107–8.

"La Mort de Rachilde." *Mercure de France* 1077 (May 1, 1953): 185.

Moses, Claire Goldberg. *French Feminism in the Nineteenth Century*. Albany: State Univerity of New York Press, 1984.

Mugnier, Abbé. *Journal, 1879–1939*. Paris: Mercure de France, 1985.

Murat, Princess. *La Vie amoureuse de Christine de Suède, la reine androgyne*. Paris: Flammarion, 1930.

Nadeau, Maurice. *Histoire du surréalisme*. Paris: Seuil, 1964.

Nahas, Rebecca, and Myr Turley. *The New Couple: Women and Gay Men*. New York: Seaview, 1979.

"Nécrologie." *Le Monde* Apr. 7, 1953: 5.

Noailles, Anna de. *Anna de Noailles–Maurices Barrès: Correspondance, 1901–1923*. Paris: L'Inventaire, 1994.

Nola, Jean-Paul de. Rev. of *La Jongleuse*, by Rachilde. *Studi Francesi* 28 (1984): 596.

Nye, Robert A. *Masculinity and Male Codes of Honor in Modern France*. New York: Oxford University Press, 1993.

O'Brien, Sharon. *Willa Cather: The Emerging Voice*. New York: Oxford University Press, 1987.

O'Farrell, Mary Ann. *Telling Complexions: The Nineteenth-Century English Novel and the Blush*. Durham: Duke University Press, 1997.

Ogrinc, Will H. L. "A Shrine to Love and Sorrow: Jacques d'Adelswärd-Fersen (1880–1923)." *Paidika* 3.2 (winter 1994): 30–58.

O'Monroy, Richard [vicomte de Saint-Geniès]. *Monsieur Mars et Madame Vénus*. Paris: Calmann-Lévy, 1878.

Orenstein, Gloria. "The Salon of Natalie Clifford Barney: An Interview with Berthe Cleyrergue." *Signs* 4 (1979): 484–96.

Organographes du cymbalum pataphysicum 18 (Sept. 8, 1982), 19–20 (Apr. 4, 1983). Number 18 is devoted to the Rachilde-Jarry correspondence, nos. 19–20 to Rachilde.

Oriol, Philippe. *A propos de l'attentat Foyot: Quelques questions et quelques tentatives de réponses ainsi que quelques documents reproduits dont le "Journal des interviews."* Paris: Editions du Fourneau, 1993.

Orliac, Antoine. "Médailles symbolistes: Rachilde." *Mercure de France* 281 (1938): 294–99.

Paillet, Léo. *Dans la ménagerie littéraire*. Paris: Baudinière, 1925.

Palacio, Jean de. *Figures et formes de la décadence*. Paris: Séguier, 1994.

———. *Les Perversions du merveilleux*. Paris: Séguier, 1993.

———. *Pierrot fin-de-siècle*. Paris: Séguier, 1990.

Paperno, Irina. *Suicide as a Cultural Institution in Dostoevsky's Russia*. Ithaca: Cornell University Press, 1997.

Paris, Paulin. "Aimeri de Narbonne." *Histoire littéraire de la France.* Paris: Firmin Didot; Treuttle & Wurtz, 1852. 460–70.

Pau, Marie-Edmée. *Histoire de notre petite soeur, Jeanne d'Arc, dediée aux enfants de la Lorraine.* Paris: Plon, 1874.

———. *Le Journal de Marie-Edmée.* Paris: Plon, 1891.

Perloff, Marjorie. *The Futurist Movement: Avant-Garde, Avant Guerre, and the Language of Rupture.* Chicago: University of Chicago Press, 1986.

Perrot, Michelle. "The New Eve and the Old Adam: Changes in French Women's Condition at the Turn of the Century." *Behind the Lines: Gender and the Two World Wars.* Ed. Margaret Randolph Higonnet and Jane Jenson. New Haven: Yale University Press, 1987. 51–60.

Perrot, Philippe. *Fashioning the Bourgeoise: A History of Clothing in the Nineteenth Century.* 1981. Trans. Richard Bienvenu. Princeton: Princeton University Press, 1994.

Petitfils, Pierre, ed. *Album Verlaine: Iconographie.* Paris: Gallimard, 1981.

Pia, Pascal. "La Stratégie dans les lettres." *Carrefour* July 7, 1977: 12–13.

Picard, Gaston. "Rachilde." *Larousse mensuel* 467 (July 1953): 301–2.

Pierrot, Jean. *The Decadent Imagination, 1880–1900.* Trans. Derek Coltman. Chicago: University of Chicago Press, 1981.

Pinkus, Karen. *Bodily Regimes: Italian Advertising under Fascism.* Minneapolis: University of Minnesota Press, 1995.

Planté, Christine. "Les Petites filles ne mangent pas de viande: Tuer, saigner, dévorer dans *La Marquise de Sade* de Rachilde." *Corps/ décors: Femmes, orgie, parodie.* Ed. Catherine Nesci. Amsterdam: Rodopi, 1999. 119–32.

Ploye, Catherine. "'Questions brûlantes': Rachilde, l'affaire Douglas, et les mouvements féministes." *Nineteenth-Century French Studies* 22.1–2 (fall/winter 1993–94): 195–207.

Poe, Edgar Allan. "The Fall of the House of Usher." *Collected Tales and Poems.* New York: Modern Library, 1992. 231–45.

Poirier, Guy. *L'Homosexualité dans l'imaginaire de la Renaissance.* Paris: H. Champion, 1996.

Poirot-Delpech, Bertrand. "L'Homme-Objet en 1880: 'Monsieur Vénus' de Rachilde." *Le Monde* July 29, 1977: 11.

Pommarède, Pierre. *Périgueux oublié: 433 cartes postales anciennes.* Périgueux: Pierre Fanlac, 1988.

———. "Le Sol et le sang de Rachilde." *Bulletin de la Société Historique et Archéologique du Périgord* 120.4 (1993): 785–820.

Praz, Mario. *The Romantic Agony.* Trans. Angus Davidson. London: Oxford University Press, 1970.

Proust, Marcel. *Correspondance.* Ed. Philip Kolb. 21 vols. Paris: Plon, 1981.

Quartararo, Anne T. *Women Teachers and Popular Education in Nineteenth-Century France: Social Values and Corporate Identity at the Normal School Institution.* Newark: University of Delaware Press, 1995.

Quillard, Pierre. "Rachilde." *Mercure de France* 9.48 (Dec. 1893): 323–28.

Rachilde. "Carnet d'un officier de 1870." *La Vie* 2.13 (Mar. 29, 1913): 685–88.

———. "Questions brûlantes." *La Revue blanche* 11, no. 78 (Sept. 1, 1896): 193–200.

"Rachilde et la France." *Organographes du cymbalum pataphysicum* 19–20 (1983): 45–57.

Rauch, Karen, and Jeff Fessler. *Why Gay Guys Are a Girl's Best Friend.* New York: Simon & Schuster, 1995.

Raynaud, Ernest. *La Mêlée symboliste: Portraits et souvenirs.* 3 vols. Paris: La Renaissance du Livre, 1920.

Rearick, Charles. *Pleasures of the Belle Epoque: Entertainment and Festivity in Turn-of-the-Century France.* New Haven: Yale University Press, 1985.

Réda, Jacques, ed. *Album Maupassant.* Paris: Gallimard, 1987.

Renard, Jules. *Journal, 1887–1910.* Paris: Gallimard, 1965.

———. *Oeuvres complètes.* Paris: François Bernouard, 1925.

——— "Rachilde." *Portraits du prochain siècle.* Vol. 1, *Poètes et prosateurs.* Paris: Girard, 1894. 16.

Retté, Adolphe. *Le Symbolisme: Anecdotes et souvenirs.* Paris: Messein, 1903.

Revue Frontenac 10–11 (1993–94). Special issue with several articles on Rachilde.

La Revue indépendente. Geneva: Slatkine, 1970. A reprinting of the journal's entire run.

Rhiel, Mary, and David Suchoff, eds. *The Seductions of Biography.* New York: Routledge, 1995.

Ribadeau-Dumas, François. "Carrefour de visages." *La Revue mondiale* 180.23 (Dec. 1, 1927): 286–91.

Ribemont-Dessaignes, Georges. *Déjà jadis.* Paris: Julliard, 1958.

Rich, Adrienne. *On Lies, Secrets, and Silence: Selected Prose, 1966–1978.* New York: Norton, 1979.

Richard, Noël. *Le Mouvement décadent: Dandys, esthètes, et quintessants.* Paris: Nizet, 1968.

Ridge, George Ross. *The Hero in French Decadent Literature.* Athens: University of Georgia Press, 1961.

Roberts, Mary Louise. *Civilization without Sexes: Reconstructing Gender in Postwar France, 1917–1927.* Chicago: University of Chicago Press, 1994.

Robichez, Jacques. *Lugné-Poe.* Paris: L'Arche, 1955.

———. *Le Symbolisme au théâtre: Lugné-Poe et les débuts de L'Oeuvre.* Paris: L'Arche, 1957.

Robinson, Christopher. *Scandal in the Ink: Male and Female Homosexuality in Twentieth-Century French Literature.* London: Cassell, 1994.

Rogers, Nathalie Buchet. *Fictions du scandale: Corps féminin et réalisme romanesque au dix-neuvième siècle.* West Lafayette IN: Purdue University Press, 1998.

Rosario, Vernon A. *The Erotic Imagination: French Histories of Perversity.* New York: Oxford University Press, 1997.

Rose, Jacqueline. *The Haunting of Sylvia Plath.* Cambridge: Harvard University Press, 1991.

Rouveyre, André. *Souvenirs de mon commerce.* Paris: Crès, 1921.

———. *Visages des contemporains: Portraits dessinés d'après le vif (1908–1913).* Paris: Mercure de France, 1913.

Ruchon, François. *Verlaine: Documents iconographiques.* Vésenaz: Pierre Cailler, 1947.

Rudorff, Raymond. *La Belle Epoque.* London: Hamilton, 1972.

Sanchez, Nelly. "Rachilde ou la décadence du naturalisme." *Les Cahiers naturalistes* 73 (1999): 275–83.

Sanouillet, Michel. *Francis Picabia et "391."* Paris: E. Losfeld, 1966.

Santon, Noël. *La Poésie de Rachilde.* Paris: Le Rouge et le Noir, 1928.

Saslow, James M. *Ganymede in the Renaissance: Homosexuality in Art and Society.* New Haven: Yale University Press, 1986.

Sautman, Francesca Canadé. "Invisible Women: Lesbian Working-Class Culture in France, 1880–1930." *Homosexuality in Modern France.* Ed. Jeffrey Merrick and Bryant T. Ragan. New York: Oxford University Press, 1996. 177–201.

Sauvé, Rachel. *De l'éloge à l'exclusion: Les Femmes Auteurs et leurs préfaciers au XIXe siècle.* Saint-Denis: Presses Universitaires de Vincennes, 2000.

Schor, Naomi. *George Sand and Idealism.* New York: Columbia University Press, 1993.

Schwartz, Hillel. *Century's End: An Orientation Manual toward the Year 2000.* Rev. ed. New York: Doubleday, 1996.

Schwartz, Vanessa R. *Spectacular Realities: Early Mass Culture in Fin-de-Siècle Paris*. Berkeley: University of California Press, 1998.

Scott, Bonnie Kime, ed. *The Gender of Modernism: A Critical Anthology*. Bloomington: Indiana University Press, 1990.

———. *Refiguring Modernism*. Vol. 1, *The Women of 1928*. Vol. 2, *Postmodern Feminist Readings of Woolf, West, and Barnes*. Bloomington: Indiana University Press, 1995.

Sedgwick, Eve Kosofsky. *Epistemology of the Closet*. Berkeley: University of California Press, 1990.

Seigel, Jerrold. *Bohemian Paris: Culture, Politics, and the Boundaries of Bourgeois Life, 1830–1930*. 1986. Rpt. New York: Penguin, 1987.

Seignol, Christian. "Rachilde et le Périgord." *Périgord Actualités* Apr. 15, 1967: 1, 3.

Severini, Gino. *The Life of a Painter*. Princeton: Princeton University Press, 1995.

Shattuck, Roger. *The Banquet Years: The Origins of the Avant Garde in France, 1885 to World War I*. New York: Vintage, 1955.

Showalter, Elaine. *Sexual Anarchy: Gender and Culture at the Fin de Siècle*. New York: Viking, 1990.

Shryock, Richard. "Anarchism at the Dawn of the Symbolist Movement." *French Forum* 25.3 (September 2000): 291–307.

Shryock, Richard, ed. *Lettres à Gustave et Rachel Kahn*. Saint-Genouph: Nizet, 1996.

Sidonius Apollinaris. *Poems and Letters*. Ed. W. B. Anderson. 2 vols. Cambridge: Loeb, 1936.

Silve, Edith. *Paul Léautaud et le Mercure de France*. Paris: Mercure de France, 1985.

Silverman, Debora. *Art Nouveau in Fin-de-Siècle France: Politics, Psychology, and State*. Berkeley: University of California Press, 1989.

———. "The *New Woman*, Feminism, and the Decorative Arts in Fin-de-Siècle France." *Eroticism and the Body Politic*. Ed. Lynn Hunt. Baltimore: Johns Hopkins University Press, 1991. 144–63.

Silverman, Willa Z. *The Notorious Life of Gyp: Right-Wing Anarchist in Fin-de-Siècle France*. New York: Oxford University Press, 1995.

Sonn, Richard D. *Anarchism and Cultural Politics in Fin de Siècle France*. Lincoln: University of Nebraska Press, 1989.

Soulignac, Christian. "Bibliographie des oeuvres de jeunesse de Rachilde, 1877–1889 (édition revue et corrigée)." *Revue Frontenac* 10–11 (1993–94): 198–218.

———. "Ecrits de jeunesse de Mademoiselle de Vénérande." *Revue Frontenac* 10–11 (1993–94): 192–97.

————. *Justifications de tirage du Mercure*. Paris: Editions du Fourneau, 1991.

Spackman, Barbara. *Fascist Virilities*. Minneapolis: University of Minnesota Press, 1996.

Stanton, Domna C., ed. *The Female Autograph: Theory and Practice of Autobiography from the Tenth to the Twentieth Century*. Chicago: University of Chicago Press, 1987.

Starkie, Enid. *Arthur Rimbaud*. London: Faber & Faber, 1961.

————. *Baudelaire*. London: Faber & Faber, 1957.

Steegmuller, Francis. *Apollinaire: Poet among the Painters*. New York: Farrar, Straus, 1963.

Stillman, Linda Klieger. "Rachilde: Comment 'Refaire l'Amour.'" *Nineteenth-Century French Studies* 22.1–2 (fall/winter 1993–94): 208–19.

Stokes, John. *In the Nineties*. Chicago: University of Chicago Press, 1989.

Stora-Lamarre, Annie. *L'Enfer de la IIIe République: Censeurs et pornographes (1881–1914)*. Paris: Imago-Diffusion PUF, 1990.

Swart, Koenraad E. *The Sense of Decadence in Nineteenth-Century France*. The Hague: Nijhoff, 1964.

Talman, Francis. *Monsieur Vénus*. Paris: Editions du Fourneau, 1995.

Teich, Mikuláš, and Roy Porter. *Fin de Siècle and Its Legacy*. Cambridge: Cambridge University Press, 1990.

Thewelweit, Klaus. *Male Fantasies*. Vol. 1, *Women, Floods, Bodies, History*. Trans. Stephen Conway. Vol. 2, *Male Bodies: Psychologizing the White Terror*. Trans. Erica Carter and Chris Turner. Minneapolis: University of Minnesota Press, 1987–89.

Thomson, Clive. "Le Discours du féminin dans *Le Docteur Pascal* d'Emile Zola et *La Jongleuse* de Rachilde." *Excavatio: Emile Zola and Naturalism* 4 (1994): 13–22.

Tinan, Jean de. Rev. of *La Princesse des ténèbres*, by Rachilde. *L'Ermitage* July 1896: 56–57.

Tindall, Gillian. *Célestine: Voices from a French Village*. New York: H. Holt, 1996.

Tisdall, Caroline, and Angelo Bozzolla. *Futurism*. London: Thames & Hudson, 1977.

Torgovnick, Marianna. *Gone Primitive: Savage Intellects, Modern Lives*. Chicago: University of Chicago Press, 1990.

Toth, Emily. *Kate Chopin*. New York: Morrow, 1990.

van Bever, Adolphe, ed. *Correspondance de Paul Verlaine*. Paris: A. Messein, 1929.

Van Dusen, Wanda. "Portrait of a National Fetish: Gertrude Stein's 'Introduction to the Speeches of Maréchal Pétain' (1942)." *Modernism/Modernity* 3.3 (1996): 69–92.

van Slyke, Gretchen. "Rebuilding the Bastille: Women's Dress-Code Legislation in the Nineteenth Century." *Repression and Expression: Literary and Social Coding in Nineteenth-Century France.* Ed. Carrol F. Coates. New York: Peter Lang, 1996. 209–19.

Vasseur, Nadine. "Rachilde." *Les Nouvelles littéraires* 2751 (Aug. 28, 1980): 30.

Verlaine, Paul. *Lettres inédites à divers correspondants.* Ed. Georges Zayed. Geneva: Droz, 1976.

——. *Oeuvres en prose complètes.* Paris: Gallimard, 1972.

——. *Oeuvres poétiques complètes.* Paris: Gallimard, 1962.

Vicinus, Martha. "The Adolescent Boy: Fin de Siècle Femme Fatale?" *Journal of the History of Sexuality* 5.1 (July 1994): 90–114.

Villiers de l'Isle-Adam, Philippe Auguste. *Oeuvres complètes.* 2 vols. Paris: Gallimard, 1986.

Waelti-Walters, Jennifer. *Feminist Novelists of the Belle Epoque: Love as a Lifestyle.* Bloomington: Indiana University Press, 1990.

Wagner-Martin, Linda. *Telling Women's Lives: The New Biography.* New Brunswick NJ: Rutgers University Press, 1994.

Waldberg, Patrick. *Eros Modern' Style.* Paris: J.-J. Pauvert, 1964.

Warner, Marina. *Joan of Arc: The Image of Female Heroism.* New York: Knopf, 1981.

Waugh, Norah. *The Cut of Women's Clothes, 1600–1930.* New York: Theatre Arts, 1968.

Weber, Eugen. *France: Fin de Siècle.* Cambridge: Harvard University Press, 1986.

Weck, René de. *Souvenirs littéraires.* Paris: Mercure de France, 1939.

Weir, David. *Decadence and the Making of Modernism.* Amherst: University of Massachusetts Press, 1995.

Weiss, Andrea. *Paris Was a Woman: Portraits from the Left Bank.* San Franciso: Harper San Francisco, 1995.

"What Is 'Pataphysics?" Ed. Roger Shattuck and Simon Watson Taylor. *Evergreen Review* 13 (May/June 1960). Special issue.

Wheelwright, Julie. *Amazons and Military Maids: Women Who Dressed as Men in Pursuit of Life, Liberty, and Happiness.* London: Pandora, 1989.

White, Patricia. *Uninvited: Classical Hollywood Cinema and Lesbian Representability.* Bloomington: Indiana University Press, 1999.

Whitton, David. *Stage Directors in Modern France.* Manchester: Manchester University Press, 1987.

Wickes, George. *The Amazon of Letters: The Life and Loves of Natalie Barney.* 1976. Rpt. New York: Putnam's, 1978.

Williams, Roger L. *The Horror of Life.* Chicago: University of Chicago Press, 1980.

Winn, Phillip. *Sexualités décadentes chez Jean Lorrain: Le Héros fin de sexe.* Amsterdam: Rodopi, 1997.

Witzling, Mara R., ed. *Voicing Our Visions: Writings by Women Artists.* New York: Universe, 1991.

Woolf, Virginia. *A Room of One's Own.* 1929. Rpt. New York: Harcourt, Brace & World, 1957.

Ziegler, Robert E. "Fantasies of Partial Selves in Rachilde's *Le Démon de l'absurde.*" *Nineteenth-Century French Studies* 19.1 (1990): 122–31.

———. "Interpretation as Mirage in Rachilde's 'Le Château hermétique.'" *Nineteenth-Century French Studies* 26.1–2 (fall/winter 1997–98): 182–92.

———. "The Message from the Lighthouse: Rachilde's *La Tour d'amour.*" *Romance Quarterly* 39.2 (1992): 159–65.

———. "Rachilde and 'l'amour compliqué.'" *Atlantis* 11.2 (spring 1986): 115–24.

———. "The Suicide of 'La Comédienne' in Rachilde's *La Jongleuse.*" *Continental, Latin-American, and Francophone Women Writers: Selected Papers from Wichita State University Conference on Foreign Literature, 1984–1985.* Ed. Eunice Myers and Ginette Adamson. Lanham MD: Univerity Presses of America, 1987. 55–61.

INDEX